Readers in
Librarianship and Information Science

Published Readers in the series:

READER IN

UNDERGRADUATE

LIBRARIES

edited by

BILLY R. WILKINSON

25

Information Handling Services
An Indian Head Company
Englewood, Colorado

**LIBRARY OF CONGRESS CATALOGING
IN PUBLICATION DATA**
Main entry under title:

Reader in undergraduate libraries.

(Readers in library and information science;
25)
Bibliography: p.
Includes index.
1. Libraries, University and college — Under-
graduate libraries — Addresses, essays, lectures. I.
Wilkinson, Billy R. II. Series.
Z675.U5R43   027.7   78-9504
ISBN 0-910972-76-1

Published by Information Handling Services
P.O. Box 1276
Englewood, Colorado 80150

Printed in the United States of America.

To the Memory of

PATRICIA B. KNAPP

and in gratitude for
her friendship with and guidance of
undergraduate librarians

Contents

IV. THE UgLi AT THE UNIVERSITY OF MICHIGAN, 1958

V. THE 1960s AND EARLY 1970s—ERA OF GREATEST DEVELOPMENT: SELECTIVE DESCRIPTIONS OF INDIVIDUAL LIBRARIES

VI. INSTITUTE ON TRAINING FOR SERVICE IN UNDERGRADUATE LIBRARIES, 1970: BEGINNINGS OF EVALUATION

VII. INSTITUTE ON THE UNDERGRADUATE ENVIRONMENT, 1971: CONTINUING EXPLORATIONS AMONG STUDENTS, LIBRARIANS, AND FACULTY

VIII. A CRITICAL OVERVIEW OF UNDERGRADUATE LIBRARIES

Foreword

Unlike many other academic disciplines, librarianship has not yet begun to exploit the contributions of the several disciplines toward the study of its own issues. Yet the literature abounds with material germane to its concerns. Too frequently the task of identifying, correlating, and bringing together material from innumerable sources is burdensome, time consuming or simply impossible. For a field whose stock in trade is organizing knowledge, it is clear that the job of synthesizing the most essential contributions from the elusive sources in which they are contained is overdue. This then is the rationale for the series, *Readers in Librarianship and Information Science.*

The *Readers in Librarianship and Information Science* will include books concerned with various broad aspects of the field's interests. Each volume will be prepared by a recognized student of the topic covered, and the content will embrace material from the many different sources from the traditional literature of librarianship as well as from outside the field in which the most salient contributions have appeared. The objectives of the series will be to bring together in convenient form the key elements required for a current and comprehensive view of the subject matter. In this way it is hoped that the core of knowledge, essential as the intellectual basis for study and understanding, will be drawn into focus and thereby contribute to the furtherance of professional education and professional practice in the field.

Paul Wasserman
Series Editor

Preface

This volume records the early development of separate undergraduate libraries on university campuses, traces their most flourishing period in the 1960s and early 1970s, and examines the beginnings and continuation of evaluation of their services by bringing together for the first time the important articles and papers in the considerable body of literature now extant. Several of the papers are published here for the first time.

John R. Haak, one of the national leaders of undergraduate librarianship, has defined an undergraduate library in his paper entitled "Goal Determination and the Undergraduate Library" (included in Section VI) as "(1) a special library for undergraduate students; (2) located in a university or other institution supporting graduate work to a significant degree; (3) housed in either a separate building or in a self-contained section of a general building; (4) consisting of a collection designed to support and supplement the undergraduate curriculum, and a staff and services which promote the integration of the library into the undergraduate teaching program of the university." His definition is used here.

The selected papers are divided into eight sections beginning with the background of library service for undergraduate students in the late nineteenth and first half of the twentieth centuries. Harvard is presented as the example.

Section II next describes in great detail the first separately housed and especially designed undergraduate library on an American university campus — the Lamont Library at Harvard — which opened on January 3, 1949. Keyes D. Metcalf and others have documented the early planning, actual design, functions, book collection, and operations of Lamont.

University librarians were greatly interested in this development of library service to undergraduate students and two major symposia were held in 1952 and 1955. The papers from both are reprinted in Section III.

Then in 1958, the University of Michigan Undergraduate Library (or the UgLi as it came to be known) was opened. Section IV is devoted to the first UgLi on a large public university campus.

The papers in Section V chronicle the era of greatest development and are highly selective descriptions of a few of the thirty-seven currently operating undergraduate libraries in the United States and Canada.

Just as the two symposia were significant in the 1950s, two institutes in the early 1970s were critical in undergraduate librarianship. The Institute on Training for Service in Undergraduate Libraries sponsored by the University Library of the University of California at San Diego, August 17-21, 1970, was both the culmination of the period of greatest development and the beginning of evaluation and self-criticism. Four of the six papers presented at the Institute are published for the first time in Section VI.

A pre-conference institute sponsored by the University Libraries Section of the Association of College and Research Libraries, American Library Association, continued the explorations begun in the San Diego gathering in Dallas, Texas, June 18-19, 1971. Appreciation is expressed to the Association of College and Research Libraries and to each of the individual authors for permission to publish for the first time in Section VII three of the major papers given at the Dallas sessions.

Incidentally, in tracing the historical development of undergraduate libraries, one notices the small, but important, change in the use of prepositions. The speakers at the symposia in the 1950s discussed library services *to* undergraduates. By the time of the institutes in the 1970s, the literature usually concerned services *for* undergraduate students. It is not too much to read into these prepositions a change in attitude from paternalism to service. The activists in the undergraduate library movement wish that library services might be carried one preposition further in the 1970s and 1980s. They want it to be librarians *with* students: undergraduate librarians in touch with students and truly working with them — students learning from librarians and librarians learning from students.

Finally, Section VIII brings together other evaluations and critiques and includes material on British undergraduate libraries.

This *Reader,* thus, ranges from the earliest concern for undergraduate library services to the opening of the well designed Sedgewick Library at the University of British Columbia in 1973. It closes on a note of evaluation and self-criticism. The next several years will reveal whether a second volume of readings will be necessary to chronicle continuing development of library service on university campuses *with* undergraduate students or whether this volume is sufficient because undergraduate librarianship was only a specialty which flourished in the 1960s and early 1970s. Perhaps undergraduate libraries and other libraries on university campuses will evolve into real service libraries as the "hard times" of the late 1970s and the 1980s decree that there will only be a few great national research libraries on university campuses and that the larger number of universities will spend their resources on good institutional libraries aimed at serving the basic library needs of students and faculty. It is hoped that this volume of readings will be insufficient to present the continuing development of library services on university campuses, particularly where undergraduate students are concerned.

In addition to being very grateful to the Association of College and Research Libraries as noted above, I wish to express sincere thanks to each author or publisher who kindly granted permission to reprint articles and thereby make this volume possible. I am also, as ever, grateful to my wife, Ann M. Wilkinson, for assistance and encouragement.

BILLY R. WILKINSON

Chicago, Illinois
April, 1978

Part I.

Library Service for Undergraduate Students in Late Nineteenth and Early Twentieth Centuries:

The Harvard Example

Part I: Introduction

Before concentrating on the development of library service for Harvard under-graduate students in the late nineteenth and the first half of the twentieth centu-ries, the historical precedents of library service for undergraduate students in English and American colleges and universities should be briefly summarized.

Wagman[1] has traced the idea of a separate undergraduate library back to the early years of the seventeenth century in England. Sir Thomas Bodley made his famous proposal in February, 1598 to Oxford University to restore the library. For the next fifteen years, Bodley made the Oxford library the "one passion"[2] of his life. Even before the opening of the library in 1602, he had hired Thomas James as his librarian to assist in this passion. It was as first Keeper of the Library that James recommended in 1608 the establishment of an undergraduate library to serve the younger students at Oxford. Bodley, however, refused to approve the idea, writing to James:

> Your deuise for a Librarie for the yonguer sort, will have many great exceptions, & one of special force, that there must be an other keeper ordeined for that place. And where you mention the yonguer sort, I knowe what bookes should be brought for them, but the elder aswell [as] the yonguer, may have often occasion to looke vpon them: and if there were any suche, they can not require so great a rowme. In effect, to my understanding there is muche to be saide against it, as vndoubtedly your self will readily finde, vpon further consideration.[3]

There was so "muche to be saide against it" that little was done for Oxford undergraduates for the next 150 years. Finally, in 1856, the statutes of the Bodleian Library were changed to allow undergraduates as well as graduate stu-dents to study in the library.[4] The Radcliffe Camera was the reading room in which the undergraduates might read if they presented a written note from their tutors and wore their gowns. Only fifty seats were available for all readers. The number of undergraduates admitted to the Camera in the 1860's averaged only eighty per year.[5] But by 1872 the graduates complained that they were being inconvenienced by the undergraduates.

With the appointment of Edward Williams Byron Nicholson as Librarian of

---

SOURCE: The introductory material to this Section is from Chapter 2 of Billy R. Wilkin-son's *Reference Services for Undergraduate Students: Four Case Studies*, Metuchen, N. J., Scarecrow Press, 1972, pp. 20-23, and is reprinted by permission of the publisher.

3

the Bodleian in 1882, a librarian with more sympathy for the needs of under-graduates took charge of the Radcliffe Camera. He wanted many more books on open shelves: a select collection for undergraduates, a reference library for researchers, and a periodical reading room. Nicholson immediately selected some 6,000 volumes as a students' library and placed them on open shelves in the Camera. This was, however, a short-lived period of open access. In 1894 he was forced to lock up the collection because of book losses.[6]

American Colonial Colleges

On the American scene, nine colleges have had a continuous history from before the revolutionary war with Great Britain. Harvard, established in 1636, is the oldest American college. A grant of four hundred pounds from the Massachu-setts General Court was the initial gift in 1636. Two years later, the "Rev. John Harvard, of Charlestown, gave by his will the sume of £779.17.2 in money, and more than three hundred volumes of books."[7] Thus was begun the first college library in this country. Shores[8] has chronicled the early history of Harvard Col-lege Library and the libraries of William and Mary, Yale, Princeton, Columbia, Pennsylvania, Brown, Rutgers, and Dartmouth. The various rules, regulations, and codes of these libraries clearly reveal that the undergraduate student was not a pampered library patron. Libraries existed primarily for the faculty. The early college libraries also had very small collections. Harvard, the largest, had only 13,000 volumes before 1800; Rutgers, the smallest, had a few hundred volumes. The other seven colonial college libraries had holdings ranging from 1,000 to 4,000 volumes.[9]

There were two responses to this inadequate service for undergraduate stu-dents: the segregation of books into a separate library for students and the founding of society libraries by the students themselves.

As early as 1765, the separation of books considered most suitable for use by students was required by the laws of Harvard College Library.[10] "There shall be a part of the Library kept distinct from the rest as a smaller Library for the more common use of the College."[11] This was not very effective because Harvard librarians, throughout the succeeding years, continued to recommend the same measure as a way to serve undergraduates.

In reaction to the restrictive nature of the regulations of use and the small number of volumes available to them, students began to found society libraries. For example, Yale College students Timothy Dwight, Nathan Hale, and James Hillhouse began the Linonia Society Library in 1769; the Brothers in Unity Library was begun later.[12] Both of these student society libraries were housed in separate wings of the college library building. In later years, they were combined in a browsing room of Yale's Sterling Library.

Harvard College

The society libraries, however, were not the magic answer to the library problems of undergraduate students. Harvard students, who were provided with a small collection in the anteroom of the College Library in Gore Hall and also had their own society libraries, drew up in 1857-58 a proposal calling for an undergraduate library in a separate building which would be free from the restrictions of the College Library.[13] These nineteenth century students, using the tactics of twentieth century students, condemned the "utter inadequacy of the College library to meet the wants of undergraduates in their last two years."[14] Their own society libraries were also found lacking: "The Society libraries, intended to supply a want which the College library cannot, are in this College few and confined either to a half or to a small minority of the upper classes."[15]

Again in the same year, students petitioned

> that the lower story of Holden Chapel, when no longer needed for its present use, be granted to the Senior Class, as a Reading Room, Club Room, and Undergraduate Library, to be open in regular course to every member of the two upper classes.[16]

A faculty committee to investigate the situation was appointed. The committee succeeded in getting the faculty and the Harvard Corporation to approve some extension of hours and greater accessibility of current periodicals.[17] Protests by the undergraduates simmered down for several years.

Then, in 1870, the students petitioned again. This time they were promised the lower floor of Massachusetts Hall if the students themselves would come forward with sufficient money for the support of the reading room. In 1872 the students organized a Reading Room Association, raised enough money to furnish the room, pay a student attendant, and subscribe to several periodicals and newspapers.[18] The quarters in Massachusetts Hall were officially granted, but the Reading Room Association was short-lived.

Although Harvard has been used as the exemplar in the section, Columbia University's early twentieth century library service for its undergraduate students is also significant.

The Columbia College Study

Another prominent ancestor of the separate undergraduate library on American university campuses was the Columbia College Study established in Hamilton Hall in 1907. It became the Columbia College Library in 1934, moving into its present quarters in the Butler Library. "Columbia was the first American university to provide special library facilities for its undergraduates (1907)."[19] To borrow a phrase from the musical *Guys and Dolls,* the Columbia College Library is the "oldest, established, permanent, floating" undergraduate library on the campus of an American university.

James H. Canfield, Librarian of Columbia, 1899-1909, stated the case for a library for Columbia College students in his 1905 annual report:

> There is again a demand for the establishment of departmental libraries in that building [Hamilton Hall] for the convenience of officers and students. The distance from the Library building, and all the other usual arguments, are being put forth in favor of this demand.
>
> I beg leave to suggest that a proper treatment of this subject will involve the use of one of the large rooms at either end of the building, say, on the second floor, as a reference library for Columbia College. In this may be placed the books now in the undergraduate Historical Reading-Room, and any other books available for undergraduate work — either by duplication or by temporary withdrawal from the main Library. By a system similar to that which enables us to place on special reserve the texts referred to by instructors, this collection could be kept fresh from term to term and from year to year, and would exactly meet the daily demands of both officers and students. A thoroughly trained and expert custodian should have charge of this room, with at least one page, and with local telephone connections with each department. It is not too much to say that the service thus made possible would surpass in convenience and satisfaction any service which could possibly be rendered by and through the departments themselves, with smaller collections in each department: and would be free from the objections to this latter plan, upon the score of extraordinary expense in duplication, or in care, and from the inevitable delay and annoyance caused by the necessary overlapping and interlacing of the interest of departments.[20]

Only two years later, Canfield happily reported:

> The establishment of the College Study — undoubtedly the best lighted, best ventilated, and most commodious reading room on the campus — is an excellent illustration of our desire to help undergraduates to help themselves, our constant effort to develop in the student self-reliance in the selection and use of books. It also enables us to test a theory which is not new, but which thus far has never been put into actual practice. That is, that a collection of not to exceed 6,000 volumes, carefully selected and kept fresh and up-to-date in every sense of the word, is sufficient to meet all ordinary demands of the undergraduates of the average college. This has been given just a half year's trial, and the result is entirely satisfactory. In a certain sense this is a branch library. From another standpoint it is an undergraduate seminar. Books are classified and shelved according to subjects of instruction and are held for reference only. The open-shelf system prevails, except as to something less than a thousand volumes, which are in such constant demand that the special reserve scheme seems necessary there. It has been our good fortune to have Mr. [C. Alexander] Nelson, the head reference librarian of the University, as the administrator of this new undertaking, in which his wide and varied library experience has been of great value. The use of this collection has increased steadily since its opening day, averaging nearly 1,100 readers each week; and from officers and students alike come words of commendation and satisfaction. Many of the books have been purchased expressly for the College Study, but a large number are loans from the

main Library, returnable to the Library, when the course of instruction changes. Undergraduates are not forbidden to use the main Library; but this special collection fitting so admirably their daily work, in the building in which their classes and lectures are held, proves far more convenient and far more attractive than the Library itself. We have every reason to be satisfied with this experiment.[21]

Upon reading Canfield's praises of the Columbia College Study in 1907, the present day undergraduate libraries do not seem so pioneering. At this early date Columbia had already established an undergraduate library in a classroom building, appointed a librarian of the College Study who seemed attuned to the needs of students, and gathered a collection of books based directly on the curriculum which were freely accessible to the students. However, it should be remembered that the library was only one study room with a very small, noncirculating collection.

Undergraduate Quarters within University Libraries

During the first half of the twentieth century, other university libraries began to set aside reading rooms, special collections, and reserve books for their undergraduate students. Often these undergraduate quarters were within the main university library. In other instances, such as at the University of Colorado and the University of Nebraska, the reader services for all students and faculty were organized into a divisional plan.[22] Open-shelf collections and service were divided according to broad subject areas (usually three divisions: humanities, social sciences, and sciences). Literary form (periodicals, monographs, reference volumes, or documents) or library function (reference assistance or circulation) were no longer the criteria for the library's organization. Improved library service for undergraduates was a factor in the conversion to a divisional plan. In still other universities with relatively small numbers of undergraduate students, such as Princeton, there was no need for separate collections or services for undergraduates.[23] Open access by undergraduates to the stacks was the policy.

In the following pages Robert W. Lovett picks up the Harvard saga in his "The Undergraduate and the Harvard Library, 1877-1937" which is reprinted here from the *Harvard Library Bulletin.*

"The Undergraduate and the Harvard Library, 1937-1947" by Keyes D. Metcalf completes the pre-Lamont Library story and this section.

Notes

1. Frederick H. Wagman, "Library Service to Undergraduate College Students, a Symposium: The Case for the Separate Undergraduate Library," *College and Research Libraries* 17 (March, 1956): 150.

2. Donald G. Davis, Jr., "Problems in the Life of a University Librarian: Thomas James, 1600-1620," *College and Research Libraries* 31 (January, 1970): 44.

3. Sir Thomas Bodley, *Letters of Sir Thomas Bodley to Thomas James,* ed. with an Introduction by G.W. Wheeler (Oxford: Clarendon Press, 1926), p. 183.

4. Sir Edmund Craster, *History of the Bodleian Library, 1845-1945* (Oxford: Clarendon Press, 1952), p. 145.

5. Ibid.

6. Ibid., pp. 240-41.

7. Samuel A. Eliot, *A Sketch of the History of Harvard College and of Its Present State* (Boston: C.C. Little and J. Brown, 1848), p. 6.

8. Louis Shores, *Origins of the American College Library, 1638-1800* ("Contributions to Education, George Peabody College for Teachers," No. 134; Nashville, Tennessee: George Peabody College for Teachers, 1934.

9. Ibid., p. 229.

10. Keyes D. Metcalf, "The Undergraduate and the Harvard Library, 1765-1877," *Harvard Library Bulletin* 1 (Winter, 1947): 29-30.

11. Harvard University, *College Book No. 7,* pp. 145-150, quoted in Louis Shores, *Origins of the American College Library, 1638-1800* ("Contributions to Education, George Peabody College for Teachers," No. 134; Nashville, Tennessee: George Peabody College for Teachers, 1934), p. 186.

12. Shores, pp. 224-25.

13. Kimball C. Elkins, "Foreshadowings of Lamont: Student Proposals in the Nineteenth Century," *Harvard Library Bulletin* 8 (Winter, 1954): 42.

14. Harvard University, *Harvard College Papers, 1857,* "Considerations in Favor of an Undergraduate Library and Reading-Room," quoted in Kimball C. Elkins, "Foreshadowings of Lamont: Student Proposals in the Nineteenth Century," *Harvard Library Bulletin* 8 (Winter, 1954): 43.

15. Ibid.

16. Harvard University, *Harvard College Papers, 1857* [Petition], quoted in Elkins, p. 46.

17. Elkins, pp. 49-51.

18. Ibid., p. 52.

19. Columbia University, Library, "A Description of the Libraries" (Columbia University Library, February, 1967): p. 6. (Mimeographed.)

20. Columbia University, Library, *Report of the Librarian for the Academic Year Ending June 30, 1905,* pp. 243-44.

21. Ibid., . . . *June 30, 1907,* pp. 184-85.

22. Frank A. Lundy, "Library Service to Undergraduate College Students, A Symposium: The Divisional Plan Library," *College and Research Libraries* 17 (March, 1956): 145.

23. William S. Dix, "Library Service to Undergraduate College Students, a Symposium: Undergraduates Do Not Necessarily Require a Separate Facility," *College and Research Libraries* 17 (March, 1956): 149.

Robert W. Lovett

The Undergraduate and the Harvard Library, 1877-1937

A professor of history and a new librarian of Harvard College Library finally combined to give the students better library service. In 1875, Professor Henry B. Adams, who as a student had signed the student petition of 1857-58, petitioned the Harvard Corporation for reading space for his students in the College Library. President Charles W. Eliot backed Adams and the Library was soon cleared of showcases and other fixtures and given over to more accommodations for readers. Then, Justin Winsor, who had been head of the Boston Public Library, was appointed Librarian of Harvard in 1877. Winsor began a reserve book system, extended the hours of opening, and by 1880 admitted students to the stacks for limited periods of time. William Coolidge Lane followed Winsor and Abbott Lawrence Lowell became President. Finally in 1915, the Widener Library was completed. Complaints, however, continued about library service for undergraduates.

Between 1877 and 1937 the Harvard Library grew from a collection of 414,215 volumes and pamphlets, the bulk of them kept in a building already forty years old and open only during daylight hours, to a collection of 3,863,150, scattered for convenience in many places, but the greater part housed in a relatively modern building, kept open until ten at night.[1] Of course the undergraduate enrollment increased during this time too; from 813 to 3,735, to be exact. But whereas there were 509 books for each undergraduate in 1877, there were 1,034 in 1937. However, had the complexities inherent in a great collection of books offset the more liberal provision of material? Both the Faculty and the students were

SOURCE: From Robert W. Lovett, "The Undergraduate and the Harvard Library, 1877-1937," *Harvard Library Bulletin* 1 (Spring, 1947), pp. 221-237. Reprinted by permission of the publisher.

aware of this problem and attempted in various ways to meet it. These included, in the early part of the period under consideration, subscription libraries managed by the students, and reserved books; later, class-room and laboratory libraries; and finally, Widener's great reading room, a separate library for freshmen, and the House libraries. No one of these was ever the complete answer, but during two thirds of the period the main effort was directed towards the attainment of a single large reading room, while it has been of recent years that the value of smaller, more strategically placed libraries has been realized. Changing methods of instruction have been reflected in the library system; and through all the expedients, the gropings, the heated discussions, real contributions to librarianship and to education have emerged.

The modern conception of the relation of the college library to the undergraduate is generally credited to Justin Winsor, who became Librarian in 1877, after nine fruitful years as head of the Boston Public Library. But just as some of President Eliot's reforms were foreshadowed during the administration of his predecessor, Thomas Hill, so some of Winsor's were attempted under Librarian Sibley, though not, probably, with his wholehearted consent. The obstacles to the free use of books by students from the building of the second Harvard Hall to the retirement of Sibley have been portrayed by the present Librarian in an article in 1947.[2] One compensating factor, as he points out, was the 'society libraries of the students'; in 1873, the last year they appear in the college catalogue, they numbered 16,000 volumes. But these were not available to all students, nor could they keep up with current publications. Accordingly, in 1872, the students organized their own Reading Room Association, designed to supply current newspapers and periodicals for the sum of two dollars a year. The *Harvard Advocate* took up the cause; President Eliot agreed to allow the use of the lower floor of Massachusetts Hall. Four hundred subscriptions were raised, enough to furnish the room, to pay a sophomore curator $2.50 a week, and to buy subscriptions to a respectable number of newspapers, including foreign. But difficulties soon arose over persons who tried to use the room without subscribing. And after a lapse in 1879 and a reorganization in 1883, the Association dissolved for good in 1884.[3] Presumably the newspapers went to the College Library. Another library open only to subscribers was that of the Harvard Union, established in 1901. That too finally was taken over by the University; quite rightly, libraries-by-subscription were not to be the answer to the problem of the student and the library.

The introduction of the reserved book system, and of the methods of teaching which it implies, was first undertaken by Professors Henry Torrey and Henry Adams of the History Department. Writing in the *Boston Evening Transcript* of 5 November 1913, 'K.V.S.' recalls: 'There came Torrey, watchful for his history alcove that it be supplied with everything new and valuable . . . It was he who first took down the "No admittance" bars and opened his alcove for the free access of his students, placing in it tables and chairs, and making it attractive, that his classes might love to live with the books and not merely refer to them.'

The contribution of Henry Adams to the new methods of teaching is well known; he describes it himself in the *Education:* 'Since no textbooks existed, the professor refused to profess, knowing no more than his students, and they read what they pleased and compared their results.'[4] Dissatisfied with conditions in the Library, Adams in 1875 addressed the following petition to the Corporation:

> The Undersigned, Assistant Professor of History, respectfully presents the following petition to the Honorable the Corporation of Harvard College.
>
> The Undersigned has the duty of instructing a number of students in the department of History. He requires of them that each one shall use to the utmost possible extent the resources of the College Library. Without doing so, they cannot acquire the training which it is his principal object to give them.
>
> As the Library is at present arranged it is impossible for them to use it to proper advantage. The students require room, especially table-room, which is not given them.
>
> The Undersigned respectfully represents that this inconvenience is wholly unnecessary. One half the floor of the library is now occupied by show-cases, stands, or other fixtures, which do not necessarily belong there and which add nothing to the proper usefulness of the institution.
>
> The Undersigned respectfully requests that these cases, &c, may be removed and that a long table may, so soon as the Honorable Corporation think proper, be substituted. If this be done, the Undersigned believes that the students will have sufficient accommodation for all their immediate wants.
>
> Respectfully presented
>
> Cambridge. 14 Decr. 1875   /s/Henry Adams[5]

The petition brought action, for President Eliot, in his report for 1876-77, states that the floor has been cleared and 'is to be given up entirely to the accommodation of persons who are consulting books.'

Justin Winsor, himself a scholar, approved completely of the new methods of teaching and the system of reserved books. An excellent statement of his attitude is to be found in his preliminary report to President Eliot, for 1876-77: 'Books may be accumulated and guarded, and the result is sometimes called a library: but if books are made to help and spur men on in their own daily work, the library becomes a vital influence; the prison is turned into a workshop.' Winsor soon did away, as he had already done at the Boston Public Library, with the calling in of books for annual examination and the closing of the Library for cleaning. He inaugurated a system of 'Notes and Queries,' whereby questions could be posted, for anyone with the requisite information to answer. By 1880 students were being admitted to the stacks; tickets were given for limited periods of time. Of his extension of the alcove and reserved book collections, he writes in his first complete report, for 1877-78:

> The students can handle — this absolute contact with books is, in my judgment, humanizing — the newer books, as they stand on certain shelves, for a while after their accession; and alcoves, with tables, are also given to an ever-changing collection of books, designated by the several professors as collateral reading for their

classes. These latter books, now conspicuously labelled with a different color for each professor, are retained from circulation, except at hours when the Library is not open . . . With this rearrangement of the hall, I had reserved in my mind the series of lower alcoves — removing the present central cases and substituting tables — to contain a succession of collections of the most useful books in all departments of knowledge, each alcove being given to a particular branch, of which the students could have unfettered enjoyment. I think there can be no difficulty about sufficient oversight; and I have confidence that it will stimulate inquiry, and give new resources to the instructors. I would not have these collections permanent, but shifting from year to year. Ten and even twenty thousand volumes can thus, I judge, be most profitably disposed.

The results of Winsor's activity were described by Henry Ware in the *Harvard Register* for October 1880:

> The books have been re-arranged in the new wing since his accession; the old Gore Hall has been devoted to the purposes of a reading-room; the hours of use have been extended, so that the doors are open even in vacation nearly as many hours as they formerly were in term time. Sunday even sees them open; and, as soon as proper means of lighting are devised, the evenings as well as the days can be devoted to study within the walls of the library. A new life and spirit seem to pervade the place; and it is safe to say that a public library does not exist to which readers are more cordially welcomed, or more intelligently and courteously aided in their researches, than the library of Harvard College under its present enlightened and modern management.

The new Librarian had the full support of the President, who, in his report for 1877-78, rejoiced that 'the Library gives abundant evidence of the inventiveness, experience, and energy of the Librarian.'

Problems raised by overcrowding, which were to plague the Library authorities for the next thirty-five years, soon faced Winsor. Space gained by the addition of 1877, in which modern stack construction was used for the first time in America, was soon filled up. Here, in a letter from Winsor to Eliot, dated 29 October 1892, is a typical statement of the case: 'I wish to notify you that of this day, at the beginning of cold weather, we are all blocked in our Reading Room, and every chair, we can find space for on the floor and in the gallery is filled, and many of the sitters are without table facilities. Our Cloak room is packed, and we have been obliged to let students carry their overcoats into the reading room. Our delivery room is crowded to the detriment of its administration. Our stack is gorged, and confusion is increasing. The thought of what we shall experience a few weeks hence is alarming.' That part of the quotation referring to crowded conditions in the reading room might easily have been written today. Without electricity, the Library had to close before four o'clock on some winter afternoons. Though an effort was made to raise funds for lighting in 1886, and the students petitioned that lights be installed in 1889, the Corporation, with an eye on the College treasury, was reluctant to go ahead. The plaster was crumbling (Sibley had noticed this back in the seventies); and on Thanksgiving Day, 1889, a fifty-pound corner ornament fell onto a table in the reading room, 'where on ordinary days a student might be sitting.'[6] Planning and hoping for an addition, or even a new building, became the Librarian's chief concern.

Early plans for enlargement hinged on a separate reading room, perhaps with smaller rooms for class libraries opening off it. Winsor favored this arrangement; writing in the *Harvard Register* for January 1880, he states: 'We can hardly hope our college libraries will do all that they should in connection with the classes, until libraries are built with class-rooms contiguous to the alcoves. A disused apartment in the Harvard Library has been divided into three stalls, with shelves about the tables to hold a large number of books; and here the professor brings his class, and illustrates the modes of research.' President Eliot, in his report for 1883-84, urged a separate reading room. If the new building had ample coat-rooms and dressing-rooms, he felt that 'students who had no rooms in Cambridge might find themselves comfortably provided for at the reading-room during the whole working day.' Still no donor came forward, and in 1890 the students started a subscription. They raised $3,530; a subsequent appeal to the alumni brought in an additional $18,000. Even in those days this was much too little; so everyone took heart when it was rumored that a donor had been found. Plans were actually drawn up for an octagonal building, to be located on the hill towards Quincy Street. It was to be connected to Gore Hall by a lean-to, which would house the delivery desk. The prospective donor[7] died, however, before the gift was made. Although the failure to obtain a new library at this time was a heavy blow, it now seems obvious that the plans were such that deferment of the new building was really a blessing.

Finally, in 1895-96, the Corporation, using the money raised by subscription in 1890, plus some of its own, renovated Gore Hall. Part of the old lofty reading room was turned into stacks and a new reading room constructed across the top of the former. This provided seats for 225 students, while the History Room, over the Delivery Desk, accommodated 50 more. And at long last the Library was wired for electricity. It was realized that the reading room arrangements were only temporary; in fact, ventilating problems soon made the use of the large reading room in summer almost impossible. A rotary fan proving unsuccessful, a large awning like a tent-fly was spread over the entire roof. All of this was too much for the editors of the *Lampoon,* who, in a fake issue of the *Crimson,* dated 30 May 1901, ran a scratched-up picture of a monumental room, which purported to be a new reading room for Gore Hall offered by an unknown donor. 'The present accommodation having become manifestly insufficient,' the news item states, 'it was deemed advisable to remove the stacks in Room E, to the left of the present reading room, as one enters. The books have been placed in carefully sealed boxes in the basement, until suitable accommodations can be obtained for them. The desks are to be of hard Georgia pine, and are fitted with a new system of drop lights, as seen in the cut.'

Balked in his efforts to obtain a new building, Winsor turned to the multiplication and strengthening of the class and laboratory libraries, outside Gore Hall, and to the provision of special collections within. Libraries in United

States History and in Political Economy were the first two class-room libraries of importance. They had been set up in University Hall in 1886; shortly they were transferred to Harvard Hall where, with collections in Social Questions and European History, they formed a reading room for the elementary courses in the social sciences. The Social Questions books were transferred to Emerson Hall in 1905, but the other collections remained in Harvard Hall, which grew more and more crowded, until the construction of Widener. In 1897, the Child Memorial Library, a collection of books in English literature, was opened as a tribute to Professor Francis James Child. Special collections in French, German, Romance, and Sanskrit were established in Warren House in 1899. Some of these were closed collections, open to graduate students with keys, and so became the ancestors of the rooms on the top floor of Widener.

Efforts to make more books available to undergraduates within Gore Hall itself included selections of reference books, periodicals, and modern literature, maintained in the reading and delivery rooms. Reporting on this material for the year 1886-87, Winsor wrote: 'In addition to the books reserved by instructors, now amounting to 6280 volumes, there are in the reading-room 1784 volumes carefully selected for students' reading by the instructors in the several departments. Of these, 1300 are English, 335 French, 105 German, and 44 Italian. The use of these books is not governed by the restrictions applied to reserved books, but the books may be taken out as other books are.' Here, perhaps, is the ancestor of the browsing collections so common today. With the construction of the Union, a student activities center, in 1901, recreational and extra-curricular reading was made much more attractive. In his first report, for the year 1897-98, Librarian Lane wrote of these collections: 'To these [reserved and reference books] should be added the books in the Harvard Hall reading-room (3,959) and those in the other class-room and laboratory libraries (16,546), making altogether, at present, about 40,000 volumes which are directly accessible in an informal manner to the members of the University.' In spite of the disadvantages of breaking up the collections, not wholly offset by centralized cataloguing and supervision, these class-room libraries have increased, accounting now for a large part of the fifty-two special libraries in the Harvard Library system.

Winsor died in 1897, just after his return from England, where he had represented the American Library Association at an international conference. Though his chief contribution to the Harvard Library was the liberalizing of the lending of books, he still believed there was no substitute for owning them. He wrote to Eliot: 'The pressure is constant to buy duplicates. It is met sparingly . . . I deem it one of the most unsatisfactory phases of our student life that there is a disinclination to count the ownership of books among the necessities of a college course.'[8] His successor was William Coolidge Lane, Librarian of the Boston Athenaeum, and a former member of the Harvard Library staff. As Winsor's extra-curricular interests lay in American history, particularly of the period of exploration, so Lane's lay in antiquarian investigations, especially into Harvard history. From his first report, it was evident that Lane meant to follow the paths laid out by Winsor. And during the next dozen years, as during the previous twelve, the Library's history may be written in terms of the need of larger quarters. But now the basic purposes of a college library came up for consideration, and President Eliot at times found himself on the opposite side of the fence from the librarians.

Hints of Eliot's position are to be found in his report for the year 1885-86: 'The justification of the enormous expense which is involved in the accumulation and maintenance of a great university library is not to be found in the daily use which the mass of the students will make of it. A much cheaper instrument would serve them. The justification must be found in its indispensableness to teachers, authors, and other thorough scholars, and to students having exceptional work in hand.' In his report for 1892-93, however, the new methods of instruction receive his complete support: 'However troublesome and costly it may be to teach thousands of students the abundant use of books, it is the most important lesson that can be given them during their student life.' By 1898-99 he was willing to put some limit upon the number of books to which the students need access: 'A library for the use of young students feels the encumbrance of masses of dead books on the shelves, and of useless cards in the catalogue drawers more than any other sort of library; for large bodies of young men in process of education want easy access to many live books in rapid succession, but have small interest in superseded books.' Addressing various library clubs in 1902, Eliot advocated a division of books into 'live' and 'dead', and a storage of the dead ones in economical fashion. Many librarians jumped to the defense of their complete collections. And Professor Kittredge marked in the backs of the books which he consulted in the stacks of Gore Hall the date and his initials, so that they at least would not be considered 'dead.' Today, in somewhat modified form, President Eliot's suggestion has been acted upon by a group of libraries in the Boston region, including Harvard.

So much for the public record. In private, Lane wrote to Eliot; 'Should not the primary object of a great university library be to supply the needs of professors and advanced students? By a selection of books placed in the Reading-room, or elsewhere, by special lists, and by personal guidance, the Library meets the needs of beginners. Hence the accumulation of books in a library does not work to the injury of elementary students, for their wants are served in a different way.'[9] To which Eliot replied: 'I agree with you that the primary object of a university library should be to supply the needs of professors and advanced students; but the way to do that seems to me to get the additional books which such persons need at the moment, and not to undertake to make huge collections in advance of the expressed wishes of the professors and advanced students.'[10] With such a difference of opinion as to methods, if not ends, between President and Librarian, it was obvious that more study was necessary. So began the period of committees. The first committee was weighted in favor of the Librarian, for it was made up of the Librarians of the Law, Divinity, Museum of Comparative Zoology, and College Libraries, plus the Director of the Observatory, and Lane was Secretary. Its recommendations were:

I. Two or more large reading rooms, in which are to be kept general reference books and current periodicals, and reserved books for all the elementary courses and for some of the more advanced courses; — with provision for 500 readers, and shelving for 35,000 volumes.

II. A series of rooms of moderate size having as far as possible the privacy and attractiveness that belong to a good private library, one or more for each of the departments that maintains or desires to maintain a separate working reference library for its advanced students.[11]

Here Widener, with its large reading room and its departmental libraries, is definitely foreshadowed.

Deciding it would be wise to have these findings checked by outside authorities, the Corporation appointed another committee, consisting of Herbert Putnam, Librarian of Congress, John Shaw Billings, Librarian of the New York Public Library, Edward C. Pickering, Director of the Harvard Observatory, and Lane. The last two named had been on the earlier committee. Lane objected to the appointment of Billings, whose field had been medicine, for fear that the committee would be overweighted in favor of science. As it happened, Billings turned in a minority report advocating a limit, within the next twenty-five years, of 500,000 volumes for the University Library. In the call for the committee, the Corporation had stated: 'The President and Fellows are ready to spend money in order to procure one handsome reading-room, but, in general, they feel compelled to be distinctly frugal and to consider very carefully the running expenses of the projected building.' In the majority report, the proponents of library expansion stated: 'We believe that a collection of books indefinitely growing, containing also the material precious from its form or from association, is a cultivating influence which ought not to be withdrawn from the student body.'

So far neither of the committees had actually decided the question of keeping Gore Hall, though both had recommended the employment of an architect to study the subject. The Corporation's views at this time appear in a letter from Eliot to Lane, dated 21 June 1904: 'Moreover, there is not a single member of the Corporation who is converted to the opinion that it would be expedient for Harvard University to maintain an immense, very comprehensive library in the College Yard.' And in his report for 1902-03 Eliot was of the opinion that 'a million books would seem to be a reasonable current stock to be kept on hand from generation to generation in the same building with the administrative offices and the reading-rooms.' Therefore, Lane began consulting with Herbert L. Warren, Professor of Architecture, on the enlargement of Gore Hall. Warren drew up plans for a series of additions, which would eventually surround that building completely. The Committee of 1901 was asked to study these plans, and found them not wholly satisfactory. So outside professionals were again called in, in the persons of Guy Lowell, Désiré Despradelle, and Charles A. Coolidge, architects. Their reports once and for all banished Gore Hall; their plans, in fact, became the basis for Widener Library. One of the few differences in the over-all plan is that they placed the delivery desk in the position occupied by the memorial room in the finished building.

During this period of planning, the Library continued to function as best it could in Gore Hall. In 1900, Librarian Lane was wondering why 501 students out of 1,092 did not use the Library. 'Most of them, probably all,' he wrote in his report, 'used the reading-rooms and class-room libraries, but it is a little remarkable that so many should have been satisfied with this, and not have been tempted to borrow additional books. The fact that several of the social clubs now support much larger and better selected libraries than they formerly did is doubtless one reason why many students do not find occasion to borrow from the College Library.' One way to bring more students into the Library, he suggested in his report for 1901-02, would be to provide a more comprehensive collection of books in the reading room. 'In the meantime,' he wrote, 'it is fortunate that the library of the Harvard Union has begun to offer some of the advantages of such a collection, and especially in fields which the College reading-room has not attempted to occupy.'[12] These fields included literature, biography, history, travel, and sport, and the collection was an open-stack one. Some of the decline in the circulation of books from the main library Lane attributed to this fact, finding it 'striking evidence of the greater pleasure to be had in picking out one's own books from well selected open shelves, even though the books must be read on the premises, than in sending for them by messenger after searching in a card catalogue, though the stock to select from be larger and though the books may be taken to one's own room and kept for a month.'

In 1907 there occurred one of the frequent waves of complaint concerning the service to students. A member of the junior class wrote to the Librarian: 'It would be asking none too much, I think, to ask for freer access to the shelves, for the priviledge [sic] of taking out one book for each course pursued (perhaps with the restriction to the number of four), for the removal of the high and inconvenient fences placed along the center of all the tables in the reading room, for a better form of chair in place of those on spindles and above all for prompt and courteous attention.'[13] A graduate student who was later to meet academic administrative problems of his own came to the Library's defense, in a letter printed in the *Crimson* for 13 May 1907: 'I beg to testify to the uniform courtesy of the hard-worked men, women and boys who make the Harvard Library the most efficient and the most liberal circulator of books I have ever seen.'[14] It is significant that it was the undergraduate who was attacking, the graduate who was defending the Library. That the undergraduate had some reason on his side is to be seen in the following description of the old Gore Hall reading room, taken from the *Boston Traveller* for 6 September 1912. 'The bare reading room,' the reporter states, 'with its poor lighting arrangements, its uncomfortable, stiff-backed swivel chairs, its inconvenient, antiquated racks and its inevitable susurrus of subdued voices has not been an incentive to earnest study.'

New names and faces appeared on the scene during the years just preceding the building of Widener; many were to come into close contact with the students. In 1904 Charles A. Mahady became Superintendent of the Reading Room, a post he held until his retirement in 1943. In 1909 President Eliot was succeeded by Abbott Lawrence Lowell. The next year Professor Archibald Cary Coolidge, for some time a benefactor of the Library, was appointed to the newly-created post of Director. Finally, in the summer of 1912, came the announcement of a new building, the gift of Mrs. George D. Widener, in memory of her son, Harry, who had been lost in the sinking of the 'Titanic.' The books were removed from Gore Hall without delay, two thirds of them going to Randall Hall (now the home of the Printing Office), the rest to Andover, Robinson, and other buildings. Reading rooms were set up in Massachusetts Hall during the three-year building period. (Massachusetts Hall, in the course of its varied history, had served as a reading room during the reconstruction of 1896, and also as the home of the students' library in 1872.)

The new building represented a compromise between the library theories current at the time and the necessity that it be a memorial.Trumbauer, the Philadelphia architect, drew heavily on the plans of the earlier committees, especially that of the architects prepared in 1910. The belief that a reading room should be large and monumental was deeply entrenched. Putnam, the Librarian of Congress, told the Overseers in 1903 that the present reading room 'lacks the large spaces conducive to meditative study, and is barren of the architectural beauty and dignity which in a great library can exercise a practical influence for good.'[15] It was hoped that the fine new building would meet the needs of both undergraduates and scholars. But as is so often the case with ends that are not wholly compatible, one soon outdistanced the other. It was inconceivable that the Harvard Library should not be a great scholarly library; all its past history pointed towards that goal. The *Boston Transcript* for 5 September 1912 had this to say of the proposed building: 'It is to be not merely a storehouse for books, not merely a place where the undergraduate may go to read, or the instructor to study. It will be a centre for the ripe scholarship of the world, a workroom and a laboratory for the men who are to give direction to the world's thought.' At last there would be studies enough for the professors (though not for long), cubicles for graduate students, and separate rooms for seminars. Anxious to defend the displacement of the delivery room in favor of the memorial library in the heart of the building, Lowell wrote to Putnam, on 30 October 1912: 'My interest in the arrangement of the library is centered about making it as useful as possible for scholars who are engaged in study by providing them with working rooms, and with stalls or cubicles, leading off the stacks. The arrangement of the delivery room has seemed to me less important.' Lane, writing in the *Library Journal,* May, 1913, echoes this argument. But many a student must have counted wearily the 68 steps to the delivery desk, and the 46 additional to the top floor, where the Business School Library was housed until 1927.

In spite of the emphasis on use by scholars and graduate students, many innovations on behalf of undergraduates were introduced into the new building. The History Library was moved from Harvard Hall and installed on the ground floor, with a convenient entrance. Here it remained until expansion of the Treasure Room required its transfer to nearby Boylston Hall in 1929. From the start, it was planned to furnish a room in the new library solely for recreational reading. In 1916, Mr. and Mrs. William Farnsworth made it possible to equip this room, adjacent to the main entrance, in memory of their son Henry, who was killed while serving with the Foreign Legion. Under the guidance of Mrs. Florence Milner, this room became a model for several similar collections in colleges across the country. Her experience was valuable when it came to establishing the Freshman and House Libraries. A somewhat similar room, for the reading of verse, was dedicated in 1931, in memory of George Edward Woodberry. Changes were made in the organization of the reference service, partly as a result of a survey of the Library made by two Business School students in 1914. Though their report is mainly concerned with the technical processes of the Library, the authors do say of the service to students: 'It seems that the treatment of students is the most serious problem in this library. Every effort should be made to overcome this defect. A reference department should be organized and a competent man with a strong personality put in charge. The circulation department should be organized so as to give efficient and willing service and should be under the control of the reference librarian.'[16] This recommendation was carried into effect the following year with the appointment to this post of Walter B. Briggs. Visiting scholars and students alike found Mr. Briggs ever ready to help them. In another effort to acquaint the students with the Library, a pamphlet, 'Notes on the Use of the Harvard College Library,' was issued in 1915; several new editions have since appeared. It has also long been the annual custom at Harvard for freshmen in small groups to be taken on a tour of the Library early in the college year. These remedies helped, but could not cure the basic disease of bigness.

The new building, which was dedicated in 1915, had not been in use long before flaws began to appear. The *Crimson* became particularly adept at picking them out; many of them petty, some serious. Almost every editorial board or group of candidates tried its hand on the subject of Widener. Just how much these editorials represented the feelings of the undergraduates as a whole would be hard to say. On smaller matters, we find noise in the reading room a subject of discussion in 1922, censorship in 1924, various utilities in 1925, ventilation in 1926.[17] It is interesting, in the midst of such criticism, to find the *Crimson* editors in 1923 approving the purchase of unique books for scholars, rather than the duplication of texts for students. 'The University's debt to the general cause of learning,' says an editorial, 'is greater than to the personal convenience of a few students.'[18] But in 1925, urging the appointment of a Professor of Books, an editorial states: 'The Widener of today is cold, formal, business-like, if not super-efficient. It is a ponderous mechanism which only the skilled graduate can rightly use. It should be the heart and soul of the University. It should be a treasure trove of knowledge, but not one that is locked to all but the initiated.'[19] This is the perennial complaint, presented in humorous form by the *Lampoon,* 19 May 1926. A student is shown requesting a copy of Plato at the delivery desk and is told: 'Sorry, we haven't any Platos today. It's either lost, strayed, stolen or reserved. Couldn't interest you in O. Henry could I?' To correct the complaints based upon the size of Widener, little could be done, except to develop library facilities outside the building. Complaints about the impersonality and quality of the service were another matter; here the administration and the students might well differ as to the degree of difficulty.

With the physical expansion of the University under Lowell in the twenties, the Library also expanded. In 1926 a separate library for freshmen was opened in McKinlock Hall; this was a double collection, one for the large survey courses, and one for general reading, somewhat like the Farnsworth Room. When the Houses for upperclassmen were completed and the freshmen concentrated in the Yard, these libraries were transferred to the Union. Of this move, Mrs. Milner wrote, in the *Harvard Alumni Bulletin* for 14 February 1936:

> The most interesting development since moving into the Union has been the steady increase in general reading. For the first year [1931] the men seemed quite unconscious of anything on the shelves except books needed for courses. The change has come about largely through the generous buying of new books by the Union Committee and by calling especial attention to them. On shelves opposite the desk, so placed that everyone entering the rooms must pass them, is kept a constantly vitalized selection of recent acquisitions. These shelves usually contain about 350 volumes, which circulate constantly. The habit is also growing of wandering through the alcoves in search of older books of interest and in becoming familiar with what the Library offers.

Too many freshmen became satisfied with the Union Library, and remained almost completely ignorant of Widener. The fault was not wholly theirs.

Plans for each of the seven Houses called for a library of from seven to ten thousand volumes. The selection included many of the books needed in course and tutorial work, as well as reference sets, and books for general reading; the furnishings suggested a club or private library. As many freshmen did not venture from the Union Library, so many upperclassmen came to prefer the House Libraries to Widener. Those electing to try for honors their senior year, however, welcomed the temporary permits admitting them to Widener's stacks. For besides the improved facilities offered to students for the reading of books, there were also changes in the methods of instruction, resulting generally in the increased use of books. These included the Tutorial System and the Reading Period. In most fields, students were assigned to tutors who were to guide their out-of-course reading. And for most courses, the two weeks prior to mid-year and final examinations were allotted to extra reading. The Reading Period, as it was called, began in 1928, the same year that Professor Robert P. Blake succeeded Mr. Coolidge as Director of the Library. Of its effect, Mr. Blake wrote as follows in his first report: 'In spite of the great strain put upon the Reading Room staff through this important innovation in college teaching, the Reading Rooms, although crowded to their utmost capacity (especially during the midyear period), functioned smoothly during this time. There were almost no complaints that books were not available and the majority of the readers were pleasantly surprised to find how liberally the books were issued to them . . . . This last fact [the purchase of books by students] shows clearly that students are being brought in contact with more books they wish to own.'

It is well the expansion came when it did, for during the depression years the Library had to economize. The Widener building was closed at six for two years, arousing such a storm of protest from the students that the Corporation was relieved to be able to open it for the usual hours in 1934. So many books were lost that it became necessary in 1930 to install turnstiles at the exits. The students accepted the necessity for this check with a minimum of grumbling. The administration, in fact, showed itself sympathetic to several of the demands of the *Crimson* during the thirties; though the improvements would probably have come anyway. New lights were installed in the reading room in 1935, lights which are already outmoded; the loan period was cut from a month to two weeks in 1938; a study was made of the time required to obtain a book, and a simplified charging system introduced. Some improvements were made in the number and currency of newspapers, and in provisions for using them. A book chute was installed, so books could be returned at times when the Library was closed. Most of these changes benefited users of the Library in general as well as the undergraduates. It would be a mistake to assume any real division between the treatment of undergraduates and that of graduate students and scholars. For though the undergraduates in general used the reading rooms and House Libraries, many were admitted for special periods to the stacks; and the graduate student might often have occasion to consult a reserved book in the main reading room.

However, the question of whether the undergraduates were making the best use of Widener, or whether Widener was really effectively usable by the undergraduates, still remained. Mr. Blake's report for 1932-33 underlined previous observations that students were to a large degree merely reading their own notes and textbooks in the Library, and not using the Library collections. In the *Critic* for 15 December 1932, the members of the National Student League held: 'The simple fact is that the course system at Harvard so emphasizes reading for examinations and so discourages independent research that only a few students utilize Widener to full advantage.' Finally, at the close of the period under discussion, the *Crimson* carried a series of editorials on the coldness and impersonality of Widener. 'Alumni and visitors,' the first editorial states, 'are awed by its murals, marble, and majesty, by its steps and circumference, its showcases and treasures. But, except at reading and examination periods, they may well wonder at the scarcity of students amid the swarm of employees and professors . . . Widener is wondering, too, and very much interested in finding the answer . . . First, is the old recommendation for personalization. Like Grand Central Station, Widener is big, moving, and impersonal, and it is difficult to add a "homey" note to a building constructed for dignity rather than coziness.' The final editorial in the series asserts that improvement 'can only come through a basic change in the library's attitude toward the undergraduate. Until the latter feels that the library is his, that attendants are there to help and not restrict him, he will continue to regard the friendly and hospitable air of the Farnsworth Room as an oasis in an otherwise grim and inhuman desert.'[20]

In such quotations as these, written by the students themselves, lies the justification for a new and radical attempt to solve the difficulty. The great specialized collections in the stacks, the extensive catalogues, are invaluable to the scholar; for the undergraduate they all too often serve to confuse and discourage. The lack of contact with books, which the reading rooms and even the House Libraries cannot wholly remedy, is the most serious loss. The provision of reference assistants, the compilation of a guide book, the tours for new students, all these help, but until the student can live with a goodly collection of books he is missing an important part of a college education. And so the experiments and the makeshifts, from which many lasting benefits have come, still leave the University the problem with which this paper started; how best to bring the student and the books together.

Notes

1. These figures include all the University Libraries, for undergraduates may use the Departmental Libraries, if necessary, and cards for these libraries appear in the Union Catalogue at Widener.

2. Keyes D. Metcalf, "The Undergraduate and the Harvard Library, 1765-1877," *Harvard Library Bulletin* 1 (1947): 29-51.

3. Notes on the reading room appear in the *Advocate* for 22 December 1871, 9 and 20 February and 22 March 1872. The annual *Harvard Index* contains lists of officers of the Association.

4. *The Education of Henry Adams* (Boston and New York, 1918), p. 303.

5. This petition, with similar documents quoted in this account, is preserved in the Harvard University Archives.

6. Letter of Winsor to Eliot, 2 December 1889.

7. Later identified as Frederick L. Ames, '54, Fellow of Harvard College 1888-93.

8. Letter of Winsor to Eliot, 17 October 1887.

9. MS memorandum to Eliot on the President's report for 1900-01.

10. Letter of Eliot to Lane, 26 February 1902.

11. Submitted 31 March 1902; quoted in Lane's fifth report (1901-02), p. 214.

12. In connection with the work of the Committee of 1902, Lane questioned the members of the Faculty as to the use of the Library by their students; unfortunately only one reply has been found.

13. Walter M. Stone, '08, to Lane, 21 May 1907. The reference to one book for each course seems unjustified, for students then were allowed to take out three books at a time, and to keep them for a month.

14. Henry N. MacCracken, Ph.D. 1907.

15. Quoted in Lane's sixth report (1902-03), p. 199.

16. Ralph Fensterwald and Marion Folsom, Final Thesis, 9 April 1914.

17. *Crimson,* May 1922: 18 November 1925; 25 March 4, 22, 26 May 1925; 2 December 1926; 13, 14 January 1927.

18. *Crimson,* 5 February 1923.

19. *Crimson,* 22 January 1925.

20. *Crimson,* 14, 19 October 1937.

About the Author

Robert W. Lovett was Assistant, Harvard University Archives, 1937-1942. After service in the U.S. Army, he returned to become Senior Assistant from 1945-1948. Since 1948, Lovett has been Chief of the Manuscripts Division of Baker Library, Harvard Business School.

Keyes D. Metcalf

The Undergraduate and the Harvard Library, 1937-1947

The Director of the Harvard University Libraries summarizes the library facilities available for undergraduates from 1932 until the opening of the Lamont Library in 1949 and observes that "A student at Amherst, Williams, Dartmouth, Bowdoin, Oberlin, or one of the better women's colleges has at his or her disposal a much larger and better collection of books than has the Harvard undergraduate." He concludes that even the "central collection is so large that it cannot be opened to the undergraduate except under very special circumstances, and as a result there is no large general collection freely accessible to the undergraduate at Harvard — no collection which will include a large share of the volumes that the student will need in any of his work or in the general reading which is desirable for him to do when in college."

The two previous articles in this series[1] brought the story of the undergraduate and the Harvard Library up to the year 1937. The only significance in that date lies in the fact that the present writer's first-hand knowledge of the situation began in the autumn of that year; 1932 or any year thereafter down to and including 1947 would have done just as well, for there have been no important changes in the service to undergraduates since opening of the House Libraries in 1930-31, and none can be expected before the autumn of 1948 at the earliest, when there is a possibility that the new undergraduate library will be ready for use. This article, then, is not a record of progress that has been attained in recent years. It consists simply of a rather detailed description of the service given in the 1930's and early 1940's, supplemented by an account of the history of the

SOURCE: From Keyes D. Metcalf, "The Undergraduate and the Harvard Library, 1937-1947," *Harvard Library Bulletin* 1 (Autumn, 1947), pp. 288-305. Reprinted by permission of the publisher.

plans for the future which are now taking physical form in the southeast corner of the Harvard Yard.

As noted in the preceding article, the transfer of the Undergraduate Reading Room for the beginning courses in History, Government, and Economics (ie., History I, Government I, and Economics A, as they are known) from the basement of Widener to Boylston Hall took place in the autumn of 1929, when the space in Widener was needed for additional quarters for the Treasure Room. A little later — 1930-31 — the seven House Libraries were opened. With their opening, the Library in the Harvard Union became available for the Freshman Library, and from 1931 until the present time no major changes have been made in the library facilities for undergraduates except for the temporary closing and opening of reading rooms, the former made possible by the reduced number of students during the war years, and the latter required by the greatly increased post-war attendance.

Reference should be made at this point to the tentative plans that were never carried out for the use of the great hall in Memorial Hall as a library stack to care for the overflow from Widener, and for the use of the old kitchens in the same building as an undergraduate reading room. This was proposed by Professor Robert P. Blake during his Directorship of the University Library. It would have provided a very satisfactory emergency measure, but was not undertaken because it was realized that, while it would help with the library space problem temporarily, the results could never be completely satisfactory. It must be admitted at this time that any addition to the space devoted to the library in an institution adding over 100,000 volumes a year may seem to be only temporary.

A fairly full description of Harvard undergraduate library facilities as they stood after 1932 and as they now stand in 1947 follows. They are many and complex, but they fall into four main groups.

1. Those in the Harry Elkins Widener Memorial Library, which houses the larger part of the central collection of the Harvard University Library which is called the Harvard College Library.
2. The reserved book reading rooms and collections that represent primarily an overflow from Widener, and are found in Boylston Hall and in the Union.
3. The House Libraries.
4. Other libraries, special and departmental, throughout the University which provide a greater or lesser amount of service to the undergraduate students.

The Widener building was completed and occupied in the autumn of 1915. From the time of the opening to the present, the large reading room on the second floor, which is unfortunately 75 steps above the street level, has been used very largely, though not exclusively, as a reserved book reading room for undergraduates. Around the walls of the central portion and the west end of the room are 85 full sections of book shelves, plus 60 shelves under the 15 windows, all filled to capacity most of the time with books containing the assigned reading in the various courses of the College. These books are arranged first by the College Department, then by the number of the course in the Department, and under each course by the author of each volume. The books are changed as assignments change, but in most cases are put out for a full semester, with return between times to shelves in the main stack area or elsewhere in the building. These books for assigned reading number up to 12,000 at one time and between 20,000 and 25,000 in the course of a year. In earlier years these books, with rare exceptions, were circulated out of the building only after 9:00 in the evening Monday through Friday for overnight use, and after 5:00 o'clock in the afternoon on Saturday for the weekend, for return at 9:00 o'clock the following morning or Monday morning respectively. They are now circulated somewhat more freely in inverse ratio to the demand for them. Many of them are let out any time after 2:00 p.m. Monday through Friday and any time after noon on Saturday. The Main Reading Room is open during term time from 8:45 in the morning until 10 at night Monday through Friday, and until 5:30 on Saturday. It has not been open on Sunday since 1931, first because of the cost of keeping such a large building open for the comparatively small number of students who have cared to use it, and second because the general feeling of the students has been, when the problem has been referred to them, as it has been from time to time, that they would prefer to be able to draw the reserved books out for the weekend than to have to return them for use in the building on Sunday.

In addition to the books for assigned reading around the walls of the Reading Room numbering anywhere between 500 and 2500 volumes, (the number varying according to the time of the year and the assignments) are books which are kept behind the desk in the center of the room. These books number perhaps 1000 different titles, and 10,000 different volumes, in the course of a year. They are the books assigned in the large courses for which the demand is greater than the number of copies at hand will supply without restrictions in use. They are shifted constantly to meet the demand as the assignments change. They are available on request by the signing of a call slip for use within the Library, or outside of the building after 9:00 in the evening or noon on Saturday. As many as 1200 books from the closed and open shelf reserve sections are sometimes drawn out on a Saturday, most of them between 12 and 12:30, and one of the best ways to obtain an idea of the quantity of service given by the Library is to stand in the Reading Room at that time. As no record can be kept of the use within the building from the open shelves, no worthwhile statistics of the total use of the Main Reading Room are available. Additional closed reserve collections are found in Boylston Hall Library and the Freshman Union Library. They will be mentioned again later.

Service to undergraduates provided in other parts of the Widener building may be summarized as follows:

The Farnsworth Room, which is made up of a general reading collection for browsing purposes, has occupied the room just to the right of the main entrance since the opening of the Widener building. A note in regard to this room appeared in the Winter 1947 issue of the HARVARD LIBRARY BULLETIN. The room is endowed in memory of Henry Weston Farnsworth, A.B. 1912, a member of the Foreign Legion of the French Army, who was killed in action 28 September 1915. It is believed to be the first World War memorial to have been established in the United States, and one of the first, if not the first, of the browsing rooms in a university library. It is designed for pleasure reading, with surroundings as nearly as possible like those of a home library. The books are all on open shelves, and include standard and modern works, chiefly in biography, travel, science, history, and literature. A large percentage of them are in English. This room was closed during most of the second World War, because of lack of demand and in order to accumulate funds that could be used to further the collection. The room seats about 35 readers at a time; the total per day has averaged 100 during the past year. The Farnsworth Room is to be transferred to the new undergraduate library.

A large part of the top floor of the Widener building has been used for undergraduate libraries from the time the building was first opened. These collections have changed from time to time, and no attempt will be made here to give a detailed record of them, but a statement about them as they stood during the college year 1946-47 is appropriate.

The Child Memorial Library, occupying the northwest corner of the floor, houses the English seminar and tutorial collections. An attendant has been in charge for all the hours that the building is open during term-time, and the room has been used extensively by undergraduate as well as graduate students.

The corresponding room in the northeast corner is the Classics seminar room, called the Herbert Weir Smyth Classical Library. It has not had an attendant and the door is locked, but undergraduates majoring in the Classics can obtain permission to use the room, which contains a good standard collection of books in the field.

Along the east side of this floor can be found the French, Romance Languages tutorial, and Lowell Memorial collections, used as one of the headquarters for the Romance Languages, particularly the French. The two rooms housing these collections have been kept open with attendants during the past year and for more limited hours in other years. Special shelves are provided for books reserved for assigned reading in French courses.

On the same side of the building may be found the German seminar and the German tutorial rooms, available for use under certain restrictions by undergraduates.

On the south side of this floor there has been the Mathematics seminar room with the tutorial collection in that field, which is open under certain restrictions to concentrators in the field of mathematics.

During the past year two other rooms on this side of the building have been used as an overflow reading room, with over 50 chairs. An attendant has been in charge and reserved books taken from the Main Reading Room have been placed on the shelves.

The Winsor Memorial Map Room occupies the southeast corner of this floor, and is used to a considerable extent by undergraduates to pursue studies in this field beyond the range of the limited collection of maps and atlases in the Main Reading Room.

The three rooms at the southwest corner of this floor were until recently occupied by the Theatre Collection, which finds a good share of its use by undergraduates interested in the history of the theatre and current activities in this field. The headquarters for the Collection were moved to the Houghton Library in January 1947, and the bulk of the collection itself will be placed in the storage stack underneath the new undergraduate library when that building is completed.

Along the west side of the top floor of Widener are the two rooms occupied by the Poetry Collection, which was endowed by Harry Harkness Flagler in memory of George Edward Woodberry. These rooms are open during limited hours. A large percentage of their use has been by undergraduates. The collection will be shifted to the new library.

As has already been stated, the undergraduate reading room for beginning courses in History, Government, and Economics was moved from the basement of Widener to the west end of the first floor of Boylston Hall in the autumn of 1929. This room has seats for approximately 175 readers. It has contained, in addition to the reserved books for the courses just mentioned, a general collection in the field of some 4,000 volumes. The room has been very heavily used — although it was closed during part of the war years when the number of undergraduate students was greatly reduced.

In the Freshman Union there are two libraries: first, the Freshman History Library with some 4,000 volumes, largely made up of books for assigned reading in History I; and second, the Harvard Union collection, which became the Freshman Library when the House Libraries were opened, containing some 18,000 volumes with particular strength in the field of English literature. These reading rooms, with the overflow that is possible into the halls and other rooms in the Union, provide seats for over 200 students. They and the Boylston Hall Reading Room may be considered as overflow rooms from the Widener building as far as the assigned reading work is concerned, and all the services that they provide will be shifted to the new library.

The third group of library services for undergraduates at Harvard consists of the seven House Libraries. In summary:

1) they each contain from ten to twelve thousand volumes for general reading and tutorial work;

2) while they do include some books for assigned reading, they were not organized with that in mind;

3) they have been a very successful part of the library development at Harvard and there is no reason to believe that the new library will affect their use in any way or change the arrangements for them.

The fourth group of library services for undergraduates at Harvard is provided by some forty other libraries connected with the University. It will not be possible in this article to deal with these in detail. All of these libraries are available to undergraduates if they present themselves properly introduced, but it can be readily seen that some of them, particularly those connected with the departments of the University rather than the departments of the College, are used very little by undergraduates. Among these are the Blue Hill Meteorological Observatory Library at Blue Hill, the Libraries of the Arnold Arboretum in Jamaica Plain and the Medical School in Boston, the Libraries of the Astronomical Observatory and the Gray Herbarium a mile north and west of the Yard. In addition it can be stated that several of the large libraries north of the Yard — the Law School, the Graduate School of Education, the Engineering School, the Farlow Herbarium, and the Museum of Comparative Zoology — also come within this group. The same holds true for a number of the smaller libraries, such as the Geographical Laboratory Library now at the Institute of Geographical Exploration, the Physics Research Library in the Lyman Laboratory, and the Isham Library of Early Instrumental Music in the Memorial Church.

Many of the other parts of the University Library, however, are used to a considerable extent by undergraduates. These include the student library for Physics in the Jefferson Laboratory, the Tutorial Library for Biochemistry in Holyoke House, the Tutorial Library for Astronomy at the Observatory, and those for Psychology (now in the basement of Memorial Hall, where it has been combined with the new Library of the Psychological Laboratories), and for the Classics in Sever. There are many other special libraries connected with the departments of the College which have reserved book shelves for undergraduates and are heavily used: the Music Library in the Music Building; the Robbins Library of Philosophy and the Social Relations Library in Emerson Hall; the Mineralogical Laboratories Library in the University Museum; the Biological Laboratories Library in the Biology building; the Chemistry Department Library in Converse; the Library of Anthropology in the Peabody Museum; the Graduate School of Public Administration Library in Littauer Center; the Fine Arts Library in the Fogg Museum; and such collections as those of the Modern Language Center (Cannon House, Divinity Avenue) and of Warren House, headquarters of English A. Other libraries giving service to undergraduates are those belonging to the Departments of Military and Naval Science. In addition, a number of the departmental libraries belonging to departments of the University, and having little or no direct connection with the Harvard College Library, are used to a considerable extent by undergraduates. This is true for the Architecture Library, where perhaps one third of the use has been by undergraduates; the Library of the Departments of Landscape Architecture and Regional Planning; the Andover-Harvard Theological Library at the Divinity School; and the Chinese-Japanese Library of the Harvard-Yenching Institute in Boylston Hall. These libraries belonging to the departments of the University will of course be continued after the undergraduate library is completed, and it is yet uncertain how much of the undergraduate use of these libraries will be transferred. For the special libraries earlier described the same holds true. The undergraduate library will be ready to take over as much of the service to undergraduates as the other libraries are ready to give up, and it seems probable that in most cases the reserved book shelves for at least the beginning undergraduate courses will be transferred. It may be several years before all the details of these changes will be worked out.

The provisions for undergraduates that have just been listed would seem to be not only extensive but varied enough so that they should take care of all reasonable needs, but they have not enabled the Library to give what has been felt to be adequate service, and this was true even before the present greatly increased student enrollment. Why are the present conditions not satisfactory? Why is it necessary to make plans for changes? Why should a university which until 1946-47 never had more than 8500 students, and which has nearly 5,000,000 volumes in its collections, with library units of some importance in forty different buildings, and with 4500 seats in these libraries, want another library building with more books and more seats for students? There are a number of reasons which, added together, made it evident as much as ten years ago that changes were desirable.

1.   Experience has shown that the very great scattering of reading room facilities reduces the use of the Library by the undergraduate, who in most cases works in more than one field. For the student in one of the graduate or professional schools, with all or practically all his work in one field, the departmentalization is on the whole a convenience rather than an inconvenience, but if the undergraduate, with courses in two to five different departments, can go to one building, not five different ones in widely scattered locations, and find there all the material for assigned collateral and general reading that he needs, it is a great help and he will make more use of books.

Another complication, and under present circumstances a serious one, is the fact that the large number of reading rooms, in scattered locations, requires a much larger staff to give good service than would be needed if the rooms were combined under a single roof. The additional costs that make necessary an endowment for a new undergraduate library building come almost entirely from expenses for building maintenance, not from those for library service.

2.   A student at Amherst, Williams, Dartmouth, Bowdoin, Oberlin, or one of the better women's colleges has at his or her disposal a much larger and better collection of books than has the Harvard undergraduate. The House Libraries with 10,000 to 12,000 volumes each, and the Union Library with 18,000, are the largest general collections completely available to the undergraduate student, and this in spite of the large number of different facilities described earlier in this statement, and in spite of the fact that the students use freely the main reading room in the Widener building, which itself contains in its chief stack area 2,000,000 volumes and pamphlets. This central collection is so large that it cannot be opened to the undergraduate except under very special circumstances, and as a result there is no large general collection freely accessible to the undergraduate at Harvard — no collection which will include a large share of the volumes that the student will need in any of his work or in the general reading which it is desirable for him to do when in college.

3.   The lack of freedom of access by the undergraduate to the main collection in Widener is only part of the story. To obtain books from this collection, the

student must select them from the large public catalogue on the second floor in the Widener building. This catalogue contains some 5,000,000 cards, with complexities of arrangement which present difficulties even to the faculty and staff, to say nothing of the graduate and professional school students. A large proportion of the freshmen find the catalogue so perplexing and overpowering on their first attempt to use it that they give up and never try again. No way has yet been found at Harvard or elsewhere to make the catalogue for a great collection of books simple enough in construction so that it can be used to advantage by an undergraduate student in his late teens or early twenties.

4. The attempt to combine the library services for undergraduate and graduate students in the same room has never worked out successfully at Harvard or elsewhere. It always seems to result in one group or the other feeling that it is neglected and left out in the cold. Widener is now the library headquarters for both graduate and undergraduate students, and with the tremendous demands from the graduate school students and faculty, it has generally been the undergraduates who have been neglected, not intentionally, but because of the plan of the building and the intensity of the demand by the older groups.

5. Even more pressing than any of the four arguments already presented has been the question of space. A survey of the question made in 1938 and 1939 indicated five needs:

a) Better physical facilities for rare books
b) Cheap storage for less-used books
c) More space for the staff
d) Book storage within the Yard for books that were used too often to go to the warehouse
e) Better facilities for undergraduates. More space for them was required and the construction of a building for them would help the whole situation, being much cheaper than a new central building, as well as being the only satisfactory solution to the problem of library facilities for undergraduates.

Plans and suggestions for the improvement of library service for undergraduates at Harvard have been outlined down to 1937 in the preceding articles. A brief account of the plans that have been made during the past ten years will now be presented. The first statement during this period dealing with the problem is found in the letter written by the Librarian of Harvard College to President Conant on 14 March 1938:

> The Widener building which houses the main part of the College Library is in some ways ill-adapted to the uses to which it is put, and will within a few years be outgrown. The terms of the gift state that no addition shall be made to it. Within a short time the University must decide on a course of action to be followed when the building is full. We have attempted to make it the headquarters for both graduate and undergraduate library work, and have not been altogether successful in either field. Sooner or later, I believe the building should be devoted to one or the other.

On 24 May 1938, the Librarian, in a letter dealing with the Chinese-Japanese Library in Boylston Hall, addressed to Mr. John W. Lowes, Financial Vice President of the University, wrote as follows:

> In any plan dealing with Boylston, we should remember that the undergraduate work in the Widener Reading Room should in the near future be moved from its present location because of the pressure from graduate students and the need for a better reference room. This means that the Reading Room in Boylston should be very much enlarged or a new undergraduate library provided somewhere. We should keep in mind in this connection the History Reading Room in the Freshman Union Building, the Sociology and Philosophy Libraries in Emerson Hall, and the Municipal Research, French, and probably the Child Memorial Rooms in Widener. These rooms are not particularly satisfactory, and are expensive to keep up as separate units with attendants.

In the spring of 1939, many talks and discussions took place between Mr. Conant, Mr. Lowes, Mr. Shepley and Mr. Abbott of the firm of Coolidge, Shepley, Bulfinch and Abbott, and the Librarian, dealing with plans for the extension of the space devoted to the Library. A series of proposals was made for annexes to the Widener building. Drawings for buildings where Boylston Hall now stands and where the Houghton Library now stands were prepared, as well as for a very large building in the southeast corner of the Yard where the undergraduate library is now rising. Consideration was also given to two sites on Mt. Auburn Street. During this same period, the Librarian presented a series of reports covering the problem of space in the College Library. (As has already been indicated, the question of space for the College Library and the University Library as a whole will be discussed in a later article, and only the section dealing with facilities for undergraduates will be considered here.) In one of these reports, the Librarian wrote:

> Space for readers is a more serious problem. For many years there has been a shortage of studies and stalls for professors and graduate students. The studies in the Littauer building will help [the Littauer building was new at that time], but will not entirely relieve the situation as far as officers or professors are concerned. No adequate periodical room and no satisfactory reference room are available [in Widener]. The main Reading Room, which might serve for these purposes, is used largely for assigned reading by undergraduates. While it is convenient to have this service provided in the central building, it is not necessary. If it could be transferred elsewhere, sufficient reading room space would be available for many years to come, and it would be possible to assign tables and shelves to graduate students who cannot be cared for in the [stack] stalls. So far as space for readers is concerned, then, it is fair to say that if the assigned reading now carried on in the Reading Room could be transferred to a place out of the building, fairly good arrangements for all other readers could be made for at least another ten years.

Later in the same report the following statements appeared:

It becomes necessary sooner or later to use one of the three following methods [to provide additional space]:

1. Add to the present building. If this cannot be done because of the terms of the gift under which the building was accepted, an annex might be placed as near as possible to the present building with access to an underground passage or possibly a bridge connecting one or more of the upper floors. Additions of this kind could be placed on either or both the east or west sides of Widener. These additions would provide reading rooms for undergraduates . . . A brief description of a proposal of this character will be found in Appendix B accompanying this report . . .

Appendix B. If it is decided to solve the College Library space problem by providing additional facilities in the southeast corner of the Yard, a first unit (a) should be completed within five years. It might be placed on the present location of Boylston Hall and should contain approximately 1,000,000 cubic feet. The first and most essential feature would be reading room facilities for undergraduates and should include four reserved book [assigned reading] reading rooms seating 200 to 225 men each, a reference room and a periodical room, each with a capacity of 50 to 75 readers. These rooms should be as close to the ground level as possible. Underneath them space could probably be found for three levels of stack holding approximately 500,000 books.

Subsequently, a more detailed statement about a proposed building for undergraduates was prepared. It read in part as follows:

1.   It would relieve the pressure in Widener and should make it possible to continue that building as a central library of the University during the next generation. With the relief provided by an undergraduate library, Widener would be a very satisfactory research library center, and indeed with the arrangements that have been planned, it should be more satisfactory than it has been ever since it was opened.[2]

2.   The second reason for the undergraduate library is the fact that Widener has not been, and never can be, a satisfactory headquarters for undergraduate library service. It was planned and built with the graduate students and faculty in mind. It has a tremendously large catalogue that is over the heads of the majority of the undergraduates. It has a collection of 2,000,000 books to which it is impossible to grant free access to undergraduates. They need a library of perhaps 100,000 volumes, mostly of modern, replaceable books, to which they can be given ready access and for which a catalogue of its own will be made. At present, without stack access, and with a catalogue built for research workers, and with a building that was not planned for their needs, our undergraduates are less well cared for than those in any of the better colleges of the country such as Amherst, Williams and Wesleyan. There is no question in my mind about the need for an undergraduate library, and with one I see no reason why the Widener building should not last for many years as the central research library of the University.

The Undergraduate Library, as it has been planned tentatively, will provide four 'reserved books' reading rooms, seating altogether over 600, a reference room, a browsing room, and a periodical room, together with a large smoking room in the basement. There will be a stack with completely free access, housing perhaps 75,000 volumes, so placed that it will be used as a passageway for the men going to the reading room. If the College thinks it desirable, there can be two or more floors above the reading room levels for a center for tutorial work . . . The building may well be placed in one of the blocks facing on Mt. Auburn Street where it would be between the Yard and the Houses. The cost of the building is estimated at $1,000,000. If the tutorial rooms are omitted, that should be ample, but it would probably be safer to say $1,250,000, with a possibility of an extension to $1,500,000 if the College decides to build the tutorial rooms. To this should be added $250,000 for equipping the new building, buying the books and cataloguing them, and making the alterations that would be desirable at Widener when the undergraduate work is moved from it.

To endow the undergraduate library suitably would take $1,500,000. The actual cost of operating it and providing service would be $80,000 a year but some $20,000 of this would be saved through closing up libraries elsewhere in the University that would no longer be needed.

Summing up the cost involved in the new building, we need from one million to one million and a half for the building itself, $250,000 for equipment and alterations, and $1,500,000 for endowment, or approximately $3,000,000 in all.

Report followed report, each going into somewhat more detail. Early in 1940 the Librarian sent the following statement to Mr. Lowes:

The pressure for space in the Widener Memorial Library building has become so great that in some way relief must be obtained. A study of the situation indicates that one method of relieving the congestion and at the same time improving the service given by the Library is the construction of an Undergraduate Library Center.

The need for such a building goes back beyond the present congestion in Widener. The attempt to provide adequate library service for undergraduates in the same building that houses a great research collection and cares for graduate students and a large faculty complicates matters in many ways. It means, in the first place, that no general stack access can be given to the undergraduates and that the average undergraduate goes through his college course without ever being directly exposed to a large general collection of books. It means that the catalogue must be made more expensive, as it must be planned for use by both advanced students and by undergraduates. It costs more and is less satisfactory for both groups. It means that two types of reference service must be given, and in a building like Widener, it means that the charging desk becomes congested and the reading room which should house a great reference collection is used for assigned book reading.

With the above in mind, plans have been developed for an undergraduate library building. A study of the situation indicated that the building should provide:

1. A seating capacity in the reading rooms for 800 to 900 students. These should be in rooms none of which seated over 200, and none of which could be called monumental in character.

2. The reading room facilities should include, in addition to the general reading rooms for assigned reading, a good reference room with space for 5000 to 7500 volumes; a good periodical room; and a good browsing room. Among the 800 to 900 seats specified under (1), 150 should be comparatively easy, but not lounging chairs.

3. The stack room in the building should have direct access from the reading rooms with no restrictions of any kind, and arrangements should be such as to encourage the students to go through the stack rather than to discourage them.

4. There must, of course, be adequate toilet facilities, and in addition a large smoking-room; the latter can properly be in the basement.

5. The reading room should be as close to the street level as possible.

6. The library should contain a good collection of books for general reading; all books needed for tutorial work; and all books for assigned reading which students are not expected to purchase for themselves.

7. There must, of course, be provision for a catalogue, but it will not be extensive . . .

On 16 February 1940, the Librarian, the Library Council, and the Administrative Board of the College met in the office of the Dean of the College and discussed various plans for relieving the pressure on the Widener building. Following this discussion, it was voted that the assembled Boards approve the plan of a special library for undergraduates; the Librarian reported to Mr Conant that this vote was unanimous, and that, as far as he could tell, everyone seemed to approve of it heartily. Later in the spring, the problem was presented to the Committee on Instruction, with similar results. The report of the Librarian for the year 1939-40 included a further detailed statement about the proposal. The President and Fellows of Harvard College approved of the plan in theory and were ready to go ahead with the building if money became available. But by this time the war in Europe was reaching a crisis. No funds for an undergraduate library were in sight, and postponement of construction seemed inevitable.

During the next period, the Librarian brought the matter up at various meetings of alumni when the opportunity presented itself, as well as before the Library Council and the Committee of the Overseers to Visit the Library. At a meeting in the Harvard Club in New York City, the Librarian was seated beside Mr. Thomas W. Lamont, '92, and told him in some detail of the plans and hopes for the undergraduate library. Mr. Lamont expressed great interest.

With the completion of the Houghton and the New England Deposit Libraries early in 1942, the space situation was relieved for the time being. The United States had entered the war, and any active planning for the undergraduate library was shelved. Then, in the autumn of 1944 the Librarian had another talk with Mr. Lamont about library needs and went over with him in some detail the plans for the undergraduate library that had been developed four years earlier. Mr. Lamont again expressed interest, and hoped that he would be able to help in making the building possible at a later time. Correspondence with him continued, and on 24 July 1945 he wrote as follows:

> Now that the burden on the colleges for service training is beginning to let up a bit, I am wondering whether you at Cambridge have gone further in your minds in the matter of a Library for undergraduates. Perhaps my inquiry is emphasized by the announcement made by Dean Buck's committee as to possible changes in the curriculum set-up — changes designed in part, I should think, to encourage wider undergraduate reading.
>
> What are your estimated money requirements today for your project? If a million dollars were in sight, would you go ahead with it? If not, what is the figure, and have you several important sources of gift in mind?

Don't let me interrupt your holiday. There is no hurry about an answer. And you must not take my inquiry too seriously, though I am much interested.

Correspondence and talk between Mr. Lamont and Mr. Conant and the Librarian continued during the summer and autumn, and, the estimates of cost being satisfactory, on 21 November 1945 President Conant was able to announce that Mr. Lamont had given to the University $1,500,000 to be used for the construction of an undergraduate library.

The selection of the architect, Mr. Henry R. Shepley of Coolidge, Shepley, Bulfinch and Abbott, was made almost immediately. The next problem was the site. The first to be considered was that of Boylston Hall, theoretically the one best adapted for the building. However, it was found impossible to place a building there large enough for the purpose without tearing down not only Boylston but Grays and Weld as well, and so it was reluctantly given up. Two sites on ends of blocks facing Mt. Aburn Street were then considered. They seemed to have the advantage of being approximately half way between the freshman and the upper class dormitories, and the size and shape of the building would not be limited by the surroundings; but either of them meant that the freshman and commuters must cross Massachusettes Avenue to reach the Library, and that the new building would be far from the Library center, the classrooms, and the laboratories. There were also serious practical complications in connection with the use of each of the lots.

The fourth location considered was the southeast corner of the Yard, the corner of Quincy Street and Massachusettes Avenue, which was occupied by the Dana-Palmer House and its attractive grounds. There were several disadvantages. The Dana-Palmer House must be destroyed or moved; the wooded grounds must be lost. Removal of the house to another site would be expensive. The situation in the Yard limited the ground area that could be covered and the type of architecture that could be used. The site was a considerable distance from the living and dining quarters of the upper classmen, who with the exception of those from Adams House would have to cross not only Massachusetts Avenue but Mt. Auburn Street to reach the Library. The use of this site would also involve removal of the Dudley Gate. However, the site had the very great advantage of being near the Library center, which would simplify administration and save considerable space in the new building. It was the only site available on even a small hillside which might make possible readily accessible entrances on two different levels, an arrangement which was regarded as highly desirable for expediting the tremendous traffic that was expected. It was so placed that under it a two-story stack could be built and used as a much needed overflow for books from the Widener and Houghton buildings, with connection to those buildings by tunnel. This two-story stack would then become the first of the underground stacks which were a part of the general plan for the development of the University Library. (In this connection it should be remembered that it is much easier and less expensive to place underground stacks beneath a building than elsewhere, and that the time to do it is before the building is constructed.) Further, this site fixed the southeast corner of the Yard for library use, and so concentrated the space occupied by the Harvard College Library near the center of the University. Of greatest importance, it was in the Yard, close to the freshman dormitories and dining hall, and also where it could be reached between classes with a minimum of time by all the students. The heaviest use of the Library by undergraduates has always been in the morning between classes. Before a decision was made, the problem was talked over in detail not only by the Corporation and members of the Library staff, but by a committee of the students, and finally this site was selected, with considerable reluctance because of the necessity of disposing of the Dana-Palmer House. Complaints about the possible destruction of the house soon appeared in the *Harvard Alumni Bulletin,* and Mr. Lamont came forward again and generously offered to provide the funds for moving it. A site was selected across Quincy Street between the Union and the Faculty Club, where it is to serve as a guest house for the University.

It was at once evident to the architect and the Librarian that help in making the plans was desirable. The Dean of the Faculty of Arts and Sciences was asked to appoint a committee of the Faculty to work with the Librarian, and the Dean of the College was asked to make arrangements with the Student Council for a student committee. In the meantime the Librarian talked over with members of the College Library staff the different problems that arose.

The general principles of arrangement for the building were determined quickly, but many details remained to be worked out. It was realized from the beginning that the success of the building would depend very largely on:

1. The efficiency of the ventilation system
2. The lighting
3. The sound absorption qualities of the walls and ceiling
4. The ease with which the students could find their books for assigned reading and obtain them.

A large share of the efforts of the architect, the Librarian, and the various groups interested has been concentrated on these problems. The question of coat rooms and of smoking facilities also received considerable attention, as did the problem of making the storage stack to be placed under the building easily available for those who wanted to use it without complicating the use of the rest of the building by undergraduates.

From the beginning Mr. Shepley gave a great deal of attention to the outside appearance of the building, in order that it might fit into the general spirit of the Yard. Questions of shape, bulk, and color were all carefully studied. Special features of arrangement desired by the Librarian complicated the problem. The early plans called for the second entrance of the building directly from Massachusetts Avenue through the Class of 1880 Gate, known as the Roosevelt-Bacon Gate. This was given up, although it would have meant the shortest possible distance to be traversed by many of the men from the Houses, because the width of Massachusetts Avenue at this point made it seem unwise to do anything that would encourage crossing, and the second entrance was shifted to the west side between Wigglesworth and Houghton, placing it farther away from the other entrance on the floor above and making it unnecessary to break through the center of the large reading area on the ground floor.

In June 1946 the plans were taken to Princeton by the Librarian and talked over in detail with the Committee of Librarians and Architects that has been working for several years past on university library planning, aided by a Carnegie grant. Criticisms of the plan there brought about a change of arrangement of the stack on the three reading room levels from long parallel stack ranges to the alcoves that had been suggested in 1939.

By way of present conclusion, it may be stated that the main objects of the building are:

1. To concentrate as far as is practicable the library service undergraduates uates in a central location
2. To make the books readily available to the students
3. To encourage general and recreational as well as assigned and collateral reading.

In addition, there is the fact already stressed that the establishment of a separate undergraduate library seemed to be the most suitable way of obtaining relief from the pressure upon the Widener building, and so of making the latter a satisfactory center for those research activities of the University which fall within the scope of the Library.

To the building which, directly and indirectly, will effect this signal twofold advance will be given the name of Lamont, in token of the perennial gratitude of the University to the alumnus who has made the advance possible.

Notes

1. *Harvard Library Bulletin* 1 (1947), 29-51, 221-237.

2. It should be stressed here that from the outset of planning it was clearly understood that undergraduates would always be welcome in Widener whenever they needed material not available in any separate library established for them.

About the Author

Keyes D. Metcalf, Professor of Bibliography, Director of the Harvard University Library, and Librarian of Harvard College. He was appointed at Harvard in 1937 and served until 1955. From 1913-1937, he was assistant to the Chief of the Reference Department, The New York Public Library. Before and since his retirement from Harvard, Metcalf has been consultant for hundreds of library buildings. He is the author of *Planning Academic and Research Library Buildings* published in 1965.

Part II.

Lamont Library, 1949

Part II: Introduction

The previous excursions into the past history of college and university libraries in England and the United States confirm the fact that undergraduate libraries were not a new concept in university library service. The Lamont Library at Harvard was not itself a new idea; it was rather the scale on which Lamont was envisioned and then built that was the new development.

The background of this development began in 1937 when Keyes D. Metcalf was appointed as Librarian at Harvard College and Director of Harvard University Library. By that time, the Widener Library was regarded as too large and impersonal for undergraduates. It was also full. Metcalf's first decision was whether or not to plan on the construction of a new central library for Harvard. He later wrote:

> This, let us say, would have been the conservative thing to do. It would have followed standard practice, and would have made possible greater centralization in a university library system which had become too decentralized. But all idea of a new, central library building at Harvard was given up 'for our time.' To start with, the cost was prohibitive. It was then [1938] estimated that $10,000,000 would be required for the first unit of a new building.[1]

The fact that there was no suitable site in a central location was another deterrent. "A third and equally important reason was that a building of the size needed would be so large as to be unwieldy from the standpoint of service."[2] For these reasons, the idea of a new central library was dropped and another plan was developed.

A study of Harvard's library situation revealed that more space was needed for books, staff, and readers. Two other problems demanded solutions: the Widener Library lacked adequate quarters for valuable collections of rare books and manuscripts, and it did not provide adequate quarters and services for undergraduates in a building where the needs of researchers were so demanding, where undergraduates had to use a catalog containing millions of cards, and where, it was thought, they could not be given direct access to the stacks.

With all this in mind, a master plan was developed to house parts of the Harvard Library. Four new units were recommended:

1. The New England Deposit Library for the storage of little used material;

2. The Houghton Library for rare books and manuscripts;
3. Undergraduate Library;
4. Underground stacks in the college yard for the expansion of the Widener collection.[3]

The Houghton Library for rare books and manuscripts and the New England Deposit Library were both opened in 1942, leaving completion of the undergraduate library and underground stacks for Widener's collections until after World War II. The Lamont Library was not an isolated event in itself, but was part of a four part solution to the many library problems facing Harvard.

Lamont was planned on three suppositions:

1. That undergraduates would make more and better use of a library designed expressly for them;
2. That it would be the best way to relieve the pressure in the Widener building and make unnecessary a new central library building; and
3. That, if that pressure were relieved, the Widener Library building would become a more satisfactory research center than it had been in the past.[4]

The architect of the Lamont Library, Henry R. Shepley, writes:

> The philosophy on which the functioning of the Library was based required, first, that it be conveniently located and inviting of access. It should be on one of the main undergraduate traffic routes, and there should be no flights of steps to the entrance or monumental vestibules or foyers to traverse before coming to the books. Second, once within the Library, the student should find the entire book collection as accessible as possible.[5]

Construction of the "first library building to be devoted primarily to undergraduate needs"[6] began with the announcement of a major gift from Thomas W. Lamont. Keyes D. Metcalf in the section's first article outlines in considerable detail the functions of this undergraduate library.

Ceremonies dedicating the completed Lamont Library were held on January 10, 1949[7] and a conference on "The Place of the Library in a University," March 30-31, 1949, celebrated the completion of the building program which had included the Houghton, Deposit, and Lamont libraries.[8]

Harvie Branscomb, Chancellor of Vanderbilt University, one of the participants in the conference asserted that he was "confident that this new Lamont Library will have a great influence on American education."[9]

The early planning, the actual design, the functions, and the dedicatory celebrations are all well documented in the literature. In fact, the Lamont Library is probably one of the most thoroughly documented events in the history of American libraries. Metcalf and the other librarians and officials associated with Lamont, perhaps sensing the importance of what they were doing, took time to record it. From this wealth of documentation, "Lamont Library: The First Year" by Philip J. McNiff and Edwin E. Williams and "The Selection of Books for Lamont" by Williams have been selected. McNiff's "Lamont Library, Harvard College" presented at the 1952 Symposium on Library Service to Undergraduates, is also included in the next section. Finally, an outsider to the Harvard scene, Charles A. Carpenter, Jr. concludes Section II with "The Lamont Catalog as a Guide to Book Selection" as viewed from his position in the Cornell University Libraries.

Thus, in the late 1940s Harvard had started something — in fact, she greatly influenced several ideas which have been very much with us in the world of university libraries. Separate undergraduate libraries, separate buildings for rare books and manuscripts, storage libraries, and underground libraries all got an early boost from Harvard. Indiana with its Lilly Library and Yale with the Beinecke Library are other very famous examples of separate rare book libraries. Several libraries have gone underground; the best illustration is the Undergraduate Library at the University of Illinois which was built under the quad because a sacred experimental corn plot on the campus could not be shaded by a new building. Even Harvard has recently gone underground again with the Nathan Marsh Pusey Library joining the earlier underground stacks. There are also many examples of storage libraries, such as the ones at the University of Michigan and Princeton. After all, as Akenson and Stevens declare in their *The Changing Uses of the Liberal Arts College,* it is Harvard which establishes "a pattern that will eventually be repeated in most of the better colleges in the country."[10]

The idea of a separate undergraduate library got the biggest boost of all by the building of the Lamont Library at Harvard. As Branscomb predicted, Lamont was to have a great influence on American education. Almost overnight Lamont became a beautiful legend; it was idealized. Many librarians and university officials made pilgrimages to the shrine. However, no university actually built a separate undergraduate library during the next nine years even though there was great interest among university librarians in this approach to library service for undergraduate students. (The University of Minnesota did, however, open its Freshman-Sophomore Library in 1952 in a classroom building.)

Notes

1. Keyes D. Metcalf, "Harvard Faces its Library Problems," *Harvard Library Bulletin* 3 (Spring, 1949): 185.

2. Ibid.

3. Philip J. McNiff, "Library Service to Undergraduates, a Symposium: Lamont Library, Harvard College," *College and Research Libraries* 14 (July, 1953): 269.

4. Metcalf, "Harvard Faces Its Library Problems," p. 187.

5. Henry R. Shepley, "The Lamont Library, Part I: Design," *Harvard Library Bulletin* 3 (Winter, 1949): 5.

6. Keyes D. Metcalf, "The Lamont Library, Part II: Function," *Harvard Library Bulletin* 3 (Winter, 1949): 29.

7.   "The Dedication of the Lamont Library," *Harvard Library Bulletin* 3 (Spring, 1949): 304.

8.   "Conference on the Place of the Library in a University," *Harvard Library Bulletin* 3 (Spring, 1949): 305.

9.   Harvie Branscomb, "The Future of Libraries in Academic Institutions, Part III," *Harvard Library Bulletin* 3 (Autumn, 1949): 339.

10. Donald H. Akenson and Lawrence F. Stevens, *The Changing Uses of the Liberal Arts College: An Essay in Recent Educational History* (New York: Pageant Press, International Corp., for Harvard College, 1969), p. 4.

Keyes D. Metcalf

The Lamont Library
II. Function

The Director of the Harvard University
Library continues his complete documentation of library services for Harvard undergraduate students. Here he describes the new
Lamont building and takes the reader on a
tour of all its levels and functions.

In the article 'The Undergraduate and the Harvard Library,' covering the period
1937-1947, the history of developments leading to the Lamont Library was outlined, the question of its location was discussed, and the following statement was
made:

> It was realized from the beginning that the success of the building would depend
> very largely on:
> 1.   The efficiency of the ventilation system
> 2.   The lighting
> 3.   The sound absorption quality of the walls and ceiling
> 4.   The ease with which the students could find their books for assigned reading
>   and obtain them.[1]

The article also listed these main objects of the building:

> 1.   To concentrate as far as practicable the library service for undergraduates in a
>   central location
> 2.   To make the books readily accessible to the students
> 3.   To encourage general and recreational, as welll as assigned and collateral read-
>   ing.

With these principles and objects in mind, plans for the new building were
developed. The Lamont Library has now been completed and is in use. It is air-
conditioned throughout by the system used successfully in the Houghton
Library; the lighting installations were decided upon after very careful study;
and every effort was made to provide quiet floors and sound-absorbing ceilings.

SOURCE: From Keyes D. Metcalf, "The Lamont Library, II. Function," *Harvard
Library Bulletin* 3 (Winter, 1949), pp. 12-30. Reprinted by permission of the publisher.

45

If the solutions to these problems are not successful, it is not through lack of attention to them.

The Lamont Library building has eight levels, made up of basement and mezzanine, ground floor and mezzanine, first floor and mezzanine, second floor, and roof house. The upper six levels, beginning with the ground floor, are designated First Level, Second Level, etc. The two lowest levels, the basement and its mezzanine, are known simply as the Widener Stack and the Houghton Stack in the Lamont Library. The Main Entrance, on the north side of the building, brings the visitor into the first main floor, or Third Level; a second or West Entrance gives access to the ground floor, or First Level.

The building is divided into four rather distinct functional sections, irrespective of the eight levels. The first section has no connection with the provision of library facilities for undergraduates; the second is not necessarily connected with the Lamont Library, but is quite logically placed in an undergraduate library building; the third is still closer to the general conception of an undergraduate library; and the fourth, which is much the largest and most important part, controlling the character of the entire building, is made up of undergraduate library facilities.

The first of the four sections consists of the basement and basement mezzanine of the building, or the Widener Stack and Houghton Stack, as indicated above. These levels are completely underground, corresponding in this way to the stack in the Houghton building and the two lowest decks of the stack in the Widener building. These Lamont stacks provide storage space for books that belong to other parts of the College Library and are included in the new building simply because it was cheaper to build storage space under a structure that was being erected than to place it there or elsewhere at another time. The basement, or lowest level of the Lamont building, is connected with the Widener building by tunnel and will be used to house overflow books from Widener. At the present time only fifteen percent of the shelving has been put in place, and it is used to care for the part of the library's collection of modern newspapers that is in demand too frequently to be sent to the New England Deposit Library. The stack in the Widener building has no special section for the shelving of bound files of newspapers, and there will be considerable saving in over-all space by placing this collection in Lamont on shelves especially designed to receive it. Two tables with seats for seven readers each are available for those who wish to consult newspapers. When the other shelving on this level is installed — and this may not be needed for another five years — twenty-seven stalls for graduate students will be included. Access to this basement level in the Lamont building will be available to those who have stack access cards in Widener, and it may be reached through the tunnel from D floor in the Widener building, or from a stairway behind the charging desk near the West Entrance of the Lamont building.

The basement mezzanine in Lamont has been assigned to the Houghton Library, with which it is connected by tunnel. About forty per cent of the shelving for this level has been installed. It houses the major part of the Theatre

Collection, which formerly occupied quarters in Widener; the early American newspaper collection, which since 1942 has been in Houghton; the Archives of the American Board of Commissioners for Foreign Missions, part of which have been in Widener and part in Houghton; the Harvard Library's sheet music collection; and the Lincoln collections that were formerly in Widener. The remaining shelving will not be installed until it is needed, some five years hence.

The second of the four main divisions of the Lamont Library consists of accommodations to be used in connection with the General Education courses of the College. The space assigned for this purpose includes an office suite for the General Education Committee, with a room for the Chairman, one for his secretary, one for mimeographing, and a Committee Room which can also be used as a conference room. This space is on the upper of the three main floors, or the Fifth Level, on the Quincy Street side. In addition, there are ten conference rooms for use by sections of the General Education courses. These rooms seat from twenty to thirty students comfortably. Six of them are in the roof house, or Sixth Level, and the other four are on the mezzanines (Second and Fourth Levels) on the Quincy Street side. Much of the work in the General Education courses is based on library material, and it seems appropriate to have the conference rooms for this work in the undergraduate library building. The close relationship of the General Education work with library facilities for undergraduates was very definitely in Mr. Lamont's mind when he made his gift.

The third functional section of the building consists of two large rooms that may be used for more than one purpose. To the left of the West Entrance there is a room fifty by thirty feet in size which is designated 'Smoking Area' on the plans and which can be used for any purpose which later proves to be desirable. This room has no windows but is well ventilated and lighted. It is available as a reading room in which smoking is permitted unless other uses are found for it. It seemed unwise to construct a building the size of the Lamont Library without providing space to care for potential if undefined needs.

The other double-purpose room is directly over the Main Entrance and is known as the 'Forum Room.' It is available for use by students in connection with activities that bear some direct relation to the Library, and should relieve the pressure on the Lowell House Common Room which has been used in the past for activities of this kind. The room seats one hundred and eight comfortably when used as an auditorium, with the possibility of adding forty more chairs. It is equipped with a blackboard, a motion picture screen, a projection room, and a loud speaker for use with phonograph recordings. It can be turned on short notice into a reading room for sixty students, and it is anticipated that this use will be made of it during the reading examination periods, if and when the undergraduate student body numbers more than four thousand.

The fourth and largest division of the building provides regular library facilities for Harvard undergraduates. It occupies most of the three main floors and their two mezzanines, designated as the First through the Fifth Level, as already explained.

At each of the two public entrances mentioned there is a charging desk, which also has the function of caring for closed reserve books; those for the large beginning courses in History, Government, and Economics are adjacent to the West Entrance, and those for other courses are behind the desk in the lobby at the Main Entrance on the Third Level.

The First, Third, and Fifth Levels each have a large reading room extending the full length of the Massachusetts Avenue side of the building. These rooms are all the same size and have approximately the same accommodations for readers. The rooms on the First and Third Levels are fourteen feet seven inches and fifteen feet one inch in height respectively, but the room on the Fifth Level is only nine feet six inches high. Each of these reading rooms has a stack area through which it is approached. The arrangements in these stacks and reading rooms are described below. Each of the mezzanines (Second and Fourth Levels) also has a stack area.

Connecting the five levels are five sets of stairs: one in the front of the building leading from the Main Entrance lobby; one at each end of the main corridor that runs the length of the building on the First, Third, and Fifth Levels; and one from each end of the reading area. These stairs are so arranged that a reader passes through a stack area on entering or leaving one of the reading rooms.

Toilet facilities are provided on the First, Second, Fourth, and Fifth Levels, in their northeast corners. Smoking is permitted throughout the upper six levels except in the three main reading rooms and the stack areas.

On the First Level there is a fair-sized room in which is installed a hand printing press and a good supply of type for use by students who wish to learn at first hand how books are made. Here also is the janitor's room with a separate entrance. On this level is found the Smoking Area, already described, and a machinery room for part of the air-conditioning apparatus. There is a second machinery room in the roof house. It should be added at this point that some of the air-conditioning machinery and apparatus is in Widener, thereby reducing the space used for this purpose in Lamont.

The Second, Third, Fourth, and Fifth Levels have large areas at the west end in which both smoking and talking are allowed. Taken with the Smoking Area on the First Level, they provide smoking rooms on each of the five levels. The smoking rooms on the Second and Fourth Levels each have five sound-proof cubicles for typing. The rooms on these levels are equipped with semi-lounge chairs, those on the other levels with regular reading room tables and chairs.

Immediately to the right of the Main Entrance on the Third Level there is a long narrow room which contains the card catalogue, a special case for maps and atlases, the reference collection, which is nearly as large as the one now provided in the Widener Library, and the periodical section with the current numbers of some three hundred periodicals. Altogether there are seats for sixty-three readers, seventeen of them at individual tables in the reference section and twelve in semi-lounge chairs in the periodical section. A balcony over the south side of this room forms a part of the Fourth Level; it has four alcoves, housing special collections.

On the Fifth Level, immediately over the Reference Room, is the Woodberry

Poetry Room, which has been on the top floor in the Widener building in the past, and the Farnsworth Room, which has also been transferred from Widener, where it occupied the room just to the right of the main entrance.

It has already been said that one passes through the stacks in going to or from the large reading rooms. A primary concern in the planning for Lamont was to make the books for general reading as readily accessible as possible. To this end, the stacks are arranged quite differently from those in other libraries. Each of the First, Third, and Fifth Levels has three wide corridors leading through it to its reading room. The walls of the middle one of these on each of these levels are lined with the open reserve books, there being room for some 15,000 volumes in all, 5,000 to a level. The main part of the stacks is made up of twelve alcoves on each level, three opening on each side of the other two passageways. This makes thirty-six alcoves for the three levels, each of which has space for some 1,500 volumes, a small table, and several chairs. The stack areas on the two mezzanines (Second and Fourth Levels) have space for some 30,000 volumes each, as well as for seven small library tables seating four readers each, and for nearly fifty tables for single readers in stalls. All the books in these stacks are accessible without restriction to any Harvard undergraduate student.

The three large reading rooms differ from standard reading rooms in a number of particulars. The outside walls, instead of having shelves with reference or assigned reading books, are lined by stalls with tables for single readers so arranged that the reader is shut off on three sides from his fellows. On the Third Level, where five great windows run the height of the room, ten of the stalls, two for each window, are replaced by an equal number of semi-lounge chairs. Each of the three reading rooms is divided into three parts by screens which project into the room in order to minimize as far as possible the 'railroad station' effect that is found in many large reading areas. These screens are flanked by individual tables, which, however, do not have partitions attached to them and so give less privacy than the stalls on the outside walls. Distributed through the nine subdivisions (three in each reading room) are eighteen pairs of tables each seating twelve readers, or two hundred and sixteen altogether, and in between the sets of tables are groups of semi-lounge chairs provided on the premise that a fair proportion of the readers in an undergraduate reading room will not be taking notes and will prefer to sit in comfortable chairs without a table rather than in regular reading room chairs at a table. (It was found that the cost of table space for one reader, added to the cost of a reading room chair, was nearly equal to the cost of a semi-lounge chair.)

On the stack side of each of the three reading rooms are four half-alcoves, eleven feet four inches wide by five feet deep. Books shelved here are so placed that their use should not prove a disturbance to the occupants of the reading room. Two of the alcoves in each room are provided with duplicate copies of dictionaries and encyclopaedias, which should be immediately adjacent to any reading room. Throughout these reading rooms and stacks, distances between chairs and tables are greater than those considered standard in libraries. But by this rather unusual arrangement, it has been possible to give semi-private accommodations to a third of the readers, unusually comfortable chairs to a fifth of them, and still have more readers in the space than could be cared for if the rooms were fitted out in the regular way.

Exhibition cases have been provided on the First, Third, and Fifth Levels. They will be used by the Department of Printing and Graphic Arts, by the Theatre Collection, and for miscellaneous exhibitions of interest to undergraduates. Five public telephones have been installed in the stairways adjacent to the reading room of the First Level. There is a drinking fountain at each end of the first five levels, and one on the Sixth.

A number of special problems arose in connection with the planning of the building, problems for which there is no one correct answer, and many of which must be faced in the planning of most library buildings. The more salient will be discussed here briefly.

No provision was made for a check room for coats, books, etc. This decision was taken, after consultation with committees representing the students, on the ground that undergraduates are unwilling to use a check room because of the delay involved. Students come to a library and leave it in tremendous numbers at the periods between class hours, and no checking system has been found that can care for hundreds of people in a few minutes. (Part or all of the Smoking Area on the First Level can be turned into a check room if it seems desirable later. It is adjacent to the West Entrance of the building.) Facilities for handling coats have been provided, however. In both of the north corners of each of the three reading rooms there are fixtures on which to hang coats which taken together have a greater capacity than a large check room. These racks are fairly inconspicuous, but within sight of most of the readers. In addition, each of the two hundred and thirteen stalls that have been placed around the reading rooms and in the stacks has a hook on which a coat and hat may be hung.

Only in comparatively recent years has smoking been permitted in any library, because of the fire hazard, and the accompanying dirt and smoky air. In a modern fireproof building, the fire risk does not seem to be serious, and the addition of air-conditioning should eliminate the problem of dirt and smoke to a considerable extent. The committees appointed by the Student Council in each of the three academic years while building plans were under consideration recommended that smoking be permitted in certain areas. It was finally determined that smoking should be allowed throughout the undergraduate levels except in the main reading rooms and their adjacent stacks, as noted above. Smoking areas would then include the five special smoking rooms, in which it is planned to permit subdued conversation, the conference rooms, the Farnsworth Room, the Poetry Room, the Reference Room, and the Periodical Room. With these arrangements in mind, the air-conditioning equipment was installed in three units. The first cares for the storage stacks in the basement, where smoking is not permitted. These two levels of stack are completely underground and are well insulated. Their occupants will be few in number, and the air-conditioning is a comparatively simple task. The second unit cares for the sections of the upper part of the building where smoking is permitted, and the third unit for the upper stacks and the large reading rooms where smoking is not permitted. It will be possible at a later time to make some changes in the areas served by these different units if it seems desirable to modify the smoking regulations.

The amount of elevator service to be provided was another difficult question. The Main Entrance to the building is only one step up from the Yard level, and there is a ramp here that will permit entrance by wheel chair. The rest of the building, as far as the undergraduate library facilities are concerned, is up or down no more than one full floor from the Main Entrance so that the use of stairs has been reduced to a minimum. Under these circumstances, it did not seem necessary to provide regular public elevator service, but there is an elevator at each end of the building, access to which is by key, and each of these is available for staff use and for students and faculty who are unable to travel up and downstairs because of physical handicaps.

The five sets of stairways in the building have already been noted. While stair-climbing by students will not be as extensive as in many other buildings, particularly in the Widener Library, there will be a fair amount of it altogether. The stairs, therefore, have been distributed as widely as possible throughout the building, and it is hoped that the arrangement of the collections is such that the traffic between them will be divided fairly equally, and that the peak load on no one of them will be too great. None of the stairways is monumental in character.

It will be noted that there is very little space in the building for staff use; in addition to the two charging desks, there is a small work room adjacent to the desk on the Third Level, offices for the Librarian and his secretary, two staff rest rooms, and a locker room. It has been possible to plan the building in this way because the order and cataloguing work and the preparation of books for the shelves will be carried on in Widener.

One of the most difficult decisions made was whether or not the building should be used by Radcliffe students. The decision has been to exclude them, at least for the time being for three reasons:

1. Radcliffe maintains an undergraduate library of its own with a collection larger than the one now installed in Lamont, and as large as the Lamont collection is expected to be in the future.
2. The money available would not provide for a building large enough to care for both the Harvard and Radcliffe undergraduates.
3. Experience here and elsewhere has shown that a library for men only or for women only can be administered with almost no supervision in the reading rooms, but that a coeducational library requires supervision if reasonable quiet is to be preserved. In order to achieve most efficiently its primary aims, Lamont has been designed in such a way that the staff would have to be doubled if adequate reading room supervision were to be provided on a coeducational basis.

The optimum size for the building was another problem for which it was difficult to obtain a solution. The use of a college library varies greatly from hour to hour during the day, from day to day during the week, and from month to month during the year — to say nothing of from year to year. The peak loads of Widener always came in the mornings. However, use at all hours increased greatly during the reading periods and at the time of the mid-term and final examinations. Space that would be adequate during other times of the year would then fall far short of requirements. With this in mind, plans were made by which the Forum Room and the Smoking Area could be turned into regular reading rooms at least during the busy periods. It will also be possible, if it is found necessary, to add chairs in the forty alcoves that make up the stacks, and in the broad corridors that lead from the front of the building to the large reading rooms. In case of emergency, the ten conference rooms can be used for reading during most of the day, and it is expected that one or more of them will be used frequently as rooms in which students with limited eyesight can be read to.

The selection of furniture for the building raised many problems. Over sixteen hundred chairs and nearly five hundred tables have been provided. The latter vary in size from two by three to four by nine feet. Very few library chairs and tables, except those of stock design, had been built in the last decade. The possibility of selection was limited, and manufacturers did not seem to be interested in new designs. Those in charge of planning the library felt that the selection of furniture was a matter of importance and that for each piece there were five considerations, no one of which could be neglected: sturdiness, because the wear and tear on furniture in any library is great; comfort, because students often stay in a library for hours at a time; appearance, because, while there was no desire to build a luxurious library, it was important to have the building as a whole attractive; cost, because the funds available were limited, and if they had been larger, the librarians at least would have preferred to spend the additional money for books or service; and finally, variety. Readers come to libraries for many different purposes, and a variety of accommodations should make the building a more desirable place to study, and go a long way in increasing its use. There seemed to be a place for small light chairs immediately adjacent to the stacks, so that a student who wanted to consult a good many books on the same subject could sit beside them while doing so. Many men not only prefer to work at a table by themselves, but will do better work under such conditions. The semilounge chairs that have been used in many places throughout the building were designed with especial care for comfort, but not for the inducing of sleep. It is hoped that each student can find accommodations for his particular need at a particular time.

The above descriptions of the Lamont Library as a building and as a library have attempted to cover its essential features. Two general points should be emphasized in connection with them.

1. The Library was planned from the inside out, not the other way round, which is so often the case, and on that account the architect was confronted with an exceedingly difficult problem when he designed the exterior. The Librarian wishes to go on record in this connection as follows:

The architect accepted the Librarian's specifications of needs and adapted his plans to them instead of insisting on changes that would simplify his problem. The results were satisfactory to Mr. Lamont as far as he saw them in drawings and in the form of a model, and to the Librarian. There have of course been criticisms of the building by alumni and others, but as it has taken shape it has received much favorable comment. The proportions are pleasing, and the awkward squarish shape, which the Librarian called for, has been successfully handled. The brick work is some of the finest at Harvard and seems to be generally admired.

2. As was stated in the first section of this article, the Lamont Library is the first library building to be devoted primarily to undergraduate needs, and as such there were no traditional lines to follow in the interior arrangements. Those responsible for the plans found themselves pioneering at every turn. They hope that the results, when put to the test of heavy use, will be satisfactory and that a real contribution to library planning has been made. They realize that firsts of all kinds are sure to have flaws — flaws that at a later time seem to be self-evident. This is equally true with a new style of automobile, a new bridge, or a new library. It will be strange if the Lamont Library does not have serious defects in its planning, but what these mistakes are, time will tell. It is hoped, however, that the advantages that will result from free access to the books will far outweigh any disadvantages that come from mistakes in planning, and that the Harvard undergraduates in the future will have available to them, as they have not had in the past, a library service as satisfactory as that provided to the student in any other institution of learning.

Notes

1. Harvard Library Bulletin 1 (1947): 304.

About the Author

Keyes D. Metcalf, Professor of Bibliography, Director of the Harvard University Library, and Librarian of Harvard College. He was appointed at Harvard in 1937 and served until 1955. From 1913-1937, he was assistant to the Chief of the Reference Department, The New York Public Library. Before and since his retirement from Harvard, Metcalf has been consultant for hundreds of library buildings. He is the author of *Planning Academic and Research Library Buildings* published in 1965.

Philip J. McNiff & Edwin E. Williams

Lamont Library: The First Year

Two Harvard library staff members report on the reality of the first year's operations in this experiment in undergraduate education. After a brief review of Lamont's background and earlier planning, they discuss matters ranging from wear and tear on the furniture to the use of the various areas of the building. They conclude that there are "remarkably few and insignificant regrets to feel after a year of experience with a new building."

Lamont is more clearly experimental than most new libraries because it is the first to be designed entirely for the benefit of a university's undergraduates and because it embodies an untried combination of ideas. Consequently college and university librarians everywhere have been interested, as well as students who use it and Harvard alumni, many of whom contributed to its endowment. Some results of the experiment can be estimated by any visitor, but other facts are apt to be discovered only by members of the staff responsible for operating the library. Perhaps those who are eager to make Lamont a success, particularly those who also had a hand in planning it, cannot hope to qualify as its severest critics, but there seem to be good reasons for reporting as objectively as possible what has been learned in the course of the first year's work in the building.

Earlier issues of the Harvard Library Bulletin have provided a comprehensive background for this report by publishing the thirteen articles dealing with undergraduate library services that will be cited here. College records for 1765 appear to contain the first definite indication of need for an undergraduate library, and the history of the subject from that date onward has been traced by Messrs. Metcalf and Lovett.[1] They report a gradual extension of library hours and liberalizing of borrowing privileges, and a certain amount of disappointment with Widener, which proved to be large and impersonal, and in which most undergraduates could be allowed direct access only to reserved

SOURCE: From Philip J. McNiff and Edwin E. Williams, "Lamont Library: The First Year," *Harvard Library Bulletin* 4 (Spring, 1950), pp. 203-212. Reprinted by permission of the publisher.

books, the Farnsworth Room's recreational reading,[2] and a few other volumes. The main reading room in Widener was never wholly satisfactory as a reserved book center,[3] and it had to be supplemented by collections for large beginning classes in Boylston and the Union. The latter also housed a general collection that was particularly helpful to freshmen, for whom there is no House Library.[4]

Ample quarters for reserved-book reading and a large open-shelf collection for undergraduates might have been included, with many other things, in a great new central library for Harvard that would have had to be several times as big as Widener. Instead, Mr. Metcalf proposed that Widener be retained as the general research library and that it be supplemented by a building for rare books and manuscripts, storage facilities for little-used materials, a separate undergraduate library, and subterranean stacks. Houghton and the New England Deposit Library were built as the first two supplements; Lamont constitutes the third and, with the two levels of stack beneath, the initial unit of the fourth.[5]

The three major objectives of the Lamont Library were stated by Mr. Metcalf as follows:

To concentrate as far as is practicable the library service for undergraduates in a central location

To make the books readily available to the students

To encourage general and recreational as well as assigned and collateral reading.[6]

One can easily demonstrate that Lamont has meant a great deal of progress in these general directions. It combines the undergraduate reserve collections from Widener, Boylston, the Union, and several special libraries. Its general collection contains material in some subjects, notably the sciences, that students used to have to obtain from laboratory collections north of the Yard. Centralization, of course, was never intended to swallow up the seven House Libraries,[7] but Lamont can offer them help in book selection. The House Libraries continue to thrive, and undergraduate services are continued by libraries in certain fields such as fine arts, because decentralization is desirable in some circumstances, not because it is imposed by lack of space at the undergraduate library center.

The ready availability of books was assured by the basic plan of the building,[8] which provides an alcove-type stack through the center, open on one side to the major reading areas and on the other to entrances, the reference room, and special collections. Users of the library, almost as often as they enter, move from one room to another, or leave, can hardly avoid passing through corridors or alcoves lined with books.

The third objective is very broad. Undergraduate reading of one kind or another may be encouraged to some extent by the smallest detail that makes any reader more comfortable and may be discouraged at least slightly by the mildest annoyance or smallest inconvenience. There is statistical evidence that general undergraduate reading increased materially after Lamont opened; Widener outside charges dropped only slightly in 1949, and the total for Widener and Lamont was 37,000 volumes greater than the Widener figure for 1948, when Lamont was not yet available. In addition, 94,000 overnight charges for reserved books during 1949 represented an increase of more than 17,000 over the preceding year, in spite of the fact that there were 500 fewer students and that such books are not allowed to leave Lamont until 9:00 p.m. except on Saturdays. There can be no doubt that undergraduate use of books within the Library also increased, for Lamont has had more than 800 readers at once on several occasions — a hundred more than could have been crowded into the areas formerly available to undergraduates even if everyone else had been excluded from the main reading room in Widener.

Centralization, because it brings greater convenience, has undoubtedly contributed to these results. So has the availability of books and the improvement of the book stock by increased duplication of heavily used titles. This duplication has made it possible to restrict to closed shelves (behind the charging desks in Lamont) fewer reserved books than ever before. Books for the large survey courses, reading period books, and a few titles in short supply were held behind the desks at the start of 1949. During the summer, however, all books were placed on open shelves, and this policy was continued during the fall except for courses in which excessive pressure developed and for reading period assignments in history, government, economics, and social relations. As was to be expected, some students cause trouble by breaking even the most liberal rules; the staff must watch closely and be ready to shift books to closed reserve whenever the demand in any course becomes too great. Closed reserves can probably never be abolished completely, but they can be reduced in number still further as enrollment falls to the normal level and as more of the books that are needed come back into print.

The chief complaints with regard to reserved books come from patrons of Widener rather than Lamont, and arise when copies of a title are not available in the former building either because it has seemed necessary to shift all copies to reserve in Lamont or because the Widener copy has been borrowed or lost. The establishment in Widener of a non-circulating collection of copies of reserved books ought to do a good deal toward solving this problem; meanwhile every effort must be made to correct mistakes and replace losses. The general collection in Lamont, it should be emphasized, was assembled by purchase and by the transfer of duplicates, not of unique copies, from Widener.[9] Some increased annoyance is probably inevitable in any case, for, if two collections have copies of a book yet both fail to produce one for him, the scholar's frustration is greater than if there had been but one place in which to seek it and be disappointed.

Availability implies not only open shelves but a minimization of all other barriers between readers and books. Enormous catalogues such as those in Widener serve as invaluable keys for scholars, but are necessarily so complex that they are discouraging and time-consuming barriers to undergraduates. The Lamont catalogue is small; moreover, facilities are provided for by-passing it whenever possible. Visibile indexes at the charging desks just inside the entrances to the building list reserved books by author, and the books themselves are arranged alphabetically by author under each department of instruction rather than under individual courses. Annotated copies of reading lists are also provided.

The classification scheme for the general collection was prepared to fit the library in which it is used,[10] and indexed copies are at hand in each stack alcove. Bulletin boards on each of the three main levels contain floor plans, a topical index to the classification, an index to the location of book collections, and a directory.

Reference service is also more readily available to undergraduates than it was in Widener, where faculty members, visiting scholars, and graduate students tended to monopolize it. There has been a gradual but distinct rise in the number and quality of reference questions since Lamont opened, and it is hoped that this will continue as students develop the habit of turning to librarians for bibliographical help.[11] The Reference Department maintains a visible index to the periodical collection, for which it is responsible, and a small pamphlet file. The latter is an innovation that deserves to be further developed, and several current lists are being checked for new material. A good deal of work has also gone into building up the back files of serials. Since Lamont periodicals do not leave the library they are often consulted by graduate students and other scholars who find that volumes from Widener sets have been charged out. Still another duty of the reference staff is the ordering (usually by means of telephone calls to local dealers) and processing of books needed on short notice for required reading. Regular acquisition and cataloguing work for the library is done in Widener.

One more contribution to the availability of books is the simplicity of the charging system[12] and the fact that the only control points are at the exits from the building. A student can take books anywhere in Lamont without formalities; when he wishes to take them from the building he need only fill out a simple slip for each and have the attendant charge them as he leaves.

Certain other features that are meant to encourage reading may be grouped under the heading of comfort. Light and air are important items here, and it is good to be able to report that the lighting throughout the building appears to have been satisfactory, and the air-conditioining system has worked well.

Since students are not all alike and since many an individual's wants vary with the type of reading he happens to be doing, variety in facilities can contribute a good deal to comfort. Smoking areas have been provided on each level and, while they have been well filled at times, they never seem to have been inadequate in size. The ten typing cubicles on the mezzanine levels have also sufficed to meet the demand.

The furniture seems to have been generally satisfactory, and to have provided for a variety of needs. The individual stalls along the outer walls of the three large reading areas and on both sides of the mezzanine levels have been the most popular study accommodations, particularly during reading and examination periods, when semi-privacy seems to be at a premium. Next have come the individual study tables along the north window of the Reference Room and along both sides of the screens that divide the reading areas. The armchairs provided in the stalls and at most of the tables in the building are good looking, comfortable, and, it is believed, durable. The eight sloping-top tables have been used to some extent, but not enough to suggest that there ought to have been more of them. There has been heavy use of the semi-lounge chairs, which come in both large and small models and are covered with red, green, or brown leather. These are relatively less popular during reading and examination periods, but some experts at note-taking by means of clip-board and knee prefer them at all times. It might be added that there are those who seem to find two such chairs essential to complete comfort.

The light natural finish of all the woods that have been used helps to avoid the institutional look associated with dark furniture, but blemishes, of course, show up clearly on the light surfaces. A year may be too short a period to indicate how serious this factor will be. Some of the chairs and tables on the third level were not sufficiently rugged at first, but this defect was easily remedied by the substitution of longer screws or of bolts for the original screws or glue.

Nearly all the furniture on this level was designed by Mr. Alvar Aalto, the famous Finnish architect, and made in Sweden. Of the same origin are the small chairs with red or green leather seats at the individual tables in the Reference Room, in the Forum Room, and in each alcove of the stack, where they have been particularly convenient for students consulting the lower shelves.

Two special rooms add to the variety that distinguishes Lamont. Some confusion might be avoided if it were customary to speak of the Farnsworth collection rather than the Farnsworth Room, for the new Farnsworth Room in Lamont, finished in natural cherry, differs a good deal from its smaller predecessor of the same name in Widener. The collection was renovated during the war years before it left Widener;[13] the furniture, though out of keeping with the style of the new room and of the building, was perforce transferred also, but will be replaced shortly through the generosity of Mrs. Farnsworth Loomis, daughter of the original donors of the Room. Students undoubtedly have welcomed the repeal of bans on smoking and note-taking. Still, when one recalls that few books except the open reserves and the Farnsworth collection used to be directly accessible to undergraduates, it seems remarkable that now, in a building with open shelves holding nearly 100,000 volumes, the Farnsworth Room is more popular than ever.

The Woodberry Poetry Room, next door to Farnsworth, also contains a collection formerly housed in Widener. Its new setting in Lamont was designed by Mr. Aalto with the approval and generous assistance of Mr. Harry N. Flagler, who established the room in 1931 in memory of his friend and teacher, George H. Woodberry. The beautifully grained woods used in paneling, bookshelves, cabinets, and furniture, and the unusual imported lighting fixtures have attracted a good deal of attention. There are 3,500 volumes of modern poetry and more than 1,100 records of poetry readings, folk ballads, and Shakespearean plays. Four turntables, to each of which eight sets of earphones can be attached, are provided for the playing of records; in addition there are four chair stations, each accommodating four sets of earphones, which can be tuned in to any one of the turntables. Loudspeaker equipment in the Forum Room next door provides for listening by classes or other groups.

The Poetry Room is now open all day, and it is heavily used. More than 8,500 students listened to records during the first ten months in Lamont, and this figure does not include visitors or students who merely sampled the equipment. All four of the turntables are often in use at once. The wear and tear on records and machinery will lead to bills for replacements, but expenditures necessitated by heavy student use are certainly justifiable.

Additional variety in Lamont is offered by the exhibits, for which twelve built-in cases were provided along the east-west corridors on the three main levels. A permanent display on the first level, arranged by Mr. Philip Hofer, Curator of Printing and Graphic Arts in the College Library, deals with the making of prints and reproductions and letterpress printing. The rest of the cases were given over when the library opened to 'The Undergraduate and the Harvard College Library.' During the year that followed, exhibits were sponsored by the Crimson Photographic Board, Ivy Films, the Philatelic Society, and the Harvard Photographic Society; members of the library staff have arranged exhibits on spring sports at Harvard before 1900, the history of the Summer School, seventy-five years of Harvard football, and the George Brinton Beale Circus Collection.

Not all of the building is devoted to facilities for the reading, housing, or display of books. The Forum Room, which seats 150 and has both loud-speaker and motion-picture projection equipment, has been mentioned as an adjunct to the Poetry Room's record collection, but it has several other uses. Various groups that have met in it include classes, student organizations, and librarians. The dedication program for the Lamont building took place in the room on 10 January 1949, and the successful completion of the Lamont Endowment Fund Campaign was announced there on 10 March 1949 by Mr. Dwight P. Robinson, Jr, Chairman of the Harvard Fund Council, at a meeting of Class Agents. University presidents and librarians from leading institutions throughout the country met there during March, 1949, for the Conference on the Place of the Library in a University.

There are also smaller meeting rooms and offices, and it should be noted that librarians are by no means unanimously of the opinion that it is desirable to provide such rooms in a library. Mr. Lamont was interested in developing a close relationship between the General Education program and the undergraduate library, since he realized that the new curriculum was designed in part 'to encourage wider undergraduate reading.'[14] Members of the faculty who are giving General Education courses occupy the office space in Lamont, and section meetings of some General Education courses, as well as other small classes, use the ten conference rooms, each of which seats from twenty to thirty students. The movement of groups to and from classrooms has caused no trouble; since hundreds of readers sometimes leave the building on the hour to go to classes elsewhere in the Yard, it would have been necessary in any case to provide exits capable of handling heavy traffic.

Some courses have not used the building because women are not admitted to it at most times. Many students and faculty members deplore the exclusion of Radcliffe from Harvard's new library, but exclusion was decided upon by administrative authorities of the two colleges before the building was planned. Radcliffe, it is pointed out, maintains its own undergraduate library, and is not prepared to help support a second. Consequently Lamont's size was determined by estimates based on Harvard enrollment alone, and no provision was made for supervision of reading areas. Satisfactory quiet has prevailed in these areas as was anticipated, but the experience of other colleges indicates that coeducational use would bring conversational disturbances. Women attending the Summer School use the building, however, and visitors of both sexes are admitted on Saturday afternoons throughout the year.

The classrooms and Forum Room were particularly popular during Lamont's first summer, when there was unusually warm weather and the new library offered the only air-conditioned meeting places at Harvard. It is expensive to cool a building, and Lamont would have been closed if the Harvard Summer School had not been willing to underwrite the additional cost. This investment seems to have been a good one. The preliminary announcement for 1950 has a picture of Lamont on the cover and refers to it as 'in many ways the new core of the Harvard Summer School.' A memorandum prepared by the Summer School Office, after pointing out that heat has always been one hazard that must be overcome if academic standards for summer work are to be maintained, states that modern, air-conditioned reading facilities in a student-centered library resulted in a four-fold increase in book use, and there was 'a significant decline in the number of failures and unsatisfactory work.'

It might seem appropriate to conclude with this gratifying testimonial, but some readers — particularly librarians who have to plan their own new buildings — may think criticisms more instructive than praise. It must be confessed, however, that an attempt to find flaws has yielded only distinctly minor ones that affect those who operate the building rather than those who read in it. There are four that ought to be mentioned:

Light colored rubber-tile treads were placed on the double stairways at the east and west ends of the building in order to distinguish each step clearly; unfortunately they look very dirty after a few hours of use. Adequate maintenance will continue to require a good deal of work unless a more effective cleaning compound can be discovered.

The light switches are not in the same place on each level, and some of them are awkwardly located.

Facilities for the staff are scattered through the building; some staff time might have been saved if they had been centered at the east end of the fourth level.

The storage room provided for the janitor and cleaning staff was intended to accommodate trash barrels in addition to supplies. Experience has taught, however, that refuse, when it consists largely of the contents of ashtrays and smokadors, stinks and ought to be kept outside the building. Therefore plans are now being made for an outdoor receptacle for trash barrels. It might have been preferable to have the service entrance on the same level as the janitor's quarters, but supplies for the most part come from Widener via tunnel, and no difficulties have developed.

These are remarkably few and insignificant regrets to feel after a year of experience with a new building. The staff's pride in the library seems to be justified, and anyone who examines circulation statistics or walks through the reading areas will find evidence that Harvard students are not neglecting the opportunities provided them by those who helped to create or maintain the Lamont Library. There is now a collection of books chosen for undergraduates, and barriers to its use have been minimized; competition with more advanced scholars for reference services is no longer necessary; and each student — with exceptions including those who prefer to read in bed or with feminine companionship — should be able to find furniture to suit him within a few steps of the shelves.

Notes

1. Keyes D. Metcalf, 'The Undergraduate and the Harvard Library, 1765-1877,' *Harvard Library Bulletin* 1 (1947), 29-51; Robert W. Lovett, 'The Undergraduate and the Harvard Library, 1877-1937,' *Harvard Library Bulletin* 1 (1947): 221-237; Keyes D. Metcalf, 'The Undergraduate and the Harvard Library, 1937-1947; *Harvard Library Bulletin* 1 (1947): 288-305.

2. David McCord, 'The Farnsworth Room, 1916-1946,' *Harvard Library Bulletin* 1 (1947): 109-111.

3. Philip J. McNiff, 'Reading Room Problems of the Harvard College Library, 1942-1947,' *Harvard Library Bulletin* 1 (1947): 254-256.

4. Robert W. Lovett, 'The Harvard Union Library, 1901 to 1948,' *Harvard Library Bulletin* 2 (1948): 230-237.

5. Keyes D. Metcalf, 'Harvard Faces Its Library Problems,' *Harvard Library Bulletin* 3 (1949): 183-197.

6. *Harvard Library Bulletin* 1 (1947): 305.

7. Frank N. Jones, 'The Libraries of the Harvard Houses,' *Harvard Library Bulletin* 2 (1948): 362-377.

8. Henry R. Shepley and Keyes D. Metcalf, 'The Lamont Library,' *Harvard Library Bulletin* 3 (1949): 5-30.

9. Edwin E. Williams, 'The Selection of Books for Lamont,' *Harvard Library Bulletin* 3 (1949): 386-394.

10. Richard O. Pautzsch, 'The Classification Scheme for the Lamont Library,' *Harvard Library Bulletin* 4 (1950): 126-127.

11. Morrison C. Haviland, 'The Reference Function of the Lamont Library,' *Harvard Library Bulletin* 3 (1949): 297-299.

12. Philip J. McNiff, 'The Charging System of the Lamont Library,' *Harvard Library Bulletin* 3 (1949): 438-440.

13.   Cf. McCord, op. cit. (note 2 above).

14.   *Harvard Library Bulletin* 1 (1947): 302.

About the Authors

Philip J. McNiff held several library positions at Harvard and was Librarian of the Lamont Library, 1948-1956. He also held the position of Assistant Librarian at Harvard from 1949 until 1956 when he was promoted to Associate Librarian. In 1965, he was appointed Director and Librarian of the Boston Public Library.

Edwin E. Williams was Assistant to the Librarian of Harvard College from 1940 until 1950; Chief of the Acquisitions Department, 1950-1956; Assistant Librarian for Book Selection, 1956-1959; and Counselor to the Director for Collections, 1959-1964. In 1964, he was appointed Assistant University Librarian. During 1947-1948, Williams was in charge of the project for selection of the Lamont Library book collection.

Edwin E. Williams

The Selection of Books
for Lamont

The following is a first-hand account of the building of the Lamont collection by the project director, the two major portions already in existence
when the selection project began: The House
libraries and the Shaw *List of Books for College
Libraries*. Faculty participation, final acquisition,
and the enunciation of several principles and
reservations are examined.

Undergraduates are the primary concern of hundreds of college libraries, but
even when an institutuion offers no graduate courses of any kind, its library
normally must give some attention to faculty needs. The Lamont Library is in a
different situation. It is contributing to the bibliographical well-being of the faculty and of graduate students by relieving Widener and some other Harvard
libraries of heavy use by undergraduates, and it is sometimes visited (as the
reserved collections in the Widener Reading Room used to be) by instructors
and graduates when they require copies of books in great demand; but books
ought to be placed in Lamont only because they will be wanted by undergraduates.

There is another distinction. Elsewhere, when a student wishes to use books
that are not in his own college library, he must generally, if he is to borrow them
at all, call upon some other institution at a distance from the campus. Here,
however, if Lamont does not have what an undergraudate wants, Widener,
Houghton, and other Harvard libraries are nearby, and they have not curtailed
the privileges he had during the pre-Lamont period when he was entirely
dependent on them.

If individualism and diversity are desirable in colleges, it may be argued that no
two college library books collections ought to be identical. Lamont, in so far as
its purposes and milieu are unique, is clearly entitled and obligated to differ
from its fellows even more than they differ from one another. Hence *extenuation*

SOURCE: From Edwin E. Williams, "The Selection of Books for Lamont," *Harvard
Library Bulletin* 3 (Autumn, 1949), pp. 386-394. Reprinted by permission of the
publisher.

1 for the defects of its collection may be offered: There was no model to be copied.

Reservation 1 might follow: Two major portions of the collection were already in existence when the selection project began under the supervision of the author of this paper.

The books on reading lists for undergraduate courses, many of them already on reserve, obviously would be needed in the new library, and the Superintendent of the Widener Reading Room (now Librarian of Lamont) made sure that all of which copies could be acquired would be found there. This accounted for approximately 4,500 titles (which duplication brings to 22,500 volumes) on reserve, and for more than 5,000 additional titles in the general Collection. Reading lists, of course, are a faculty product, so selection by librarians was not involved.

Recreational reading was to be furnished by the Farnsworth Room (about 5,000 volumes) and the Poetry Room (about 3,000 volumes), both of which had been operating in Widener for years. The former collection had been weeded and renovated while the room was closed during the war, and both are kept up to date by a 'Curator of the Poetry Room and Subject Specialist in English Literature in the Harvard College Library.'

At first glance the reservation might seem to make a special selection project unnecessary. Students, like other men, presumably read for profit, for pleasure, or for some combination of the two. Widener, next door, can supply extraordinary needs; with normal required and recreational reading in Lamont cared for already, what more is needed? This question should, at least, suggest *reassurance 1:* It is unlikely that anyone will be irreparably damaged by omissions or other results of poor selection in the general collection for Lamont.

Still, from the premise that no single volume in it can be termed essential, it does not follow that a general collection is undesirable. Perhaps students ought to read more than is required; in preparing term papers, for example, they may often have to turn to books that no instructor has recommended or assigned for any class as a whole. Moreover, interest in chosen subjects may lead a student to find pleasure in volumes that do not divert enough of his classmates to warrant their inclusion in a Farnsworth Room.

Whether or not access to their stacks can be permitted, Widener and other research libraries are so large that the best books on most subjects are submerged in the highly technical, the obsolescent, the mediocre, and worse. A specialist needs the inferior as well as the great books, and should be competent to find his way among them; but an undergraduate faces wasteful and discouraging searches unless he can start with selection of the most useful material on any field of interest to him. If he exhausts the selection and desires to investigate further it is then time for him to call on the research collections, and his reading in the Lamont stacks ought to have made him enough of a specialist to do so effectively. Indeed, while the new building can greatly facilitate both his required and his unspecialized recreational reading by offering better physical accommodations, the general collection, which did not exist before, may be called Lamont's major bibliographical contribution to the undergraduate.

Picking out this general collection might have been an enjoyable task for a man who knew enough to do it, particularly if he were also interested in exerting a salutary influence on future generations of Harvard students by sparing them authors, ideas, and subjects obnoxious to him, while providing generous quantities of those his tastes approved. Instead, the work of coordinating selection devolved upon one who not only lacked these qualifications but who thought it desirable for students as well as prudent for himself to follow a procedure that would shelter him beneath *reservation 2:* The faculty has been responsible for Lamont book selection.

It might have been simple to go to each instructor or department and request a list of the books that ought to be acquired. But, no matter how well he knows the literature of a subject, a specialist may not be prepared to think of all the books on it that ought to be in a library. Perhaps a better job could be done more easily if fairly comprehensive lists could be submitted to the faculty for revision. Unsuitable titles then might readily be crossed out, and some, at least, of the omissions would probably be suggested by the titles at hand.

Fortunately, members of the Harvard faculty had already done work that could be utilized in compiling such preliminary lists. Each of the seven Houses has a collection of more than 10,000 and fewer than 13,500 volumes; in his article describing these libraries, Frank N. Jones has stated that 'the project of getting together the books for the first two Houses enlisted at one time or another the active cooperation of a hundred or more Faculty members . . .'[1] All seven have had the benefit of faculty advice at least to some extent throughout their history, and, though they differ widely, all have been selected with the needs of Harvard students in mind; consequently it was believed that a large proportion of the books owned by the Houses would prove to be desiderata for a general undergraduate collection. Typists began early in 1947 to copy main-entry cards for all books in the Adams House Library; then the six others were incorporated one by one until a card file had been made covering all volumes in the seven Houses, with symbols indicating in which of the libraries each title was to be found.[2]

The second major source of titles for consideration was one to which at least a few members of the Harvard faculty had contributed. The Carnegie Corporation of New York, when making grants-in-aid to colleges for book purchases, financed the preparation and publication in 1931 of *A List of Books for College Libraries,* edited by Charles B. Shaw, and containing more than 14,000 titles selected by two hundred faculty members of Harvard and forty-nine other American colleges and universities.[3] A supplement, also edited by Shaw, and listing nearly 4,000 new books that had appeared between 1931 and 1938, was prepared in the same manner and published in 1940.[4] The second step in the Lamont selection project was to annotate cards that had been copied from the House library catalogues and type new ones until the file included a record of everything in these two 'Shaw lists.'

A third source of suggestions was needed to provide for the years since 1938. More than one hundred and fifty scholarly journals, including the fifty-four in which the Shaw supplement cites book reviews, were chosen for checking. Reviews (many of them by members of the Harvard faculty) in issues of each journal from 1939 to date were read, and cards were made for all books that had been favorably reviewed and did not seem obviously unsuitable. Fourteen professional members of the library staff were called upon to help with the review checking when it was seen that the supervisor of the project would not finish soon enough if he attempted to do it all himself. No effort was made to be very selective; the librarians inevitably were unfamiliar with many of the subjects in which they had to examine reviews, and the faculty evidently would find it easier to eliminate titles that need not have been listed than to add those that ought to have been brought to their attention but were not.

Finally, the cards were annotated to show which titles were already assured of inclusion in Lamont because they were on required-reading lists. Since no decisions would be needed on these, this was a means of saving some time for the judges; moreover, it might have been unwise to select books on a subject without taking into account those that had been chosen in advance.

When the file was completed late in 1947 it was found to consist of nearly 44,500 cards, each indicating whether or not the title it listed was in Shaw or on a required-reading list, which Houses owned it, if any, and (for books less than nine or ten years old) which of one hundred and fifty journals had favorably reviewed it. The titles then had to be classified and sorted by subject; in the process it was possible to discard more than 4,000 as surely unnecessary because they were out of date, inferior editions, or too specialized. Most of the latter were volumes that presumably had strayed into one or another of the Houses by gift.[5]

In January 1948, 40,290 cards, now divided into fifty-four subject files, were ready for submission to those who would select. Each department of the Faculty of Arts and Sciences had been informed of the project and asked to appoint one of its members as a representative with whom the Library could deal. The twenty-eight departments[6] could be counted upon to handle thirty-five of the subjects — philosophy, psychology, social relations, government, economics, comparative philology, mathematics, astronomy, physics, chemistry, mineralogy, geology, biology, anthropology, medicine, engineering, fine arts, achitecture, music, geography, history, and the following languages and literatures: American, English, German, Scandinavian, French, Italian, Spanish, Portuguese, Latin, Greek, Celtic, Semitic, far Eastern, and Indic. Useful arts were attached to engineering; the Biology Department was asked to pass on palaeontological and agricultural materials; and a member of the History Department covered Slavic.

It was not difficult to make less formal arrangements for expert selection in most of the other subjects by asking for help from the Curator of the Nieman Fellowships, the Librarian of the Houghton Library, the Curator of the Department of Printing and Graphic Arts, the Director of the Andover-Harvard Theological Library, officers giving instruction in military and naval science, the Dean and the Librarian of the Graduate School of Education, the staff of the

Harvard Archives, the Managing Editor of *Isis,* the Librarian of the Blue Hill Meteorological Observatory, the Assistant Director of Physical Education, the Curator of the Theatre Collection, and an Associate Professor of Public Speaking. A few miscellaneous or small groups of cards were handled by members of the Widener Library staff.

The collections of cards with which members of the faculty were confronted ranged in size from two dozen to nearly seven thousand. Each department, of course, was free to deal with them as it chose, and there was no uniformity in the procedures adopted. In some cases the chairman or his representative did the work himself; other departments appointed committees to serve as juries; and the cards for some subjects were further sorted in order that a specialist in each subdivision of the field could examine those in the area with which he was most familiar. Many professors called informally on one or more of their colleagues for advice. Consequently it is impossible to make a complete list of the individuals to whom the Lamont Library is indebted for help.

It should be emphasized, however, that the work of selection was done by officers of the University who were asked, either directly or through their departments, to assist; this request in, every case, meant an unexpected addition to normal teaching and administrative duties, yet there were no refusals to cooperate and, in most cases, the selection was made very promptly. The last of the cards were returned by the end of April 1948, less than four months after the first of them had been distributed.

Probable use by Harvard undergraduates was the criterion for selection, rather than any theory of what would constitute an ideal book collection. Education, for example, is not an undergraudate field of concentration at Harvard, but is heavily represented in the Shaw lists; the preliminary card file for education was, therefore, ruthlessly weeded until only 290 titles were approved of the 880 that had been suggested.

Other accidents of time and place influenced selection. Harvard students of fine arts spend a good deal of time in the Fogg Museum using its collections of originals, slides, etc.; the Fogg is across the street from Lamont; and fine arts books are very expensive. Consequently the list approved in this field was smaller than it would have been if there were no fine arts library at the Fogg. German books are hard to obtain at present, so the German collection in Lamont has been smaller to start with than would have been desirable. In French, on the other hand, the Department of Romance Languages authorized the transfer of books freely from the Lowell Memorial and French Libraries on the top floor of Widener, so the Lamont collection of French literary classics is a more extensive one than would have been assembled by purchase alone.

Cards were not duplicated; each title appeared in only one subject file, and there was some mis-classification. It was not surprising, therefore, that a number of the additions suggested by faculty members proved to be titles that had been submitted to and approved (in most cases) by another department. Of the 40,290 titles assembled for faculty consideration, approximately 7,700 were rejected, and *net* additions to the list by the selectors amounted to 3,809; hence a total of

36,399 titles were approved for inclusion. Many rejections were to be expected in the sciences, where books become out of date most rapidly; in some other subjects a majority of the titles rejected were judged too specialized for undergraduate needs. The linguistic attainments of the average student in each field were, of course, an essential factor in deciding on books in languages other than English.

It should be noted that two special portions of the general collection — the periodicals and the reference books — had been selected for the most part before faculty advice was sought. It was believed that back files of serials, unless indexed, would be used very little by students; therefore inclusion in *Poole's Index*, the *Reader's Guide*, or the *International Index to Periodicals* was an essential consideration in deciding which files would be desirable, and an important one in choosing current subscriptions. It will take many years, of course, to collect all the back files that are wanted. It was thought that the best judges of reference books would be librarians who have been answering undergraduates' questions and helping them find information. Cards for reference items, like those for required reading, were included in the lists submitted to the faculty for their information rather than for decision.

While every book recommended by the faculty had been placed in Lamont if it could be obtained, there are inclusions (besides those just mentioned) that were not specifically recommended by the faculty. Large gifts of books had to be sorted before the lists had been approved, and volumes selected for Lamont from these gifts were processed at once. Undoubtedly faculty members would have differed with the supervisor of the project in some cases. Perhaps, however, he would not have been unanimously overruled on many items, for it was instructive to see how frequently a professor, overlooking the symbol indicating required reading, would attempt to reject cards for volumes that one or another of his colleagues assigns to undergraduates.

Of the 36,399 approved titles, 9,832 were already on required reading lists or in the reference collection. Checking indicated that 4,392 more had already been catalogued for Lamont, chiefly as a result of the gifts that have been mentioned, and that duplicate copies of another 6,364 were available for transfer from Widener. Normally, a book was not transferred to the general collection in Lamont unless there was a duplicate of it for Widener to retain, but it has not seemed practicable to establish any inflexible rule that Lamont shall contain only copies of books kept in the Widener stacks. The Farnsworth and Poetry Rooms have never been so restricted. A book must go to Lamont if it is on reserve and additional copies of it cannot be bought. Moreover, when hundreds of undergraduates have assignments in the same book, it does little good to tell the graduate student or faculty member who needs it that Widener has a copy, for that copy, no doubt, will already be in the hands of an enterprising undergraduate. Finally, Lamont has purchased a good many books, particularly in the sciences, that Widener would never have bought; in these fields, Lamont represents a duplication for the undergraduate's benefit of special and laboratory collections.

Acquisition was a separate project, but it should be observed that, of the 15,811 titles remaining to be purchased after transfers had been made, nearly 3,500 were published abroad and more than 5,000 were out-of-print American books. It is not surprising, then, that something like 4,000 of the books wanted could not be obtained at reasonable prices in the second-hand market by the time the new library opened. This supplies *extenuation 2* for Lamont's deficiencies: Many of the volumes selected are not there yet. On the other hand, it is clear that better administration of the selection project[7] by the writer would not only have given the faculty more time and more satisfactory lists on which to work, but would have left a longer period after selection, during which additional hundreds of out-of-print books could have been tracked down.

The hunt for titles remaining on the desiderata list will continue. Selection of new books will be based on reviews in the current issues of the journals used to supplement the Shaw lists, with continued advice from the faculty. Lamont is not designed to house more than 100,000 volumes, and it opened with more than 80,000; thus it must fairly soon begin to discard old books as rapidly as it adds new ones. A research library grows and tries to preserve almost everything that comes to it; an undergraduate library can be kept at the same size because no volume in it need remain there always — one may hope that there will be many copies of Homer in Lamont as long as the building stands, but, even in ten or twenty years, they will not be the same copies of the same editions that were there in 1949.

This may be summarized as *reassurance 2:* The collection is impermanent; so, therefore, are its present deficiencies. All those who use it (or whose students use it) can help to improve Lamont's book collection, which, in a few years, will reflect the original selection less than the later criticisms and suggestions made from day to day by students, librarians, and members of the faculty.

Notes

1. 'The Libraries of the Harvard Houses,' *Harvard Library Bulletin* 2 (1948): 368.

2. These cards could now be used as the basis for a Union Catalogue of House Libraries, which might be kept up to date in Lamont, but it seems doubtful that such a catalogue would be worthwhile.

3. Shaw, *A List of Books for College Libraries* (Chicago, 1931).

4. Shaw, *A List of Books for College Libraries 1931-38* (Chicago, 1940). Preliminary checking had shown that little could have been added to Shaw by using Foster E. Mohrhardt's *A List of Books for Junior College Libraries* (Chicago, 1937).

5. Cards for all House library titles that were not approved for Lamont by the faculty have been collected in a file that may be useful to House librarians who wish to weed their collections.

6. For the departments then existing see *Harvard University Catalogue, November, 1945,* pp. 158-159.

7. The clerical employees are to be congratulated on having done an excellent job, particularly Miss Gladys Wells, who was with the project longer than any of the others.

About the Author

Edwin E. Williams was Assistant to the Librarian of Harvard College from 1940 until 1950; Chief of the Acquisitions Department, 1950-1956; Assistant Librarian for Book Selection, 1956-1959; and Councilor to the Director for Collections, 1959-1964. In 1964, he was appointed Assistant University Librarian. During 1947-1948, Williams was in charge of the project for selection of the Lamont Library book collection.

Charles A. Carpenter, Jr.

The Lamont Catalog as a Guide To Book Selection

From a Cornell University perspective, Carpenter appraises the published *Catalogue of the Lamont Library, Harvard College.* He points out its virtues, questions the inclusion of some titles, and warns against accepting the *Catalogue* as a "work of great reliability before its reliability has been definitely established."

The most useful volume available to the book selector in college and undergraduate libraries is *The Catalogue of the Lamont Library, Harvard College.*[1] As the collaborative product of Harvard specialists, the Lamont catalog has become, in effect, the successor to the long authoritative Shaw lists.[2] Its use as a checklist for evaluating and detecting gaps in book collections is outstanding since it contains three times as many titles as the Shaw volumes; furthermore, as Philip J. McNiff, librarian of the Lamont Library, notes in his introduction to it, the Lamont catalog has distinctive value as "an actual, working list rather than an ideal, theoretical listing of books."[3]

There is a danger, however, that the Lamont catalog will be accepted as a work of great reliability before its reliability has been definitely established. In order to use this kind of bibliography with the best results, the book selector must have a thorough understanding of its nature: he must know what it is supposed to be, how it was developed, and what it actually is.

The *Catalogue of the Lamont Library* is intended to list books which will be *used* by Harvard undergraduates. The fullest statement of the criterion for selection has been given by Mr. McNiff:

> The Lamont Library . . . contains a live, working collection of books selected to serve the required and recommended course reading needs of Harvard undergraduates in addition to a good general collection of books.[4]

SOURCE: From Charles A. Carpenter, Jr., "The Lamont Catalog as a Guide to Book Selection," *College and Research Libraries* 18 (July, 1957), pp. 267-268, 302. Reprinted by permission of the author.

The supervisor of the selection project, Edwin E. Williams, has made it explicit that "books ought to be placed in Lamont only because they will be wanted by undergraduates."[5]

Mr. Williams has described in detail the process of selection. A file of titles compiled by librarians was turned over to faculty members, who made final additions and deletions. The initial file was assembled from reading lists prepared by professors for undergraduate courses, from catalogs of house libraries, from the Shaw lists, and from favorable reviews in about 150 journals since 1939. Fields such as art, education, and agriculture were represented by minimum collections because of particular local conditions.

In attempting to determine what the Lamont catalog actually is, viewed in terms of its purpose, one must not be critical of its omissions. More than four thousand titles originally selected were unobtainable at the time the catalog was prepared.[6] In the French literature section, for instance, there are striking gaps, but out-of-print books in foreign languages are difficult to procure.

Representative of the omissions are some very useful American literature titles: Alfred Kreymborg's *History of American Poetry,* Margaret Mayorga's *Short History of the American Drama,* Emery Neff's volume on Robinson, and Irving Howe's study of Faulkner; critical anthologies such as Harry H. Clark's *Major American Poets* and Allan G. Halline's *American Plays;* the "inclusive edition" of Whitman's *Leaves of Grass,* edited by Emory Holloway; the American Writers Series volumes for Bryant, Cooper, Emerson, Holmes, Irving, Longfellow, Lowell, Poe, Thoreau, Twain and Whitman; and, to choose one novel, *The Just and the Unjust,* by James Gould Cozzens. The catalog lists an impressive percentage of essential books in the American literature field, but there are important omissions. A book should not be underestimated simply because it is not "in Lamont."

It is presumptuous to contend that a particular book will not be used by Harvard undergraduates, but we may question the inclusion of titles in the catalog with regard to their probable use by undergraduates in general. For example, do students now read Lafcadio Hearn and Agnes Repplier enough to justify eleven volumes by Hearn and twelve by Miss Repplier? A more realistic estimate might call for no more than one or two volumes by each author.

In the American Literature—History and Criticism section of the Lamont catalog, the titles by Bronson, Ellsworth, Farrar, Mitchell, Overton, Richardson, White, and James Wilson are highly questionable inclusions. The books by Cooper, Halsey, and Lawton in Collective Biography, and those by Onderdonk and Otis in Poetry are similarly suspect. It is difficult to imagine a rationale for their inclusion in an undergraduate library collection.

How often do students study the works of minor nineteenth- and twentieth-century novelists? Will forty volumes by Francis Marion Crawford, fourteen by Silas Weir Mitchell, twenty-six by Frank Stockton, ten by Charles Brockden Brown, and nine by Joseph Hergesheim be used by undergraduates?

Compare the list of books about Walt Whitman, particularly the biographies, with the comments in Gay Wilson Allen's *Walt Whitman Handbook*[7] or in the

Literary History of the United States.[8] The best titles up to 1953 are there (with the exception of an excellent study by Frederik Schyberg), but so is one of the least trustworthy (Frances Winwar's); the essential books are in the library, but so are the unessential (those by Bailey, Barton, Carpenter, Masters, and Morris). The same observation can be made about the secondary works listed under Emily Dickinson, Emerson, Hawthorne, Longfellow, Melville, Poe, Robinson, Thoreau, Whittier, and Wolfe.

This excess is not found only in the section on American literature. As evidence, see the bibliographies for Kant and Kierkegaard in the Philosophy section, for St. Francis of Assisi and Pascal in Religion, for Homer and Virgil in Classics, for Chaucer and Lawrence in English literature, and for Diderot and Hugo in French literature.

Possibly there are convincing reasons for including such a wide range of material in a library for undergraduates. Some of these books might be recommended, or even required, at Harvard. But the selector using the Lamont catalog must be aware that not all of the titles listed are essential, or useful, or even "good" by modern standards.

One source of a large percentage of these superfluous titles might be the 1931 *List of Books for College Libraries,* which was duplicated in the file checked by Harvard faculty members. In many respects, this volume is as out-of-date as a 1940 treatise on polio prevention. Many authors considered important in the nineteen-twenties are no longer read except by literary historians; critical and interpretive works have been replaced by more recent studies.

Both the Shaw list and the Lamont catalog include large portions of the work of Louise Imogen Guiney, Margaret Deland, and Richard Gilder, for example, the above-mentioned novelists, as well as Lafcadio Hearn and Agnes Repplier, are represented by disproportionate amounts of their writings in both bibliographies. The titles from the History and Criticism, Collective Biography, and Poetry subdivisions cited above are all in the Shaw volume. We know, at least, how these particular books happened to be considered for inclusion in the Lamont Library.

"The faculty has been responsible for Lamont book selection."[9] This fact is so impressive that one is inclined to accept the catalog as a thoroughly reliable guide. Certainly there is no doubt that the Harvard staff possesses an adequate knowledge of books. But how effectively will a scholar apply this knowledge to the selection of a library for undergraduates?

Even the finest scholar-teacher is hampered in this effort by his own concept of a book's usefulness. The specialist, who is able to discriminate between reliable and questionable material, is bound to regard some books as useful which are of little value to the student; in fact, what is necessarily vital to the scholar is often beyond the comprehension of the undergraduate.

Consider how important the monumental eight-volume *Text of the Canterbury Tales* would be to the specialist. How often will the undergraduate use it? Apply this same test to the ten volumes of Emerson's *Journals,* or to the fragmentary *Life of Poe* by Thomas Holley Chivers, or to the reminiscences of Thomas

Wentworth Higginson—or, for that matter, to the minor writings of any author.

These titles, and many others of a similar nature, are in the Lamont catalog. They indicate that the scholar's concept of a useful book sometimes has little relation to the needs of students. If it is true that "an undergraduate faces wasteful and discouraging searches unless he can start with a selection of the most useful material on any field of interest to him,"[10] it would seem that many of the books which are in the Lamont Library are not intended to be there. The generally distributed quality of profusion in the collection actually makes the Library better adapted to the needs of graduate students than to those of undergraduates.

There is no denying, however, that the catalog itself is more useful because of this profusion. Its value as a list from which to choose appropriate titles for any library far surpasses that of more selective bibliographies. Some of the questionable items should be deleted from later editions of the catalog, but its succeeding editions will be welcome, whatever revisions are made.

Notes

1. Philip J. McNiff, ed., *The Catalogue of the Lamont Library, Harvard College* (Cambridge: Harvard University Press, 1953).

2. Charles B. Shaw, comp. *A List of Books for College Libraries* (2nd ed., Chicago: American Library Association, 1931); [Supplement] 1931-38 (1940).

3. McNiff, p. vii.

4. Ibid.

5. Edwin E. Williams, "The Selection of Books for Lamont," *Harvard Library Bulletin* 3 (1949): 386.

6. McNiff, p. vii.

7. Gay Wilson Allen, *Walt Whitman Handbook* (Chicago: Packard, 1946), pp. 96-102.

8. Robert E. Spiller *et al.*, eds. *Literary History of the United States* (New York: Macmillan, 1948), 3, 759-768.

9. Williams, p. 388.

10. Ibid., p. 387.

About the Author

Charles A. Carpenter, Jr. was Librarian of the Goldwin Smith Library, Cornell University, when this article was written. He later received his doctorate in English from Cornell and became a member of the faculty of the English Department, State University of New York at Binghamton.

Part III.

Symposia on Library Service to Undergraduate Students 1952 and 1955

Part III: Introduction

In addition to the individual visits by many librarians to Lamont Library at Harvard College, to see for themselves the new and separate approach to library service for undergraduate students developed there, the keen interest of university library administrators is further evidenced by the symposia held in the decade after the opening of Lamont Library.

The first such discussion was held on July 1, 1952, when the University Libraries Section of the Association of College and Research Libraries at its annual program meeting had a symposium entitled "Library Service to Undergraduates." It was chaired by Arthur M. McAnally, then Director of Libraries, University of Oklahoma. He briefly described the background of library service to undergraduate students. Stanley E. Gwynn presented the viewpoint of the University of Chicago which had long experience with an undergraduate library unit in different campus locations. Philip J. McNiff next reviewed the Lamont Library experience. William S. Dix, who was formerly Librarian of the Fondren Library at Rice Institute, discussed undergraduate service in a library which was partially subject-divisional in nature and partially open or interspersed. Finally, Wyman W. Parker gave his views on undergraduate service from the perspective of one who had moved from a small college library with excellent service to a large municipal university.

The second major symposium on service to undergraduate students was held on July 5, 1955. Once again, it was under the auspices of the Association of College and Research Libraries and jointly sponsored by the Junior College, College and University Libraries Sections of the Association at their annual meeting in Philadelphia.

SOURCE: From "Library Service to Undergraduates: A Symposium, University Libraries Section, Association of College and Research Libraries, July 1, 1952 (Introductory Remarks by Arthur M. McAnally; The College Library at the University of Chicago by Stanley E. Gwynn; Lamont Library, Harvard College by Philip J. McNiff; Undergraduate Libraries by William S. Dix; and The Vital Core by Wyman W. Parker)," *College and Research Libraries* 14 (July, 1953), pp. 266-275. Reprinted by permission of the authors.

Edward B. Stanford, University of Minnesota, chaired the program. Frank A. Lundy, Director of Libraries, University of Nebraska, discussed library service to undergraduate students in a divisional plan library. William S. Dix, University Librarian, Princeton University, presented a viewpoint which he entitled "Undergraduates Do Not Necessarily Require A Special Facility." The final speaker was Frederick H. Wagman, Director of Libraries, University of Michigan, Ann Arbor, who gave "The Case for the Separate Undergraduate Library." The working architectural drawings were then being prepared for the Undergraduate Library on the Ann Arbor campus. The first real daughter or son of Lamont was about to be born.

Arthur M. McAnally

Library Service to Undergraduates: A Symposium, July 1, 1952 Introductory Remarks

In order to provide background for the problem of library service to undergraduates, it is necessary to go back in history to the time when most university libraries were small and were either informal or else were organized for service on the alcove principle. Collections were not large, the proportion of graduate students was small and their number negligible by modern standards, and the library served both the graduate and undergraduate more or less equally. The duration of this era varied among institutions.

Beginning in the 1870's, however, when Harvard University introduced the tiered bookstack, the larger university libraries entered upon a long era in which primary emphasis was placed upon the development of great research collections and upon specialized service to the users of these collections. The undergraduate student's library needs tended to be overlooked and his access to the collections gradually reduced, not through deliberate choice but by the trend of events.

By the 1930's, many university librarians began to realize that in the development of their great collections the undergraduate had been neglected, that he was the larger clientele of the two groups of users, and that service to him should be improved. Books were not very accessible to the undergraduate and reserve room service, which was about all most of them got freely, was not very satisfactory educationally. Of course the enterprising undergraduate could surmount the obstacles of huge card catalogs, impersonal circulation desks, etc., but he was discouraged at every hand.

Some university libraries therefore developed browsing rooms, dormitory collections and the like. These were admirable in their way but no real answer to a real problem.

The search for a method of providing satisfactory library service to undergraduates has led many universities to establish libraries specifically for undergraduates. The same objective also has been a factor in the adoption of the subject-divisional plan of organization in medium-sized and small universities. Separate undergraduate libraries have existed for many years, but have been commonly accepted only since 1945. At least four new ones were established during the school year 1951-52.

The statements below discuss this relatively new development from several different approaches: first, from the viewpoint of the University of Chicago, which has had long experience with such a library unit in different locations on the campus; second, from the point of view of a well-planned undergraduate library in a separate building planned for it (The Lamont Library at Harvard); third, as seen by a librarian whose library is partly subject-divisional and partly open or interspersed (The Fondren Library of Rice Institute); and finally, as viewed by a university librarian fresh from a college library which provided excellent teaching service to students but now in the University of Cincinnati which has not provided so well for undergraduate students.

About the Author

Arthur M. McAnally received his doctorate in Library Science from the University of Chicago. From 1945-1949, he was University Librarian, University of New Mexico. In 1949, he accepted the position of Assistant Director for Public Service at the University of Illinois Libraries, Champaign-Urbana. McAnally became Director of Libraries at the University of Oklahoma in 1951. He was an exponent of the Library Faculty and has written and worked extensively in the field.

Stanley E. Gwynn

The College Library at
the University of Chicago

The Assistant Director for Reader Services at the
University of Chicago Library traces the history
of its College Library during an existence from
1931-1949 and then asks a series of questions
(such as "Should we not accept the fact, made
clear by numerous reading studies, that only a
relatively few undergraduates read beyond the
course requirements?") which continue to be valid
today.

The college library at the University of Chicago existed for a period of eighteen
years — from 1931 to 1949. Although it was always a small operation, I believe
that a brief account of its history and of the actual use made of it will throw light
on what I, at least, conceive to be the real problem of the undergraduate library.

The first college library at the University of Chicago was established in 1931, at
the time the Chicago Plan for undergraduate education was introduced. The
library had two main purposes. The first was that of making easily available a
large number of required books, for many of which every student would be held
responsible in the comprehensive examinations. Yet, the college library was not
merely a reserve collection, for its second purpose was the provision of a large,
carefully-selected collection of optional reading, designed to enrich the curriculum by filling gaps in the indispensable readings, or between courses, and by
affording opportunity for the individualization of a highly-prescribed course of
study through independent reading.

The collection numbered about 12,000 volumes initially, but grew to about
20,000 volumes in the course of a few years. Extensive duplication was necessary, and the original 12,000 volumes included only 2000 different titles. Of these
titles, only one in ten was indispensable or required reading, and this ratio
between the required and the recommended readings persisted throughout the
first phase of the college library.

Actual use by the college students averaged 70 to 80 volumes per student per
year. This was a relatively high rate, but not much beyond the upper range of
student withdrawals in other colleges as reported by Branscomb in *Teaching
With Books*. More important is the kind of materials withdrawn by the students.

81

A special study, made in 1937-38, indicated that, although the 1239 students in one Humanities general course and in two Social Sciences general courses withdrew 29,000 books in one quarter, only 635 of these titles were in the carefully-selected and highly-recommended optional reading category. This is a rate of about one and one-half volumes of non-required reading per year per student. Since we know that typically a few students read a relatively large number of titles, we also know that many of these Chicago students read no optional materials at all. In general, therefore, the students under the Chicago Plan, like college students everywhere, borrowed from their library only the books they were required to read.

In 1942, the college library as described above was abolished, partly because of war-induced pressure for space, but more importantly, because a shift in the college program and teaching methods had greatly diminished demands upon the library.

However, in September, 1943, a new college library, which was also intended to be a source of free reading for the entire university, was created. The core of this library consisted of the 2000 titles of recommended readings in the current college syllabi. To these were added another 2000 titles of material of general current interest, including standard and good recent fiction. The assumption was that a collection of this kind could satisfactorily serve both the college students and the other members of the university. Although the capable librarian worked closely with the college faculty and students, a reading study made throughout the first year showed that college students accounted for only 36% of the use of this library and, moreover, that 71% of the students in the college borrowed not even one book. The carefully-selected recommended readings circulated hardly at all.

As a consequence of her observations over a period of more than a year, the librarian concluded that neither the college faculty nor the library staff really knew what kind of library was needed for the college, and what any college library should properly do in the educational program beyond the provisions of required readings. She suggested that a capable research man with faculty rank be appointed full time to study the problem. This was not done, but for the next few years it was arranged that the college librarian should also be a teaching member of the college faculty and should devote the major portion of his time to thinking through the problem of what kind of library our kind of college should have. Two men held this post in succession. I was the second, serving in the year 1946-47. Both of us failed to accomplish our assignment, largely because each of us served only a year, and because too much of our time was taken up by teaching or by other university library problems. College use of the library continued at an even lower level, and in 1949, when space problems again arose, the dean of the college consented to the disestablishment of the college library, stating that while desirable, it was not necessary to the work of the college at Chicago.

Although I failed to produce an answer to the problem assigned me, I did come to several conclusions regarding the problem of the undergraduate library in general.

It seems to me that the problem of the undergraduate library is *not* the simple problem of physical arrangement with which we have been occupying ourselves lately. It is quite possibly desirable, in a large university at least, to provide a separate, selected, easily-accessible collection of books that will appeal to the undergraduate and to the general reader in the university regardless of his status. Whether this is a browsing room or a divisional reading room or a Lamont Library is not really important, just so those who really want to read can find good and interesting books when they want them.

Nor is the problem that of conjuring up devices (some of them misguided) designed to lure undergraduates into the library.

The problem is that academic librarians generally have not defined and faced the real problem. They have adopted the goal of *more books and more readers* without ever questioning the applicability of this goal to the undergraduate library. In doing so, I am sure that they have puzzled a good many faculty members, who in general display a far more rational view of the library's function than do librarians.

I think there *is* a problem of the undergraduate library, and I hope that the committee of this section appointed to study that problem will isolate it and will outline steps toward its solution. If they do this, they will probably find themselves considering matters of the following kind:

1.   Should we not accept the fact, made clear by numerous reading studies, that only a relatively few undergraduates read beyond the course requirements?

2.   Should we not consider that perhaps these are the only students who should do such reading?

3.   Should we not acknowledge a fact we already know but refuse to accept, that in adult life only a relatively few people read and utilize the knowledge gained from reading, and that these people are the intellectual leaders of our society, wielding an influence greatly disproportionate to their numbers? Should we not ask whether *reading or not reading* is associated with the basic temperament and personality and mental equipment of the person and is therefore a characteristic incapable of alteration by librarians or anyone else?

4.   Finally, should we not put these ideas together and assume — tentatively, until the matter is demonstrated or disproved — that, once good books have been made available, the limited staff and the limited budget of the undergraduate library should be used for one primary purpose: To make certain that we and the faculty together find all the true readers or potential readers in the undergraduate population, and that we see that they get the books they want and whatever special treatment may be desirable — the opportunity to discuss these books, and broaden their reading, and grow intellectually to the limit of their natural endowment?

If this is the thing to do and we do it, we will be doing what the college faculty and the college curriculum already do: provide the same basic intellectual menu for everyone, but make available for those who want them and are capable of utilizing them, those special nutrients above and beyond the standard diet that develop the exceptional student and the exceptional man.

If it turns out that this is what we should do, we will not do it merely by providing a separate undergraduate library, useful though that may be. The questions of what we should do in the areas outlined above, and how we can translate into action what we learn, are difficult ones. Their isolation, their investigation, and their solution, constitute the immediate problem of the undergraduate library.

About the Author

Stanley E. Gwynn received his AB degree in English Literature from Northwestern University. In 1936, he was Assistant Reference Librarian of the National Safety Council, Chicago. From 1937-1943, he was Reference Librarian at the Newberry Library. From 1943-1945, he served as Test Operator and Process Engineer, Buick Motors Division, General Motors, Chicago. He became associated with the University of Chicago Libraries when he was College Librarian and Instructor in the Humanities in 1946-1947. Mr. Gwynn was Chief of Readers Services, 1947-1949 and Assistant Director for Readers Services from 1949 until his recent retirement.

Philip J. McNiff

Lamont Library, Harvard College

The Librarian of the Lamont Library, with over a three-year perspective since its opening, describes the building and services, states the library's objectives, and concludes that "staff experience and student response seem to indicate that Lamont fulfills these objectives."

There is no one solution to the problem of undergraduate library service in a university. Institutions differ in their organization, finances, building facilities and curricula. With these, among other factors influencing the type of library service which can be given, each university has to determine its own method of library service to undergraduates. Harvard decided to build a separate library for its undergraduates.

The idea of such a library was not new. The college records of 1765 contain the first reference to the need of separate library facilities for the undergraduates. In the *Harvard Library Bulletin* a series of articles on the history and development of library services in Harvard College, traces the growth of the collections, the lengthening of hours of service, the extension of borrowing privileges, and the rise of reserved book, classroom and laboratory collections.

With the dedication of the Widener Library in 1915, it was hoped that the library problem at Harvard had been solved for a great many years to come, but this proved not to be the case. The report of the director for 1927-1928 cited the need for more space. The new building had many drawbacks to undergraduate library service. It was too large and impersonal; the college students had direct access only to reserved reading books and a small browsing collection. The large reading room on the second floor proved to be unsatisfactory as a reserved book center and collections serving the survey courses were established in two other buildings. The increased demands of faculty members, graduate students and visiting scholars pushed the undergraduates further and further into the background. The result was that Harvard students were not receiving the quality of library service enjoyed by students in the better four year liberal arts colleges.

By 1937 the space problem was acute and Mr. Metcalf after a careful survey recommended a four point program:

1. The New England Deposit Library for the storage of little used material
2. The Houghton Library for rare books and manuscripts
3. Undergraduate Library
4. Underground stacks in the college yard for the expansion of the Widener collection

The idea of an undergraduate library was approved in 1940 by the Library Council and the Administrative Board of the College. The planning of the library was accelerated with the announcement of Mr. Lamont's gift in 1945. Faculty and student committees were formed to consult with the library staff committee on matters of lighting, smoking and furniture.

So much for the background. The building itself has eight levels. The two lowest levels are underground stacks. One level is connected by tunnel to Widener and the other to Houghton. This supplies the expansion noted on point four above. The undergraduate library occupies three main floors and two mezzanines. The remaining level is a roof house which contains six classrooms and a fan room for some of the air conditioning equipment. Stacks are placed in the center area of the building on five levels; on the north side of the building on the main levels are located special rooms and on the south side are the three large reading areas. There are three wide aisles on each main floor leading through the book stack areas to the reading areas. This means that students must pass through the book stack areas to the reading areas. The stack areas on the main levels are divided into 12 alcoves; on the mezzanines there is a regular stack arrangement. Each of the three large reading areas has a row of stalls around the outside walls and a variety of tables and easy chairs. Smoking is allowed in the special rooms on the north side and in the rooms at the west end of the building. Each of the mezzanine smoking rooms has five typing cubicles with sound proofing on the walls and ceiling.

The motivating ideas behind the planning of the library were well expressed by Henry R. Shepley, the architect, when he wrote, "The philosophy on which the functioning of the library was based required first, that it be conveniently located and inviting of access. It should be one of the main undergraduate traffic routes and there should be no flights of steps to climb to the entrance or monumental vestibules or foyers to traverse before coming to the books. Second, once within the library, the student should find the entire book collection as accessible as possible."

Let us see how well the library fulfills this philosophy. The building is situated in the south-east corner of the Harvard Yard and is directly across the street from the Union, the dining hall for freshmen. This means that all the resident freshmen who live in the yard dormitories must pass the front entrance of the library on their way to and from meals. Many of the more heavily used classrooms are located in the vicinity of the library, thus insuring use of the building between classes. There is but one step outside the library, and a ramp is available for students in wheel chairs. Standing outside the glass doors of the main entrance the student sees a functional lobby, reserve desk and book stacks. All books, with the exception of those on a closed reserve section are readily available on open shelves, and may be taken to any area in the building.

The theme of this ALA conference is "Books are Basic." Harvard, believing in this slogan, tries to eliminate all barriers between the student and the book. The establishment of reading habits which will follow the students into their post college years is one of the most important functions of an undergraduate library. Required reading, motivated by tests and reports, presents the library with the problem of adequate supply and efficient distribution. The professional staff concentrates its efforts on the encouragement of general and recreational reading. The accessibility of a carefully selected collection of books is the first requisite. Add to this an efficient ventilating system, good lighting, a building made quiet by the use of sound absorbing ceilings and floors and inviting color treatment of walls and stacks, a variety of reading accommodations and the stage is set for the alchemical reactions described in Lawrence Powell's talk on "The Alchemy of Books."

Extra-curricular interests in books and reading are encouraged further by such features as book displays, exhibitions arranged by student groups, the record playing facilities of the Poetry Room, the home atmosphere of the Farnsworth Room — a browsing collection, and the Printing Room. In three and one-half years of operation, 25,000 students (exclusive of class groups) have made use of the Poetry Room listening facilities. Surely they have achieved a deeper appreciation of poetry and it may even be hoped that the library has contributed some small part to the development of poets of the future. The small group of undergraduates interested in printing as an avocation are instructed by the Library's Department of Printing and Graphic Arts. The Forum Room, which seats up to 175 people, is available to undergraduate organizations. This room is equipped with a dual turntable and loudspeaker, screen and projection booth and an FM radio has just been installed in order to make available to students some of the programs offered by Boston's new educational FM station. The broadcast of the Boston Symphony Orchestra's Friday afternoon concerts will replace the weekly music record hour offered by the library.

The Lamont Library uses simplified cataloging and a numerical classification scheme which has not more than one decimal place. This scheme is not a classification of knowledge but a means of making it easier for students to find the books for which they are looking. Copies of the scheme with its alphabetical index — a subject guide to the collection — are scattered throughout the building for students to use at the shelves.

The objectives of the library are: (1) to concentrate as far as practicable all undergraduate activities in one place; (2) to make books readily available to students; and (3) to encourage general and recreational reading as well as to supply required reading books. Staff experience and student response seem to indicate that Lamont fulfills these objectives.

About the Author

Philip J. McNiff, after serving in several library positions at Harvard, was Librarian of the Lamont Library from 1948-1956. He also held the position of Assistant Librarian at Harvard College from 1949 until 1956 when he was promoted to Associate Librarian. In 1965, he was appointed Director and Librarian of the Boston Public Library.

William S. Dix

Undergraduate Libraries

Dix proposes that an "old fashioned" method of
service for undergraduates, under certain conditions and at smaller institutions, may be more
effective than the divisional or segregated
arrangements. He describes the Fondren Library
at Rice and its service to undergraduates, graduate students, and faculty via the L.C. classification
with open stacks.

At the risk of seeming conservative and even obstructionist, I should like to propose that under certain conditions a quite old-fashioned method of handling the
undergraduate library in the university might be more effective than some of the
newer divisional arrangements and segregated collections. Now I am quite
aware that the arrangement which I propose would not work in a library system
the size of that of Harvard, but after all I regret to say that there is only one
Widener Library. In the smaller libraries in the smaller universities I wonder
whether any very special treatment of the undergraduate library is really
necessary.

This is, I take it, largely an experience meeting. People get tired of hearing
"This is the way we do it," but a brief description of the Rice Institute Library
will illustrate my point. May I say again that I am sure that our system would
not work everywhere else. Rice, like most other universities, is a special place.
We have a student body of about 1500; including some 200 graduate students,
pursuing a rather limited curriculum with professional schools only in engineering and architecture. The Ph.D. is offered in mathematics, physics, chemistry,
biology, English, and history, and there is somewhat more faculty and graduate
research than one would expect in so small an institution. Our library of some
225,000 volumes is housed in a new, postwar building.

My point here is that in a library of this size I see no reason for making any
special provision for the undergraduate. The total collection is housed in one
building, with completely open stacks. It is my feeling that with a little care and
planning there is no reason for the undergraduate to become lost in working
with a unified collection numbering not more than, say, a half million volumes.

In principle we feel that the undergraduate should be constantly confronted by
books a little beyond his grasp, that we are not concerned primarily with his
finding specific books but with instructing him to learn to think, to use the
library, and to grow intellectually. Thus when he goes to the shelves for a particular elementary book he finds there also the major standard works on the same

subject. What if any of these are written in a language which he does not read or are accounts of original research which he cannot understand? He at least becomes aware of their existence and if he is of the material from which scholars are made, there is just a chance that he might be led gradually into deeper waters. Such an effect cannot be reproduced if the undergraduate works entirely with a few basic books which have been placed on reserve and in which chapters have been assigned by his instructors, or if he works entirely with a small collection supposedly within his grasp. If the library is thought of as an enlarged textbook only, I do not see how it can be expected to produce a student who has anything but a textbook-memorizing kind of mind. Therefore in the Fondren Library at Rice we deliberately left out any provision for a reserve reading room. Our list of books on reserve at no time reaches more than two or three hundred.

Of course, this concept of the use of the total library as a unit demands that the books on the shelves be arranged in such a fashion that the student may use them easily. To effect this end we have again used an old-fashioned device. The entire collection is arranged strictly according to the Library of Congress classification scheme, with the single major exception of basic reference tools. Now no classification scheme is of course perfect; the important thing in such an arrangement is to follow carefully whatever system is in use. In the Fondren Library all books on physics, for example, including all journals, are shelved in the same area. The student who wants material on nuclear physics finds both the books and the special journals together. Current issues of physics journals are also shelved nearby. We have no periodical room as much. Major reference tools are given prominence by separate shelving, still in the same area. In other words we do have something like a divisional plan, but the divisional library includes not a selection of books and journals, but *all* materials on the subject and it is arranged so that it falls into its proper place between mathematics and chemistry in the LC system.

Such a system presupposes a building which lends itself to the arrangement: open stacks, adequate reading and study space in each area, some provision for the shelving of current periodicals in such areas throughout the building. On the other hand, it saves a substantial amount of effort in locating books. There is no cumbersome system of location symbols; one does not have to check the card catalog to find the location of a book, if he knows the general area where it is supposed to be. There is one place and one place only on the campus for a particular volume, and that is where the LC system puts it.

Aside from this overall simplification, this arrangement provides several intangible benefits, as I have indicated. It is not only stimulating for an alert student to find books slightly beyond his grasp, but it is also perhaps good for him to see graduate students and faculty members working at the same table and in the same part of the building on problems like his except more advanced. With such an arrangement it is almost impossible for a student majoring in any field to graduate from college without becoming at least familiar with the backs of the major research tools in the field.

Of course this system does presuppose faculty approval and interest. If the classroom instructor merely wishes his student to absorb a specified number of pre-digested pellets placed on reserve, he will resent the fact that his students have to handle ten books to get the one they want. If the instructor wants his students to see only the best book on a subject, he will not understand the librarian who thinks that students should also see some other books not quite so good and thus learn for himself that the printed word is not always infallible. But if the instructor is interested in teaching the student to think rather than memorize or to study the sources and arrive at his own conclusions rather than accept blindly the opinions of the one "official" text, he will work enthusiastically with the librarian who administers such an arrangement.

I insist again that the provision for the undergraduate library in the university which I am describing is not applicable to every university and is not something new. It seems to me merely a return to some of the principles of those who first developed systems of library classification, an attempt to reduce all learning to some kind of order. I see no reason why we should abandon this simple orderly arrangement so long as it works. It does seem to be working with us. In the space of two years after we set up this system and abandoned a series of departmental libraries scattered over the campus, our circulation more than doubled, although the size of the student body remained the same and the new building provided vastly improved facilities for using books without charging them. For Harvard, the Lamont Library, or something like it, was a necessity. For the library of less than a half million volumes in the smaller institutions to adopt any system which permits students to use anything less than total collection seems just a bit foolish. The function of the university library is education, not facilitating access to the one "best" book on a subject.

About the Author

William S. Dix earned his Ph.D. in English from the University of Chicago. He was Associate Professor and Librarian, Rice Institute from 1946 to 1953. From 1953 until his recent retirement, he was University Librarian, Princeton University.

Wyman W. Parker

The Vital Core

The author contrasts a "small liberal arts college having a strong library program [Kenyon College] with a large municipal university having no special undergraduate library policy [University of Cincinnati]."

My assignment is to comment on the difference between college and university libraries, specifically contrasting a small liberal arts college having a strong library program with a large municipal university having no special undergraduate library policy. In relation to our topic, that of considering a library from the undergraduate's viewpoint, this tends to become an investigation on ways to humanize and make attractive our noble Gargantua, the university library.

College and university libraries do in fact have similar aims. Both are concerned with undergraduate study where the library reduced to its most basic and unromantic terms is a laboratory for discovering facts or a depository of what has been said and thought throughout the ages. However there is always implied the idea that the library is available for the leisurely investigation by the individual of ideas and subjects that are especially intriguing. In other words the library should be a source of inspiration and enjoyment over and above the exact word as promulgated in the class room. Sir Antonio Panizzi in giving evidence before a Select Committee of the House of Commons in 1836 had this ideal well in mind as a function of the British Museum when he said, "I want a poor student to have the same means of indulging his learned curiosity, of following his rational pursuits, of consulting the same authorities, of fathoming the most intricate enquiry, as the richest man in the kingdom so far as books go. . . ."[1] In the United States this is carried even further and, although awarding no door prizes as do our movie theaters and gas stations, libraries do try to intrigue the student with exhibits, satisfy him with modern reproductions, and entertain him with music and possibly movies. Most libraries encourage the individual to come and just plain sit in the hope that some of the ideas in nearby books may penetrate by a kind of osmosis. Of course we hope that the sitter will pick up a book, trusting the while that this library novice will not become too interested in it so that he walks out with it illegally. So few of the students ever do take a book out of the library that in moments of despair I sometimes wonder if the $37.00 average per student operating expenditure for university libraries would not be more immediately appreciated if it were spent yearly in books to be given to each student.

The university library in addition must provide for graduate research. This means more comprehensive and extended coverage on diverse levels. The earlier conception of the university library as a self sufficient entity completely covering all fields of knowledge has gone, hastened on its way by such wise cooperative ventures as the Farmington Plan and the MILC.

There is however a real difference in the actual sizes of college and university libraries. This results primarily in a university library with a large, and to the undergraduate bewildering, collection of books. Even more pertinent to this discussion is the complexity of the university library card catalog with its millions of entries subdivided in ways best known to catalogers. In fact the catalog of even a small college collection tends to be unintelligible to the average undergraduate. Perhaps we might take a hint from the public library catalog where simplicity is paramount. Another significant difference is the fact that a large collection is usually protected in closed stacks although encouraging signs of a happier trend are seen in the open stack collections at Princeton and Iowa City. Closed stacks make for less spontaneous browsing although the rewards may be greater in the larger collections once the barrier is passed. At Kenyon College we felt happy to have portfolios of the Catlin Indian scenes and Catherwood's . . . *Ancient Monuments* . . . on the open shelves. Unsuperivsed rarities are not usually found on the shelves of a university collection although one of our departmental libraries at Cincinnati does have early 16th century Aldines and the Pickering Diamond Classics in its open shelf collection. Such items are usually consigned to the Rare Book Room where the university student can consult even more costly treasures like the Kingsborough *Antiquities of Mexico* or, in a few fortunate libraries, the Audubon elephant folio.

These complexities of library detail result in the conclusion that it is a privilege for the undergraduate to work in a selected library. This was readily apparent before the turn of the century to Daniel Coit Gilman, once librarian of Yale. In his address at the opening of Cornell University Library in 1891, Gilman, then president of Johns Hopkins, said, "What then can keep the shelves from encumbrance? Only constant elimination, convenient storage, frequent rearrangement. The books less wanted must be stacked away . . . and the books most valued must be brought forward. Constant readjustments are essential to the healthy vitality of a library."[2] Certainly this is even more logical these days when our every waking moment entails selection. Why should we not enlist the aid of our professors and our librarians in choosing a collection which will represent our basic knowledge which is our heritage? Henry Stevens of Vermont, representing American culture in London as a prominent nineteenth century bookseller, put this very nicely in his usual fresh way, "A nation's books are her vouchers. Her libraries are her muniments. Her wealth of gold and silver, whether invested in commerce, or bonds, or banks, is always working for her; but her stores of golden thoughts, inventions, discoveries, and intellectual treasures, invested mainly in print and manuscript, are too often stores somewhere in limbo, . . . where, though sleek and well preserved, they rather slumber than fructify."[3]

Certainly our undergraduates should be privileged to see together those books which people of culture consider part of our common knowledge. They should be chosen in generous numbers by each institution's own faculty. The "Great Books" chosen by the Chicago group will be here too but let us not tend toward regimentation especially in the liberal arts. Let us have lots of books and particularly let us not rely on the horrible idea that anything not analyzed to the 102 ideas in the *Syntopicon* need not be considered. Our collection will not be rigid but will change as do our professors and our trends in literature. For example, we have seen in recent decades the revival of interest in Melville and James and an increasing pre-occupation with the metaphysical poets. Our reaction from the sentimentality of the nineteenth century is certainly most apparent in the recent interest in the feverish, feckless, Fitzgerald era and in the currently popular unselective realism of our war novels such as *The Naked and the Dead* and *From Here to Eternity*. There is need and room for varieties of expression in our representative collection.

There are various ways to attack this problem. The happiest solution seems to be the separate building housing the undergraduate library of which Lamont with its collection of about 80,000 volumes is the prototype. An earlier solution is the separate library within the main university building such as that so successfully used at Columbia, known as the Columbia College Library, with its collection of about 35,000 volumes. Most recent of all is what might be termed a department-of-all-knowledge area known at Iowa as the Heritage Collection which will have a varying number of books, probably around 20,000 volumes. A comparable scheme which we hope to put into effect at Cincinnati is to set up a separate collection of about 10,000 volumes physically tied in with our special collections. We plan to house this collection in rooms flanked by a popular browsing room and the rare book room, the whole complex of rooms to be open to undergraduates for study and lounging.

Any undergraduate library, no matter where it is housed, would be expected to have its books shelved as an entity. In this fashion the undergraduate has the opportunity to see together those books that form our intellectual heritage. Thus the undergraduate has a touchstone, an ideal collection roughly comparable to the library of a truly cultivated man. Of course this representative library would have its own simplified catalog, its own librarian, and its own reading area.

A municipal university presents a special problem for the call of home is strong and students and faculty have a tendency to evaporate rapidly as the day progresses. Therefore it is apparently necessary to trap the undergraduate between classes or before the comforts of home become too appealing. Thus it is desirable to introduce a more intimate atmosphere than has hitherto been customary so that when the rest room stop has been accomplished the student may be led into other rooms of less necessity and more culture. Once the individual enters the library portals it is possible to intrigue the inquiring mind by means of exhibits which in large cities can be tied up with civic projects and by calling upon both museums and business firms for illustrative and eye-catching material. A browsing room may be utilized as a come-on. Every store has its system of loss-leaders. Why cannot the library buy books of less than permanent nature to attract its students? I think of such items as the books of cartoons, the lavish picture and photograph books, and those all too few books of humorous essays.

Most important in any library is the atmosphere of hospitality where there may be a cordial exchange of ideas and suggestions. There is a special difficulty of communication in a university where so much is occurring in myriad directions. A library wants the special knowledge and support of the faculty and the administration in its programs. In a college the word gets about very quickly as to new attitudes and approaches within the library. It is truly a wonderful feeling to be the focal point of an institution which was briefly the case at Kenyon when we hung an Alexander Calder mobile in the library with an accompanying book display. According to all the books of theory the library is the center of the campus but we all know this as being unapproachably utopian. We occasionally received intimations of such an ideal courtesy of a provocative exhibit which would be discussed in sundry classes. I remember a particularly successful one on the "Horrors of Book-Making" which could have been equally well entitled "Excesses of Taste." Any fresh presentation that stimulates the student to think in new paths is a forward step.

In preparing areas for undergraduates there are fortunately numerous truisms which we find effective in this mid-century period. For example, in physical details such things as alcoves rather than large reading rooms are almost universally preferred by today's students. Modern library design has accepted the fact that movable bookcases make attractive and utilitarian partitions to form alcoves within large areas. Of course, books are our best and richest decorations. (Parenthetically I might add that books are likewise the most satisfactory decorations of the mind.) Soft chairs, footstools, and adequate indirect lighting are all eminently acceptable to the student generation of these days. Individual desks and carrels are very popular with the serious student with special work to get done. Seminar rooms containing a permanent collection in a special area, such as the Elliston Poetry Room at the University of Cincinnati or the Woodberry Poetry Room in the Lamont Library have been found to provoke healthy and profitable discussion. If a faculty member is in the habit of dropping by to chat with the students that makes for even a better brew. Smoking appears to be the most essential requirement of the undergraduate in this type of area. Rooms for the projection of films, such as those interesting ones released by the Museum of Modern Art, and others for playing recordings are additional attractions for the undergraduate. At the University of Cincinnati we are even now refitting the Stephen Foster Exhibition Room so that students in a comfortable and attractive atmosphere can hear recordings of poets reading their own works. Incidentally I believe that few people can be completely equipped to comprehend the twentieth century unless they have heard T. S. Eliot's majestic rendition of *The Wasteland* as recorded in the Bollingen series of the Library of Congress.

It is the privilege of our newest librarians to carry the word to the undergraduates of a library where books are most easily available and librarians more cordial with an interest in the undergraduate and his problems. Making important and interesting books easily available to students is half our battle. The rest is done at the appropriate time by the skillful suggestion of librarian and professor.

People are naturally curious about books, a fortunate inheritance from the Renaissance when only the privileged could read. Fortunately for librarians, students are interested in books in spite of everything that has been done in the past to discourage them. I do not agree with the late Hon. James Walker who is reputed to have said that he never heard of a girl being seduced by a book. People can be seduced by books although I prefer to say they are stimulated by books. That is why a library should contain all viewpoints and why our Intellectual Freedom Committee is presently so active. I believe in the innate goodness of the human mind and that our students when given the facts will make the right and proper choices and thus continue to build toward a healthy national future.

Notes

1.   Gt. Brit. Parliament. *Sessional Papers. House of Commons.* 1836, v. 10, p. 399.

2.   Gilman, Daniel Coit, *University Problems in the United States* (New York, 1898), 249-50.

3.   Stevens, Henry, *Photo-Bibliography* (London, 1878), p. 12.

About the Author

Wyman W. Parker was Librarian of Middlebury College from 1938 to 1941; Kenyon College, 1946-1951; University of Cincinnati, 1951-1956; and Wesleyan University, Middletown, Connecticut, 1956-1976.

Frank A. Lundy

Library Service to Undergraduate College Students: A Symposium, July 5, 1955 The Divisional Plan Library

After citing five fallacious assumptions that influence contemporary academic librarianship, Lundy gives a "Constructive Philosophy" in the context of the subject division organized library, such as those at the Universities of Colorado and Nebraska.

Introduction

I shall discuss with you the idea of the divisional library. These remarks might be entitled: "Do undergraduates deserve an education?"

In approaching the problem of providing good undergraduate library service, let us first examine several fallacious assumptions which influence contemporary college and university librarianship.

Five Fallacious Assumptions

1. *Undergraduates don't count.* First among these is the common notion that undergraduate students don't count. We are interested only in our graduate students and in the research carried on by the faculty. How often one hears remarks like these on the university campus. Here, for example, is a great state university in the Middle West with nearly 20,000 students on its campus, almost 15,000 of

SOURCE: From "Library Service to Undergraduate College Students: A Symposium," Association of College and Research Libraries, 1955 ("The Divisional Plan Library" by Frank A. Lundy; "Undergraduates Do Not Necessarily Require A Special Facility" by William S. Dix; and "The Case for the Separate Undergraduate Library" by Frederick H. Wagman) *College and Research Libraries* 17 (March, 1956), pp. 143-155. Reprinted by permission of the authors.

them undergraduates. It boasts a new multi-million-dollar library building designed, it is said, to serve research carried on by graduate students and the faculty. Undergraduates don't count. In practical effect it would be better if they weren't there. I have heard remarks like these many times on the campus of the great state university on the West Coast where I labored early in my career. And I have heard them repeated and amplified on many other campuses.

2. *A college education is completed in four years.* Second, an education is completed in four years of college. A college education consists of courses of study which can conveniently be measured in units and graded numerically for quality. In general these courses are related to each other and grouped together in terms of prerequisites and majors. Outside the major field of study, the history of our culture and the broad view of our contemporary society are served by a few more or less unrelated units of "this, that, and something else," selected in amounts appropriate in size to fill the package. The completion of a major entitles the student to enroll for graduate or professional training in the same specialty. If he does not choose to do so, and the majority do not, he can put his education on the shelf and forget about it. His education was completed in four years. He is an educated man.

3. *The library is a warehouse of books organized for the convenience of the library staff.* Third among our fallacious assumptions, the university library, speaking collectively for the library complex, is the warehouse for books and periodicals. It must be organized to suit the convenience of the librarians who work there. The convenience of the students and faculty is secondary. The convenience of undergraduate students in particular is hardly worth considering. And so it follows that reference books, which are for the most part encyclopedias and other compendia, fill the reference room, as it is so called. Unbound periodicals come in quantity and pose a special problem in record keeping and are therefore routed to a periodical room. Assigned readings are segregated from all other books and fill a reserve book room. Documents, which in the library world mean simply any printed item with a government imprint, enjoy a special distinction in housing and service in this strange caste system. The student in search of an idea is given quite a run-around. Only in the central book stack are books arranged in accordance with the ideas which they contain. Nearly all of the stock of readable books is in the book stack. And, of course, on most campuses undergraduate students are not given free access to the book stack.

4. *Librarians are custodians, not educators.* Fourth, librarians are not educators. They are custodians. Their work is clerical. They function in an environment full of negative rules framed to protect the book from student and faculty alike. Books are acquired by the library in order that they may be preserved. Their preservation requires a complicated set of descriptive records, duplicated and re-arranged, entirely or in part, many times over. Rule keeping and record making are so absorbing of time and energy that none is left for taking part in the educational process involving faculty and students. Nor are librarians capable of such participation. Their professional education has not prepared them to assume a position of such responsibility in the academic community. The

thought that they should be given academic status with appropriate ranks is shocking and abhorrent.

5.   *Cataloging and reference work are in no way related.* Fifth and last among primary fallacious assumptions that are presently influential in our university libraries is the notion that the technical services and the public services must exist in separate sovereignties with a minimum of communication between them. Cataloging is an esoteric art. Only a true initiate can understand the cataloging process, or for that matter the end product, the catalog card. Perhaps it isn't necessary to be peculiar in order to be a cataloger, but it helps. Reference work, on the other hand, enjoys a special prestige. Perhaps reference librarians are born. Certainly they do not need to labor in the bibliographical process in order to acquire competence in the interpretation of the library's collections. A reference librarian would rather be dead than be seen cataloging a book.

A Constructive Philosophy of Librarianship

Stated in this manner, these five assumptions or principles appear to be somewhat ridiculous. And yet, in their general application to our universities, and to their libraries, these assumptions are true to a surprising degree. Among universities with more than 5,000 students the exceptions to these generalities are still so few in number that they are conspicuous. With library service to the undergraduate student uppermost in mind let us examine these five assumptions. Let us restate them in support of a more positive view of general education and a more constructive philosophy of librarianship.

Universities and their libraries must serve students at all levels and must support both teaching and research. The divisional plan library provides effective library service.

First and foremost, if we may speak for a moment of tax-supported institutions, a state university has three major obligations. It must provide a good general education for the young men and women who are residents of the state. This implies good teaching, with libraries organized to lend effective support to the education of these students. The university must also train professional students and graduate students in the methods of research and must support faculty research in the interest of local and national welfare. A university is *per se* a community of enquiring minds. No field of knowledge is closed to its enquiries. Finally, in addition to teaching and research, a state university renders a wide variety of services to the citizens of the state.

Clearly, the university has an obligation to offer its undergraduate students the opportunity of acquiring an education. We must hear no more talk to the effect that undergraduates don't count. These students are the future citizens and from their ranks come our leaders, not to mention our professional students and even our graduate students. A university which recognizes no obligation to these students is dishonest in accepting their money and their time. Such loose talk about their insignificance in the academic community could bring swift retribution from the taxpayers.

The university library can and must serve the university program — that is, teaching and research — both on and off the campus. Honest analysis indicates clearly that emphasis has thus far been placed upon service to graduate students and faculty members through such devices as closed stacks, carrells, seminars, faculty studies, the reference collection, extended borrowing privileges, and an elaborate system of small, specialized, and restricted branch libraries. A few concessions have been made to the undergraduate student in the form of the undergraduate reading room with a small collection of materials, a few thousand reserve books on open shelves, and here and there a browsing room of general nature. No one could possibly say that these devices represent an honest effort to provide good over-all library service to the undergraduate student body.

The University of Colorado experimented with a pilot plant to house an adequate undergraduate library. Barriers between books and students were removed by placing the books on open shelves in large enough quantity to reflect the entire undergraduate curriculum, including books of general interest as well. And the word "books" was reinterpreted to include all forms of print immediately pertinent to the program; that is, books, periodicals, pamphlets, reference sets, and so on. These were brought together not by format and process, but by content and idea. Large workable collections were brought together by subject matter to serve groups of related departments of instruction — hence the phrase divisional plan. Harvard University has carried the idea forward with a model undergraduate library of 100,000 volumes in a separate building, an ideal arrangement but for most of us an expensive one.

The University of Nebraska has adopted and developed the Colorado plan with a divisional library serving the humanities, the social studies, and science. At Nebraska practically all of the vestigial organs of the traditional library have been eliminated. At the same time Nebraska has steadily improved all of its library services in support of graduate study and research. It is of interest here to note that an expanded divisional plan will be housed in the new building at Michigan State College.

Education is a lifelong process. The divisional library encourages and develops the reading habit.

Brief attention can be given here to the fallacious proposition that an education consists of prescribed courses which can be completed in four years of time serving. A college education should awaken a student's curiosity and train his mind to enable him to continue educating himself throughout his lifetime. If the habit of reading is to be acquired in college then every opportunity in that direction must be made attractive. In this the library can exert leadership.

A professor said to me, not long ago: "The only books that are of any importance to my students are the ones I assign to them to read." If this were true, a few books on reserve would serve all undergraduate needs. We should recognize, however, that there are few college courses in applied science or social science that are not quickly out of date.

In the past, perhaps unintentionally, insurmountable barriers were placed between the student and his books. Closed stacks and a complex organization of service by form and process such as reference, periodicals, documents, and reserves were among these barriers. At Nebraska these barriers have been removed. One hundred thousand books and other materials, carefully selected for the purpose from the million or more in the stacks, are arranged by content in a series of large reading rooms. Comments from many students and faculty members lead us to believe that in this study environment students are reading more books and books of wider variety than heretofore.

Be it noted here that these materials have been carefully selected for what we call the college library. Other approaches to this problem are being tried elsewhere. At Princeton and Northwestern, for example, there are no divisional reading rooms, but the book stacks are open to all students. We believe that it is no service to the undergraduate student with a problem to solve or a paper to write — particularly to the lower division student — to turn him loose among a million books consisting mostly of research materials. In Nebraska, where many of our students come from Clay Center and Beaver Crossing, from Ogallala and Wahoo, we are certain that this is true. We carefully guide these students into the university curriculum and we must also guide them into the world of print. We regard the completely open book stack in the large university as a lazy man's way of solving the problem of undergraduate library service, or as an admission that there are simply not enough funds to tackle the job. Let me add, however, that no student at Nebraska is ever denied his right to browse among the stack collections if he wants to do so.

The library is the students' laboratory.

In contrast to the attitude that the library is a warehouse for books and that its contents must be arranged for the convenience of the staff who manage it, let me suggest a businessman's approach. Books are the basic tangible commodity on the campus. The library is a merchandising center. Books should be well displayed to attract the customer. By this we do not mean *a few books,* or a shelf of *new books,* but *all the books* in the college library. Librarians are the sales force. Their function is to bring books and readers together. Librarians should, therefore, be trained to defer to the personal needs and tastes of the student and to apply their expert knowledge in his interest, with tact and discrimination.

In the social science reading room, for example, we are presenting the undergraduate student with a workshop of printed materials in this broad field. This is his laboratory. Here he will accomplish most of his reading in the social sciences and here he will write his term papers. Here in convenient arrangement are books, periodicals, and newspapers; pamphlets and other vertical file materials; encyclopedias and indexes. When we talk about a convenient arrangement of materials we are thinking primarily of the student's convenience. His assigned readings are on open shelves in call number sequence with the rest of the collection. Only a few titles are segregated behind a desk on two-hour reserve. These few are the books in very heavy demand. All overnight, three-day, seven-day, and two-week books are in the open shelf collection. Librarians determine the nature and content of these various groups of materials, including the two-hour reserve collection. Librarians consult with faculty and students to solve their library service problems, but authority in the arrangement and distribution of materials rests with librarians.

Shelving the majority of assigned readings on open shelves has the advantage of enabling students to help themselves. Shelving these books in call number sequence with the rest of the collection has the added advantage of continuously acquainting the student with other books on the same subject. One book leads to another. In such circumstances browsing among books becomes a part of the daily study routine, and this leads to scanning books that catch the eye, and thus the reading habit is launched.

The large reading room is broken up into small study areas through thoughtful use of free-standing book cases. Students work in small groups in small areas where they are literally surrounded with books of interest to them. Acoustical plaster on walls and ceiling and rubber tile on floors eliminate noise and distraction. Soft white fluorescent lights create the illusion of continuous daylight. The several reading rooms are contiguous and freely accessible to all students. All circulation procedures have been concentrated at the single central loan desk. There is only one inspection point, at the exit. The reserve book room has been abolished and its room space converted to an unsupervised study hall, complete with lounge corner and with coffee, coke, and apple vending machines. When conversation must flourish it can flourish in this study hall. Here, too, is a battery of typewriters freely available to all students.

In such a building, with emphasis upon service throughout, graduate study and faculty research also have greatly improved accommodations. At Nebraska the book stack is now a place of relative quiet. The former problem of paging books from the stacks in great numbers has now been transformed into a comparable problem of housekeeping in the reading rooms where the students are encouraged to leave books on the tables. When the new central library was built provision was made in the stacks for a book escalator. It has not been necessary to complete and operate this equipment because the problems of getting books is no longer concentrated into the book stack. In the reading rooms this problem of finding books has become much less a problem because the principle of self-help is applied extensively under the watchful eyes of a competent staff. In the book stack are more than a hundred carrells. On the fourth floor are 16 seminars which serve also as graduate study rooms. On the fourth floor, too, are 40 faculty studies — separate private rooms, which are, in the words of several of our scholars, the finest improvement on the campus in their lifetimes.

At this point one or two misconceptions about the divisional plan should be cleared away. Is the divisional plan expensive? Isn't it more expensive to operate than a traditional library? The answer is, no! The cost of a competent public service staff is directly related to the size of the student body, to the length of the schedule of hours of public service, and to the quality of the service program. Many libraries are trying to do too much with too few. The reference librarian is expected to cover all fields of knowledge. A divisional librarian restricts his service to a broad but limited field of knowledge, and with correspondingly greater competence. One should bear in mind, too, that there is no prescribed number of divisions and reading rooms. A divisional plan can be set up and operated in one room. Or, if circumstances seem to warrant, it can be set up in three, or six, or some other number of divisions.

Finally, how about the cost of duplications? To this we would say that no more duplication is implied in the divisional plan than would be necessary for adequate service under any other plan or organization. Many libraries appear to be reluctant to face the cost of necessary duplications.

Through training and experience librarians in the divisional library must acquire sound academic judgment and must exercise broad professional competence. They must be recognized as bona fide members of the academic community.

The organization and direction of a library division call for imagination and creative energy. The public service staff in a divisional library must be adequately trained in subject matter and in librarianship. The humanities librarian, for example, does not need to know more than any citizen should know about atomic energy or federal reserve banks, or about the sources of such information. But he must be deeply interested and widely read in all language and literature, in philosophy and the fine arts. It is highly desirable that the humanities librarian and his staff have at least master's degrees in the subject matter of the division. And in the same breath let us mention that a master's degree in librarianship is indispensable.

Theirs is not custodial work. These librarians must be competent to a high degree in the educational process. Their work requires that they be educators. In this, their professional and academic attainments must be matched with mature and pleasant personalities. Under their general supervision the housekeeping chores are delegated to clerical employees, to student pages, and to building custodians.

Into the hands of the divisional librarian and his staff flows the entire book selection process. Daily conversations with members of the faculty over the development of the collections have become a regular if not a routine activity. Assistance to students at all levels and to the faculty in the interpretation of the collections — that is, help in finding what they need — is a continuous process. Staff assignments are limited only by the boundaries of broad fields of subject matter, such as the humanities or the social sciences, and never by the format of books, or by their imprint, or by the accident of their location in reading room, book stack, or branch library. In order to assure a careful correlation of all the book collections and related library services we have subordinated all departmental and laboratory libraries to their appropriate divisions. The chemistry, physics, botany, zoology, and geology libraries are, therefore, administratively supervised by the head of the science division. With respect to our principal branch libraries in law, medicine, and agriculture, the relationship is defined as a staff rather than a line relationship.

The public service staff in the divisional library is recruited for broad competence in librarianship and in subject matter. Similar competencies are highly desirable in the technical services, in solving difficult problems in bibliography, and in the cataloging and classification of materials. Only a few of the larger libraries can afford to duplicate such qualifications between the public and the technical services. We believe that a better solution lies in assigning the same staff to both of these areas, and this we have done at Nebraska. Our public service staff catalogs and classifies all books and assists with difficult problems in bibliography in the order department. We believe that the reference librarians become competent in bibliographical knowledge and technique through experience in cataloging. We believe also that catalogers produce a more usable catalog when they have the continuous experience of helping students and faculty to find materials.

It must be obvious by now that the staff that participates in divisional librarianship as described in this paper must be or must become competent to a high degree in the educational process. It is our hope that their academic and professional growth are continuous. They are daily engaged in library operations of a wide variety and with student and faculty contacts of widely varying degrees of intensity and difficulty. Such a staff soon becomes an indispensable part of the academic community and academic activity tends to center in the library.

It only remains then to recognize these librarians in their true role as educators. At Nebraska all librarians are members of the faculty and all have appropriate academic rank. Some 15 or more are *bona fide* members of the University Senate. They serve on various university committees. Several have recently achieved the rank of associate professor and now have tenure.

Conclusion

The divisional plan can consist of two or three reading rooms, with books on open shelves and a staff employed to watch them and with everything else in the library as usual. On the other hand, the divisional plan can become the basis for a new and expanded plan of library service throughout the university — a new philosophy of librarianship. The ultimate implications of the divisional plan at Nebraska have led to a broad view of our individual responsibilities and have led each of us into the practice of librarianship "clear across the board." In so doing it was inevitable that we have closed ranks with the faculty and now work together in a common cause.

About the Author

After holding positions at the University of Arizona Library, Los Angeles Public Library, University of California at Berkeley, and University of California at Los Angeles, Lundy was appointed Director of Libraries at the University of Nebraska in 1944.

William S. Dix

Undergraduates Do Not Necessarily Require A Special Facility

From his Princeton experience (see the earlier article in this Section for his Rice Institute perspective), Dix describes the 1,250,000 volume open-stock collection for 2,900 undergraduates and 500 graduate students at the New Jersey University. He concludes that he suspects that the range of performance between different systems of organization, whether unified collection, divisional plan, or special undergraduate collection, is considerably less than the difference in performance caused by a host of other factors, and further that it is "solemn nonsense to pretend that there is much sicence at work in the selection of any form of arrangement."

All of this has a strangely familiar feeling, like one of those recurring dreams in which one walks through a haunting landscape amid reflected faces and echoing voices. I hear my own voice coming back to me: "For the library of less than a half million volumes in the smaller institutions to adopt any system which permits students to use anything less than the total collection seems just a bit foolish." Then I remember that at another hot meeting in New York almost exactly three years ago we went all over this same ground. Only the faces on the platform are different — except, alas, my own.

I was then at the Rice Institute, and I described briefly how about 1,200 undergraduates were served by a collection of considerably less than a half million volumes with no special provision for undergraduates. Now I am at Princeton, trying to serve about 2,900 undergraduates with about a million and a quarter volumes. If I could just say that I had changed my opinions, I might have something to talk about. Unfortunately, I have not. If I were really honest, I should simply refer you to COLLEGE AND RESEARCH LIBRARIES, volume XIV, number 3 (July, 1953), pages 271-72, and ask you to read there what I said three years ago, multiplying as you read all of the figures by three. Then I could sit down and both of us would be better off.

Actually, I am not quite that honest, and I'll try to say the same thing in different words. My own feeling is simply that for purposes of education and for purposes of research the larger the collection the better, within reason, if it is well arranged and if other conditions are optimum. Today, based on my own experience, I'll interpret "within reason" to be less than a million and a half volumes. This is *not* the best system for quick reference, but I take it that our business in the university library is either education or research and that we shall naturally take care of the quick reference function by a careful selection of certain handy tools for some sort of reference room. I take it also that the process of undergraduate teaching — at least insofar as the library is concerned — is improved as its methods approach those of research. One may *indoctrinate* and even *train* by lecturing at large groups of students and having them memorize facts from a textbook, but one can *educate* better by turning them loose in a good library and letting them really learn under the careful guidance of mature scholars. These are my premises.

Now for the confessional aspects of the program, the feature we always seem to come to: "This is what *we* do." It is my understanding that Princeton has always had essentially open stacks from 1756 when the library occupied a little room on the second floor of Nassau Hall — even though the whole library was open only one hour one day a week and no frivolous reading on Sunday. Similarly, it has always been first of all an undergraduate college, with 2,900 undergraduates and 500 graduate students today. Variations from the concept of the unified single collection have been in the direction of special facilities for advanced work rather than for the undergraduate. Some ten subject field collections outside the main building have developed, always because of geographical convenience and the needs of research, principally in the pure and natural sciences. Within the building are a number of other special collections housed in graduate study rooms, almost all duplicated in the main collection. A few special interdepartmental programs for undergraduates have separate collections, but here again all duplicated and designed primarily for advanced work. The process of fragmentation at Princeton has been from the top down, rather than from the bottom up.

This, I think, follows the structure of organized knowledge; as the cliché has it, "the scholar is a man who knows more and more about less and less." At least to the extent to which this is true, it seems sensible to divide, if at all, along the lines of the scholar's interests. To divide at the other end of the scale, where we aim at "general education" or whatever is the popular term at the moment, seems to me just a bit more of an expedient than a virtue. At least, I am fairly confident that the next big division at Princeton will be again at the top: the segregation of seldom-used books into some sort of compact storage area.

Does it work? I can only say that I think so, in the absence of any statistics. I know that I pick up more expressions of dissatisfaction from our graduate students than from our undergraduates, who do use the library with considerable intensity.

Having said all of this, and sounding perhaps as if my notions were absolute dogma, let me add that I am not at all sure of my conclusions. I happen to have spent all of my professional life as a librarian and a considerable part of my life as a student, teacher, and semi-scholar in collections managed as I have indicated. I have found them satisfactory and considerably more usable than the fragmented libraries in my personal experience. Perhaps I am rationalizing.

I really suspect that the range of performance between different systems of organization — unified collection, divisional plan, special undergraduate collection, or what you will — is considerably less than the difference in performance caused by a host of other factors, and further that we are talking solemn nonsense when we pretend that there is much science at work in the selection of any form of arrangement.

The essential thing is that the good library develops through the years to meet ever more precisely the needs of its constituents. In special situations, like the wonderfully special one at Harvard, of course a Lamont Library is a great idea. In other special situations it might be utter nonsense. I'm afraid that we don't have any coherent body of theory to argue about, only details, which are less fun but usually important.

About the Author

William S. Dix earned his Ph.D. in English from the University of Chicago. He was Associate Professor and Librarian, Rice Institute, 1946-53. From 1953 until his recent retirement, he was University Librarian, Princeton University.

Frederick H. Wagman

The Case for
the Undergraduate Library

The author reviews the history of special libraries
for undergraduates beginning with Bodley's
Library in 1608 and then concentrates on the
problems of educating students at the larger
American universities. He outlines the planning
process from 1953-1955 at the University of Michigan for a 2,500-seat Undergraduate Library
which will serve the 10,500 enrolled students in
the University's lower divisions and then projects
the Library's services and philosophy in detail.

Discussion of the advisability of special libraries for undergraduates occurs earlier in the literature of librarianship than is generally supposed. In 1608, when
Thomas James was appointed to Bodley's Library, he proposed the establishment of an undergraduate library to help the younger students. But Sir Thomas
Bodley was opposed, and wrote him:

> Your deuise for a Librarie for the yonguer sort, will haue many great exceptions,
> & one of special force. That there must be an other keeper ordeined for that place.
> And where yow mention the yonguer sort, I knowe what bookes should be bought
> for them, but the elder as well [as] the yonguer, may haue often occasion to looke
> vpon them: and if there were any suche, they can not require so great a rowme. In
> effect, to my understanding there is muche to be saied against it, as vndoubtedly
> your self will readily finde, vpon further consideration.[1]

Three hundred and forty-seven years later there is still "much to be said against
it." Certainly, the size of the university, the educational aims of the institution,
the nature of the curriculum and of existing library facilities, the pattern of
instruction followed by the faculty, the extent of the book collections, the geography of the campus, the availability of libraries in halls of residence are all considerations that must be taken into account by any institution that considers the
advisability of establishing a separate undergraduate library.

Justification for the separate undergraduate library may be offered on two levels. One involves the argument of practicality. In some situations the problem of
providing adequate physical facilities for library service to undergraduate stu-

109

dents may be solved most efficiently and even economically by a circumflex separate library. The other justification is more theoretical and relates to the role of the library and the librarian in the education of the undergraduate student. If the latter seems to us more difficult to defend, the cause may be an unconscious diffidence on the part of librarians regarding their own importance for the educational process.

Existing patterns of library service for undergraduate students are extremely diversified. At one end of the scale are the notable libraries found at some of the small liberal arts colleges, where the collections have been highly selected and developed over a great many years with a view to serving the requirements of the college student and the needs of his instructors for materials to support the work of instruction. Here, in the best examples, the library is an important adjunct to the teaching program. The reference staff devotes considerable effort to helping the individual student find his way to books that will relate to his course work and broaden his interests. The student is conscious of few barriers between him and the books. The faculty members are aware of the library's educational potential and take it into account in planning their courses, frequently consulting with the librarian, whom they regard as a member of the teaching staff. The emphasis at such institutions is on teaching rather than on research. The liberal arts, humanistic tradition is strong here and stresses the importance of books and reading in the process of education.

At the other end of the scale is the library of the behemoth university which developed during the past century under the influence of the German university pattern. Here the emphasis is on research and publication to a far greater extent. The faculty is interested for the most part in its advanced courses. As far as the undergraduates are concerned, the library often is not closely integrated with their instruction and is usually not well adapted to their needs. The functions of such a library are diversified since it must serve students in the professional schools, the faculty, graduate students, and staff members of research institutes. The undergraduates comprise a heterogeneous group, ranging from the student who hopes to acquire a liberal education in four years to the student who is training himself to manage his uncle's drug store and is impatient with the general education requirements of his curriculum. Here, also, the liberal arts tradition is cherished within the literary college but that college is, to a certain extent, the servant of the professional schools and must adapt some of its courses to the special requirements of those schools.

The reputation of such a university usually rests less upon the quality of its instructional program for college students than it does on the international renown achieved by its scholars and research staff. The faculties of such universities usually demand that the library maintain the quality of its research collections, even when this limits expenditures for multiple copies of books that might be useful in undergraduate instruction. As a consequence, the teaching of undergraduates frequently relies, to a far greater extent than is wise, on textbooks and canned material. The collections of such a library are huge and its catalogs are complex. The books are usually shelved compactly in stack areas to which it is unfeasible to admit the thousands of undergraduates. Moreover, large segments of the collections are dispersed among divisional and departmental libraries, which exist to make the use of books and journals more convenient to research workers, and some parts of the collections are usually in storage.

Apart from these inherent disadvantages of the very large university libraries, it must be remembered that the tax-supported universities which cannot fully control their enrollments are facing the prospect of a tremendous increase in their campus populations within the next 15 years. Relatively few of the larger universities are blessed with library facilities adequate to meet the demands of present student bodies and the problem of providing meaningful service to undergraduate students is likely to yield, ten years from now, to the more pressing problem of how to provide any service at all for the entire group.

Despite the handicaps just enumerated, the large university must try to offer the benefits of the good small college library for its undergraduate students. It may never succeed fully in this aim since reading and study are not mass activities. They flourish in solitude, not in concert, and it is difficult to make books and library services available to thousands of students in an atmosphere conducive to study and reflection. But the university's obligations with respect to the general education of the undergraduates as well as their specific course work compel it to rely heavily on the library. For the humanities and the social sciences, the library serves as laboratory. The course work in these fields should be planned in terms of extensive reading. Textbooks, anthologies, and syllabi have serious shortcomings as a substitute for the original full-length works on which they are based. Lectures are extremely useful in organizing and outlining information and in stimulating the student to read and investigate on his own, but in all subject fields other than the sciences, mathematics, and elementary language training the undergraduate curriculum must depend heavily on good books.

With respect to the general liberal education of the undergraduates, the university must make a determined effort to counteract the frightening phenomenon of our age that Clifton Fadiman calls "the decline of attention." It must try to resist the displacement of the students' faculty of attention "away from ideas and abstractions toward things and techniques;" to offset the constant indoctrination of the student by society "with the virtues of . . . attentiveness to thins, techniques, machines, spectator sports, and mass amusement."[2] The job of the university teacher is to start the student on the process of self-education through attentive reading of the works that represent the best expression of our wisdom and creative imagination. The aim of college education should be "to provide all students with a broad intellectual experience in the major fields of knowledge and to insure that every graduate has a personal experience with the content, methods, and system of values of the various disciplines by which men try to understand themselves and their environment."[3] For this the right books must be available, and the students must be induced to read them. I say "induced" advisedly, for the majority of undergraduates are not motivated to read.

The problems encountered in educating undergraduates at our largest universities do not derive solely from the great size of these institutions. Some of these universities maintain as high a ratio of teachers to students as do very small colleges. If the educational experience of the average undergraduate at a large university is inferior to that enjoyed by his counterpart at the small liberal arts college, the reason may be sought partially in the fact that the larger institutions seem to find it difficult to influence their students to read. To some extent this may be the fault of the library, which at some institutions has been relatively passive as regards its profound obligations to the undergraduate.

In order to stimulate or induce the undergraduate to read books that require attention and mental effort on his part, it is essential that such books be made attractive and easily available to him. How shall this be done?

It has been suggested that every student be required to buy himself a private library. This is an excellent idea but we cannot expect most students to buy any significant number of the books that they should read, become familiar with, or examine in the course of their four years at college.

Another solution often mentioned is the dormitory or house library. These have the virtues of smallness and of convenience. At a large university it is questionable how many such dormitory libraries the institution can afford to maintain if any of them are to be adequately stocked and managed.

A third solution is the absorption and distribution of undergraduate library services within the whole service complex provided by the main generalized library and its subject-specialized branches — the existing pattern at most universities. The defects of this arrangement for the very large university are exemplified by the present situation in which the University of Michigan finds itself.

The University of Michigan has an enrollment of 10,500 undergraduates, and more than 7,000 graduate students. There are, in addition, several thousand staff members with library privileges. The general library building book stacks are crowded by approximately 1,200,000 volumes and the same number of volumes are dispersed among 22 divisional and departmental libraries, four study halls for undergraduates, and three graduate reading rooms. The Literary College has 6,000 undergraduates for whom specifically there are provided far less than a thousand library seats and one open-shelf collection of approximately 3,000 volumes. All but a few of the divisional libraries are required to serve undergraduates as well as graduate students and faculty. Audio facilities for students of music literature and music appreciation, and for listening to recorded drama and poetry, are inadequate. There is little exhibit space. In order to maintain the qualitative level of the research collections, the library committee of the Literary College has ruled against the purchase of more than three copies of any one book at the request of any one department. The existing study halls discourage reading because of their uninviting character and the paucity of their collections. Over 4,500 graduate students and staff members have stack passes in the main building, and it is impossible to admit undergraduates to the stacks except on Sunday, or in unusual cases.

Because it has not been possible to buy multiple copies of books, nor to give them shelf space, nor to provide adequate reading space for the students, the faculty has been relying more and more heavily on textbooks for the course work. This situation, the dean of the Literary College and a considerable percentage of the faculty find deplorable. It is quite possible at present for a student to spend four years as an undergraduate at the University of Michigan without once entering the general library building.

The inadequacies of existing library facilities have a serious effect also on the service provided for the graduate students and faculty. Since the undergraduates must make use of the divisional, specialized libraries, these have a divided function. Their staffs must spend a high percentage of their time serving the needs of the undergraduates and are free to develop relatively few services for advanced students.

The administration of the University of Michigan has been aware, for some time, that its library has not been contributing as it should to the intellectual development of the undergraduate student. It has realized for some time also that by 1970 there might be 20,000 undergraduates enrolled at the University of Michigan and that expansion of library facilities is a matter of extreme urgency. As a consequence, it has given the program of library development a high priority and has been strongly supported by the Board of Regents and by the State Legislature.

In planning for the future, it soon became evident that modification of the existing pattern of library services would be necessary. The general library building is so situated that no significant expansion of it is feasible. On the other hand, many of the colleges of the university are scheduled to have new and larger buildings in which it will be possible to provide spacious divisional libraries. A number of these colleges are to be removed to a new campus four miles from the original 40 acres. The principle is firmly established at Michigan that campus expansion will not be inhibited in order to keep library services centralized. The library system simply must provide service where it is needed.

These various considerations led to decisions that transform necessity into virtue. The divisional libraries are being strengthened and given full custodial responsibility for the materials in their disciplines. They will become almost exclusively graduate research libraries. The general library building will remain the administrative and technical services center for the university library system and also the graduate research center for the humanities and for most of the social sciences. Little-used material is already being drawn off from the general library and the divisional libraries to a stack building on the new campus.

It was clear by 1951 that additional new facilities would have to be developed for the undergraduates. The idea of providing scattered study halls for the undergraduates to supplement those already in existence was promptly rejected. Such study halls have been unsuccessful at Michigan in the past. No one of them contains an adequate library collection or sufficiently diversified services. Moreover, the cost of providing enough seating space in such rooms would go far toward paying for a much better library for undergraduate use.

The possibility of furnishing libraries within halls of residence also was rejected because of the rather staggering fact that the undergraduates already reside in 19 residence halls (three of which are enormous and comprise 20 houses), in 64 undergraduate fraternities and sororities, and 13 "league houses." This excludes the many private rooming houses and cooperative houses and does not take into account the men and women who live at home or commute.

There seemed to be no hope of caring for both present and future undergraduate library needs without erecting a new and separate library building. At the same time, it seemed likely that by concentrating the books and other materials needed by the undergraduates in one building, by providing as many copies of each book as are needed, and by employing an energetic staff to work intelligently with both faculty and students, it should be possible to relate the library more closely to the students' course work and to the interests stimulated in the classroom, and to induce the student to give more attention to books that exercise the intellect and the imagination.

Planning of such a separate library began in 1953 and the working drawings are now being prepared. The separate undergraduate library seems to me the most practical answer to Michigan's pressing problem but it has an even more profound justification in educational terms. The new library will give the faculty members much greater freedom to shape their courses as they should. At the same time it will serve as an intellectual center for the undergraduates. The building will be designed, frankly and unashamedly, to induce the students to enter it and read. It will offer a collection of the best books produced by our civilization, exhibits of various kinds, facilities for listening to music, recorded drama, and poetry, facilities for viewing documentary films and for student participation in discussion groups. It will provide, we hope, a quiet, inviting atmosphere for study and reflection. It will, if we succeed, give the undergraduate student a proprietary feeling toward it, the impression that the staff, the collections, and the facilities are all adjusted to serve him specifically and to enable him to make the most of his educational opportunities. The books he needs, as well as all those his teachers think he should be exposed to, will all be convenient and accessible in open shelves rather than dispersed over the campus, and there will be an adequate number of copies to support assignments made by his teachers, either as required or suggested reading.

This library will seat approximately 2,500 students with ease, ample space for the present undergraduate population. For the time being, and probably for the next ten years, an engineering library will occupy two floors. Within the next 15 years, the School of Engineering and several of the other professional schools will move to the new campus. By that time there may be 12,000 undergraduates in the Literary College alone and the two floors of the undergraduate library building initially devoted to the engineering library will become available for the increased number of undergraduates in the Literary College.

Administratively, this library will be under the direction of the University Library, whose technical services departments will acquire and catalog the books for it. The staff of the undergraduate library will be concerned exclusively with book selection and custodial and reference services. We hope to persuade the teaching faculty to work closely with the staff in terms of developing reading lists and exhibits, and in encouraging use of the library through classroom stimulation, and assigned and suggested reading.

The most difficult problem that we face, of course, is the question of book selection. For this the help of almost the entire teaching staff of the Literary College has been solicited. Funds have been provided to pay part of the salaries of approximately seven members of the Literary College faculty who will work with their colleagues and the library staff to elicit and coordinate recommendations for inclusions in the collection. Each department of the Literary College has begun checking the catalog of the Lamont Library, the catalogs of various publishers, and the reading lists presently used by the departments. This is being done also by the staffs of all the other colleges that have an undergraduate enrollment, since their students also will use this library, at least until they move to the new campus. Each member of the faculty is being asked to re-think his method of instruction in terms of making the best possible use of the future undergraduate library and to suggest the books and periodicals that he feels should be available in the collections, including not only those that he will require his students to read but any others in which he would like to interest them. Several departmental libraries which exist chiefly to serve undergraduates are also being carefully weeded by the departments concerned, and existing print and phonorecord collections used in the instruction of undergraduates will eventually be moved, after weeding, to the new building. It is likely that, apart from the engineering collection, the content of the undergraduate library will total between 100,000 and 150,000 volumes.

The plans do not include a separate reserve book room despite the fact that all required reading material for courses which include undergraduates will be kept in this library. Provision is being made for a limited, controlled collection of reserve books against the possibility that some required reading may simply not be available in an adequate number of copies. For the most part, however, required or collateral reading which must be provided in multiple copies will be kept in its proper place on the open shelves, the spines of the books marked to indicate that they may be charged out only overnight.

Final arrangement of the books has not yet been settled. The site for the building and the space requirements have governed its shape and the number of stories, but it is completely flexible and it should lend itself to arrangement of the books in a divisional pattern.

We have not planned for a separate browsing collection. In a broad sense, the entire collection will be a browsing collection for the whole campus. The library will contain not only the best books of the past but those of the present, since it is our firm belief that the students' education not only should give them a sense of history but should make them aware of the best current thinking on the issues and life of our times.

It is not intended that the undergraduates be restricted to this building. On the contrary, it is hoped that their experience in the undergraduate library will stimulate them to make advantageous use of the research collections. They will be welcomed at all branches of the library system when they have a serious purpose in using them.

The solution that we have adopted may not be viable on many other campuses. I am certain, however, that it will help the library share in importance and effectiveness with the inspiration of good teaching in educating the undergraduate students at the University of Michigan.

Notes

1. *Letters of Sir Thomas Bodley to Thomas James,* edited by G. W. Wheeler (Oxford: Clarendon Press, 1926), p. 183.

2. Clifton Fadiman. *Party of One* (Cleveland: World Publishing Company, 1955), p. 355.

3. University of Michigan. *General Register,* Section II, 1954, p. 24.

About the Author

Frederick H. Wagman held the following positions at the Library of Congress from 1945-1953: Acting Director of Personnel and Administrative Services; Assistant Director, Reference Department; Director, Processing Department; Deputy Chief Assistant Librarian of Congress and Director of Administration. In 1953, he became Director of Libraries, University of Michigan, Ann Arbor.

Part IV.

The UgLi at the University of Michigan 1958

Part IV: Introduction

At the Conference on "The Place of the Library in a University," held in the Lamont Library, Harvard University, March 30-31, 1949, Donald Coney, University Librarian, University of California at Berkeley, said that "Harvard's Lamont Library solution to the undergraduate library problem is notable for its adequacy and directness."[1] He then asked: "Can this solution hold hope for those of us in state-supported universities?"[2]
Coney responded to his own question:

A test of the Lamont solution in its application to the mass campuses is its reduction to dollars. I assume that Lamont, with its 1,100 seats and 80,000 volumes, is substantially Harvard's provision for undergraduate library service. How many undergraduates does Harvard have? Something in the neighborhood of 5,000. But a Lamont Library on the Berkeley, or Minnesota, or Illinois, or Michigan, or Texas, or Wisconsin campus would have to be large enough to accommodate three, four, or five times as many readers, if equal facilities were to be provided. A crude cost estimate of Lamont's five undergraduate levels suggests that this space runs to something like $1,300,000. Thus, the cost of construction alone, on a large state university campus, would be of the order of three to five times as much, i.e., from four to six and one-half million dollars. In addition to the building, a book collection and its catalogue are required. Lamont's 80,000 volumes may easily have cost $240,000; its catalogue, even at an unrealistic minimum of 25 cents per volume, would add another $20,000 to the cost. Perhaps these are books enough for the largest undergraduate enrollment likely. The get-ready cost, therefore, of a Lamont Library for a campus such as Berkeley's (with more than three times Harvard's undergraduates) would be, at a minimum, four and a quarter millions of dollars.

I do not say that such order of expense is impossible for state universities; but the magnitude of enrollment, translated into the magnitude of dollars, sets the scale of the solution's cost. A Lamont Library can be realized on state university campuses only if administrators and librarians are skillful in presenting the library needs of the state's youth so persuasively that legislatures will see the light, for it is to state legislatures — and not to private wealth — that the state universities must turn for the provision of this library essential to undergraduate education. More important than this act of persuasion, however, is a decision which must be taken earlier, and by librarians and university administrators. I mean the decision that, important as it is to have libraries for books, it is also important to have libraries for people.[3]

The University of Michigan at Ann Arbor was the first state university which tested the "Lamont solution in its application to the mass campuses."

William Warner Bishop, University Librarian at Ann Arbor, has been credited with the idea for a Michigan undergraduate library.[4] Frederick Wagman has also attributed the Michigan proposal to Harlan Hatcher, University President and Charles Odegaard, Dean of the College of Literature, Science and the Arts.[5] It was clear to these University administrators by 1951 that undergraduates could no longer be ignored. They drew up a plan for a storage library on the North Campus in Ann Arbor and for a separate undergraduate library on the main campus. Actual detailed planning did not begin until the arrival of Wagman as Director of Libraries in 1953.

The second separate undergraduate library in the country—and the first descendant of Lamont—was opened for use on January 16, 1958. The Michigan students soon were calling it the UgLi. James Davis recently and correctly observed that "Although the Lamont Library was the first, the University of Michigan Undergraduate Library may with some justification be considered the prototype of most undergraduate libraries. The classification system there follows more closely the one that prevails in other libraries on the campus, and a comprehensive program of reference assistance is provided."[6]

In this section, Frederick Wagman describes the Michigan UgLi, under the guidance of Roberta Keniston, the dynamic first head librarian, from his perspective as Director of Libraries.

Incidentally, the Michigan UgLi was built at a cost of $3,105,000 for the building, furniture, and equipment with the entire amount furnished by the State Legislature. A building of 145,036 square feet on five floors with 2,250 seats was achieved. The initial cost of the book collection was $200,000 with another $200,000 invested in acquiring and cataloging the opening day collection. Coney's 1949 estimate for a campus such as the University of California at Berkeley had been $4,250,000, although UC at Berkeley was not to build its Moffitt Undergraduate Library until eighteen years after the Michigan UgLi became the first separate undergraduate library at a state university.

Notes

1. Donald Coney, "The Future of Libraries in Academic Institutions, I," *Harvard Library Bulletin* 3 (Autumn, 1949): 328.

2. Ibid.

3. Ibid., p. 329.
4. Irene A. Braden, *The Undergraduate Library,* ACRL Monographs No. 31 (Chicago: American Library Association, 1970), p. 29.
5. Ibid.
6. James Davis, "The Changing Role of the Undergraduate Library in Universities," *New Dimensions for Academic Library Service,* Edited by E.J. Josey (Metuchen, N.J.: Scarecrow Press, 1975), p. 64.

Frederick H. Wagman

The Undergraduate Library
of the University
# of Michigan

Wagman, Director of Libraries at the University
of Michigan, describes the first separate undergraduate library on a state-supported university
campus. The background, planning, and actual
detailed dimensions of the UgLi, as it was chris-
tened by Michigan students, are detailed.

In 1952 the University of Michigan set aside a plan, developed over about a decade, for the enlargement of its general library building. The remodeling and
expansion of this building, at very high cost, would have improved it greatly for
use by the graduate students and faculty but would not have provided for undergraduate needs to any significant extent. A substitute program was drawn up
calling for some remodeling of the General Library; for construction of a library
storage building and bindery; and for a separate undergraduate library building.

The program written subsequently for this undergraduate library stated, as
basic principles, that everything possible should be done in the architectual
planning and in the selection of books and staff to make the library inviting and
easy to use; to give the students the impression that the librarians were employed
to assist rather than supervise or monitor them; and to help the undergraduates
develop a proprietary interest in their library. To insure maximum flexibility of
the space provided, a modular building was called for. The rectangular form and
orientation of the only site available governed the shape of the building and even
its external appearance. The desire to avoid producing a structure that would be
offensive in appearance between the buildings on either side and the limitation

SOURCE: From Frederick H. Wagman, "The Undergraduate Library at the University
of Michigan," *College and Research Libraries* 20 (May, 1959), pp. 179-188. Reprinted by
permission of the author.

on the appropriated funds available for the construction governed the number of floors that could be provided above and below grade respectively. Accommodation of the plan to the various strictures resulted in a structure 240 x 120 feet, built on a module 30 x 24 feet, with four stories above grade and one below. The building contains 145,000 square feet, most of it in the form of a large undifferentiated area on each of the four lower floors which can be adapted for almost any conceivable use. Lighting, air conditioning, and liberal provision of electric and telephone outlets will make possible the erection of partitions in almost any pattern desired in the future.

It was decided early in the planning that the entire book collection would be placed on open shelves. To facilitate the finding of books, the floor plan was simplified to the ultimate degree and no sacrifice of this simplicity was subsequently permitted for the sake of architectural effect. Critical examination of the reasons usually advanced for keeping reserve books behind a barrier led to the conclusion that it would be feasible, although more costly, to place the reserves where they belong in the classification system, on the open shelves, provided one marked them with a distinctive symbol and controlled the exits from the building. Exception to this rule has been made only for occasional items such as reprints of journal articles lent to the library by the faculty for class use. The planning committee decided also that the only argument against allowing the students to smoke anywhere in the air-conditioned building was the janitorial cost of emptying ash trays at night and that this argument was not compelling. Similarly, it seemed foolish to make students who were spending long hours in the library leave the building in order to get a cup of coffee, so a coffee shop was provided even though this meant extra floor washing in one room.

Since the ideal of complete privacy, a separate room for every reader, is unattainable, a compromise was effected. The large reading area on every floor is broken by a row of group study rooms along one wall, each of which can accommodate eight students, by the ranges of book shelving and by placement of colorful "space-breakers" or screens. As a result one is not given the sensation of sitting in a very large room in any reading area. One-third of the seating provided is at individual tables attached to the screens or along the walls. The rest of the seating is at tables designed for four students, except that the arrangement of tables is interrupted by occasional groupings of lounge furniture. Despite the disproportionate ratio of seating to book space, the reader is conscious of the proximity of the books in all parts of the reading areas.

All tables were designed to offer each reader 3 x 2 feet of work surface. The chairs were designed to provide maximum comfort over long periods of time and yet to serve as an important ingredient of the decorative scheme through their colored upholstery. Careful selection of flooring material, ceiling construction, and lighting has resulted in glare-free even illumination and an extremely low noise level. The grouping of special purpose rooms at one end has simplified the traffic patterns and provides maximum flexibility of space in the reading areas. Decoration was achieved through the use of color in the upholstery, on the "space breakers," and on the rear wall of each room. The total effect is one of lightness and of pleasant, colorful, informality. Despite the constant stream of students in and out of all parts of the building there is little impression of confusion.

It was agreed that the book collection should represent the best in the human record of the past and in current thought. With the aid of hundreds of faculty members and a process of book selection that went on for more than two years, an initial stock of 60,000 volumes and 150 periodical titles was assembled and cataloged. Important omissions from this collection are being corrected currently and it is the intention to keep the collection current by the addition of new books that contribute to knowledge. Inasmuch as the entire collection is a browsing collection, in effect, no separate browsing collection was provided and no special "recreational" reading collection, based on the notion that "recreational" is synonymous with "second-rate" or even with "meretricious."

The faculty members were asked to rethink their courses and submit new required or recommended reading lists. An attempt was made to procure one copy of each of these titles for every twelve or thirteen students enrolled in the respective course. In addition a substantial collection of reference books was placed on the open shelves where they are accessible to both staff and students. It has been found necessary to augment the reference collection rapidly. The problem of helping a student halfway to an answer and then referring him to the General Library for additional assistance becomes intolerable in practice if not in theory.

Books and periodicals are not the only library materials undergraduates need or should be exposed to, and a special room was provided for listening to recorded music, poetry, and drama. Equipped with 151 seats, 72 turntables, at each of which two students may listen with earphones, 7 cubicles for listening to loud-speakers, and a control room from which programs may be played over 13 channels by record or tape and tuned in at each of the seats, this facility provides library support for the popular courses in music literature which enroll hundreds of students each year. A multipurpose room equipped with 200 stacking chairs, motion picture projectors, and public address system is used by the students for lectures, discussion groups, motion pictures, or for any affair which concerns undergraduates and the library. Additionally, one room was equipped with four motion picture projectors on which several students may view different documentary films simultaneously, listening to the sound through headphones, or where a small class may watch a documentary film. On the main floor of the library an exhibit area was provided where the Fine Arts Museum staff arranges small monthly shows of prints, most of them brought to Ann Arbor on loan. On the top floor a large display room was made available to the fine arts department. Equipped with museum benches and tackboard on the walls and on several large screens, it offers an ideal space for five hundred students to study the prints and photographic reproductions with which they must familiarize themselves for their fine arts courses.

For a few years, until a new classroom and library building can be provided on the University's new north campus for the School of Engineering, the library of that school is being housed on the third floor of the Undergraduate Library. Similarly, the Transportation Library is being housed temporarily on the fourth floor.

The Undergraduate Library was opened on January 18, 1958. The response of the students was overwhelming and a dramatic revelation of past inadequacies. Prior to this date there had been available for the use of the undergraduates, apart from the main reading room in the General Library and the numerous branch libraries, three reading rooms seating 489 students in crowded fashion, housing negligible collections of books, and staffed by library science students or other student assistants. The new building seats 2,200 very comfortably and is staffed with ten professional librarians who provided reference aid and supervise a large staff of clerical and student assistants. Both building and staff have proved to be much too small.

In the first year of operation, the library counted 1,420,865 users. More than 9,500 students have used the library on one day and on many days the number ranges between 8,500 and 9,000. It should not be suspected that the volume of "visitors" bears no relation to use of the collection. During this first year the Undergraduate Library circulated 134,719 volumes for home use. A total of 280,037 volumes were used in the building and had to be reshelved by the staff. How many additional volumes were used and properly reshelved by the students themselves cannot be determined. In short, at least six and one-half times as many volumes were used or borrowed by the students as the collection contains. Meanwhile, circulation in the branch libraries and in the General Library has not declined. Home circulation from the Undergraduate Library and General Library combined exceeded the total home circulation from the General Library alone for the corresponding period in the previous year by more than 135 per cent. Analysis of the circulation for home use indicated that 37.7 per cent represented voluntary reading and 62.3 per cent was course-related. Further analysis of the course-related reading reveals that a very large part of this also was not required but apparently was stimulated by the course work.

The statistics quoted above reflects use of the new library in its infancy and before a considerable part of the faculty had begun considering its potentialities as an aid to their teaching. The rate of both building and book use has been climbing steadily and threatens to be phenomenally high this spring. Many students have already adopted the practice of arriving at 6 p.m. to insure that they will have a seat available for the evening. On numerous evenings in recent weeks students have been observed sitting on the stairs and floors to read, because the chairs were all occupied.

Other less measurable effects of the new library are noteworthy. It has definitely become the hub of undergraduate activity on the campus. Its central location has made it possible for the students to spend the hours between classes reading in the library and thousands of them do so. Many students are now using the library who confess that hitherto they had preferred the movies to the study halls and had rarely or never ventured into the General Library. Obviously, also, the undergraduates are reading a great many more good books than before and under the guidance of the reference staff, short-handed as it is, are learning how to use a library catalog, indexes, bibliographies, and other reference works. Psychologically, the effect of this library on the students has been extremely gratifying. Formally, through the spokesmen for their organizations, they have, of course, indicated their appreciation of this new facility but, more important, many of them individually have made it a point to tell the staff that the new library has made a tremendous difference in their daily lives. Moreover, the success of the Undergraduate Library has stimulated the students to plan the development of small libraries in the dormitories which they will administer themselves. A committee is at work enthusiastically on plans for a series of such house libraries.

It had been feared that free access to the reserve books would result in their rapid disappearance and, in fact, one per cent of the total book stock did disappear in the spring semester last year. As a result, the Regents of the University approved a new regulation that any student who mutilated a book or removed it from the building without charging it would be fined $100 or would be suspended. The penalty has been imposed twice this semester and indications are that book losses have decreased. At the same time, the fine for late return of books was increased sufficiently to make it painful and late returns have also decreased. Both new regulations were endorsed by the students, most of whom seem to resent the theft of needed books from their library even more, perhaps, than do the librarians. Also, contrary to the fears of some that the permissive attitude as regards smoking, the provision of a coffee shop and the absence of supervision would lead to mistreatment of the furniture, books, and the building itself, there has been no damage as a result of student neglect or indifference and there seems to be no reason to fear that the students' proprietary interest in the library will not continue. Finally, the fear that the library would serve primarily as a social club, an ideal place to meet one's date or make new friends, especially in the winter months, has proved to be needless. Of course, students do meet in the library and the "study date" continues to be a popular custom, but this is an earnest generation. The first group of students admitted to the library on the day it opened included an astonishing number who went directly to the bookshelves or catalog without even taking time to tour the building. They typify the undergraduate today better than the image most of us have carried in our minds since our own undergraduate days. Moreover, in these times, at a university which provides almost thirteen hundred apartments on its campus for married students, the boy and girl holding hands while they read Gesell and Ilg may well be husband and wife preparing simultaneously for their next class and for a future, predictable "act of God."

The effect of the new library on the faculty has been equally interesting. While the building was under construction a very considerable number of professors understood its potential value and were eager to have it completed. There were a few others, however, who were convinced that the project was a wasteful diversion of funds which might better be used for other library purposes. On several occasions, members of the library staff found it necessary to meet with apprehensive faculty groups and reassure them that the book collection would not represent transfers, for the most part, from the research collections and that if any such transfers were to be made, the departments most concerned would be consulted beforehand.

It is apparent now to all that the percentage of extra copies in the new collection is not so heavy and that the book collection of the undergraduate library is a welcome addition. Over and over again it became apparent that copies of notable books purchased for the new collection were not really additional at all; the older copies recorded in the General Library catalog all too often had been lost, stolen, or worn out. More important, however, an increasing number of members of the faculty (including professors in the sciences) are "teaching with books." Courses represented by reading lists in the library increased one-third this fall as compared with the preceding spring semester and faculty interest in using the library as an aid to their teaching has begun to exceed the library's ability to keep up. This past fall, the University of Michigan was compelled to work with a reduced budget. It was not possible to staff the undergraduate library without reducing services in, and book funds for, the General Library and the branches which serve the faculty and graduate students. Regrettable though this was to all concerned, there was no resentment over the sacrifice. Indeed numerous professors have assured the library staff that the new library simply must be well supported, and almost every week members of the faculty propose additional services for their students which would require that the new facility be given an even larger share of the library budget.

The effect of the new building on the General Library and the branch libraries has been as anticipated. These are now used predominantly by graduate students and faculty. The stacks of the General Library have been opened to all and it also is now, for the most part, an open-shelf library. Graduate students have been working in the General Library and the branches in much greater number than ever before and it has become possible to adapt much of the space formerly pre-empted for undergraduate reading rooms to special uses. The reference department and the branch librarians have more time to spend on service to faculty and graduate students and on bibliographic enterprises. It has been possible to curtail the staff of the circulation department in the General Library despite the fact that circulation of books from that collection has not decreased.

The value of the Michigan Undergraduate Library as an example is not to be sought primarily in its solution to the various specific problems of architecture or librarianship. Errors were made in both respects, of course, that will be avoided in newer libraries and a number of problems have not yet been perfectly solved. Nor should it be assumed because it is proving to be successful on one campus that an identical library is needed or would be justified at all other large universities. Its importance lies in its clear demonstration of the fact that a greater investment in library service to undergraduate students on the very large university campus will elicit a dramatic response from the students in terms of their attitude toward course work and toward the process of education generally and an equally gratifying response from the faculty in terms of their teaching with books. It offers a warning also. The cost of the building, books, and staff is far higher than experience would allow one to estimate on any campus where frustration of undergraduate students in their effort to use the library has been a condition of many years standing. A building that contains 145,000 square feet and cost $3,105,000, an initial book collection that cost $200,000 and approximately the same amount again to acquire and catalog, a very heavy investment of staff and faculty time in planning and book selection, and a budget of $138,000 per year for staff (apart from janitorial and maintenance costs) are not adequate to satisfy the need at the University of Michigan. The potentialities for service are only gradually being realized by the Michigan librarians and faculty in this very early stage of the new library's existence and the annual cost of operation is almost certain to increase steadily as both students and faculty discover increasingly how helpful the new library can be.

About The Author

Frederick H. Wagman held the following positions at the Library of Congress from 1945-1953: Acting Director of Personnel and Administrative Services; Assistant Director, Reference Department; Director, Processing Department; Deputy Chief Assistant Librarian of Congress and Director of Administration. In 1953, he became Director of Libraries, University of Michigan, Ann Arbor.

Part V.

The 1960s and Early 1970s —
Era of Greatest Development:
Selective Descriptions of
Individual Libraries

Part V: Introduction

What might be pompously labeled as the New Age of the Separate Undergraduate Library began with the opening of the Lamont Library in 1949. But it took some years before real development of the idea gained momentum. In 1955 Taylor surveyed the libraries of thirty-six institutions belonging to the Association of American Universities to determine the status of library services for undergraduate students. Responses were received from twenty-nine large university libraries throughout the United States and indicated that only ten of the twenty-nine libraries had their stacks open to undergraduates.[1] However, "fifteen of the twenty-nine universities responding to the questionnaire have developed separate collections for undergraduates."[2] These collections were usually in the main university library.

Within a few years this situation was to change drastically. As discussed in Section IV, the University of Michigan opened its UgLi in 1958; during the next decade and a half many other universities opened separate undergraduate libraries. Undergraduate libraries in new buildings were built on the campuses of the University of South Carolina (1959), University of Texas (1963), Stanford University (1966), Ohio State University (1966), University of North Carolina at Chapel Hill (1968), University of Illinois (1969), University of Tennessee (1969), University of California at Berkeley (1970), University of Wisconsin (1970), University of Maryland (1972), University of Washington at Seattle (1972), and University of British Columbia (1973).

Other universities built new research libraries, extensively remodeled their original main libraries, and reopened them as undergraduate libraries. Universities that chose this alternative were Cornell University (1962), Michigan State University (1965), University of California at Los Angeles (1966), University of Hawaii (1968), Emory University (1970), and Duke University (1970).

The University of Nebraska remodeled over one-half of the largest building on campus to create an undergraduate library-museum-classroom facility. The University of Florida constructed a graduate library and used its older main library as an undergraduate library, but did not refurbish it. The University of California, San Diego, created a new research library and moved its Cluster I Library into the building formerly occupied by the research collection.

The trend toward separate undergraduate libraries has not been entirely unquestioned. The University of South Carolina opened its undergraduate

library in 1959 in an Edward Durell Stone designed building but later centralized library services and eliminated the undergraduate library as a separate entity. Indiana University created an undergraduate library which opened in 1963
but has now vacated it upon the completion of a new university library designed
to serve the entire university community. (A five-story tower provides undergraduate service and houses its collection; an eight-story tower houses the general book collection, seminars, carrels, and faculty studies. Connecting the two
wings are public service departments and staff work areas.) New York University and the Universities of Notre Dame, Miami, and Iowa have also elected to
follow Indiana's approach.

The Age of the Separate Undergraduate Library was concurrent with the
Golden Age of the 1960s — the Age of Higher Education — when funds seemed
to automatically increase each year. From the resulting profusion of libraries for
undergraduate students, five examples have been selected for this Section. Two
universities remodeled and refurbished their old "main libes" into undergraduate libraries (the Uris Library at Cornell and the College Library at UCLA) after
they had built new libraries on the campus to house the research collections and
services. Billy R. Wilkinson at Cornell's Uris Library and Norah E. Jones at the
UCLA College Library describe the system from their vantage points. Two other libraries which were built specially for the purpose of serving undergraduates
are also reviewed at considerable length. It must, however, be remembered that
these are partisans describing their own libraries somewhat uncritically. Jean
Cassell, who oversaw the selection of its collection describes the University of
Texas Undergraduate Library. Lucien W. White, then Associate Dean of
Library Administration, surveys the University of Illinois Undergraduate
Library. Finally, the Sedgewick Undergraduate Library, a new building
designed for undergraduates at the University of British Columbia in Vancouver, is critiqued and applauded by Ellsworth Mason from his perspective as a
building consultant.

Notes

1. Constance M. Taylor, "Meeting the Needs of Undergraduates in Large University
    Libraries" (unpublished Master's thesis, Graduate School of Library Science, Uni-
    versity of Texas, 1956), p. 51.

2. Ibid., p. 74.

Billy R. Wilkinson

The Uris Library, Cornell University

The founding and development of "this easy-going, loose-jointed institution" (as Carl Becker characterized Cornell) is summarized and the evolution over the years of the University's library is outlined. The Uris Undergraduate Library is then described. The library's function as study hall, social center, reserve book dispenser, browsing collection, and audio-visual facility is reviewed in detail. A statistical summary of the first seven years concludes the article. Reference services in Uris Library are not discussed here, but are thoroughly analyzed in Wilkinson's paper in Section VI.

Brief History of the University

Two very dissimilar men — Ezra Cornell and Andrew Dickson White — founded Cornell University in 1865. Cornell, an upstate New York mechanic and farmer, left Ithaca in 1842 to seek his fortune. When he returned thirteen years later, he had made a considerable one as a builder of telegraph systems with Samuel F. B. Morse.[1] He purchased land and began to farm it scientifically. Wishing to benefit his fellow citizens, Cornell in 1863 "proposed to build, and to endow, a great public library for Ithaca and Tompkins County."[2] Later in November, he was elected to the New York State Senate. Here he met Andrew D. White, Chairman of the Senate's Committee on Literature when Cornell's bill to incorporate the library was referred to White's committee. A partnership unique in the annals of American higher education was formed.

White, a wealthy and scholarly Yale graduate who had taught at the University of Michigan, already had an

idea of the great work that should be done in the great State of New York. Surely
. . . in the greatest state there should be the greatest of universities; in central New

---

SOURCE: From Billy R. Wilkinson, "Case II: Cornell University," *Reference Services for Undergraduate Students: Four Case Studies* (Metuchen, N.J.: Scarecrow Press, 1972), pp. 139-173. Copyright 1972 by Billy R. Wilkinson. Reprinted by permission of the publisher.

York there should arise a university which by the amplitude of its endowment and by the whole scope of its intended sphere, by the character of the studies in the whole scope of the curriculum, should satisfy the wants of the hour.[3]

After Cornell's first philanthropic venture — the public library — he still had a great desire

to dispose of so much of my property as is not required for the reasonable wants of my family, in a manner that shall do the greatest good to the greatest number of the industrial classes of my native state, and at the same time to do the greatest good to the state itself, by elevating the character and standard of knowledge of the industrial and productive classes.[4]

Thus a university "where any person can find instruction in any study"[5] became a reality with Ezra Cornell's endowment, plus funds from the sale of western lands provided in the Morrill Act of 1862, and with the leadership of Andrew Dickson White as the first President. Cornell University opened on October 7, 1868 with 412 students (332 freshmen, 80 with advanced credit); a small faculty (one member being Daniel Willard Fiske, Professor of North European Languages, Librarian, and Director of the University Press); and two completed buildings.[6]

From these auspicious and innovative beginnings, the University has flourished during the past century.

For perhaps the first time in history, courses in agriculture, engineering, and veterinary medicine were taught on a level with the humanities. It is unique today in its peculiar and diverse organization, where we find certain units — the College of Arts and Sciences, the Medical College, the Law School and the School of Hotel Administration, and the Colleges of Architecture and Engineering — existing as private, endowed colleges, while others [the College of Argiculture for example] are supported as "contract colleges" by the State of New York.[7]

The main Ithaca campus of more than 90 major buildings and 700 acres is now home to twelve schools and colleges. The School of Nursing and the Medical College are in New York City. During the Fall semester, 1969, 10,042 undergraduates and 4,098 graduate students were enrolled for a total of 14,140 students on the Ithaca campus. Men numbered 10,743; there were 3,397 women.[8] During the same semester, 1,805 full-time faculty members were employed in Ithaca.[9] The number of part-time faculty was approximately 2,000.

Cornell University is accredited by the Middle States Association of Colleges and Secondary Schools.

The College of Arts and Sciences

A single faculty guided Cornell until 1887 when the College of Law separated. In 1896 other departments and colleges were formed with the Academic Department as the forerunner of the College of Arts and Sciences.[10] (The official renaming came in 1903). The College had 631 undergraduate students by 1898/99; 1,424 by 1915/16.[11] Throughout its history, the College has attracted a distinguished faculty and offered its students, through one of the freest of elective systems, a wide range of courses. In addition to the education of its own students, the College plays a second role as a university college and is responsible for the education of all Cornell students in liberal subjects.

In the 1969 Fall semester, 3,241 undergraduate students were enrolled in the College of Arts and Sciences. There were 1,139 women and 2,102 men. The freshmen numbered 770.[12] The full-time College faculty members totalled 622 in the same semester.[13]

This, briefly, is Cornell University and its largest component, the College of Arts and Sciences. The 10,042 university undergraduates, and more particularly the 3,241 underclassmen of the College, are the largest group of potential library users at the University.

The Cornell University Library

Few universities have had a President who believed so strongly in and worked so successfully for a great university library as Cornell had in its first President, Andrew Dickson White. To White "the ideas of a university and a great library were so inseparably related that one predicated the other."[14] In his organizational plan for the University, he wrote:

> A large library is absolutely necessary to the efficiency of the various departments. Without it, our men of the highest ability will be frequently plodding in old circles and stumbling into old errors.[15]

The Board of Trustees backed White with funds, appropriating in February, 1868, $11,000 for the purchase of books. In the Spring, White traveled over Europe shopping for books and equipment. Having already collected a fine personal library, "he knew how to buy well, occasionally indulging in a bibliophile's weakness for the care and scholarly volumes which are today Cornell's treasures."[16] When he had spent the appropriated funds, he used his own money or appealed to Ezra Cornell.

The first of the Library's great collections was a gift by Cornell before the University opened. He purchased in July, 1868, the 7,000-volume library of classical literature collected by Charles Anthon of Columbia College. White recorded that Cornell's

> liberality was unstinted . . . . Nothing could apparently be more outside his sympathy than the department needing these seven thousand volumes; but he recognized its importance in the general plan of the new institution, bought the library for over twelve thousand dollars, and gave it to the university.[17]

The President and the Founder were soon joined by the first Librarian to form a trinity of extraordinary library benefactors. White invited Willard Fiske, an old friend from their boyhood days in Syracuse, to the staff of the University.

An excellent linguist, he was fitted for his professorship of north European languages. Well trained in the best American scholarly library [seven years as Assistant Librarian of the Astor Library in New York], and a true bibliolater, he was equally well equipped to establish Cornell's Library. A practiced journalist, he could supervise Cornell's publications and serve as an unofficial Director of Public Information.[18]

The University Library's home was in Morrill Hall, the first building on the campus. "By January, 1869, the Library numbered 15,400 volumes — more than Columbia College had acquired in a hundred years."[19] In June, 1871, there were 27,500 volumes. The Library then moved to McGraw Hall when it was completed in 1872.

The Cornell Library was a reference library, patterned on the Astor and the Bodleian Libraries. With this concept of non-circulation, there was a need to make the volumes available to the faculty and students. Fiske from the first had the Library open nine hours each day — longer, he boasted, than in any other American university.[20]

Together Fiske and White continuously and systematically strengthened the collection. Goldwin Smith, the brilliant professor from England who taught at Cornell, gave his personal library. The Franz Bopp philological library and the Kelly Collection of the history of mathematics and the exact sciences were purchased; Samuel Joseph May, the abolitionist, gave his Antislavery Collection; the Jared Sparks Collection in American History and the 13,000-volume Zarncke library of German literature came to Cornell; and other collections enriched the holdings.[21]

This progress in the development of the Cornell Library, however, was interrupted. Rita Guerlac has recorded the extraordinary events:

In the 1880's the Cornell University Library was the center, and Willard Fiske one of the principal figures, of a drama which rocked the University and the community. John McGraw, one of the first trustees of the University and the donor of the building which first housed the Library, died in 1877, leaving his whole estate to his only daughter Jennie. Jennie McGraw had been a friend of the University since its founding, and had given the chime of nine bells that rang out for the first time at the inauguration exercises. . . . In 1880 she married Willard Fiske in Berlin; she died a year later. Her will, after bequests to her husband and her McGraw cousins, left to Cornell University the residue of her estate, amounting to almost two million dollars, part of which was designated for a library and other gifts and the rest for unrestricted use. It was a princely bequest. 'The creation of such a library would have been the culmination of my work,' wrote White. 'I could then have sung my *Nunc dimittis.*'

But a question arose as to the legality of the University's accepting the bequest, because its Charter restricted the size of the Corporation's endowment. While the University turned its attention to this problem, personal complications arose between two of the trustees and Willard Fiske. Mr. Fiske, indignant, and not without provocation, resigned from the University in 1883 and undertook to break his wife's will; the McGraw cousins, on the advice of trustee Henry Sage, joined him in his suit. Ithacans took sides and feeling ran high; outsiders followed the story in the press. The case was contested over seven years, and went finally to the Supreme Court of the United States, which, in May 1890, decided against the University. The litigation had by then consumed almost a quarter of the estate; half went to the McGraw heirs and the final quarter to Willard Fiske.[22]

All was not lost to the University and its Library. The legal limitation on the size of the University's endowment was removed. But more importantly, Henry W. Sage decided to pay for the new library building which Jennie McGraw Fiske had intended in her will. A site on the main quadrangle was selected and William Henry Miller was chosen as architect. The stone building with its tower was completed and opened on October 7, 1891. Sage gave the University $260,000 for the construction costs and $300,000 as an endowment — the interest would purchase books annually for the collection.[23] The local newspaper described the building as being "somewhat in the form of a Greek cross, . . . treated in a style that may be called modified Romanesque."[24] The Library had a stack capacity of 475,000 volumes, or over four times the 1891 holdings (ca. 114,330; 84,330 volumes in the main collection and some 30,000 in the White Historical Library) .[25] The new Library

> soon enjoyed a national reputation . . . when Secretary Thwaites of the Wisconsin Historical Society returned to Madison in 1895 from a visit to fourteen Eastern and two Southern cities . . . he reported to the Wisconsin Board of Library Building Commissioners regarding the Cornell Library: '. . . This is by far the best planned and best built university library building in this country.'[26]

President White gave his personal collection of 30,000 volumes, 10,000 pamphlets, and many manuscripts. "Called the most valuable private historical library collected in the United States"[27] it was installed in a special room — "a delightful example of Millerian gothic-romanesque-baroque"[28] — in the new building.

Willard Fiske, who had retired to a villa in Florence, left the University a large bequest upon his death in 1904. But to the Library he bequeathed four magnificent collections which are particular treasures: his 7,000-volume Dante Collection, a 3,500-volume Petrarch Collection, a library of Rhaeto-Romantic literature, and his 10,000-volume Icelandic Collection.[29]

In his 1905 *Autobiography,* Andrew Dickson White wrote of his pride in the development of the Library:

> The library has become, as a whole, one of the best in the country. As I visit it,

there often come back vividly to me remembrances of my college days, when I was wont to enter the Yale library and stand amazed in the midst of the sixty thousand volumes which had been brought together during one hundred and fifty years. They filled me with awe. But Cornell has now, within forty years from its foundation, accumulated very nearly three hundred thousand volumes, many among them of far greater value than anything contained in the Yale library of my day.[30]

George William Harris succeeded Fiske as Librarian. He served the Library for forty-two years, thirty-two of them as head Librarian. After the move into the new building, there was a period of "largely uneventful years, devoted to keeping the Library going rather than growing."[31] Harris continued the policy of a non-circulating, reference library until 1908 when the Library Council decided to permit home loans. The inevitable flaws were found in the building: poor ventilation in certain rooms, the need for more radiators in the stacks, and an overestimation of the stack capacity (by 1904 Harris begun requesting more stack space). Harris is most remembered, however, for the book classification system he adopted — a fixed shelf location device based on the British Museum scheme.[32]

The period from 1915 until 1946 was a general decline into chaos. The Librarians—Willard Austin, 1915-1929, and Otto Kinkeldey, 1930-1945 — pleaded for more space, more funds, and more staff, but their pleas were unanswered by University administrators. "The space nightmare took on a Kafkaesque quality. The Library was bulging."[33]

The University Library, 1946-1969

Once again, a "forceful and imaginative Librarian and a President who [believed] in the Library and its central importance to the intellectual life of the University"[34] came together to bring order out of chaos. President Edmund Ezra Day in 1946 invited Stephen A. McCarthy to take charge of the Library. With Day's promised support, McCarthy directed the Library toward recovery. The administration of the Library was reorganized and new staff members were appointed: Felix Reichmann and G. F. Shepherd, Jr. in two key positions and Frances W. Lauman and Josephine M. Tharpe as Cornell's first reference librarians. Studies were made of the space problem and a survey[35] by outside experts gave recommendations for improving the Library and "strong support to the initiative of the new Librarian."[36] On January 1, 1948, the staff began the use of the Library of Congress classification and the long task of reclassifying all pre-1948 holdings from the Harris system to that of the Library of Congress.

It was President Deane W. Malott, 1951-1963, however, who "saw the central importance of the Library and the urgency of its problems, made their solution his first priority, and quietly carried it through to a splendid conclusion."[37]

During the McCarthy years, all campus libraries were completely rehoused in new or renovated quarters. Beginning in 1950 with the A. R. Mann Library, which serves the colleges of Agriculture and Human Ecology, the building program culminated with the 1961 opening of the John M. Olin Library (the "first university library building in this country designed and constructed for research"[38]) and the 1962 reopening of the renovated main library building as the Uris Undergraduate Library. The Olin Library, built and furnished at a cost of $5,700,000, occupies a prominent position on the College of Arts and Sciences quadrangle. Its seven floors and two lower levels have a stack capacity of two million volumes.

When Stephen A. McCarthy resigned as Director of Libraries in 1967 to become Executive Director of the Association of Research Libraries, a distinguished era in the development of the Cornell Libraries ended. Under his leadership the collections more than doubled (1,206,195 volumes in June, 1946; 3,067,073 in June, 1967); the number of professional staff members doubled (62.5 in October, 1947; 120 in 1967); reference questions tripled (28,939 in 1950/51; 92,217 in 1966/67); total recorded use was 2.2 times greater (526,361 in 1950/51; 1,172,530 in 1966/67); and library expenditures in his last year were eleven times more than his first year ($361,251 in 1946/47; $4,096,779 in 1966/67).[39]

During 1967/68, G. F. Shepherd, Jr., Associate Director, was Acting Director. David Kaser became Director of Libraries on August 1, 1968.

Table 1 shows the growth and use of the University Libraries during their first century.

The Users

A survey[40] of all persons entering the Olin Library was conducted January 10-13, 1967. Of the 5,251 persons who answered the brief questions concerning their status at the University and their purpose in coming to the Library, undergraduate students were most numerous (47.3%). Graduate students (38.2%) and faculty members (11.7%) were the other major users with the research staff (0.5%) and others (2.3%) forming very small proportions.

When all users were asked what they planned to do in the Library, the responses were:

Course assignment or class preparation	25.3%
Research	27.4
Some of both	11.4
Other plans	10.1
No response to question	25.8

During the same period, 511 persons asked questions at the Olin Library reference desks. Their university statuses were:

Undergraduates	42.7%
Graduate students	31.9
Faculty	17.0
Others	8.4

The categories of borrowers of 3,906 volumes at the Olin circulation desk during January 10-13, 1967 were:

Undergraduates	40.3%
Graduate students	40.8
Faculty	12.3
Others	6.6

Table 1 — Volumes and Recorded Use, Cornell University
Libraries, 1869-1969[a]

Year	Volumes on June 30	Total Recorded Use of Materials During Previous Year
1869	18,000	...
1876	39,000	...
1891	96,000	...
1900	250,000	...
1920	655,000	...
1940	1,063,000	...
1946	1,206,195	...
1951	1,505,728	526,361
1958	1,967,599	744,656
1959	2,043,026	811,182
1960	2,116,230	873,903
1961	2,198,654	958,946
1962	2,278,046	967,515
1963	2,413,369	1,060,554
1964	2,577,296	1,140,085
1965	2,725,624	1,203,690
1966	2,892,539	1,178,885
1967	3,067,073	1,172,530
1968	3,257,399	1,269,052
1969	3,444,570	1,310,509

[a] Cornell University. Library. *The Cornell University Library, Some Highlights* (Ithaca: The Library, 1965).
Cornell University. Library. *Reports of the Director of the University Libraries.* 1950/51-1968/69.

The Staff

In 1969, the staff of the University Libraries was composed of 136 professionals and 251 full-time non-academic employees. Many part-time employees (in full-time equivalents: 92.25) worked a total of 189,915.75 hours during 1968/69. The total number of FTE staff members was 479.25.[41] The professionals have the following titles: Assistant Librarian, Senior Assistant Librarian, Associate Librarian, and Librarian. These staff members work in the Olin Library, the Uris Library, and thirteen other libraries on the Ithaca campus.

Library Budget

During the early 1960's, with the opening of the Olin and Uris Libraries, substantial increases in funds were allocated by the University for library personnel. Funds for books and other materials were also increased. In 1959/60, the total library expenditures (including the Medical Library in New York City and other non-Ithaca libraries) were $1,650,995. By 1962/63, when both new libraries were in operation, the total library expenditures were $2,711,166. During 1968/69, $5,011,500 was expended for the entire library system.[42]

The Future

Adequate space for housing the Cornell collections has again become a problem. Six linear miles of new shelving are required each year to keep pace with the present rate of growth in the campus libraries. In order to plan for the future needs of the libraries, the University appointed a 15-member faculty-administration Library Study Committee in the Fall Semester, 1969. Under the chairmanship of Professor Francis E. Mineka, the Committee began a year-long study of the problem.[43]

The Uris Library

There were a series of abortive plans going back to 1925 for relieving the crowded conditions of the University Library. The schemes were either additions to the building, the use of Boardman Hall (the neighboring building on the quadrangle) as an annex, or the construction of a new building. After the appointment of McCarthy as Librarian, further efforts were made to solve the Cornell library problem. Finally, Keyes D. Metcalf and Frederic C. Wood[44] were retained as consultants to restudy the situation.

> The two consultants visited the campus, conferred with library and administrative officers, reviewed previous plans, studied the present library building, proposed sites, etc. The consultants also conferred with each other. Each consultant submitted his own report, and both participated in a joint meeting of the Administration and the Library Board on July 21 [1955], at which the reports were presented orally and discussed. The recommendations of the consultants won the full support of the Administration and the Library Board.[45]

The recommendations made by Wood and Metcalf were:

1. Retention of the main library by conversion into an undergraduate library, and

2. demolition of Boardman Hall and use of its site for the construction of a new research library which would primarily serve graduate students and faculty.[46]

Their plan had excellent points in favor of its adoption: the old Library with its tower which had become a landmark and the symbol of Cornell would be preserved; Libe Slope, a lovely hill behind the Library, would not be violated (it had become hallowed ground to many generations of Cornellians as the scene of commencements and reunions in the Spring and tray-sliding in Winter); and the two-building central library complex could serve all members of the University community in its choice location on the main quad.

The plan had one great disadvantage: the demolition of Boardman Hall. Although the building was old, needed extensive repair work, and had much unusable space, it was also venerated as the previous home of the Law School and later as home to the Departments of History and Government with the offices of such illustrative professors as Carl Becker.

The Executive Committee of the Cornell University Board of Trustees adopted the Wood-Metcalf proposals on October 13, 1955 — "a two-building central library, consisting of a new Graduate and Research Library on the site of Boardman Hall and the present Library Building remodeled and converted into an undergraduate library"[47] became official policy.

Efforts were concentrated on the research library building after the drafting in 1956 of a preliminary program[48] for the undergraduate library which "served as a basis for the schematic plans developed by the architect in connection with the planning of the Research Library."[49] In 1958 a Committee on the Undergraduate Library, organized as a subcommittee of the Library Board (an advisory group of faculty members), was appointed by the Provost of the University. Professor Robert M. Adams chaired the committee of six faculty members and three librarians (Stephen A. McCarthy; G. F. Shepherd, Jr.; and Charles A. Carpenter, Jr., Librarian of the Goldwin Smith Library). The subcommittee reviewed the preliminary program and approved a final program[50] for the conversion of the old Library into an undergraduate library. The program called for 1,000-1,200 seats, capacity for 100,000-150,000 volumes, audio equipment, a room for library orientation and other lectures, and various reading rooms. The program stated that

The Reference Department performs the chief teaching function of the Library. The Reference Collection will consist of 2000-3000 volumes of bibliographies, indexes, encyclopedias, handbooks, etc. The Reference Room should be close to the card catalog and the Circulation Department.[51]

The Building

The architects of the new John M. Olin Library— Warner, Burns, Toan, and Lunde — were appointed in June, 1959 to draw plans for the major renovation. When the Olin Library was completed in early 1961, all volumes and equipment were moved through a new tunnel connecting the two libraries. The old Main Library was closed on Feburary 1, 1961 after seventy years of service. Later that year, work was begun on interior renovation; the exterior of the 1891 building was to remain unchanged.

For a total expenditure of $1,232,192 (including $144,375 for furnishings),[52] Cornell University created an undergraduate library of 50,000 square feet with 1,067 seats and a book capacity of 125,000 volumes. A major portion of the costs was given by Harold D. and Percy Uris, for whom the building was named the Uris Library. Arthur H. Dean also contributed substantially and the main reading room was named in his honor.

At 8 A.M., September 19, 1962, the Uris Library quietly opened for use (the fanfare being saved until October 9-10, when the Olin and Uris Libraries were dedicated in a long-remembered program climaxed with a special concert by the Philadelphia Orchestra). In contrast to its forebears — the Lamont Library and the University of Michigan Undergraduate Library — the Uris Library was not a modern building designed to meet the needs of undergraduates, but

> it is generally agreed that architect Charles Warner and his associates were pecul-
> iarly sensitive in planning the remodeling in that they preserved and enhanced
> many of the fine architectural features of the building and yet produced a good,
> functional, modern library.[53]

The Collection

The Goldwin Smith Library — a select collection of 8,000 volumes (6,200 titles) strong in American and English literature, philosophy, and drama, situated in a classroom building with a reading room for undergraduate students, and the reserve book desk of the University Library for courses in the Departments of English, Speech and Drama, Romance Literature, German Literature, Philosophy, and Classics—was the foundation upon which the collection for the Uris Library was built. In May, 1959, the Subcommittee on the Undergraduate Library proposed to the faculty of the College of Arts and Sciences that the shelflist of a recently established undergraduate library be obtained, divided among the various disciplines, and distributed to the departments for revisions and additions. Assured of the faculty's cooperation, the shelflist of the University of Michigan Undergraduate Library was distributed in September, 1959, to be used in the selection of titles. Charles A. Carpenter, Jr., Goldwin Smith Librarian, also compiled a list of approximately 11,000 titles. To this file were then added titles from reserve book lists, syllabi, and recommended reading lists.

When the faculty recommendations were returned, the Library had its shopping list for the undergraduate collection.

The purchase of the stock of the Pyetell Bookshop in Pelham, N.Y., the transfer of duplicate copies from the research library's collection, the purchase of in-print titles, the cataloging and processing of the volumes, and other details of assembling the collection — all done under the direction of Felix Reichmann — are described by Irene A. Braden.[54]

A committee of the library staff selected the periodical titles which would be duplicated in the Uris Library. Approximately 250 titles were initially selected (some 80 of these were designated to have complete or 10-year backfiles). A list of the desired backfiles were sent to the faculty and also appeared in the *Cornell Alumni News*. These appeals prompted numerous gifts.

Recommendations for the reference collection were made by the reference staff in the Olin Library. When Frances W. Lauman, Associate Reference Librarian, was named Reference Librarian-designate of the Uris Library in July, 1961, she assumed the task of final selection for the reference collection, which numbered approximately 1,780 volumes during the first year of operation.[55] The spoken arts recordings for the Listening Rooms were selected by the Uris Library staff. No musical recordings were included because the Music Library maintained an extensive collection.

The Uris Library was to contain no microforms or bound backfiles of newspapers. The Department of Maps, Microtexts, and Newspapers, in the adjacent Olin Library, would serve undergraduates needing these materials.

The Uris Library opened with a book collection of 42,722 volumes. The main collection was housed in one wing of the building on seven levels of bookstacks. The holdings have increased to 83,485 volumes (June 30, 1969). Table 2 traces the yearly growth.

Upon the opening of Uris Library, the professional staff members began to assist the Undergraduate Librarian in selecting titles to be added to the collection. In addition to recommending current publications, several librarians with special subject backgrounds strengthened portions of the collection by recommending retrospective titles. Individual faculty members have also surveyed a subject area and suggested purchases.

Table 2 — Volumes and Titles in the Uris Library, Cornell University, 1962-1969[a]

Year	Volumes on June 30 of Each Year	Titles
1962	ca. 30,000[b]	..
1963	46,404	..
1964	52,032	..
1965	57,103	..
1966	64,517	42,587
1967	71,906	47,493
1968	79,038	52,421
1969	83,485	55,123

[a] Cornell University. Library. Uris Library. *Annual Reports.* 1952/63-1968/69.
[b] On September 19, 1962 (Opening day) there were 42,722 volumes.

Subscriptions for additional periodicals were also continually considered. By June 30, 1965, the number of periodicals received had reached 282; by June 30, 1969, 347 periodicals were received.[56] In 1969, the Uris Library received 10 newspapers.

The Staff

No formal studies were done of undergraduate use of the old Main Library in order to gather data for estimating the size staff necessary for the Uris Library.[57] The chaotic, crowded conditions during the building's last ten years of service precluded any meaningful studies. As the planning of the Uris Library progressed, the top University administrators asked Director McCarthy and his associates for an estimate of the staff needed to operate Uris Library for its first several years, not just the opening-day staff. The University administrators realized that the Library "had been running at a very low level for a long time and was staffed at approximately that low level."[58] It was completely understood that the two new buildings would require a substantial increase in the number of staff members. During 1960/61, McCarthy submitted an estimated salary budget for the Undergraduate Library staff. It was then planned that the staff would "consist of 23-25 members, approximately 10 of whom will be professional librarians and the remainder clerical or subprofessional."[59] Funds were then officially allocated for a staff of 22 full-time persons (9 librarians and 13 subprofessionals). All were new positions in the library system. Wages for part-time student assistants were also budgeted.

Several years before the opening of Uris Library, Charles A. Carpenter, Jr. was named as Librarian-designate of the Undergraduate Library. When he resigned to work on a doctorate in the Department of English at Cornell, Billy R. Wilkinson was appointed in July, 1961 to succeed him. During the 1961/62 academic year, Wilkinson was in charge of the small Goldwin Smith Library and assisted the Library administration in planning the the service program and assembling the book collection of Uris Library, then under renovation. Frances W. Lauman was also designated as the future head of reference services in Uris Library, over a year in advance of the opening. During 1961/62, she continued as Associate Reference Librarian in the Olin Library. By April 4, 1962, five additional staff members had been selected to transfer to Uris Library on September 1, 1962.[60] Experienced librarians thus formed the nucleus of the first Uris Library staff. A search was then begun for librarians for the other positions. During the summer of 1962, applicants for the non-professional positions were invited.

During 1962/63, the Uris staff was comprised of 9 librarians, 13 non-professional staff members, and approximately 50 part-time student assistants. By June 30, 1969, the full-time staff still numbered 22 persons, but the professional positions had decreased from 9 to 7 and the non-professional positions had increased from 13 to 15. Part-time student and non-student employees worked a total of 16,116 hours during 1968/69.[61]

The Librarian of the Uris Library has always reported to G. F. Shepherd, Jr., Assistant Director for Readers Services and later Associate Director of University Libraries.

The technical service departments of the John M. Olin Library perform most of the acquiring and processing tasks for Uris Library materials. The Uris staff selects, searches, and prepares orders for its own monographs and serials, which are then acquired, processed, and returned to Uris ready for use. Two exceptions, however, have existed to this general rule: beginning in 1966, orders for Reserve Desk copies were taken directly by the Uris staff to a local bookstore and when the books were received, they were sent to the Olin Acquisitions and Catalog Departments for rush processing. From the beginning, recordings for the Listening Rooms were ordered and received directly by the Uris staff who also cataloged the recordings.

Wilkinson's Tenure, 1962-1967

Billy R. Wilkinson served as Librarian of the Uris Library during its first five years. He and the staff saw the building win acceptance by the Cornell undergraduates during the first year. During 1962/63, Uris Library had an attendance of 705,251 persons; 125,488 volumes used in the Library; 64,072 home loans; 2,247 listeners in the Listening Rooms; and 6,609 questions asked at the reference desk.[62]

During the first years, the Library had an unusually experienced staff who knew the University and its library system and who were interested in working with undergraduate students. The staff members were also flexible; during the summers when Uris Library was completely or partially closed, various staff members worked in departments of the Olin Library or other campus libraries.

The collection and access to it were kept in good order by complete annual inventories. Only approximately 1% or less of the volumes in the main collection was missing each year.

Physical improvements were made in the building. The large Dean Reading Room and other areas on the main floor were carpeted in December, 1965. One of the reading rooms on the lower level was completely redecorated and carpeted in 1966-67 with a gift from Allan P. Kirby as a memorial to his brother, Sumner M. Kirby, who had attended Cornell.

Progress was also made in improving the book funds. Allocations from the University were gradually increased and then Uris Library was endowed by Allan P. Kirby with the Sumner M. Kirby Memorial Fund of $100,000 (the yearly income would purchase volumes in American history, economics, and sociology and also refurbish the Kirby Room as necessary). Another generous benefactor was the Iota Chapter of Kappa Alpha Theta Sorority which gave in 1966 a fund of $35,000 for the establishment and support of a Cornelliana Collection in the President Andrew D. White Library — the triple-tiered "gothic-romanesque-baroque"[63] room which had been preserved in the conversion of the building into an undergraduate library. The annual income from the Kappa Alpha Theta Fund purchased books concerning the University as well as those by and about its faculty and students. The University Press also helped in establishing a collection of its publications.

Arthur H. Dean, Chairman of the University Board of Trustees, also continued his generous support. As one of his many gifts to the Library, he began a series of book collection contests in 1966. Cash awards were presented to six undergraduate students who were judged to have the best private collections. The Uris Library staff organized and conducted the competitions and the receptions held in the White Library for the participants.[64]

All was not sweetness and light, however, during this period in the Uris Library. Complaints were received from students and staff about noise in the Library, particularly at night and in the main lobby, Dean Reading Room, and adjacent areas. Installation of additional acoustical tile in the lobby and carpeting of the main floor partially alleviated the noise problem created by many socializing students.

Another problem during the first years of the Uris Library was the lack of a formal means of communication with a representative group of students. No attempt was made during 1962-1965 to initiate a committee of undergraduate students who would advise the Librarian and the staff concerning the policies and services of Uris Library. When a Committee on Undergraduate Library Service — two students, two librarians (the Undergraduate Librarian and the Associate Director of Libraries), and one faculty member — was formed in 1966, it was a substitute for the students' request for representation on the all-faculty Library Board. Five meetings[65] were held during 1966/67, but

> From the view point of both the students and the librarians, it would probably be agreed that the committee was not a smashing success. The reasons for the failure were many and complicated, but basically the whole intemperate climate of student-administration relationships kept hovering over the meetings. Perhaps the committee should be given a second year in order to function more successfully.[66]

There was no second year.

Other problems (the decline in use of the Listening Rooms, the decline in the number of questions asked at the reference desk, and the failure to develop a program of library instruction other than the one-hour orientation lecture for freshmen) are discussed in succeeding sections.

Rucker's Librarianship, 1967-

Ronald E. Rucker was appointed Acting Librarian of Uris Library on September 1, 1967 upon the resignation of Wilkinson who became a doctoral student at the Columbia University School of Library Service. Rucker had previously directed the Central Serial Record Department in the Olin Library. He was named Librarian of Uris Library in 1968.

During Rucker's tenure, the collection has reached 83,485 volumes (June 30, 1969) and the staff "embarked on a program of selective retirement"[67] of obsolete volumes. Books of little interest to undergraduates were removed from the collection, with additional weeding to be done in the future.

Improvements continued to be made in physical facilities. The lecture room on the lower level was redecorated and carpeted in 1968 with funds given by Mrs. Oscar Seager as a memorial to her husband. A long-neglected room on the ninth level of the bookstack was also refurbished the same year, with the aid of a special grant, and became the seminar room of the Greek Civilization Study Program.

The Cornelliana Collection in the White Library grew to 1,112 volumes by June 30, 1969. Frances W. Lauman was appointed Curator of the Collection in the Autumn of 1967.

The Uris staff worked intimately with small groups of undergraduates through the continuation of the Arthur H. Dean Book Collection Contest. Contact was established with three fraternities by assisting with their house libraries. Suggestions were made as to material which might be discarded and purchases were recommended for improving the small libraries. Recommendations of titles were also made for a small collection in the Noyes Center, the second student center on the campus.

Tentative planning was done for a new Commons Library, which would be a Uris Library branch situated in the residence hall complex under construction on the North Campus. Scheduled for completion in Fall, 1971, the Commons Library was envisioned by Ronald Rucker as a library of several thousand volumes where "the emphasis will be placed on a solid reference section, recreational reading and congenial study space with a highly selective collection providing the basic materials for the teaching fields of undergraduate concern."[68] However, after an indefinite postponement of the branch library because of a lack of funds, it was decided in November, 1970 to eliminate completely the Commons Library.[69]

As the financial problems of the University have affected the Uris Library in its projected branch in the new student residence area, other contemporary University problems have directly touched the Library's users and staff.

In December [1968] the deep-seated dissatisfaction with life at Cornell felt by many black students brought them to Uris among other libraries to protest the alleged irrelevance of the book collections. The demonstration, which involved piling books taken at random from the shelves on the Circulation Desk, seemed to be an early skirmish in the sequence of events that led to the occupation of Willard Straight Hall in April [1969]. As the atmosphere of tension on campus reached a peak on the Tuesday evening following the weekend of occupation, there were rumors that Uris was among the buildings to be seized.[70]

There was no take-over of Uris Library, but

In the days that followed, the Library was deserted most of the time and in fact normal levels of usage were not experienced during the remainder of the term. This situation allowed the staff considerable time to talk among themselves and a number of specific proposals were put forward concerning our response to campus events.[71]

Several of the proposals were acted upon, such as assembling a collection of books, periodicals, pamphlets, and newspaper clippings on student dissent. The materials were intensively used. However,

> There remain within the Uris staff considerable differences of opinion as to the role of the Library. Some strongly support its apolitical stance; some believe we are too bound to passivity; and others probably have simply refrained from speaking their minds. Probably to all, however, it seems necessary to re-examine what we are doing and why.[72]

Other aspects of the Rucker administration are discussed in the following sections on Uris Library's roles as campus study hall, social center, reserve book dispenser, browsing collection, audio-visual facility, and reference center.

Uris as Study Hall

The first *Annual Report* of the Uris Library recorded that:

> the Library immediately began fulfilling its functions as the much needed open-stack basic book collection and study space for the Cornell undergraduates.
> During the first year, the Uris Library had a total attendance of 705,251—an average of 2,722 for each of the 259 days open during the 1962/63 year. The highest single day's attendance on January 15, 1963 was 5,959.[73]

The attendance increased by 7.5% during the second year and then remained basically the same until 1967/68 when there was a 6.8% decrease (Table 3). The attendance decreased another 7.7% during 1968/69.

Although no formal studies have been done to ascertain the exact number of students who come to Uris Library to study exclusively from their own materials, the number is large. One survey[74] conducted January 10-13, 1967 does support this deduction. Persons entering the Library were asked "What do you plan to do in the Library today?" and were asked to check one of the following four responses: (1) Course assignment or class preparation; (2) Research; (3) Some of both; or (4) Other. Undergraduate students outnumbered graduate students 14 to 1 (5,990 undergraduates: 420 graduate students) in the Uris Library. In the Olin Library during the same four days, the number of undergraduates only slightly outnumbered the graduate students (2,483 to 2,007). In the two libraries, the undergraduates gave the following responses as to their library plans:

	Uris Library (N = 5,990)	Olin Library (N = 2,483)
Course Assign. or Class Prepar.	53.5%	35.9%
Research	5.7	16.3
Some of Both	8.5	10.7
Other Plans	7.8	10.2
Left Blank	24.5	26.9

Although the percentage of those who left the question blank is high, over half of the undergraduates in the Uris Library were doing course assignments. Much of this was probably with materials they brought with them or with reserve books. The significant difference between the undergraduates in the Uris and Olin Libraries is the larger number who intended to do "research" in the Olin Library.

If there is no exact data on the number of students using Uris Library as a place to study their own materials, the observations of past and present Uris staff members confirm that large numbers of students use it as a study hall. When asked in interviews whether the Library was a success as a study hall, the librarians unanimously agreed that it was extremely successful as a study hall. The Director of University Libraries summarized for many of the staff:

> Uris Library is very effective as a study place; the variation and kind of accommodations — the totally "camp" atmosphere of the whole building with its little nooks and crannies — make it extremely functional as a study hall.[75]

During the past three years, the Uris Library has not been open past its regular closing at 12 Midnight as a late-night study hall. In 1966/67 when the closing hour was 11:30 P.M., a study hall from 11:30 P.M. until 1 A.M. was provided during examination periods in several rooms on the lower level.

Table 3 — Attendance, Uris Library, Cornell University, 1962-1969[a]

Year[b]	Number of Persons Exiting Building	Percentage of Increase or Decrease
Sept. 19, 1962- June 15, 1963	705,251	. .
1963/64	758,331	+7.5
1964/65	752,583	-0.8
1965/66	739,126	-1.8
1966/67	742,596	+0.5
1967/68	691,624	-6.9
1968/69	638,344	-7.7

[a]Cornell University. Library. Uris Library. *Annual Reports.* 1962/63-1968/69.
[b]Uris Library has usually been completely or partially closed from the end of the Spring semester in late May or early June until mid-September.

Uris as Social Center

The rites of Spring were celebrated in the Uris Library in April, 1968 when someone anonymously distributed over the building many mimeographed copies of the following poem. (Two references in the poem may need explication for non-Cornellians: Alan Funt gave the Psychology Department video tapes prepared for his "Candid Camera" television program; Straight-shooters connotes Willard Straight Hall, the student union.)

IT'S ALL HAPPENING AT THE ZOO

Welcome to Uris
>Did you ever visit the zoo
>>Animals are ever so amusing
And Art Linkletter is quite right, you know
Ferlinghetti's island has my mind, you see
>If I knew Alan Funt was coming
>>I'd of burnt a cake
>>>But the smoke would be blinding
And there's ever so much smog about
>What with kappa cool
>>>>sigma skin
>>>>>pi protest
>>>>>>>et al.
But the minstrels are asking
>Have you noticed you're alive
And the Straight-shooters are asking
>Are you happy
But they don't care
>Nor do the animals
Of course it is said that hamsters
>Turn on frequently
And Art Linkletter is quite right, you know
>Though sad might be a better term
>>They say spring is best
Birds come out in the spring
>Like a peculiar game of show and tell
>And people watch
>To keep their minds from wandering
Instead of fixing a hole
But people should realize
>You can't keep the rain from coming in a cage
Make sure you see the shaven thighs
>And the shaven minds
>That's very painful to see, you understand
But so many dead people live at the zoo
>So it won't bother them

Then how is it that a perceptive few can say
> The beauty of the human race is here
> And you have created
After all
> Can't animals
> Think

Characterizing Uris Library as a zoo is too harsh, but the lines

> They say spring is best
Birds come out in the spring
> Like a peculiar game of show and tell
> And people watch
> To keep their minds from wandering

captures beautifully the social aspects of an undergraduate library not only in the Spring, but on some week-day nights throughout the year.

The Librarian had earlier and more prosaically described the Uris Library:

> The Library is a fine place to study from 8 o'clock in the morning until 7 o'clock in the evening.

> It is an impossible place to study from 7 P.M. until 10 P.M. on some nights of the week. Usually, there is just too much activity, too much coming and going, too much socializing. In short, too many lively and restless undergraduates. The good study conditions are shot down by the students themselves.

> Around 7 P.M. or a little earlier, the great entrance begins. It takes the next hour for everyone to settle down. When this is almost accomplished, it's time to wander around, smoke and talk in the lobbies and stairways, go to the Straight, etc., etc. This is the agenda for the next hour. We finally go through the settling down period again.

> From 10 P.M. until 11:30 P.M., the Library is a good study place again.[76]

The Librarian was naturally showing his age — perhaps he and the other librarians on duty at night at the reference desk, which is only separated by glass from the main lobby where most of the socializing takes place, were the ones who found it difficult to concentrate; the undergraduates who wanted to study may have had no difficulty.[77] But it is more likely that the Librarian was slightly exaggerating in order to make a stronger case for carpeting the Dean Reading Room, the reference room, the lobby, and other rooms on the main floor. Funds were appropriated for carpeting which allowed the continuation of the socializing at several decibels lower in volume.

During interviews in 1969, the Uris staff agreed that the Library continues to be a social center for the campus, but that it is no great problem. Ronald Rucker attributed the decrease in attendance during the past two years to a decline in socializing in Uris Library. The librarians also agreed that they did not act as monitors.

Uris as Reserve Book Dispenser

Throughout the history of Uris Library, the volumes circulated at the Reserve Desk have outnumbered the home loans from the main collection. Even when the main collection volumes used within the Library (not charged out) are added to the home loans, the reserve usage still outdistanced main collection use during the first six years. During the first year, reserve use amounted to 144,480 loans — over three times the 45,080 volumes used from the main collection (31,268 home loans and 13,812 volumes reshelved after use in the stacks). Reserve use rose during the next two years, reaching its high point in 1964/65 when 170,375 reserve transactions occurred. Since then, however, reserve use has declined during the four most recent years to a low point of 111,229 in 1968/69. For the first time, use of the main collection surpassed reserve use (111,229 at Reserve Desk; 113,758 volumes used from the main collection — 63,225 home loans and 50,533 volumes used within the Library in 1968/69).[78]

This pattern of declining reserve use was greatly assisted by a concentrated effort, begun by the Reserve Book Librarian in 1965/66, to call faculty members' attention to specific reserve titles which were never or rarely used. This pointing out of the "deadwood" was continued each year. By 1967, results began to show:

> A strong plea was made to more than eighty faculty members in the Spring of 1967 asking that they eliminate unused items from future reserve lists. The response was very good as the total of 7,391 volumes placed on reserve for the Fall, 1967 semester represents a 36% reduction over the previous Fall term. Under these conditions, much better and faster service was possible at the Reserve Desk. Whether or not our plea will have a lasting effect is uncertain.[79]

The number of items on reserve in the Fall semester, 1968, did increase to 8,661 from 7,391 in the previous Fall semester, but by 1969, Librarian Ronald Rucker saw "decreased dependence on reserve reading assignments and the limited exploration of library resources which this teaching approach engenders."[80] He also pointed out that

> The proportion of uncataloged items, mainly duplicated journal articles provided by the faculty member, is increasing rapidly while the number of books declines . . . [and] as has been true for years, too many works are placed on reserve and receive little or no use, rendering considerable staff time wasted.[81]

Judith H. Bossert, Reserve Book Librarian, recently worked with several professors who were willing to experiment with leaving the books to be used by their students in the open stacks of Uris Library. She also saw another trend in reserve book use with students who are themselves running their seminars under the direction of a faculty member. The students bring only the books and articles which will be used during a particular two-week period to the Reserve Desk for circulation to the seminar members.[82]

No records have been kept of the number of reserve titles and volumes purchased each year and their proportion of the total titles and volumes acquired during the year. However, expenditures for reserve books have never exceeded 36% of the total expenditures for books and recordings (this occurred in 1965/66 when $11,217.42 was spent on reserve books, out of a total budget of $31,237.72).[83] During most years, reserve book expenditures ranged from 20% to 29% of the total.[84]

In summary, definite progress has been made in whittling down the importance of Uris Library's role as reserve book dispenser, but much more progress must be made before the battle is won.

Uris as Browsing Collection

As noted in the preceding section, use of the carefully selected main collection has been overshadowed by the heavier reserve use during the early Uris years. During 1962/63, use of the main collection accounted for only 23.7% of the total book use. Use of the main collection gradually increased each year: by 1968/69, it was 50.5% of the total use.

Using Branscomb's finding that the "average student draws from the general collection of his college or university library about 12 books per year,"[85] how do Cornell undergraduates compare in their use of the Uris Library? During 1968/69, an average of 6.3 home loans from the main collection was charged to each of the 9,993 undergraduates on the Ithaca campus. However, when it is assumed that Uris primarily serves the 3,207 undergraduates in the College of Arts and Sciences, each of the College's undergraduates averaged about 19.7 home loans.[86] When the home loans and the building use of the main collection are combined, Arts and Sciences undergraduates had a per capita use of 35.5 Uris books in 1968/69. These computations do not account for volumes borrowed by undergraduates from other campus libraries.[87]

The home loans and book use within the Uris Library are detailed in Table 4.

The expenditures for the Uris main collection, reference collection, and reserve books in 1962/63 totalled $18,214.61 (additional amounts were spent: $1,000 for recordings and tapes; $3,836.78 for back files of periodicals; and $4,999.44 for binding).[88] By 1968/69, the total expenditures for the main collection, reference collection, and reserve books had increased to $26,276.45 (2,702 titles and 4,954 volumes were received during the year). A total of $16,227.89 was spent on additions to the main collection — 61.7% of the expenditures for books. Reserve books accounted for 27.3% ($7,185.71) of the expenditures and 10.9% ($2,862.85) was for additions to the reference collection. Additional amounts were also spent: $360.68 for recordings and tapes; $1,111.18 for back files of periodicals; and $2,576.61 for the Cornelliana Collection, for a grand total of $30,324.92.[89] Both binding and current subscriptions for periodicals are paid by general library funds and do not come from Uris Library allocations.

Although not a part of the main collection, an extensive collection of catalogs from both American and foreign universities and colleges is maintained on open shelves in Uris Library. In 1966, the collection contained 3,786 catalogs representing over 1,500 institutions. During 1966/67, in-library use amounted to 28,443.[90]

When questioned about the open-shelf main collection, Uris librarians and Cornell University Library administrators replied that in their estimation the collection was a success. Several librarians pointed to its increasing use each year during a period when undergraduate enrollment had not greatly increased as one indication of its success. Several of those interviewed thought that its greatest disadvantage had been the necessity to house the collection in a tiered bookstack because of the use of a renovated building. Although the stacks have been open to all users and have adjacent reading rooms, the arrangement was not as ideally suited to browsing as recently designed undergraduate libraries.

Uris as Audio-Visual Facility

As was the case at the University of Michigan Undergraduate Library, there was a substantial commitment to audio services and equipment in creating the Uris Library. However, whereas Michigan made limited provisions for visual materials, Cornell, in contrast, did nothing. Recording and tapes with listening equipment became a special collection in Uris Library, but films and other visual media have never been provided. A projection booth and equipment were planned for the lecture room on the lower level, but they were deleted from the plans for lack of funds. No exhibition space for art was included in the Library.

A suite of three rooms — a central control room with audio equipment and two listening rooms (one exclusively for sixteen individual listeners at carrels and the other for classes or group listening which can accommodate sixteen individual listeners when not in use by a group)—was designed on the upper level above the Library's main entrance. Eight desks in the adjacent White Library were also wired for sound, bringing to 40 the number of seats for individual listening available at one time. The lecture room (seating 50-70 persons) on the lower level was wired for group listening.

The Listening Rooms were first provided with six channels (one AM-FM radio, two phonograph record players, and three tape recorder-players). Two channels were later added, with further expansion still possible. The listener, after using the card catalog[91] of audio holdings, presents his request to the staff member in the control room who secures the tape or recording from storage,

Table 4 — Home Circulation and Book Use within the Library, Uris Library, Cornell University, 1962-1969[a]

Year	Home Circulation[d]	% Increase or Decrease	Book Use in Library[d]	% Increase or Decrease	Total Book Use	% Increase or Decrease
1962/63	64,072	...	125,488	...	189,560	...
1963/64	87,009	+35.8	130,297	+3.8	217,306	+14.6
1964/65	83,277	-4.3	183,823[b]	+41.1[b]	267,100[b]	+22.9[b]
1965/66	77,099	-7.4	174,109	-5.3	251,208	-5.9
1966/67	76,752	-0.4	169,493	-2.6	246,245	-3.0
1967/68	79,673	+3.8	168,677	-0.5	248,350	+0.8
1968/69	76,786	-3.6	148,201[c]	-12.1[c]	224,987[c]	-9.4[c]

[a] Cornell University. Library. Uris Library. *Annual Reports.* 1962/63-1968/69.
[b] 27,227 of the increase was of college catalogs which were included for the first time.
[c] Does not include 20,000-30,000 uses of college catalogs.
[d] Includes Reserve Books.

charges out a pair of earphones to the listener, and informs him of the channel number to which he should dial at the seat.

The collection in June, 1969 consisted of 1,140 albums of discs and 1,514 tapes (1,140 are duplicates of the albums). The collection consists of poetry, drama, speeches, prose literature, and other material in the "spoken arts" field. Most of the recordings are in English, but foreign literature in its original language is also included. However, there are no recordings for learning foreign languages; the Division of Modern Languages houses these. No musical recordings are included; the Music Library provides recordings and equipment for music and Willard Straight Hall also has a collection of musical recordings.

The number of listeners grew steadily during each of the first four years of operation. In 1962/63, 2,247 patrons (1,599 individual listeners and 648 students in 31 classes meeting in the Listening Rooms) were served. By 1965/66, 8,845 persons (5,571 individual listeners and 3,274 students in classes) used the Listening Rooms. Then, beginning in 1966/67 and continuing through 1968/69, the number of listeners declined each year, reaching a low of 4,102 (3,105 individual listeners and 952 students in classes) in 1968/69.[92]

Two factors may explain this substantial decline. During the Library's first five years, all freshmen attended an orientation lecture in the Uris classroom. At the end of the hour, an excerpt was played from one of the recordings in the Listening Rooms collection and a brief description was given of the audio facilities and their out-of-the-way location. This advertisement for the Listening Rooms was lost when the orientation lectures for freshmen were discontinued in 1967/68. Another factor is also important in the decline. Judith H. Bossert explained:

> We are not in the audio age. We're in a visual age — this is not the generation of students who grew up listening to the radio. I did; they watched television. The Listening Rooms should be showing films and television sets should be available. We should show films at four o'clock every afternoon in the Seager Room. University libraries are dragging their feet, absolutely dragging their feet over this . . . . The Listening Rooms, however, serve a function. The students seem to listen most to plays because listening, rather than just reading, brings them alive and brings an immediacy to them which the printed page lacks.[93]

David Kaser concurred:

> The kids who are with us today as undergraduates are totally visually oriented. They grew up, not with a radio as I did, but with a screen in front of them. They do not want to listen to anything; they want to watch.[94]

To revive use of the Listening Rooms, there has been an effort toward promoting the collection and facilities during the past two years:

> Several displays of new acquisitions were exhibited in Uris and bookmarks featuring an important new recording were available at several places in the building. In addition, spot announcements produced by the Listening Rooms staff were played

on radio station WVBR during the Fall term. As in past years, copies of the holdings list were sent to new faculty members in the humanities and social science disciplines.[95]

Statistical Summary of First Seven Years

As a summary of many Uris Library services — except reference assistance — the first year of operation is compared with the seventh year in Table 5.

The years were ones of growth in all areas, except for attendance in the Library, which decreased by 9.4% and the number of full-time staff, which remained the same. The increases ranged from a modest rise in the number of hours open to substantial increases in the size of the book collection, number of students using the Listening Rooms, home loans, and total book use.

Table 5. — Percentage Changes in Thirteen Variables From First to Seventh Years of Service, Uris Library, Cornell University[1]

Variable	1st Year (1962/63)	7th Year (1968/69)	% Increase or Decrease
Attendance	705,251	638,344	- 9.5
Home Loans from Circulation and Reserve Desks	64,072	76,786	+19.8
Book Use in Library-Main Stacks and Reserve Books	125,488	148,201	+18.1
Total Book Use	189,560	224,987	+18.7
Total Number of Listeners in Listening Rooms	2,247	4,102	+82.5
Collection Growth: Titles	Unknown	55,123	..
Volumes	46,404	83,485	+79.9
Total Seating Capacity	1,115	Slight Decrease	..

Table 5 — Continued

Variable	1st Year (1962/63)	7th Year (1968/69)	% Increase or Decrease
Average Weekly Hours Open	104.5	107	+2.4
Books and Periodical Articles on Reserve	14,000[2]	16,000[2]	+14.3[2]
Reserve Lists Received	325	406	+24.9
Total Full-Time Uris Library Staff (Does Not Include Part-Time Student Assistants)	22	22	0.0
Undergraduate Enrollment, College of Arts and Sciences	2,904[3]	3,207[4]	+10.4
Total Undergraduate Enrollment, Ithaca Campus, Cornell University	8,836[3]	9,993[4]	+13.1

1. Cornell University. Library. Uris Library. *Annual Reports.* 1962/63 and 1968/69; Letter from Ronald E. Rucker, Librarian, Uris Library, to Billy R. Wilkinson, September 21, 1970; Letter from Jack D. McFadden, Associate Registrar, Cornell University, to Billy R. Wilkinson, November 10, 1970.
2. Estimate.
3. Fall semester, 1962.
4. As of October 4, 1968.

Notes

1.   Morris Bishop, *A History of Cornell* (Ithaca: Cornell University Press, 1962), p. 19.

2.   Ibid., p. 21.

3.   George William Curtis [Address at the Inauguration of Cornell University, October 7, 1868] as quoted in Bishop, p. 40.

4.   Ezra Cornell, "Defense Against the Charge of Being the Founder of an 'Aristocratic' University, 1865" in Carl Becker, *Cornell University: Founders and the Founding* (Ithaca: Cornell University Press, 1943), p. 169.

5.   The motto on the Seal of Cornell University: "I would found an institution where any person can find instruction in any study."

6.   Bishop, p. 90 and p. 107.

7.   Rita Guerlac, *An Introduction to Cornell* (Ithaca: Cornell University, 1962), pp. 8-9.

8.   Cornell University. Office of the Registrar. "Registration — Fall Term 1969," October 17, 1969. (Mimeographed.)

9.   Data furnished by Office of the Dean of the University Faculty, Cornell University, November 5, 1969.

10.   Bishop, p. 323.

11.   Ibid., p. 352.

12.   Cornell University. Office of the Registrar. "Undergradaute Enrollment by Class—Fall Term 1969," October 17, 1969. (Mimeographed.)

13.   Data furnished by Office of the Dean of the University Faculty, Cornell University, November 5, 1969.

14.   Rita Guerlac, "Cornell's Library," *Cornell Library Journal* No. 2 (Spring, 1967): 1.

15.   Andrew D. White, *Report of the Committee on Organization* (Albany, 1867) as quoted in Bishop, p. 77.

16.   Guerlac, "Cornell's Library," p. 4.

17.   Andrew Dickson White, *Autobigraphy of Andrew Dickson White*. 2 vols. (New York: Century, 1905) I, p. 308.

18.   Bishop, p. 108.

19.   Guerlac, "Cornell's Library," p. 5.

20.   Bishop, p. 108.

21.   Guerlac, "Cornell's Library," pp. 8-9.

22.   Ibid., pp. 11-12.

23.   Henry W. Sage "Presentation Address" in Cornell University, *Exercises at the Opening of the Library Building, October 7, 1891* (Ithaca: Cornell University, 1891), p. 30.

24.   *Ithaca Journal,* June 18, 1888.

25. Sage, p. 29.

26. Jackson E. Towne, "Building the Cornell Library," *Cornell Alumni News* LV (June 15, 1953): 533.

27. Bishop, p. 271.

28. Ibid.

29. Guerlac, "Cornell's Library," p. 13.

30. White, *Autobiography,* I, pp. 421-22.

31. Guerlac, "Cornell's Library," p. 18.

32. Ibid., pp. 18-19.

33. Ibid., p. 22.

34. Ibid., p. 15.

35. Louis Round Wilson, Robert B. Downs, and Maurice F. Tauber, *Report of a Survey of the Libraries of Cornell University for the Library Board of Cornell University, October 1947-February 1948* (Ithaca: Cornell University, 1948).

36. Guerlac, "Cornell's Library," p. 27.

37. Ibid., p. 30.

38. Ibid., p. 31.

39. Wilson, Downes, and Tauber, pp. 20, 28, and 107; Cornell University. Library. *Reports of the Director of the University Libraries.* 1951/52, p. 19 and 1966/67, p. 40.

40. Cornell University. Library. "Library Use Survey, January 10-13, 1967." Ithaca, 1967. (Typewritten.)

41. U.S. Office of Education. "Higher Education General Information Survey, Library Collections, Staff, Expenditures, and Salaries." (Cornell University's Report for 1968/69.)

42. Cornell University. Library. *Reports of the Director of the University Libraries.* 1962/63, p. 33 and 1968/69, p. 29.

43. "Study Group Analyzes Libraries' Future Needs," *Cornell Chronicle,* I (November 6, 1969), 1.

44. Frederic C. Wood, "The Expansion of the Cornell Library" [Report of Frederic C. Wood, Consulting Engineer, to Cornell University, July 8, 1955]. (Greenwich: Connecticut, 1955.) (Typewritten.)

45. [Stephen A. McCarthy, "Introduction" to the] "Central Library Facilities; the Wood Report; the Metcalf Report." (Ithaca; 1955, p. 2.)   (Typewritten.)

46. Wood, pp. 3-6.

47. Cornell University. Library. *Report of the Director of the University Library.* 1955/56, p. 1.

48. Cornell University. Library. "Program for the Undergraduate Library." Draft Program, March 26, 1956. (Mimeographed.)

49. Cornell University. Library. *Report of the Director of the University Library.* ·1958/59, p. 4.

50. Cornell University. Library. "Program for the Undergraduate Library," July 13, 1959. (Mimeographed.)

51. Ibid., p. 2.

52. Cornell University. Library. Uris Library. "Costs of Remodeling the Building, 1961." [Statement prepared by Harold B. Schell, Assistant to the Director of University Libraries, July 3, 1964.] (Typewritten.)

53. Cornell University. Library. *Report of the Director of the University Libraries.* 1962/63, p. 3.

54. Irene A. Braden, *The Undergraduate Library,* ACRL Monographs, No. 31 (Chicago: American Library Association, 1970), pp. 101-05.

55. Cornell University. Library. Uris Library. *Annual Report.* 1962/63, p. 17.

56. Ibid., [Statistical Supplement], 1964/65, p. 4; 1968/69, p. 4.

57. Interview with Stephen A. McCarthy, former Director of the Cornell University Libraries, presently Executive Director of the Association of Research Libraries, Washington, D.C., December 29, 1969.

58. Ibid.

59. Cornell University. Library. *Report of the Director of the University Libraries.* 1960/61, pp. 21-22.

60. Cornell University. Library. *Information Bulletin,* No. 55 (April 4, 1962), 1.

61. Cornell University. Library. Uris Library. *Annual Report.* [Statistical Supplement], 1968/69, p. 5.

62. Ibid., 1962/63, pp. 3-4.

63. Bishop, p. 271.

64. Benjamin G. Whitten and Billy R. Wilkinson, "A Day of Books and Students," *Cornell Alumni News,* LXIX (July, 1966): 7-11.
    Billy R. Wilkinson, "The Arthur H. Dean Book Collection Contest," *Cornell Library Journal* No. 3 (Autumn, 1967): 55-56.

65. Cornell University. Library. Committee on Undergraduate Library Service. Minutes of Meetings, 1966/67. (Typewritten.)

66. Cornell University. Library. Uris Library. *Annual Report.* 1966/67, pp. 21-22.

67. Ibid., 1968/69, p. 6.

68. Ibid., 1967/68, p. 30.

69. Letter from Ronald E. Rucker, Librarian, Uris Library, to Billy R. Wilkinson, November 18, 1970.

70. Cornell University. Library. Uris Library. *Annual Report.* 1968/69, p. 1.

71. Ibid.

72. Ibid., p. 2.

73. Ibid., 1962/63, p. 3.

74. Cornell University. Library. "Library Use Survey, January 10-13, 1967." (Ithaca: 1967) (Typewritten.)

75. Interview with David Kaser, Director of University Libraries, Cornell University, December 10, 1969.

76. Cornell University. Library. Uris Library. *Annual Report.* 1964/65, pp. 38-39.

77. In April, 1966, the Librarian decided it was very easy to forget about the large majority of students who were seriously studying even at the height of the social period and commissioned a head count for 8:30 P.M. on six nights. Over 500 students each evening were quietly seated and studying.

78. Cornell University. Uris Library. *Annual Reports.* [Statistical Supplements.] 1962/63, p. 1; 1964/65, p. 1; and 1968/69, p. 1.

79. Cornell University. Library. Uris Library. *Annual Report.* 1967/68, p. 13.

80. Ibid., 1969/70, p. 8.

81. Ibid., p. 9.

82. Interview with Judith H. Bossert, Reserve Book Librarian, Uris Library, Cornell University, October 30, 1969.

83. Letter from Ronald E. Rucker, Librarian, Uris Library, Cornell University, to Billy R. Wilkinson, September 24, 1970.

84. During 1969/70, only 14.6% of the total expenditures for books and recordings was for reserve books ($4,171.14 for reserve books of a total of $28,535.02).

85. Harvie Branscomb, *Teaching with Books* (Hamden, Connecticut: Shoe String Press, 1964 [Reprint of Chicago: Association of American Colleges and American Library Association, 1940]), p. 27.

86. Cornell University. Office of the Registrar. "Registration-Fall Term 1968," October 4, 1968. (Mimeographed.)

87. In two studies of home loans from the research collection in the John M. Olin Library, where the stacks are closed to undergraduates except by special permission, undergraduate students accounted for 34% (December 6-9, 1965) and 39.8% (January 10-13, 1967) of all home loans. Of the 184,361 home loans from the research collection in 1966/67, undergraduates probably accounted for 70,000-75,000 loans.

88. Cornell University. Library. Uris Library. *Annual Report.* [Statistical Supplement.] 1962/63, p. 3.

89. Letter from Ronald E. Rucker, Librarian, Uris Library, Cornell University, to Billy R. Wilkinson, October 8, 1970.

90. Cornell University. Library. Uris Library. *Annual Reports.* 1965/66, p. 9; 1966/67, p. 8.

91. Christopher R. Barnes, "Classification and Cataloging of Spoken Records in Academic Libraries," *College and Research Libraries* XXVIII (January, 1967): 49-52.

92. Cornell University. Library. Uris Library. *Annual Reports*. 1962/63, p. 13; 1965/66, p. 4; 1968/69, p. 13.

93. Interview with Judith H. Bossert, Reserve Book Librarian, Uris Library, Cornell University, October 30, 1969.

94. Interview with David Kaser, Director of University Libraries, Cornell University, December 10, 1969.

95. Cornell University. Library. Uris Library. *Annual Report*. 1969/70, p. 14.

About the Author

After service in several positions at the Louis Round Wilson Library, University of North Carolina, Chapel Hill, and as Head, Catawba County Library, Newton, North Carolina, Billy R. Wilkinson was appointed Goldwin Smith Librarian at Cornell University in 1959. He was designated as Undergraduate Librarian in 1961 and was in charge of the Uris Undergraduate Library from its opening in September, 1962 until 1967 when he became a doctoral student. He received his doctorate from the Columbia University School of Library Service in 1971. From 1971-1977, he was Staff Relations Officer at the New York Public Library. He is now Associate University Librarian at the University of Illinois at Chicago Circle.

Jean Cassell

The University of Texas Undergraduate Library Collection

Cassell was in charge of collection building for the Texas Undergraduate Library from September, 1959 when library staff began preparation for its opening in 1963. This article describes the collection rather than the building. See the Williams and Carpenter articles in Section II for comparison with the selection of the Lamont Library collection.

On the morning of September 23, 1963, students anxiously awaited the opening of the attractive new Undergraduate Library located between the Main Building and the University Commons on the University of Texas campus.

As administrative officials, faculty and librarians watched the curious, and apparently delighted, students pour through the turnstiles, many were as excited as any planner who is about to see whether his creation will stand the test of hard use. Would the goals envisioned by Dr. Harry Huntt Ransom, Chancellor, and Alexander Moffit, University Librarian, and outlined by the Sub-committee on the Undergraduate Library be met?

The Sub-committee had conceived the Undergraduate Library as a center of learning for undergraduate students. "In this one location," its November 1958 report states, "we hope to have not only books and journals, but all types of library materials needed by the student in the preparation of his daily assignments. No barriers will be placed between the student and the selection of books he wishes to use. It is thought that in selecting specific books the student will inevitably be led to reading titles surrounding those books to which he has been directed, thus gaining a deeper understanding of the subject investigated and in all probability developing an acquaintanceship with new fields. We hope that

SOURCE: From Jean Cassell, "The University of Texas Undergraduate Library Collection," *Texas Library Journal* 39 (Winter, 1963), pp. 123-126. Reprinted by permission of the author.

use of the library will not only meet the needs for specific courses, but will also make it possible for the student to further his general education."

Scope of the Collection

The open-shelf library, housed on the first three floors of the Undergraduate Library and Academic Center Building, opened with a collection of approximately 60,000 volumes and is expected to increase in size as new books are added to become a 175,000-volume working library. Not only is the collection intended to serve curriculum and reserve book needs of the undergraduate, but to stimulate lifetime reading interests in fields outside the specific discipline of the student's major field.

The collection is not designed to serve research needs of graduate students and faculty, nor will it even fully serve the upperclassman as he advances in his study program. The General Library and its branches will continue to fill research needs. In learning to use the Undergraduate Library, it is hoped that the student will be better prepared for an intelligent use of the research facilities of the almost two million-volume General Library. As was the case at Harvard University, it is anticipated that use of the Undergraduate Library will stimulate the use of the General Library, rather than reduce it.

The collection is designed primarily to serve the needs of the undergraduates enrolled in arts and sciences courses. Students in the professional schools are already served by branch libraries, and in these subject areas the Library provides only a minimum collection — a relatively few books on the layman's level. Some overlapping is inevitable, however, especially in such fields as music and art, where the nonspecialist expects coverage of some depth.

The collection is a new one; that is, books were not transferred from the General Library, except for multiple copies of books used for collateral reading. Most books are duplicates of titles already in the University Library system. The collection was developed independently, however, without consideration of whether titles selected were already owned by the University Library.

In addition to books, the Library includes periodicals, newspapers, records, tapes, and a few scores. A vertical file is maintained in the reference section on the first floor. There are no plans at present for acquiring films, film-strips and slides, since the need for these materials is being met adequately elsewhere on the campus.

Selection Policy

The book selection policy reflects the two-fold function of the collection. In course-related selection, one copy for fifteen students is purchased for assigned readings and one copy per title for suggested readings unless otherwise noted by the faculty member. Professors must justify the purchase of multiple copies of expensive titles, works in foreign languages on reserve lists for courses other than those in foreign language and literature, and expensive scholarly sets.

In general selection, the Undergraduate Library, like the University of Michigan Undergraduate Library, "is conceived of as a large 'gentleman's library,' which contains carefully chosen books in the arts, in letters and in the sciences, on a level accessible to an educated layman who wishes to explore independently various fields of learning." Emphasis is on fine biography and history, contemporary *belles lettres,* literary criticism and reliable interpretations of science for the non-scientist. Detective and "light" fiction are usually not considered. The journalistic type book is avoided, and although very often difficult to determine, the question of a book's future usefulness and importance is considered.

The majority of periodicals are general in nature, but basic scholarly journals in a number of subjects are included. Whether or not a journal is indexed in *Reader's Guide, PAIS,* and *International Index* is an important consideration before a subscription is entered.

In the selection of musical recordings, an attempt is made to cover the various periods and forms of music of the Western world. Attention is given to performers, quality of performance and technical excellence of the recording, with quality of performance being given first place. Spoken records are in general limited to literary works, with preference given to an artist's reading of his own works. At this time, language discs and tapes are not purchased, but are borrowed as needed from the Modern Language Laboratory.

Michigan and Lamont Lists

The skeleton Undergraduate Library staff which began work in September 1959 faced the formidable yet challenging task of building the book collection. The task was also an opportunity — a once-in-a-lifetime opportunity to build and shape a collection from its very beginning.

The book selectors were not without lists to guide them. The Lamont Library has published a catalog of its collection, and from the University of Michigan Undergraduate Library we purchased a photocopy of its shelflist.

These excellent lists were helpful in book selection. However, both reflect the academic emphasis and special needs of the institutions they were designed to serve. The Lamont list is, for instance, too heavy for our needs in philosophy, and the Michigan list is heavier than we would want in psychology. The Michigan list served, nevertheless, as a basic guide in book selection; it was followed closely, if not slavishly.

Faculty Participation

Four copies of the Michigan shelflist were obtained. Two of the lists were cut into card form. One of these was arranged in alphabetical order by main entry, the other in classified order.

The classified list was divided into large subject groups, according to the University's departments of instruction. Alexander Moffit, University Librarian, called in faculty library chairmen, discussed the Undergraduate Library plans in general terms, and requested that the professors check the cards and indicate which, in their opinion, were to be included and which excluded.

At the same time he distributed special order forms for recommending titles not represented on the Michigan list. The participation of the faculty exceeded all expectation. In several departments as many as four people checked each card — not always agreeing, of course.

With the alphabetically arranged Michigan cards and with the cards returned by the faculty as a guide, the Undergraduate Librarian began checking desiderata against book resources on hand. These resources included collections of duplicates and collections acquired through gift and purchase. A careful search of all available titles was made before the purchasing of books with Library funds began in the summer of 1960.

Reserve Books

It is the policy of the Undergraduate Library to make materials freely available, but a small collection of reserve books is inevitable. Books limited to less than a three-day loan period are placed on closed reserve.

Although it was assumed that faculty members had their reading lists in mind when they examined the Michigan cards, such lists were willingly checked by staff whenever requests were made. This effort was concentrated in the summer of 1963, when multiple copies of reserve books in the General Library were recatalogued for the Undergraduate Library.

If the General Library owned only a single copy of a title, that copy was not recataloged but was simply charged to the Undergraduate Library for use; added copies were transferred and recataloged. Books on reading lists which are not immediately available for purchase or are not considered desirable for permanent inclusion in the Undergraduate Library are charged from the General Library for the current semester or as long as needed.

Special Materials

An original list of 212 periodicals was prepared following examination of the periodical lists of the Lamont Library and the Michigan Undergraduate Library, Farber's *Classified List of Periodicals for the College Library,* many of the periodicals themselves, and indexes. Members of faculty and staff were also consulted. The date set for collection and binding of the most popular titles was 1950.

The nucleus of the vertical file represents a selection of items from the discontinued Package Loan Library by the members of that staff. It is anticipated that this will grow and change as particular needs are made known to the staff.

At the time of opening 715 phonodiscs had been processed for use. Music and drama professors had submitted several lists, but the major work of selection was and is done by the library staff. At this time no tapes have been purchased. Rather, raw tape is bought and the phonodiscs are taped to preserve the discs. The Audio Room is proving to be one of the most popular features, and the collection will grow.

Directions of Growth

Staff members and patrons have found a number of "gaps" which were anticipated but not known. With the size of the undergraduate student body, it seems now that additional copies of selected titles are desirable. Interest shown in the collection by science, mathematics, and engineering faculty and students indicates that the Library may possibly need to reconsider selection policies in those fields.

In summary, the collection will grow and change as we learn of the needs of undergraduate students. While the collection may never be able to answer all those needs, the combination of improved and increased book resources and an awareness of the Undergraduate Library staff of its responsibility as a referral agency will improve library service at The University of Texas.

About the Author

After holding cataloging positions at the University of Iowa, the University of Texas, and Columbia University Libraries, Jean Cassell was Rare Books Librarian at the University of Texas Libraries from 1957-1959. In 1959, she assumed responsibility for the selection and acquisition of the collection for the Texas Undergraduate Library.

Norah E. Jones

The UCLA Experience:
An Undergraduate Library —
for Undergraduates!

Jones describes the UCLA College Library and points out that the "rather intransigent original library building" of 1929 has been successfully remodeled for undergraduate use. She then outlines specific programs and activities developed by the library staff such as the College Library Conversations; special programs for Black, Chicano, American Indian, and Asian American students; and the Current Issue Center.

The College Library at UCLA has now been in full operation for a little over four years. In this time it has developed some specific ways of relating its services to undergraduate needs which may be of interest to librarians working with undergraduates at other universities.

Discussion of these programs must, however, be prefaced by some description of the College Library itself, to give an idea of the setting in which we work.

At UCLA, as at Cornell, the rather intransigent original library building has been somewhat remodeled for undergraduate use, and a new building, modular and flexible, has been built to house the rapidly expanding research collections. The decision to use the old building as a college library was a wonderfully happy one, for it gives both a central and conspicuous location on the campus and a setting that has immense appeal to the undergraduate imagination.

The rose brick library and Royce Hall which faces it across an Italianate quadrangle, the first two buildings on the campus, were built in 1929 sharing a common architectural derivation from Sant' Ambrogio in Milan: Royce Hall has that church's twin towers, and the library has its octagonal dome. This Romanesque-Byzantine style, which so well suits the Westwood landscape and climate, is carried into the library itself in a wealth of detail. The columns with intricate basket capitals, the inlaid tile work, and the painted designs show an astonishing

SOURCE: From Norah E. Jones, "The UCLA Experience: An Undergraduate Library — for Undergraduates!" *Wilson Library Bulletin* 45 (February, 1971), pp. 584-590.

creative variety; and the fact that small Bruin bears appear occasionally among the decorative motifs, and that splendid serious owls stand as newel posts on the main staircase, proves that these are no mere copies, that the craftsmen who put them there knew that this was the library at UCLA.

By current building standards the floorplan may seem somewhat eccentric, but it has its own peculiar advantages. The concept is fairly easily described. From the entrance foyer short flights of steps at right and left lead to outer wings, while straight ahead a grand branching staircase rises to the main second floor. At the head of this staircase, on the one side through graceful arches is a lofty monumental reading room extending across the full front of the building, and on the other is a spacious rotunda of rose-colored brick ringed around with further arches. On either side of this rotunda are annex-areas leading again to the building's outer wings, and beyond the rotunda are doors to a functional but unlovely multi-tier stack.

When the University moved to the Westwood campus in 1929 the library's book collection numbered 154,000 volumes, and the idea that within thirty-five years this might increase to two million could never have presented itself to the architects' minds. They had designed a building appropriate for a library of the size later projected for undergraduate service, and the College Library inherited it with appreciation. Only minor remodeling was needed to provide open stack access, conspicuously available reference service, and comfortable and attractive reading areas.

It was just after the library had been moved into the remodeled central core in 1966 that the staff learned with pleasure that the building was to be officially named for Lawrence Clark Powell. This was of course eminently appropriate: in this building, as University Librarian, he developed UCLA's research collections to national stature; he founded the School of Library Service here; and it was he who established the College Library.

A Philosophy of Service

Something of the basic philosophy of the College Library is indicated by the choice of that name rather than "Undergraduate Library." We call ourselves "College Library" partly as an indication of the particularly strong support we try to offer to the curriculum of the college of Letters and Sciences (at UCLA our branch libraries in the sciences and fine arts have long been serving advanced undergraduates), and partly because we wish to avoid any suggestion that our library is restricted to undergraduates or limited to elementary content—or, conversely, that undergraduates should be excluded from any of the campus's research libraries when advanced work in their major fields requires specialized materials. Our function goes beyond merely supplying in open stacks those books which correspond directly to undergraduates' current needs and concerns. It is additionally, and most importantly, a teaching function: using a well-selected but deliberately limited collection as a laboratory, we try to teach students to use these resources effectively, and to reach beyond them knowledgeably when they become inadequate. The collection we are putting together attempts to include the basic classics and the best current writing in all fields. We expect that freshmen and sophomores will find their needs entirely satisfied in the College Library, but that we will be beginning to refer upper division students to the research collections in their fields of specialty. In addition, graduate students and even faculty will increasingly take advantage of our careful selection in subjects outside their own areas of expertise. We should like, then, to be a library for lively minded non-specialists, with librarians who are generalists in the best Renaissance tradition.

Such a philosophy makes us quite unwilling to acknowledge that any book which we might wish to collect could be labelled an "undergraduate" book: books, we feel, should be seen as more or less specialized, rather than as elementary or advanced, and they are likely to be of interest to students at any level. With this in mind, and because we wish to protect our collection from long-term faculty use and keep it available for undergraduates, we decided from the first that the College Library should not have any unique book materials. This policy does not mean, of course, that we are prevented from ordering anything we choose; it means, rather, that whenever we select anything which is new to the library system we must see that an order is simultaneously placed for the research collection.

Practicalities

With this as background, then, here are the specific services the College Library offers, in their present dimensions. Our basic open-stack book collection is now 137,000 volumes, cataloged under the Library of Congress system (as are their counterparts in the research collection). Two bookcases conspicuously placed in the rotunda serve as New Book Shelves. We have current subscriptions for 973 serials, and are attempting to fill in back runs to 1945. In 1969/70, over 190,000 loans were recorded from this open-stack collection, and reshelving figures indicate that another 130,000 volumes were used by readers in the stack areas without charging. Each quarter, approximately 8,000 volumes are placed on closed-stack reserve for some 250 courses, with an annual circulation of 150,000. The reference librarians have at hand their collection of over 4,000 volumes, and a series of drawers built into their desk-enclosure contains 8,000 pamphlets on current affairs. Reference statistics show that during 1969/70 the staff has dealt with approximately 75,000 questions, and they have often been too busy to record them fully. Near the reference desk, displayed on rods, are current issues of 33 newspapers from across the nation and around the world. In the west wing is an Audio Room with 36 listening stations, each with dial access to any of 24 centrally controlled tape players. The collection of about a thousand titles on tape is principally spoken-word, and is designed to extend in the audio dimension the sort of material to be found in book form — literary, dramatic, historical. While the College Library is essentially a public service unit within the library system, with order-placement and cataloging done centrally in the research library, there is a small but vital technical processing section which sees to the careful bibliographic checking of the orders submitted and maintains our public catalog. The collection grows by about 10,000 volumes a year, and systematic weeding, so far postponed, should soon be begun. To staff all of this there are 23.5 salary-roll positions (7.5 professional and 16 non-professional), with some 28 full time-equivalent of part-time student assistance. In addition, using funding allocated from student fees, small libraries in each of UCLA's five campus residence halls are maintained by the College Library.

The figures just cited are fairly respectable ones but our deepest satisfaction comes from something far less tangible yet very real to us — a sense that we are beginning to succeed in establishing a special relationship with the students and campus we serve. Change, and our adaptation to it, is so quick these days that it is hard to remember that four years ago only an occasional student wore his hair long. Still, Berkeley had had its Free Speech Movement, and "alienation" of students from faculty was a matter of serious concern. An initial idea that seemed worth trying was to invite a faculty member with an interesting specialty for a specific afternoon, and to publicize to students that they might come to talk with him informally. The faculty member would have nothing to prepare and need contribute only the couple of hours of his time, and the students would have the opportunity to meet and question him in the comparative anonymity of a small group. That first quarter four popular professors in "relevant" fields were invited, and scheduled for every second Thursday afternoon. A poster for the series and an article in the campus newspaper announced that participation in each conversation would be limited to fifteen students, and that coffee and cookies would be served. To our relief and gratification enough students actually came to keep the program viable, and the College Library Conversations became an established activity. On a campus of our size this is a tiny program indeed, involving one professor and from ten to eighteen students once a fortnight during academic sessions; but it is after all its intimacy that allows it to be effective. Each occasion, forty-nine of them so far, has developed its own special excitements, for discussions are intense and far-ranging, and individuals are directly involved with ideas. We have no doubts that our coffee and cookies are well invested.

Another much more conspicuous series was also inaugurated with faculty assistance during our first quarter. This too sprang from our desire to bring students into the building for enjoyable experiences unconnected with formal class assignments, and to make them begin to regard the library as a rich cultural center rather than as an over-complicated grade-raising mechanism. It occurred to us that our high brick rotunda should have the same live pure acoustical quality as the Romanesque churches which had inspired it, and indeed the building did lend itself perfectly to concert-giving: Thus was born a popular concert series — at least once a quarter on Saturday evenings, the one night the library does not offer regular service — which has now been running for four years.

Although faculty participation in special programs of this kind has never been hard to enlist, we found ourselves up against a blank wall in attempting to convince the faculty that there might be new and creative ways to use our library in their teaching. This is not a state of affairs that we accept, and we would have made some strenuous efforts to modify it if two years ago a great deal of our available energy had not rather unexpectedly been channeled in another direction.

Extending Our Grasp

In the summer of 1968 I was asked to join a Chancellor's Task Force that had been assigned to consider how UCLA might increase the enrollment of ethnic minorities. While efforts would certainly be made to attract minority students with the conventional qualifications, we recognized that if we were serious about bringing in substantial numbers we would have to design a program that would admit students whose past academic performance would not meet usual standards. By September the University had accepted a proposal under which fifty Black and fifty Chicano students who lacked normal entrance requirements but who showed strong academic potential would be enrolled in a concentrated program which, within a year at most, would prepare them for full participation in the regular university curriculum. The students in each component of this High Potential Program would at first be taught entirely by members of their own ethnic group, and the subject matter of their initial classes would be adapted to their special interests. We wanted emphasis placed on helping the students to understand the differing cultural values of the new community of which they were becoming a part, and we wanted them to learn to live with these without deprecating or rejecting the rich cultural heritage of their own communities. In practical application, this was to be called "playing the University game," and various confidence-building exercises in it were proposed in the planning stages. One of these, to my dismay, was to direct the student to "go to the library desk and complain about the service." It wasn't really too difficult, however, to explain that this was not the best approach, that what was wanted was to teach students to use the library effectively. And suddenly, as a special unit of the larger concept, we were talking about "playing the library game."

The enthusiasm which this idea generated managed to survive the inevitable shifts and changes and slippages as the program actually got under way, but despite frequent visitings back and forth, and discussions between our staff and the teachers in both components, we did not in that first year settle on any particular pattern of instruction in library skills. We did indeed bring all hundred students into the College Library fairly early, and in small groups they were given tours which emphasized the availability of appropriate ethnic materials. The Black component showed a special curiosity about the card catalog, and one of our staff devised an excellent lesson in its use. She chose from our catalog about a hundred cards, all representing Black studies materials and illustrating different approaches and filing conventions, and made multiple copies of these mini-catalogs. She gave them to the students so they could follow her explanations and manipulate the cards in simulation of a genuine encounter with the catalog. We were also able to collaborate effectively in a number of other assignments designed for the Black component. One especially interesting one, for which the Audio Room's resources were called upon, involved the analysis of the themes of lyrics of rock music as an introduction to poetry explication.

We came to feel a very personal interest in these hundred students (a few had taken jobs with us as student assistants), and were delighted that the great majority of them—83, in fact—successfully made the transition to regular course work. The program was more than doubled for its second year, when one hundred Blacks, one hundred Chicanos, 50 American Indians, and 25 Asian Americans were admitted.

Chicano involvement with the library this last year has been one of their, and our, major concerns. Two very lively Chicano teaching assistants had observed that their students the previous year had not profited much from the tours of the library, during which they had only been expected to follow along as passive listeners. Far better results could be obtained, the TA's thought, if each student were, over a period of time, to perform individually a series of tasks which would teach him in actual practice to use all the tools and services which the tour guide had merely described. This sounded really exciting to us, and our reference librarians immediately joined the TA's in their planning. They divided the standard library tour into fifteen units (such as "call numbers," "Reserve Book Room," or "pamphlet collection") with more than one unit assigned to use of the card catalog and basic reference tools. For each of these fifteen units we wrote a short explanation, and a good number of separate exercises or questions were developed, all focusing on some aspect of Chicano studies. As soon as the quarter began, the Chicano students were told that they were required to put in two hours of study time each afternoon in the college library, and that their TA's would be on hand to help them with their assignments. The students would be expected to do three library units each week so that in five weeks they would have completed their tour of the library. This plan allowed students to proceed at their own pace, and to go through the necessary motions without feeling that someone was standing over them. Their answers were to be written and returned to the TA's for approval. The main difficulty came when the students, enjoying the game, demanded to have more than three units a week, and threatened to outrun the frantic preparation of teaching assistants and librarians. When the initial tour was completed, the students went on to prepare bibliographies and annotate them. Future term papers should hold no library-related terrors.

Members of the Asian and Indian components, having heard the Chicanos' enthusiastic reaction to their library project, came to us with their own requests for library instruction. Their groups were fortunately much smaller, and our reference people were able to help in an individualized way with specific assignments. Each of the components is very different in its characteristics and requirements, and we find the best response comes when we are able to react flexibly and spontaneously as needs arise. The important thing is that the High Potential Program and the College Library have a sense of being caught up in an educational adventure together.

The Direct Approach

While, like many other librarians, we have often felt a sense of frustration at our lack of success in persuading the faculty to persuade their students that exploring a library can be fascinating, we have this year suddenly become aware that this was all along an unnecessarily roundabout approach — that if we wished to work with students we should quite simply seek out students directly. Again last summer I served on a Chancellor's Task Force, this time concerned with the overwhelming topic "The Reform of Undergraduate Education." Some of the student members of the Task Force were, I found, also working on an ambitious experimental course which was to be launched in the fall quarter. With funding from the Ford Foundation and provisional approval from the Academic Senate, it was to be known as HENAC (the acronym for Humanistic and Educational Needs of the Academic Community). It would carry twelve units of credit (a normal full course load in itself), and it anticipated 200 enrollees who, through a complicated interaction of seminars and discussion groups, would study in depth such areas of concern as Ecology, Urban Development, Community Involvement, and Revolutionary Non-Violence. While there would be general supervision of course content and student output by a quartet of faculty members, a corps of student initiators was to provide the actual organization and leadership.

At the time I fell into the discussions a problem had arisen because no appropriate space could be found for the "Sharing Room" the planners envisioned, where books and pamphlets could be kept and students could drop in to browse and discuss the ideas their reading generated. Could I, they wondered, find them a suitable spot in the College Library? Our east rotunda-annex seemed far enough removed from study areas to make conversation quite acceptable there, so we found them a bookcase and a few more chairs, and asked what they'd like to have to read. The conversation went something like this:

"Well . . . the College Library probably doesn't have a few of the things we have in mind . . . and maybe you wouldn't want to buy them anyway . . . "

"What are they?"

"Well . . . Lenin . . . "

"Oh, yes, we have plenty of Lenin."

"Well, Allen Ginsberg?"

"Certainly, we have Ginsberg."

"Eldridge Cleaver's *Soul on Ice?*"

"We have ten copies."

"Che Guevara?"

"Of course."

"Oh." A pause. "Well, then, could a couple of you join our directors' group?"

"We'd be happy to."

We never concealed from them that we were also well supplied with William Buckley, Robert Welch, Joseph Alsop, and the Dan Smoot Reports, but it didn't seem to matter: they accepted us. And at least eighty of their students came in regularly, and read, and discussed eagerly for two whole quarters, until the Academic Senate, overcome by doubts which we must acknowledge had their basis, withdrew further credit and halted the experiment.

The presence, through, of those independently motivated students in our east rotunda had done a great deal for our campus image. More and more our staff has sensed an easiness and a confidence in the manner of the students who bring their problems to our desks. A young man from Hillel wearing his skull cap came to ask whether he and a dozen other Jewish students could invite their rabbi to join them in the east rotunda each day at noon for the week before Passover to discuss the holiday's symbolism. Our staff made them welcome by setting up an exhibit of ceremonial seder plates and haggaddas, and by giving each of them a quickly prepared guide to our library's resources on Passover. We expect them back for Yom Kippur. Another student who had been writing letters to the campus newspaper about the need he felt for a new and separate campus library on ecology appeared lugging an enormous box containing his own personal collection of ecology pamphlets, and presented them to the College Library.

It was last spring's student strike, however, that seemed to bring us more closely in touch with our students than ever before. During the first week we set up a postcard-writing table in our foyer, with information available on pending Indo-China legislation and on addresses of government officials. In that week 871 postcards and 91 letters were sent from there. Students from the School of Library Service organized a Current Crisis Information Center and offered to do extended research for campus groups. Since their home-base in the School didn't have sufficient public visibility, a desk in the corner of our rotunda immediately exposed them to all the demand they could handle. Members of our own staff made a number of visits to the Strike Headquarters to pick up announcements and flyers; and, as we got into conversations at the Community Action table, we found students eager to make use of library resources in developing fact sheets to support their speakers' program. Old friends now involved in a Non-Violent Strike Committee asked us to set up a browsing collection on Cambodia. This was no sooner in place than a faculty organizer of a new sociology class in Community Action dropped in to say that his nearly nine hundred students needed just such a collection.

It was heartening to find so many turning to us so naturally for assistance; but it was a bit dismaying, too, to hear from others a constant expression of pleased surprise that a library should concern itself with current issues. It became very clear to us that we had taken it far too much for granted that students would understand that current materials were always available in our pamphlet and newspaper and periodical collections, and we realized that we needed to give them a much more prominent and conspicuous place in our service. In the Research Library a similar need had developed, and it was decided to form two interdepartmental Current Issues Centers, one in each building, to be staffed by volunteers from existing departments and from the School of Library Service. The Powell Building's Center, directed by a member of the College Library staff, has taken over the whole east rotunda, absorbing the Indo-China browsing collection quite naturally. Its simple equipment consists of a desk and a filing cabinet for pamphlets and clippings. The informal seating of course remains. The bulletin boards which line the walls have been given such headings as Academic Freedom, Elections, Peace, Ecology, Censorship, and so forth; and posted clippings and pictures on each board give as many points of view as possible on a particular current event which illustrates the larger issue. This bright and attractive display area has already occasioned much enthusiastic comment from students, and it is sure to be particularly appreciated next fall as election time approaches. Its educative function, however, goes beyond quick responsiveness to obvious student interest. In the thoughtful and comprehensive and non-partisan choice of the material to be posted we are able, indirectly but quite plainly, to say something very important about the philosophy of academic libraries — and, indeed, of the university itself.

I may have described our College Library in all too much detail — though I swear I have been stringently selective. But it is only by talking about these programs and activities, after all, that it is possible to convey a sense of what it is that we feel we are accomplishing at UCLA, and perhaps to define an identity for us. The College Library is not, essentially, a building — although we make resourceful and affectionate use of the lovely one we have. Nor is it, really, our book collection — for that must be carefully selected to support current interests and must be weeded and rebuilt with different emphases as interests change. It comes closer to say that the College Library is a friendly and perceptive staff involved in teaching love of books and skill in using them. At its best, though, it can quite unassumingly become a community of learning. One day last week I paused at our reference desk to speak to the librarian there. A student came up and asked, "Do we have any pamphlets on urban renewal?" "Do *we* have . . . ?" That one word, "we," tells us we're on our way.

About the Author

Norah E. Jones has pursued her professional career at the University of California at Los Angeles, with the exception of an exchange year at the University of Leeds. She was Librarian of the UCLA College Library during its developmental years in the 1960s. In 1971, she was named Head of the Technical Services Department at the UCLA University Libraries.

Lucien W. White

University of Illinois Award Winning Undergraduate Library

A senior administrator of the University of Illinois Libraries describes the underground structure of the Undergraduate Library on the Champaign-Urbana campus. A Building Data Sheet furnishes additional details.

The University of Illinois has had an undergraduate book collection since 1949 when the 25,000-volume collection of the discontinued Galesburg branch of the University was moved to Urbana and placed in a reading room on the first floor of the General Library Building.

Although the desirability of providing a more adequate undergraduate library facility was recognized from the start, strong impetus was given to this idea when the President's Third Faculty Conference, meeting at Allerton Park in 1960 to consider the topic "The Undergraduate Climate at the University," approved a resolution which recommended the establishment of a separate undergraduate library building with a book collection selected to meet undergraduate needs and organized in a less complex fashion than the General Library.

As planning proceeded, site studies pointed to the north-south mall directly east of the General Library, as the ideal location for the new building. This site was central in relation to undergraduate classrooms and residence halls, and its proximity to the General Library provided easy accessibility between the two facilities. An underground structure was planned in order to maintain the open appearance of the mall and to prevent shading of the Morrow Plots, which have provided valuable agricultural research data continuously since 1876.

The facility is of modular design and constructed to provide maximum flexibility of space. It consists of two floors approximately 217 feet by 241 feet with a 72-foot square central court and is joined to the General Library Building by a

SOURCE: From Lucien W. White, "University of Illinois Award Winning Undergraduate Library," *Illinois Libraries* 50 (December, 1968), pp. 1042-1046. Reprinted by permission of the author.

tunnel. It will provide seats for 1,905 readers and has a book capacity of 150,000 volumes. Approximately two-thirds of the seating will be at individual carrels 40 inches wide and 30 inches deep, with front and side panels extending 53 inches above the floor. The balance of the seating will be at 4 foot by 6 foot tables or in lounge chairs. The intent is to provide generous work space with as much privacy as can be arranged in an unpartitioned area. Privacy is augmented by alternating seating modules with shelving modules, creating many smaller seating areas instead of a few large ones. Acoustical ceilings and carpeting are provided throughout in order to assure a maximum of quiet.

The upper level will house the card catalog, the reference and periodical collection, a browsing collection, part of the general book collection, staff offices, and a listening center. The latter consists of a control room and 106 listening stations designed to make available audio materials of all kinds as required to supplement course lectures or for recreational purposes.

The lower level will house the major portion of the general book collection, as well as the reserve books, and provides fourteen typing carrels. Four separate rooms are also provided on this level for the use of blind readers and their assistants. Copying machines will be available on both levels. In view of the anticipated heavy use of this facility two entrances will be maintained, one on the east and one at the west, and students will be able to check books out at either side. Exits are to be controlled by electrically operated turnstiles.

House phones will be located strategically on the lower level and at the card catalog on the upper level for the convenience of students seeking help from a staff member if one is not in the immediate area. Telephone and electrical conduits are also provided for eventual use in a computerized on-line circulation system.

The new facility will be backed up by collections of the General Library and its numerous departmental branches, and it is expected that undergraduates will make increasing use of these existing facilities during their junior and senior years.

The surface area will be an attractively landscaped and lighted plaza providing bench-type seating for those who wish to read outside in fair weather, and the central court is designed to serve a similar purpose. The two pavilions not only provide cover for the stairways, elevators, dumbwaiter, and certain needs of the mechanical system, but are designed to heighten the aesthetic effect of the plaza treatment.

Construction of the Undergraduate Library was facilitated by a $1,000,000 federal grant under the Higher Education Facilities Act of 1963, and the building was selected for a first honor award in the 1966 Design Award Program of the United States Department of Health, Education and Welfare.

BUILDING DATA SHEET

Name of Library: Undergraduate Library, University of Illinois, Urbana
Architects: Richardson, Severns, Scheeler and Associates, Incorporated;
    Clark, Altay and Associates, Associated Architects
Consultants: Clark, Dietz and Associates; Robert G. Burkhardt and Asso-
    ciates, Incorporated
Interior Design: Dolores Miller & Associates, Ltd.
Population Served 22,000

Total Square Footage:
    Net usable space 67,121
    Gross 98,689

Seating 1,905

Book Capacity 150,000

Costs:
    Total project cost $4,240,125.00
        Federal share 1,000,000.00
        Local share 3,240,125.00
    Project cost per sq. ft. 42.96
    Building cost 3,150,000.00
    Building cost per sq. ft. 31.91
    Landscaping 69,000.00
    Fees 241,230.00
    Equipment and furniture 400,000.00
    Other 379,895.00

Lighting System: 2'x4' Troffer Type, recessed, prismatic lens, 90 foot can-
    dles throughout reading and shelving area

Floors: general library areas, carpet over concrete slab; toilet rooms, ceram-
    ic tile; lobby, terrazzo

Heating and Air Conditioning: four air supply units will be served by chilled
    water piped from a central University refrigeration plant; steam
    and condensate returns connected to the University steam tunnels
    will be used for heating

Shelves and Stacks: bracket-type shelving, with follower-type book support

Special Features: listening center with 106 stations wired for audio control
    from a central control room; four rooms for blind readers; master
    clock, public address and chime bell systems; typing and microfilm
    rooms; exit turnstiles

About the Author

Lucien W. White was Professor of Modern Languages at Augustana College in Illinois from 1939-1953; from 1954-1958, he was Librarian of Augustana. In 1958, he went to the University of Illinois Libraries and held the following positions during his career there: Associate Director of Public Service Departments, 1958-1965; Director of Public Service Departments, 1965-1968; Associate Dean of Library Administration, 1968-1971; and Dean of Library Administration, from 1971 until his death on March 6, 1975.

Ellsworth Mason

Underneath the Oak Trees: The Sedgewick Undergraduate Library at U.B.C.[1]

The following is a critique of one of the most recently completed separate UgLis and a "supreme exemplar" according to the author-building consultant. He begins with the site and ends with his list of the Library's achievements, having also delved into the traffic flow, visual activity, furniture, carpeting, lighting, and construction of the building. Mason predicts that Sedgewick "will be a seminal influence in the design of new library buildings during the coming years."

"I learned that form does not follow function; form follows site."

Richard Henriquez, Todd & Henriquez,
Urban Designers, Vancouver

You can tell that you're in Canada by the high quality of taxicab drivers and waitresses; that you are in Vancouver, at this point in time one of the world's most congenial and attractive cities, makes the change all the more appealing.[2] Legend has it that in the 1920s a group of students walked out from their cramped urban site and staked a squatter's claim on public land to a knoll at the western edge of the city which was subsequently validated by the Provincial government as the new site for the University of British Columbia. Whatever the actual facts, that university is presently laid out on a thousand magnificent acres

---

SOURCE: From Ellsworth Mason, "Underneath the Oak Trees: the Sedgewick Undergraduate Library, at U. B. C., "*The Journal of Academic Librarianship* 2 (January, 1977), pp. 286-292. Reprinted by permission of the publisher.

of "endowment land," fringed by the finest residential area in the city, sloping down to the Strait of Georgia on the west, with the near horizon marked on three sides by spectacular ranges of mountains.

The university is impressive even to one who grew up in the Ivy League when it still was solid ivy, and as you walk eastward across the main campus mall, the visual quality continues in the landscaping and plantings, in the arrangement and architecture of the buildings (most of them recent), and in the attractiveness and intelligence of the directional signs, which are unusually good on this campus.

The Introduction

Straight ahead beneath a mall 70-feet wide and flanked by huge oak trees, lies Sedgewick Library, marked only by two truncated cones that rise from the mall to a height of about ten feet. The truncated slices form skylights that provide views into the library. Before reaching the cones, a stairway at either end invites you down to a commodious entry area of the building. Outside of the library control point running from south to north there is an informal seating area, a snack area with lounge seating and open formal seating at small tables and carrels surrounded by the attractive octagonal group studies designed by the architects that form a distinctive feature of the furniture of this library.[3]

One level below the mall, the main entrance to Sedgewick (four double doors set in a long glass wall which faces the Main Library) provides a fine view over the terraced open-court garden between the two buildings. Early in the exploration of Sedgewick a pleasant feeling is aroused by the substitute for the chair-rail or visual-graphic barrier generally used to prevent people from walking through glass walls. Here and throughout the building we have instead a continuous line of quotations from Shakespeare (including the source), all of which contain allusions to glass or the word "glass" in handsome black lowercase letters two inches high, which reinforce intellectually the visual impression of the octagonal group studies. Here is a building, they seem to say at the very entrance, created by thought and taste to expand the capacities of the young.

The Site

An unusual combination of sensitivity and intelligence marks all aspects of the planning of Sedgewick Library, which posed from the beginning a seemingly insoluble site problem—the addition of a large undergraduate library building in a very limited area just west of the existing Main Library, where studies indicated the center of student travel was located. Almost certainly it would crowd the existing buildings around it and probably would have to encroach on the main mall of the campus, a wide walkway flanked by 40-year old northern red oaks which frame a vista that traverses the entire campus. Rhone & Iredale, the Vancouver architects assigned the task of designing a two-story building without destroying the traditional feeling of the mall and surrounding areas, detected in the course of their studies what escaped easy notice through distance—that the elevation of the mall was 12 feet higher than the entrance to the Main Library.

They concluded that excavating additional depth lower than the Main Library would allow them to build directly below the mall an underground structure not unduly submerged. By exposing both the east and west sides of the library, the only underground library to date that has done so, they changed the entire range of considerations that governed the building and allowed themselves a great deal more freedom in forming it than would have been possible in a building above the ground, where exterior esthetics would have limited the shape.[4] It gave them the freedom of irregular shaping into nooks and compartments for varied study and of providing angles on the lower floor from which the building looks back on itself (a very pleasant feeling). It emphasized the importance of views looking out from the building, which is completely surrounded by sunken courts on its open sides, and inviting glass walls that enjoy unusual freedom from sun because of the excavation. The north and south ends, of poured concrete entirely below grade, became logical places for the core units—peripheral stairs, rest rooms, utility closets, elevators, mechanical areas— and for noise producers such as typing rooms, completely removing them from intrusion on the rest of the building.

There remained the considerable problem of the trees, which were finally encased in brickwork that penetrated both floors of the library as a strong design element interrupting in most pleasing fashion the very large areas, more than 50,000 square feet, on each floor. One wonders how these spaces could have been handled without some such monumental interior design feature, here given to hand by the solution of the site problem. The simplicity and ingenuity of the architects' use of the underground concept is remarkable.

The remaining problem of the esthetics of the exterior sides that faced the courts, a problem inherent in the use of glass walls (which, on balance, the next century will probably consider the Curse of Mies), was solved by using over-hangs containing planters that produces varied and interesting facades very much in keeping with landscape gardening of the terraced courts and the well-groomed feeling of the UBC campus.

Traffic Flow

Within, the traffic flow and functional layout of the library match the general concept of the building in their high degree of success, as is seen in the main floor plans. Head on from the main entrance the tapering walls of the large trun-cated skylight cone come down through the ceiling. They are covered with the green carpeting used on floors throughout the building. Slotted windows afford a view of the lower level. To the left is the building directory, and to the right a wide natural walkway into the building leads on the oblique past a 16-foot long communication wall made of handsomely textured, vari-brown colored resawn cedar which is used throughout the building for interior separation panels. It contains a suggestion box, a wide shelf for writing, and above the shelf on P-slips clipped to the wall, typed responses to each question, over a hundred of which were posted when I was there. They make instructive reading about the building and how it works, and about the preferences of undergraduates in library facilities. Nearby is a blackboard for students to use for messages, and briefcase storage units.

This communication wall points the student toward another wall along the entrance allée from the northwest mall stairway that contains book return drops, just beyond six turnstile entrance and inspection points, which define the working areas of the library. Rolling grills are lowered from overhead to close off each exit and entrance for flexibility of control.[5] When all are lowered the library is closed to access; the elements in the main entry area then serve as an after hours study area complete with snacks, smoking areas, rest rooms, coat-hanging units, study units and book return slots, and with three different outside entrances. The fact that the area outside the working library has been arranged without clutter, and that the main entrance also provides a pleasant, visually interesting, and clear avenue leading into the library demonstrates a high degree of architectural skill.

Beyond the turnstiles we encounter the oblique angle of the circulation desk, which points us to the Reference Desk, directly in front of the small reference collection, and opposite the card catalog. Having located our call number, the next logical movement is through six doors at the end of the catalog, to the staircase, and down to the numbered books. If our need is for periodicals, they are just beside the reference collection. Sound recordings are located together with machines in the Recordings Collection that opens off the main floor beside the doors into the stairwell. From the entrance to the library, we are led past a series of specialized library facilities and directly along a traffic artery that is clearly marked, indeed, almost dictated, by the arrangement of partitions and furniture. Few library layouts are so self-explanatory.[6]

Adjacent to the Recordings Collection a lightwell extending from skylight to lower floor draws us down to the lower level by a large open spiral staircase or a smaller spiral staircase enclosed in a concrete turret.[7] A slot in the wall of the turret conceals slide and film projectors which occasionally project images high enough on the upper wall of the lightwell to be visible from outside the building. These projectors provide a prime facility to project images that produce a quick, pleasant feeling about the building on the way down to the working floor; but to date they seem to have been used for delivery of information that really requires seating and concentration to absorb.

Compartmentalization

The foot of the stairs lies between the avenue of bookstacks that run between the great circular tree drums.[8] Head on, the center aisle that penetrates the north stacks leads through stacks to seating. Beyond the stacks to the east and west extend seating areas, which provide a very successful solution to the problem of compartmentalizing large quantities of seating into humanly congenial areas. No seating group contains more than 40 seats in one visual expanse. To the east and west of the stairs seating areas on platforms raised 15 inches and surrounded by 6-foot resaw cedar panels provide bench seating on their inside and outside faces. These panels are penetrated on all four sides to provide easy access. Similar but lower bench panels are used throughout the floor to interrupt and define this very large area of more than 50,000 square feet.

In the north and south angles of this level raised floors are carved into circles, banks and steps covered with carpeting for sprawl seating. These interesting islands, together with the three-foot square hassock used throughout the building, provide materials for students to build the ingeniously tortured positions favored as comfortable by many contemporary students.[9] In the east and west angles of this floor, the octagonal study is used in clusters of six within enclosed or semi-enclosed rooms, one of which doubles as a library orientation room. Everywhere, an intelligent mixture of single or cluster carrels and tables provides a variety of writing spaces and good esthetic balance, completely avoiding the institutional feeling generally produced by heavily furnished libraries.

Visual Activity

While the feeling of the upper floor is light and airy, dominated by open traffic areas, with window walls inviting views down to the garden courts, this larger, heavily furnished floor finds its greatest interest in a range of visual activity. Beginning with the spiral staircase in the center, our first impression is dominated by the stacks, whose yellow endpanels play against the bone white tone of the shelving, the green carpeting, and white painted coffers overhead. One orange book-return shelf in the outer section of each stack range forms a pleasant pattern as the eye flows down the aisle between ranges.

At the perimeter, the glass walls look out to the east and west garden courts. Seen from this level, the west court, with its five terraced levels of retaining wall built of rough cedar, becomes five sharply stepped levels of flower and shrub planters above a court planted with moss. The east court slopes more gently in a garden-punctuated lawn flowing up to brilliant plantings and to a clock tower at the entrance level to the Main Library.

The other walls on this level, far more extensive than on the main floor, are painted white and enlivened by the purple-orange-yellow-green band of the supergraphic used on all solid walls in the library. It occasionally explodes into a fine burst of romanticism for emphasis.

The Tree Drums

The 32-foot diameter tree drums make their most striking contribution on this level, covered with a light-brown brick with a slightly red tint and a beige pepper texture. The meticulous mortar work between the bricks formalizes the drums into curving walls, as seen from any one spot. The design of spaces related to the drums, and the irregularities of the east and west window walls, with the main floor planter jutting out overhead, are used to full advantage by the architects to create effective, irregular spaces for relaxed and secluded reading, and to produce vistas of great interest from within the library back through the library. This building contains a dozen different kinds of atmospheres distinctly different from each other and varying from the most casual and informal to aloof, quiet and protected reading areas.

Furniture And Carpeting

The heights of chairs in Sedgewick Library follow the recommendations of the Arkansas Agricultural Experiment Station (with adjustment for their local students) in favor of a lower chair than is usually found at writing surfaces.[10] Since this is the only side chair used in public areas, the tables and carrel tops in this library are 27 inches high instead of the conventional 29 or 30 inches.

The library uses 4 by 6 foot tables for 4, 4 by 9 foot tables for 6, and 5-foot diameter round table with a 5-footed pedestal (which is unusually stable), but their carrel, with rear and side baffles is undersized—23¾ by 31½ inches on its writing surface, due to budgetary pressures. Since it also lacks a bookshelf, the floor around it must be littered with books and personal belongings at high-use periods. All writing surfaces are matte white plastic. Unusual furniture includes an 18 by 72 inch table 40 inches high, placed at the outside ends of bookstacks for consultation before proceeding to a seat. This excellent idea has not yet received response at Sedgewick where the table is not much used, perhaps because the loosely-packed shelves provide book-browsing niches in the stacks.

The reference area contains a good double-faced triple-shelf index table, made in units 4½ feet long and 5 feet wide, that provide 14 inches clearance for index volumes. The special microfilm tables, with two pull-out writing shelves and a reader mounted on a slide, is a failure, in my opinion.[11] A totally good microfilm reading table has yet to be designed.

The carpeting is made of polypropylene, with an anti-static wire woven in, completely without padding of any kind, cemented to the concrete floor. The lack of cushioning should have made the carpet wear out much faster, but the cost was about seven dollars per square yard, and after three years of very heavy use it has proved to be easy to maintain (it has not required cleaning yet), and except at extremely vulnerable points (at turnstiles and stairs) it has shown no signs of wear.

Interior Design

The feeling of the lower level is not dominated by the forms of furniture and equipment but rather by colors and texture—the stern grain of concrete overhead relieved by white painted coffers, the red-tinted brown of the tree drums, the green carpeting matched by the vinyl covering of the hassocks, the orange vinyl covering of bench seats, and looming everywhere the variegated brown tones and rough texture of the resawn cedar panels.

The overall effect of the interior design, which emerges most strongly on the lower level, is not completely successful. The tones of colors fall short of blending sensitively and enhancing each other. The weakest item visually is the carrel. With its baffles of an undistinguished tone of pale green and disappointing proportions it falls pathetically short of meeting the demands made by the other forms, colors, and textures. In addition, the use of resawn cedar in such numerous and prominent masses, often rising 6 feet high, overwhelms and submerges to a considerable extent other elements of the interior design. Its overabundance should have been relieved by varying its surface or color in ways that could have been managed simply.

As great as were Rhone and Iredale's contributions to this building, their interior design, planned by an architect, falls short of maximum performance. In my experience, architects have never demonstrated the refinement of taste and synthesizing esthetic skills necessary to create a totally successful integration of forms, colors, and textures into an outstanding interior design. Architects, as they must, think and feel differently from interior designers, and why they generally refuse the interior designers with whom they collaborate (even those in their own firm) enough freedom of sway to take full advantage of the distinctive sensibilities of these specialists, I am unable to say.[12]

Lighting

The fluorescent lighting, with three different light sources, is of better than reasonably good quality and intensity in most locations throughout the building. The best quality lighting is in the bookstacks, where open tubes are mounted on top of the canopies to provide indirect lighting of superb quality that provides 40 footcandles at the lowest shelves. Troffers of 16 by 48 inch fixtures, hung from the ceiling nearly to the edge of the beams, are contained within coffers formed by the T-beams. The ceilings dropped around the tree drums contain 1 by 4 foot flush-mounted fixtures. Both of these fixtures use a plastic prismatic lens with a good degree of diffusion but both lenses have overbright tube show-through, a source of reflected glare, due to the shallow (3½ inch) depth of the containers.[13]

Where the building's huge 2 by 4 foot support beams cross at right angles to the T-beams that hold the light troffers, a 6 or 7 foot stretch of ceiling has no lighting fixtures, and the intensity at reading surfaces below drops to 40 footcandles. Everywhere else, the library has intensities of 50 to 75 footcandles, even within the confines of the baffles of the small carrels. In general, the light distribution throughout the building is good and even.

All the fixtures in T-beam coffers have a sheet of colored plastic as the top of the container. Light passing through these sheets reflects the color off the white-painted coffers down to the areas below, in the first substantial use of color in library lighting in my experience. Five different colors are used, alternated in areas of three strips each—yellow, orange, red, green and blue. The sheets can be easily interchanged at will. Although this venture into overhead color was launched by the architects on very simple conceptual grounds, it is a matter of infinite complexity, requiring an oustanding degree of skill in handling colors in a total interior environment. As indicated above, no one involved in this planning had such skill.

The architects first proposed the use of color in lighting to code the areas of the library by their use—reading, book storage, service—or to code sections of the stacks by content. Since this turned out to be far too complex a problem, they settled on a theory that warm colors would invite readers who preferred "active" feeling areas for study while cool colors would invite those who preferred "quiet" feeling areas. Unfortunately, they planned the color areas too small to keep them from scattering.

Sitting at a table in a corner of the lower level, within my sight line three shafts of blue merged uneasily into three shafts of yellow which merged into three shafts of green. On my left flank, and feeling brighter because of the angle and the color, were three shafts of yellow, and through the slits above the support beams ahead appeared two slits of green and some reds. None of the colors blended especially well with the tables, resawn cedar, or concrete textures within sight. The result is scattered and unharmonious.

On the other hand, the area in which I sat was well defined as a visual unit by the support beams, tree drums and wall, and the use of a single lighting color, not juxtaposed with any other, could have lent this area a special feeling for those who prefer a change from the usual feeling produced by fluorescent lighting. Providing a few areas using no more than two different colors could add to the variety of choice already available to readers in Sedgewick. The problem would require the total elimination of contact with other lighting colors, which would make these areas emerge as color islands in the white lighting. This is a simple problem of coordinating the lighting layout with the furniture layout.

The far more complex problem, requiring the highest levels of sensitivity and taste, involves the selection of every color, texture, and form in the area below this lighting to be enhanced by the overhead color while still remaining harmonious with each other as they appear under the color tint. This early pioneering effort at UBC suffers from multiplicity of colors and from a nearly total lack of consideration of what the lighting colors would do to the furniture and equipment below. The effect sometimes impairs the achievement of the interior design which, as indicated, rises only to the middle level of success. The use of colored lighting in Sedgewick should be studied to achieve in other libraries higher degrees of success.

Construction

The very simple construction of the building resulted in a cost of $25.41 per square foot, excluding site work, landscaping and fees, in a city where costs are roughly equivalent to those in the suburban areas of New York. The lower floor slab and the end walls are cast-in-place concrete. The rest of the building is constructed of 2 foot precast octagonal concrete columns, which support 2½ by 4 foot precast concrete beams, which in turn support precast double T-beam floor panels 7 feet 4 inches wide. The downstrokes of the Ts, on about 4 foot centers, provide white-painted coffers about 2 feet deep and 40 feet long, with 3 to 3½ feet clear space between Ts. The top of each coffer is lined with white acoustical tile, which, together with the carpeting and the cedar panels, provides extremely good acoustics in the library.

The coffers hold the lighting troffers and the white ducts and diffusers of the air-handling system. At one large air-return grille on the lower level enough sound is generated to disturb a small seating area. Otherwise, the system is admirably quiet. The plumbing pipes, painted white, are also run in the coffers. No attempt is made to conceal these mechanical elements and their appearance in no way detracts from the feeling of the building. The ceilings measure 10 feet to the underbeam of the Ts and 12 feet to the coffer except for around the tree drums and along the end walls, where acoustical tile ceilings drop to about 8½ feet high.

This structural system allowed the development of very large clear spans, which use a basic module of 22 by 44 feet. Between the tree drums on both floors, where the direction of the spans is at a right angle to the spans elsewhere, the module is 22 by 52 feet. The bay containing the central stairwell is 44 by 52 feet. The spans allow total flexibility of layout for the bookstacks which at present are on 4 foot 4 inch centers. The use of precase floor panels to achieve longer spans and minimize the restriction of columns is bound to increase in library construction. This library was required to use sprinklers throughout by the local fire marshal.

Achievements

A balanced evaluation of this multifaceted library would sum up its achievements as follows:

Site—a brilliant solution that turned difficulties completely to the advantage of the building.
Traffic layout—outstanding; surpassed by no other building in my experience.
Compartmentalization—the best in any large-seating library in my experience.
Visual interest—very high.
Architectural elements—(stairwell, tree drums, window-walls, garden courts) —extremely good.
Interior design—in the medium range of success.
Lighting—better than reasonably good.
Construction—simple, functional and inexpensive.

To be able to say this much about single library is a rare opportunity; but in addition, Sedgewick Library is probably the most venturesome library built since World War II, incorporating these unusual elements, some of which are pioneering:

1. Its placement beneath an existing main pedestrian mall, without disrupting the character of the area.
2. The opening of both sides of an underground library.
3. The enclosure of existing trees in the interior of the library.
4. The variety of library elements laid outside of the control point.
5. The communication wall.
6. Unusually wide stacks.
7. Unusually long spans between columns.
8. The heights of furniture.
9. The size of the carrels.
10. The stripped, backless carpeting.
11. The four-color super graphic wall stripe.
12. The Skakespearean line window wall barrier.
13. The use of color in the lighting.

Not everything ventured has achieved maximal success, but most of the results are admirable, and everything will serve as an example to test the potential of what was attempted. If you're short of money, see how stripped carpeting and a small carrel have worked at UBC.

Those of us who have watched the amazingly high professional achievements of Canadian librarians since 1959 have urged them to step forth and teach us what they have learned by thinking originally under very different circumstances. They still defer to the long-held leadership of librarianship in the United States, although I note with interest significant articles by Canadians beginning to emerge.

It is time to recognize that during the 1960s, while the seemingly endless cornucopia of this country was blowing our brains into fatuousness and hanging Hero Medals on all the hollow men (the most disruptive period in librarianship in my lifetime, despite its material cumulations) the librarians of Canada and Great Britain were quietly laying sound, comprehensive, and long-range bases that have radically increased the potential of their libraries in a short time. The supremacy of U.S. librarianship has staggered, and we now have a great deal to learn from abroad.

Sedgewick Library will remain a supreme exemplar. It has already won the 1970 Award of the Canadian Architecture Yearbook, and the 1973 First Award of the Royal Architectural Institute of Canada, the highest architectural award in Canada in a competition including all kinds of buildings. Additional recognition will swiftly come from abroad, and Sedgewick will be a seminal influence in the design of new library buildings during the coming years.[14]

Notes

1. This article departs from a policy of silence about library buildings with which I have been connected (I refused to evaluate good library buildings at Colorado College and Hofstra University for which I was library-planner). Although I was consultant on this building for two days, my contribution was largely advice on the planning process, and very little of the detail can be attributed to me. I therefore feel capable of evaluating it objectively. The distinctly good features of the building are the result of the superlative information bases for planning generated by the UBC librarians, and the talent of the architects.

2. My travel to Vancouver was supported by Dr. Harold Gores, President of Educational Facilities Laboratories, whose small but extremely stimulating staff has had a larger impact on educational buildings and equipment than any comparable group in the country.

3. This octagonal study is esthetically the most successful component of the many devices created by the architects to compartmentalize by office landscaping methods the large number of seats (1,650) used in comparison to the small number of book-stacks (for 193,000 volumes). Its eight sides are connected by bolted braces, and it is movable. One entire room filled with these cubicles on the lower floor is cleared at the proper season to provide open space for orientation. About ten feet separates opposing interior walls, and an oval, open, step-in doorway (similar to a ship's door-hatch) provides entry. One inside wall is a chalkboard, and another a tackboard.

    These studies are furnished with a 3 by 6 foot table, which should be able to seat 6 (1 at each end and 2 at each side), but support stretchers at each end of this table prevent it from being used by more than 4, even when such groupings are desired by students (which, in my experience, is often). From the outside, the shape of the oval doorway in the 7-foot high white-painted walls, striped with the 4 color (purple orange-yellow-green) supergraphic strip used throughout the building, makes them visually striking and pleasant furniture elements.

    Their open top, thin walls and open doorway, however, make it impossible for them to contain sound, and they cannot be used for group conversations. The single most important flaw in this building is the total lack of conversationable group study rooms, where intellectual ferment can pour forth without disturbing nearby readers.

4. The University of Illinois Undergraduate Library opened the center of its underground building to bring the feeling of outdoor light into the library, which it does well. Harvard is also using this solution. The effect of opening both sides of this underground library is far superior.

5. Due to a lapse in communications during the planning of the building, these grills, intended to be stored behind an overhead beam had to be stored at the bottom of the beam. As a result, the grill in storage position allows only 6 feet 6 inches above the turnstiles, which makes for a close feeling as you pass under it.

6. This is overwhelmingly a public-use building, but it should be said that all the work areas for librarians it contains are conveniently and efficiently arranged, and sized for future expansion. The staff lounge opens onto a very pleasant cedar plank deck overlooking the west garden court.

7. Circular or spiral staircases should be avoided in libraries except where there are clearly overriding reasons for having them, because the width of treads, which vary according to the point on the tread on which you walk, is almost never a dimension that accommodates a normal stair-stride. The widths of the treads in these two spirals vary from 11 inches on the inside to 19 inches on the outside of the tread of the large staircase and 11 inches to 21 inches on the small staircase. Eleven inches is just a little too wide for a normal stride and 19 or 21 inches splits the mind between taking giant strides, 1 per tread, or mincing steps, 2 per tread. This schizophrenic choice varies slightly at other points on the tread. Consequently the use of spiral stairs inflicts a constant, if slight, discomfort on users. In addition, they take up considerably more space on each floor than comparable square or rectangular stairs.

    Balanced against these factors is the consideration that, in the hands of a good designer, these staircases can be highly ornamental. This fact alone cannot justify their use. However, in Sedgewick Library, coupled with the smaller enclosed spiral, and surrounded by a circular lightwell that extends up into the truncated cone skylight, the whole reflecting in an open form the great circular tree drums that penetrate the building, the staircases justify their existence.

    The provision of a second staircase as an alternative means of reaching the lower level, instead of a larger single staircase, resulted from questions posed by the Environmental Psychologist on the faculty of the UBC School of Architecture, about the desirability of allowing students an alternative. Since the vast majority of books and seats are on the lower level, and the student must go down to use them, and since he is totally committed to do so by the time he reaches the stairhead, providing twinned alternative routes down reflects a conception of people as incredibly delicate creatures, rather than the sturdy fellows we are, to survive all that the psychologists try to do to us.

8. Two items of the stacks are of considerable interest. I don't know what made me measure them, because three-foot wide stacks are even more maternal than motherhood, but these stacks, manufactured by Johl, are exactly 36 3/16 inches wide. If this is standard with Johl, Canadian and other librarians considering these stacks must be sure to correlate their bay systems to accomodate this dimension.

The shelves use the best end bracket I have seen, a triangle 9 inches high by 2 ½ inches at the base, fastened to the shelves in an easily removable manner. Custom made, they cost $1.68 each. When the brackets have to be removed because of crowded shelves, there no longer is any fear of books toppling over.

9. What they do to the circulatory and reproductive systems I leave to cardiologists, gynecologists, and human engineers.

10. Clara A. Ridder, *Basic Design Measurements for Sitting,* University of Arkansas Agricultural Experiment Station Bulletin 616 (Fayetteville, Arkansas: 1959). These measurements resulted from the actual choice of dimensions in an experimental adjustable chair by subjects seated in it at positions of total comfort for a chair at a writing surface. The exact complex of dimensions of the seat is given on pages 38-42 of the Bulletin. UBC had its chair made to order to its own measurements based on the Arkansas design by Flexsteel, a Canadian company, at $24 each. Its appearance is reasonably good, but not striking, as one would wish in the only side chair used, but budgetary pressures at the end of the construction also caused the development of a carrel smaller than normal.

11. The reader is mounted on rollers that move on fixed tracks parallel to the length of the table. It is difficult to push it left and right, and it allows no adjustment from front to back, making it impossible to position the reader at just the right spot in relation to the note-taking shelf.

12. The one basic lack on the otherwise outstanding planning team at UBC was a person with sure and sensitive esthetic judgment.

13. The tube should be at least four inches clear of the surface of the lens to obtain totally good diffusion and low show-through in fluorescent fixtures even if they have totally good diffusing lenses.

14. The statistics for Sedgewick Library:
Gross area—113,349 square feet.
Seating capacity—1,646 seats.
Book capacity—192,625 volumes.
Building costs—$2,880,270 ($25.41 per square foot, construction costs only).
Project cost—$3,894,808.

About the Author

Ellsworth Mason earned his Ph.D. in English at Yale University in 1948. After teaching at Williams College, 1948-1950, he held library positions at the University of Wyoming Library and Colorado College Library. He was appointed as Librarian of Hofstra University in 1958. In 1963 he was named director of Library Services at Hofstra. In 1972 he became Director of Libraries at the University of Colorado. Recently, he became Head of the Special Collections Department, University of Colorado. Mr. Mason has consulted extensively throughout his career on library buildings.

Part VI.

Institute on Training for Service in Undergraduate Libraries, 1970: Beginnings of Evaluation

Part VI: Introduction

As undergraduate libraries proliferated during the golden 1960s, their chief librarians sought each other out in order to compare notes and seek support from kindred spirits. Les Pyrénées Restaurant on Manhattan's West 51st Street was the luncheon place for the first formal gathering of five or six undergraduate librarians who were attending the American Library Association conference in New York City, July 10-16, 1966.

Under the leadership of John R. Haak, University of California at San Diego, a larger group of undergraduate librarians met at the American Library Association convention at Atlantic City in June 1969 to discuss their work. Haak then founded and edited the *UgLi Newsletter* with No. 1 appearing in July, 1969. The *UgLi Newsletter,* now edited by Yoram Szekeley, State University of New York at Buffalo, continues to be the source for current information and statistics on undergraduate libraries.

Interest in matters concerning undergraduate libraries grew and the 1970 American Library Association conference in Detroit was the scene of a program on undergraduate libraries sponsored by the University Libraries Section of the Association of College and Research Libraries. John R. Haak once again played a major role as chairman of the program entitled "The Undergraduate Library: A Time for Assessment." Kenneth Toombs, Director of Libraries, University of South Carolina, discussed the planned demise of the Undergraduate Library there. Norah E. Jones, College Librarian, University of California at Los Angeles, reviewed the UCLA successes (see Part V for her remarks). Billy R. Wilkinson, then a doctoral student at the Columbia University School of Library Service and former librarian of the Uris Undergraduate Library at Cornell University asked "Are We Fooling Ourselves About Undergraduate Libraries?" see Part VIII for his paper.)

The wide-spread interest in undergraduate libraries was turned into a fervent movement within the profession with the approval and funding by the U.S. Office of Education of the Institute on Training for Service in Undergraduate Libraries, held at the University of California at San Diego, August 17-21, 1970, under the direction of Melvin J. Voigt and John R. Haak.

In requesting the grant, the UC San Diego officials had observed that:

During the past two decades many university libraries have altered their traditional patterns of organization by creating undergraduate libraries; some forty such libraries are now in operation or in advanced stages of planning. Although millions of dollars have been invested in the book collections and physical plants, no corresponding efforts of any significance have been made to train librarians to serve in these new types of libraries. Neither a comprehensive body of literature, nor specialized courses, nor apprenticeship programs are available for training undergraduate librarians. Costly, powerful machines have been created, but no training given the engineers. The institute is proposed in order to bridge this major gap in training which has developed with the growth of this new specialty within academic librarianship.

The prerequisite of a teaching and training program is a pertinent body of knowledge, but the literature of librarianship is devoid of up-to-date and evaluative literature concerning undergraduate libraries. However, there is a substantial pool of experience which could be made available through an institute. By making possible the reporting and study of this experience, the institute would pioneer the first attempts to train librarians to be specialists in working with undergraduates, to develop standards for library service which will support the teaching function of the university, and to evaluate the record of undergraduate libraries during the past twenty years.[1]

Thirty librarians were selected to participate in the Institute. They, along with the faculty who were Melvin J. Voigt, University Librarian, University of California at San Diego; John R. Haak, Cluster I Librarian, University of California at San Diego; Irene A. Braden, Librarian for General Administration, Ohio State University; Patricia B. Knapp, Associate Professor, Wayne State University, Department of Library Science; Warren B. Kuhn, Director of the Library, Iowa State University (and formerly Librarian of the Meyer Memorial Undergraduate Library, Stanford University); and Billy R. Wilkinson, doctoral student, Columbia University School of Library Service (and formerly Librarian of the Uris Undergraduate Library, Cornell University), became the disciples who went forth from the Institute to spread the word concerning undergraduate library service. The proposal for the Institute was correct when it predicted that the "act of working together in an institute will develop among the members of this new specialty a feeling of comradeship. It is through such experience that a foundation can be laid for cooperation, the exchange of information, and the future development of the specialty"[2]

The following four papers presented at the Institute on Training for Service in Undergraduate Libraries are published in this Section:

John R. Haak, "Goal Determination and the Undergraduate Library."
Patricia B. Knapp, "The Library, the Undergraduate and the Teaching Faculty."
Melvin J. Voigt, "The Undergraduate Library: the Collection and Its Selection."
Billy R. Wilkinson, "The Undergraduate Library's Public Service Record: Reference Services."

The following papers which were also presented at the Institute are not included:

Irene A. Braden, "The Undergraduate Library — The First 20 Years."
Warren B. Kuhn, "Planning the Undergraduate Library."

Notes

1. University of California Library. San Diego. "Proposal [to the U.S. Office of Education] for an Institute Entitled Training for Service in Undergraduate Libraries, August 17-21, 1970." Director: Melvin J. Voigt. La Jolla, California, University Library, University of California at San Diego, 1969. Mimeographed.
2. Ibid., p. 16.

John R. Haak

Goal Determination and
the Undergraduate Library

Haak launched the Institute on Training for Service in Undergraduate Libraries with this major contribution to the literature of undergraduate librarianship. He discussed the creation of tangible service goals and warns against the ease with which these goals are displaced. A substantial part of the paper is concerned with the ability of the undergraduate library staff to achieve institutionalization (or to solicit and achieve support for the library's service goals from students and faculty).

Introduction

Jean Henri Fabre, the famous French naturalist, performed an intriguing experiment with processionary caterpillars. These caterpillars move in a long procession or chain; one leads, the others follow, each with eyes nearly closed and head snugly placed against the rear extremity of the preceding caterpillar. Fabre enticed a group of these caterpillars onto the rim of a flowerpot and succeeded in connecting the first one with the last one so that a complete circle was formed. Food was placed nearby and was plainly visible. The caterpillars kept circling at the same unchanging pace and continued for several days and nights. Finally, sheer exhaustion and ultimate starvation brought them to a stop. They followed instinct, tradition, or habit and followed it blindly. Although active, they accomplished nothing and in the end destroyed themselves because of failure to assess their situation and redirect their action toward a meaningful goal.

Do we undergraduate librarians have the goal of responding imaginatively to the challenges of undergraduate libraries,[1] our students, our times, our professional responsibilities, or do we, like the caterpillars, simply plod along to the beat of those who precede us? The original justification for undergraduate libraries was not just open shelves, not just books, but a program which, as a

SOURCE: From John R. Haak, "Goal Determination and the Undergraduate Library." Institute on Training for Service in Undergraduate Libraries, Sponsored by the University Library, University of California at San Diego, August 17-21, 1970. Included by permission of the author.

205

result of library-academic planning, would contribute forcefully to the educational experience of undergraduates.

With the challenge always before us to create innovative, flexible, and up-to-date libraries to serve the teaching function of our universities, it is puzzling to find that a number of undergraduate librarians are beginning to question the value of their own work specifically, and undergraduate libraries generally.

Several undergraduate type libraries have avoided using the term "undergraduate library" in their names, and librarians from libraries which have used the term are beginning to ponder its relevance. James Thompson, former Undergraduate Librarian at the University of North Carolina, (in his reply to the Robert Golter Questionnaire which appeard in *UgLi Newsletter,* no. 3, March 1970) questioned whether the term "undergraduate library" is still valid or whether such a library is simply an ancillary library to the research library by reasons of space and duplicate books. Robert Muller, in his recent article, seems to consider the highly selective and "choice" nature of the undergraduate library's book collection of greater significance than its service emphasis on undergraduates. As a result, he states:

> The designation "undergraduate library" is not entirely satisfactory since graduate students have also found such libraries useful when they had to venture into fields in which they were not specialists. Moreover, undergraduates have continued to make use of the graduate or research library on many a campus, for a variety of reasons, despite the existence of an undergraduate library. The designations "college library", "curricular library", or "general library" are equally inadequate in conveying the full flavor and the intent of these large new selective libraries and services.[2]

Problems of purpose associated with undergraduate libraries are related to a lack of definition of whom these libraries are to serve and how. While there may be no such thing as a purely undergraduate level book or even book collection, there are services which are more appropriate for undergraduates than for other members of the academic community. It is these services that make the library uniquely an undergraduate library.

For many undergraduate libraries the honeymoon period is now ending. This period may be characterized by the excitement and the frenzy of activity which is inherent in any pioneering effort. During this time the plant is developed, the staff hired, and the collection begun. Idealism, coupled with predictions of a new utopia in library service, is accompanied by the more practical impetus of a patient and cooperative library management which is willing to supply the funds, freedom, and time necessary for the library to grow up. But the day finally dawns when the issue of the undergraduate library's effectiveness is raised, and the honeymoon is over.

The uneasiness, doubt, and questioning which accompany the end of the honeymoon period spring from a number of sources. First, during the honeymoon we are dealing with activities which are more familiar to us, as librarians, and for which we find precedents in older undergraduate libraries. The processes involved in creating buildings and acquiring book collections are familiar and concrete, and their results may be viewed by visiting established undergraduate libraries or by reading about these libraries in the literature. The providing of these buildings and collections is akin to creating a stage setting for a play. The set reflects but is no substitute for the play itself. When the scene is set and it comes to creating and acting out the play itself, the undergraduate librarian is on his own. As he turns from a period of preparation to a period of production, he finds few cues to prompt him, either in other libraries or in the literature, and is often forced to learn his lines or improvise while on stage.

Second, the operation of undergraduate libraries is no longer a hypothetical activity. The hard facts of experience have shattered any fantasies which we may have conjured up in which faculty and students embrace our undergraduate libraries like a newly discovered cause. Experience shows that pious statements of purpose are not of sufficient attraction and must be followed by a solid service program. The play, to carry the analogy further, must have substance.

Finally, once the issue of effectiveness is raised, it means that a period of evaluation will soon follow. This period is bound to be somewhat painful, for organizations, just as individuals, find it more comfortable to ignore their most troublesome traits rather than to correct them.

Perhaps at this moment we undergraduate librarians are better equipped to create the set than write the play, but we are entering into a period during which the play must be written and performed. It is our responsibility to develop our specialty so that our undergraduate libraries may offer substantive service programs.

In order to support the development of service programs and to stress the importance of professional staff, this working paper will concentrate on the problem of undergraduate library goals and three related subject areas which have remained under-studied in the literature of librarianship:

(1) service
(2) institutionalization, and
(3) professional staff.

Part I: Goals and Evaluation

The Problem of Goals

Before service programs can be planned and before evaluation can take place, institutional goals must be defined. In order to stress the importance of goal definition this section of the paper will discuss some of the possible effects on service-centered institutions, such as undergraduate libraries, when they fail to specify a program of tangible service goals.

While perusing programs for a number of undergraduate library buildings, I was struck by the amount of detail they contained. They all specified the exact number of reader stations as well as the number of volumes to be contained in the buildings. Descriptions of furniture were supplied in minute detail, as were heights of doorways, locations of desks, the number of lavatory fixtures, and on and on; everything seemed magnificently accounted for.

I then began a search for comparable documents which would specify service programs, documents which would inform me of what intended results would emerge from this mixture of librarians, students, faculty, books, and buildings, and how these intended results would be produced. I searched in vain. I did find a number of phrases which expressed, abstractly, purposes or goals of under-graduate libraries. Some of the typical statements of undergraduate library goals which I found are as follows: to stimulate undergraduates to read good books, to encourage the lifelong habit of self-education through reading,[3] to be a center of learning for undergraduate students,[4] to continually respond to the changing educational needs of the students.[5] Goals such as these may be defined as intan-gible goals or goals which express intended states but do not indicate the proc-esses or activities which lead to their accomplishment. Intangible goals are extremely important, as they provide the ultimate purpose for organizational activity.

However, since intangible goals by their nature do not provide for order, direc-tion, or coherence, they cannot by themselves guide group action and therefore must be supported by sets of tangible (or operating) goals which do. For exam-ple, much religious activity has been centered around the intangible goal of "gaining the kingdom of heaven." This goal is usually supported by a set of more tangible goals to accomplish this end—the Ten Commandments, the beat-itudes, etc. in some cases, an evaluative system is even built in through private or public confession and repentance. So too, our libraries need tangible goals[6] to bridge the gap between means (acquisition, cataloging, circulation, book collec-tions, listening rooms, etc.) and the intended results as expressed in intangible goals.[7]

Most undergraduate libraries claim the intangible goal of acting as an agent for enriching the educational experience of undergraduates. But this goal is way up in the air; so how do we get off the ground? We do so through a series of related tangible goals that are subordinate to, instrumental to, this larger achievement. One such goal then becomes close faculty-librarian understanding and coopera-tion. An entire series of more specific tangible goals may be built under this heading. Another tangible goal becomes productive student-librarian relations with a ladder of varied activities leading toward this important aim. Book selec-tion is another subordinate tangible goal that can be made instrumental to the primary intangible goal. Some of the characteristics which tangible goals should possess to be both effective and practical are as follows:

1. Tangible goals should be a guide to action and sufficiently explicit to suggest a certain type of activity. Tangible goals should be helpful to decision-making and not pious statements.

2. Tangible goals should suggest tools to measure and control effectiveness.

3. The goals should be challenging. It is the goals which create organizational vitality. It is necessary to distinguish between the possible and the impossible, but to be willing to get close to the latter.

4. The whole set of goals should make sense. With rare exception, there is no single overriding goal. Goals should be balanced in relation to one another.

5. Goals must take into consideration external opportunities and constraints and internal opportunities and constraints. Experience shows that it is not possible to sit down and write a reasonable, practical and specific set of goals. It is first necessary to consider the internal challenges and opportunities as well as the external ones relating to the organization's environment.

Principles to follow in goal setting:

1. Limit initial statements of goals to questions which are of practical concern. Select a limited starting point, cover it well, and then branch out into other items on the list as the need becomes recognized.

2. Goal setting, to be effective, calls for group participation. It is a well-recognized principle that people work harder to achieve objectives which they have helped to establish.

3. Set a half dozen specific goals for each position. These goals are usually reviewed and revised annually. Users of this approach have found that it usually results in superior individual achievement. The employee not only knows the purpose of his effort but is then also able to relate his work to the overall goals of the organization.

For a more complete discussion of the process of setting goals, see: Hill, William and Charles Granger, "Establishing Company Objectives," in Maynard, H.B., *Handbook of Business Administration,* McGraw-Hill, New York, 1967, pp. 3/28-3/33.

The following program for the Earlham College Library illustrated the principles enumerated above:

1. Advise entering freshmen that they will be tested on their knowledge of the following basic reference sources: *Encyclopedia Britannica, Reader's Guide,* card catalog, and about six other sources. Freshmen who do not demonstrate competence on these reference sources are given 50 minutes of additional library instruction during freshman orientation week. This time is divided among the librarians who man the Reference Desk.

2. Give library instruction on the following basic reference sources to all

freshmen doing research papers in required courses: *Social Sciences & Humanities Index, Public Affairs Information Service, Essay and General Literature Index, Biography Index, New York Times Index,* and *Subject Headings Used in the Dictionary Catalog of the Library of Congress.*

3. Ask for invitations to give library instruction to all classes which are making intensive use of the reference services. At first, note the classes in which students ask for similar information at the Reference Desk and talk with their instructors. After you have a reputation for giving effective library instruction, ask individual instructors before a new term whether they will want library instruction.

4. Give one to ten hours of library instruction related to a course required of all majors, as they begin concentrating on their discipline.

5. Make the library instruction concrete and relevant.

   a. Ask the instructor to describe the assignment for which library instruction is needed.

   b. Meet with the class when students are beginning their literature search.

   c. Hand out annotated bibliographies especially prepared for each class. Arrange the bibliographies according to categories of reference sources in a logical order for doing a literature search.

   d. Use the bibliography to work through the literature search for a sample term paper topic. Use an overhead projector to show transparencies of sample pages from about ten of the most important and/or complicated reference sources. Do not demonstrate sources already known to most students in the class.

   e. Ask the teacher to attend this presentation and make comments.

   f. Caution students that an hour of library instruction is only the beginning.

   g. Encourage faculty to require a working bibliography at least four weeks before a major paper is due.

Creating tangible service goals requires the same attention and concentration on detail that is exhibited in building programs. It is by developing tangible goals that we make intangible goals attainable. Since this attention has not generally been displayed by the planners of undergraduate libraries and since some of the older undergraduate libraries are beginning to waver in their commitments to provide professional service to undergraduates, I wish to draw a connection between these two problems — lack of tangible goals and wavering commitment — by probing into a process described as goal displacement.

Goal Displacement[8]

Social and service organizations, such as undergraduate libraries, which orient their programs around abstract ideas are most susceptible to goal displacement. Goal displacement is a process through which means, unwittingly, become substitutions for claimed goals. For example, custodial functions tend to dispel treatment or rehabilitative functions in prisons, juvenile halls, and mental hospitals. So too, in libraries, clerical processing tasks, rules, and even the collection itself become the operating institutional goals, supplanting the more intangible service goals. Therefore, unless a structure of tangible goals or programs is developed to bridge the gap between means and ends, the means gradually surface, and, through default, function as the tangible goals.[9]

Goal displacement is not really a conscious process; it occurs gradually as intangible goals are replaced through the day-to-day decisions which create more secure operational habits and minimize uncertainty, insecurity, frustration, and risk.

Reports which emphasize activities which may be counted serve to legitimize these activities as ends, contributing to goal displacement. Annual reports of libraries often exemplify this fault. These reports generally highlight attendance and transaction counts, the number of volumes added to the collection, the number of reference questions answered, the amounts of fines collected, the problems with the building, etc. It is not that these statistics or conditions are unimportant, for this data is what our masters need to justify plant and staff. But often the data we accumulate about libraries is just a pulse-taking operation. It indicates something about the level of activity without measuring its quality or if the library is meeting its goals.

The basic result of intangible goals which are unsupported by tangible ones is goal displacement; goal displacement cuts an institution from its philosophical moorings and sets it drifting. Displacement takes its toll by directing an institution away from its original purpose and towards the means which were established to accomplish the purpose. Intangible goals contribute their own special effects. First, it is very difficult for an organization or its staff to have success experiences which can be related to intangible goals. Second, these intangible goals may be taken literally by some staff members, students and faculty, who will develop expectations that the organization will accomplish them, thus leading to misunderstanding and frustration.

Perhaps these first two effects of intangible goals provide clues to why some undergraduate librarians have become skeptical of, and frustrated with, the basic purposes of undergraduate libraries and are wavering in their commitments to them. Undergraduate libraries need goals that are attainable if they are to win staff support. Nothing is more demoralizing than to be judged according to an impossible standard.

A third product of unsupported intangible goals is that they make it possible to assume that an organization is effective. According to Warner and Havens:

> Accumulated experiences, precedents, rules, and traditions assert that certain tangible facilities, processes, and practices increase effectiveness, and these assertions are accepted as proven. . . . Obviously, assuming effectiveness as a given prevents adequate evaluation. Yet an organization is severely handicapped if its effectiveness is not tested, for lack of evaluation and feedback may force the organization and its program into more nonrational forms and programs.[10]

Therefore, goals are necessary not only to guide undergraduate library programs and to coordinate them with the programs of other campus libraries but also to evaluate results. Effectiveness then becomes a function of the degree to which an undergraduate library accomplishes its goals, and tangible goals serve as the standard for measurement.

By not rigorously examining goals, and by succumbing to the process of goal displacement, an organization risks destruction in the same manner as a home attacked by termites. It is not until the house suddenly collapses that its owner becomes aware that anything is wrong, and then it is too late. So too, undergraduate librarians who fail to assess library goals might soon find their libraries abandoned[11] by their superiors or unwittingly transformed into different kinds of libraries as commitment weakens or as goals become confused or displaced.

Part II: Service

What Do We Mean By Service?

Before tangible goals can be developed to guide the service programs of an undergraduate library, a clear conception of what is meant by service must be achieved. What do we mean by service? There is a great tendency in discussions of undergraduate libraries to confuse resources with service. Are open stacks, selected book collections, simplified card catalogs, audio rooms (all the elements we have described as providing the set for the play) services? We often speak of them as if they were.

Dr. Irene Braden, in her survey of undergraduate libraries, identified six ways in which undergraduate libraries have differed from traditional university libraries:[12]

(1)   by providing open access to the collection to avoid the difficulties of the closed stack system,

(2)   by centralizing and simplifying services to the undergraduate,

(3)   by providing a collection of carefully selected books, containing the titles all undergraduates should be exposed to for their liberal education, as well as incorporating the reserved book collection,

(4)   by attempting to make the library an instructional tool by planning it as a center for instruction in library use, to prepare undergraduates for using larger collections and by staffing it with librarians interested in teaching the undergraduate the resources of a library and the means of tapping those resources,

(5)   by providing services additional to those given by the research collection, and

(6)   by constructing a building with the undergraduate's habits of use in mind.

These six categories may be divided into two basic capabilities which the undergraduate library should have if it is to complement and support the teaching trends on campus, a self-service capability and an active-service capability.[13] The first capability provides the library with a self-service potential where the student or teacher uses, or is encouraged to use, the physical means which the library places at his disposal. The more common elements of this self-service capacity are as follows:

a. The library environment, including its location, building, atmosphere, and interior arrangement of books
b. The book and periodical collection, including the reference collection
c. The reserve book, honors, and browsing collections
d. The self-instructional devices and programs, including programmed texts, tapes, recordings, educational television, radio and films
e. The finding devices, including the catalog, periodical lists, and information pamphlets
f. Exhibits
g. Special facilities for the physically disadvantaged

Each of the elements of the self-service capacity may be approached directly by the library user without referring to the library staff. In providing these self-services the library staff acts in a technical capacity as administrator, provider, and processor. The self-service elements contribute to the teaching function of the university by providing a place for, and access to, materials which complement the classroom efforts of both students and teachers.

The second capability the undergraduate library must have to complement and support university teaching is what I shall call an active-service capability, one which revolves around the concept of the undergraduate librarian as teacher rather than technician. Active library service is totally dependent on the library staff and on its ability to work with faculty and students, and requires the participation of the librarian inside and outside of the library building. It is with these active services that the librarian binds the library to the curriculum and guides the student in the use of the library's resources. With the proper training of staff the following services can potentially be offered through the undergraduate library:

a. Teaching students, through formal or informal classes, ways to use the library effectively, including the different ways to search for information, the uses of bibliographical and informational tools and their purposes and limitations, and the features and peculiarities of the total university library system.
b. Stimulation of reading by students through counseling, library sponsored seminars, and cultural events.

c.   Providing reference and reader advisory services, including work with students on library related assignments.

d.   Serving the faculty in an advisory capacity, exploring with them the ways of using the library's staff, collection, and services to enrich the undergraduate teaching program.

e.   Working with the faculty in evaluating and improving teaching programs which require students to use the library.

By dividing goals into self-service and active-service categories, we can begin to develop appropriate tangible goals for each one as well as evaluation criteria and procedures. We can also establish appropriate qualifications for staff and can begin to assess our libraries, not only on the basis of what *they have,* but what *we do.*

Part III: Institutionalization

One of the conditions and limits of undergraduate libraries is that they have no monopoly on campus library resources. The books and periodicals in the undergraduate library collection may also be found in other campus libraries. The undergraduate library, therefore, is in a position of having to compete for clients (students and faculty). The long and short of an undergraduate library's success will rest with the ability of its staff to achieve *institutionalization*[14] or, in other words, to solicit support for the library's service goals from faculty and students.

Goals give direction to an institution and also mark a standard for its evaluation. But even if the library staff meticulously develops a program of tangible service goals, their efforts are wasted if these goals and the justifications for them are not familiar to the faculty and students and supported by them. The problem of defining goals in a service organization is not ended once a logical set of goals and priorities is set to paper. It still remains to broadcast goals and to determine whether or not these goals and the programs devised to accomplish them are meaningful and useful to the library's patrons.

People are generally more willing to accept and support goals that they have helped to set. People are also more willing to accept an institution and its purposes if they know, like, and respect its staff. On most univeristy campuses the fact that one is a librarian does not automatically place one in the center of a communication network which includes faculty and students. The librarian must work to build relationships.

Traditionally, service organizations have recognized the value of encouraging the people they serve to participate in decision-making. This practice not only keeps the organization keyed to the ever changing needs of its clients but also fosters vital personal contacts between staff and customer. Banks have on their governing boards men who represent local industrial and financial interests; federal regulatory agencies solicit advice from the industries they regulate, and their customers, as well as from related state and local governmental bodies; research libraries also have their faculty library committees. Service organizations, including libraries, which make no attempt to involve those they serve in the life of the institution, foster the attitude that the organization is created and operated for the convenience of the staff.

Most undergraduate libraries do not have an active advisory committee made up of students or faculty. Whether or not such a committee is the answer to a particular library's need to institutionalize is dependent on a number of factors, such as the inclination and the personality of the librarian, the degree of formality or informality of the campus, and the interests of faculty and students. However, if the committee method is rejected, then other ways should be found to formulate goals and programs which are pertinent to the needs of faculty and students and are acceptable to them. So too, other ways should be sought to increase personal contact between librarians and the people they serve.

Once contacts are made, support for any particular library goal is dependent on three basic factors. First, a goal is more likely to be supported if the value it implies is compatible with the values of clients. For example, if a faculty member encourages his students to read independently and explore the library collection, the librarian's role as reader advisor is much more likely to be accepted than if a faculty member binds his students to a reserve reading list. Second, goals are more likely to be supported if clients concur with the library staff in the importance or degree of emphasis placed upon them. A number of librarians have applied this principle by postponing library orientation until that point in the semester when students are assigned to write papers and so have an immediate need for help. Lastly, goals are more likely to be accepted by students or faculty when they see that librarians themselves are accomplishing them. If undergraduate libraries claim a reference service but a student's first attempts to have questions answered by a librarian are unpleasant or unsatisfactory, the student's confidence in the ability of the library to provide reference service is nil.

Several undergraduate libraries have attempted to involve faculty and students in the life of the library in a way other than through an administrative committee. This "way" is by encouraging the university community to look upon the undergraduate library as a cultural center. The Undergraduate Library at the University of Michigan provides a large multipurpose room for a variety of educational programs. The College Library at the University of California, Los Angeles for five years has had a successful series of informal seminars featuring popular faculty members as well as numerous and varied programs of chamber music. And, during this coming academic year, the Cluster Library (the Undergraduate Library) at the University of California, San Diego will begin sponsoring a series of concerts, poetry readings, informal seminars, and art exhibits.

Some university librarians as well as undergraduate librarians object to undergraduate libraries engaging in such activities. The major negative argument seems to be that these activities are really peripheral to the central purposes of an undergraduate library.[15] My view is that such events make the library visible and soften its formal institutional and bureaucratic image. These activities and the process of planning for them provide opportunities for increasing the dialogue between librarians, faculty, and students.

Institutionalization may also be increased if undergraduate librarians join social, recreational, cultural, or official campus organizations whose memberships are primarily comprised of students, or faculty, or both. It would not hurt at all if a few more librarians were good surfers, basketball players, musicians, or energetic and effective committee members. Participation in campus activities transforms the librarian from a title into a person.

Successful institutionalization is dependent on two basic factors, personal relationships and "image." Whether institutionalization is fostered through formal or informal committees, cultural events, or participation in campus activities, each one of these methods requires personal contacts between the undergraduate librarian and faculty members and students. Such personal relationships take time to develop. For this reason turnover of effective undergraduate library staff members can be particularly crippling to institutionalization. Whether we like it or not, people categorize libraries and other service institutions according to the way they perceive the staff. If the library staff members are friendly and helpful, the library is a friendly place. If the staff is arrogant, impersonal, and bureaucratic, the library is a hostile place. Let us hope that we might eventually attract for our undergraduate libraries the support recently expressed on a petition by a group of UCSD students for a cafeteria threatened with closure:

> We request that the Matthews snack bar remain open. This is the only cafeteria on campus which gives its customers friendly, personalized service. In a world where most people don't give a damn, it's great to go to a place where the employees have a smile for you and even know your name.

Part IV: The Library Staff and the Undergraduate Library

One of the barriers inhibiting the development and reward for staff in undergraduate libraries is that there has often been little recognition of the possibility that special training or skill is necessary to serve in them. A typical attitude of library administrators seems to be that any young person with an attractive personality has the necessary qualifications[16] and that "turnover is of no importance because what is important is that they are willing to help people and to go to some lengths to help them."[17] One assistant university librarian told me that a nice young person was running their undergraduate library but that the real creative work was performed by the administration before the library opened.

These views of certain representatives of library administrations are rooted in the short history of undergraduate libraries. Undergraduate libraries have often been a fashionable and practical solution to the problem of providing needed additional space for books and readers. In order to reduce development time, these libraries have borrowed from each other in cannibalistic sequence, with each new library copying much from its predecessor.

The induced birth of many undergraduate libraries has meant that they have been planned and built by the campus director of libraries or his immediate subordinates. They consult with another library director that has an undergraduate library, they select the site and develop the building program, they choose a relatively handy and up-to-date list of "basic books" to guide book purchases, and finally put the undergraduate library into business by hiring a nice but relatively inexperienced group of young people to operate the library. As a result, the post of undergraduate librarian has been seen as one where minimal creative or independent work is required.

A second attitude seems to be that, yes, a very well-qualified individual is needed to serve as the chief administrator for the undergraduate library but that the few other professional positions assigned to the library require librarians with only a minimum of experience. Undergraduate libraries expressing this philosophy place their emphasis on the novel self-service capabilities of the library rather than on the personal services that may be supplied by staff.[18]

However, as more undergraduate libraries are turned over to us undergraduate librarians to create and operate, we become the true spokesmen for these libraries rather than the general library administrator. It is up to us to develop our specialty as undergraduate librarians; to ask what is really the rationale of the movement; to build a service program of substance and worth; and to improve our capabilities in order to carry out these programs. We can begin by specifying tangible goals to guide us and to foster institutionalization. We can also begin working with one another.

The fact that the Institute, Training for Service in Undergraduate Libraries, has been funded so generously by the Office of Education, and the willingness of university librarians in sending staff to this Institute, indicates that this is an appropriate time in the history of undergraduate libraries for us to begin developing the specialty rather than working just as individuals in our own libraries. It is hoped that, as we work and learn together during the Institute, a feeling of comradeship will develop and that a foundation can be laid for improving our libraries through cooperation and the exchange of information.

Notes

1. For the purpose of this paper an undergraduate library is defined as follows: (1) a special library for undergraduate students; (2) located in a university or other institution supporting graduate work to a significant degree; (3) housed in either a separate building or in a self-contained section of a general building; (4) consisting of a collection designed to support and supplement the undergraduate curriculum, and a staff and services which promote the integration of the library into the undergraduate teaching program of the university.

2. Muller, Robert H., "The Undergraduate Library Trend at Large Universities," in Voigt, Melvin, *Advances in Librarianship* no. 1 (Academic Press, 1970), p. 114.

3. Frederick H. Wagman as quoted in Braden, Irene, *The Undergraduate Library* (Chicago: American Lib. Assn., 1970), p. 49.

4. Sub-Committee on the Undergraduate Library, *Report,* University of Texas, Austin, 1968, p. 1.
5. *Statement of Program for the Undergraduate Library,* Pittsburgh: University of Pittsburgh, p. 1.
6. Tangible goals may be stated in such a way as to be subject to evaluation, whereas intangible goals cannot. This is an important point, since it is organizational events which are tangible and measurable that are most often used in evaluation and sanctioning.
7. If the Library is to have an educational impact on students, goals must be clearly specified. If specification is lacking, students may not know whether their own purposes and those of the library coincide. For a stimulating study on the effect of goals on student values, see: Vreeland, Rebecca, and Charles Bidwell, "Organizational Effects on Student Attitudes: a Study of the Harvard Houses," *Sociology of Education* 38 (Spring 1965): 233-250.
8. For this discussion of the process of goal displacement I am indebted to W. Keith Warner and A. Eugene Havens and their article, "Goal Displacement and the Intangibility of Organizational Goals," *Administrative Science Quarterly* 12 (March 1968): 539-555.
9. Kenneth Keniston seems to argue that institutions in a technological society are culturally susceptible to goal displacement, since technological values concentrate on means rather than ends — telling us how to proceed rather than where to go. In the absence of other positive values the instrumental values of our society are often unconsciously elevated to ends. The "deification of instrumentality" has two basic aspects — pursuit of sheer quantity and the quest for expertise. See: Keniston, Kenneth, *The Uncommitted: Alienated Youth in American Society,* (New York: Harcourt, Brace & World, Inc., 1965), pp. 335-336.
10. Warner and Havens, op.cit., p. 545
11. Abandonment is not as farfetched as it sounds. The Undergraduate Library at the University of South Carolina will be abolished in 1973 and a science library will occupy the building. The stated reason for the development was that the undergraduate library was nothing but a study hall and the facilities could better be used as a science library.
12. Braden, op.cit., p.2.
13. Naturally, fundamental to both of these capabilities is the whole supportive apparatus of ordering, cataloging, binding, stack maintenance, etc.
14. *Institutionalization* may be defined as the degree to which a system of action obtains support for its decisions or goals from the environment.
15. For an example of this point of view see: Orne, Jerrold, "The Undergraduate Library," *Library Journal* 95 (/) June 15, 1970 (/) 2230-2233.
16. Braden, op.cit., p. 89.
17. Ibid.
18. The following statement of purpose appears in the 1966 Program of the Undergraduate Library of the University of North Carolina: "The Undergraduate Library accordingly aims first at providing a maximum provision of inviting study areas for a very large proportion of the undergraduate student body, and secondly, at assuming the presence of carefully selected, up-to-date books presented in utmost accessibility. A basic principle of undergraduate use in complete access with direction available but not forced. The emphasis on self-service here is only an introduction to

later personal searches by the upper class and graduate student." (Robert B. House Undergraduate Library: Final Program, 1966, University of North Carolina, Chapel Hill, mimeo, p. 2.)

About the Author

John R. Haak served as Assistant Social Science Librarian from 1962-1964 and as Mines Librarian from 1964-1966 at the University of Nevada. In 1967, he was appointed Undergraduate Librarian at the University of California, San Diego. On July 1, 1971, he was promoted to the position of Assistant University Librarian at UC San Diego. More recently, he became Associate University Librarian.

Patricia B. Knapp

The Library,
the Undergraduate and
the Teaching Faculty

With the vast experience gained in the Montieth
Library Project and from her perspective as an
outstanding social scientist and teacher, Patricia
Knapp does not wish to "discourage the undergraduate librarian who wants a more active role in
serving undergraduate education." But she provides a "dose of realism as antidote to the sort of
over-optimism which usually leads ultimately to
too-ready acceptance of defeat." With her usual
wisdom, she guides and alerts librarians at the
Institute to ways for achieving better relationships
with students and faculty members. This is a clas-
sic discourse on the trinity of the library, the
undergraduate student, and the teaching faculty
member.

Introduction

This paper presents a view not of but *from* the undergraduate library. It looks
outward — toward the faculty, the students, and the curriculum and also toward
the university as an organization and toward the university library as a total system. These elements of the academic milieu are powerful forces in determining
the role of the undergraduate library, and if that library is to go beyond providing "self-service capability" — which it has been remarkably successful in doing
— to active library service in collaboration with the teaching faculty, librarians
must understand how these powerful outside elements operate.

For those who aspire to this ideal of active library service, the prospect presented here is gloomy. For within each of the major segments of the academic milieu

SOURCE: From Patricia B. Knapp, "The Library, the Undergraduate and the Teaching
Faculty," Institute on Training for Service in Undergraduate Libraries, Sponsored by the
University Library, University of California at San Diego, August 17-21, 1970. Included
by permission of the author.

there is, it seems to me, a major thrust which runs counter to such an ideal goal. In the faculty there is an increasing trend toward "professionalization of the disciplines." Among the students, "making the grade" is an overriding influence and the "vocational subculture" is dominant. The undergraduate curriculum, lacking a unified and coherent philosophical foundation, ends up as a compromise among the various conflicting views of its purpose. As a "professionally-oriented organization" the university is fragmented and dominated by competing graduate and research interests. And, finally, the university library system is necessarily organized in an hierarchical fashion, which is out of tune with the pattern of the university organization itself; it is subject to the power of the research-oriented establishment; and its operational patterns are ill-suited to the mass requirements of undergraduate library service.

Despite the grimness of this general picture, however, I do not intend to discourage the undergraduate librarian who wants a more active role in serving undergraduate education. Instead, I hope, first, to provide a dose of realism as an antidote to the sort of over-optimism which usually leads ultimately to too-ready acceptance of defeat and, second, to point out a few bright spots in the general gloom — some minority tendencies in the clientele, some hopeful indications of change, some tactics which may be useful.

The analysis presented here is derived from reading, from observation, and from some participation in undergraduate teaching and administration. It consists mostly of personal reflections, and because it is personal, I must warn you that my bent is toward the social sciences. Like many in this field I am given to rather large generalizations. These should not be understood as anything on the order of scientific principles based on irrefutable evidence but simply as ways of looking at social phenomena and of trying to find some rational order in their complexity.

Another caveat is in order before we move into discussion, first, of the faculty. Most of the sources of information I have used are based on evidence gathered prior to 1968 — most, in fact, are based on studies conducted in the late 50's and early 60's. It is impossible to predict whether the increasing ferment in the universities during the past two years, the financial strain, the student unrest, the internal and external pressures toward social involvement and politicization — whether all these will produce significant changes. If they do, they may make the picture of the university presented here obsolete and the prospects for library service to undergraduate education will be a good deal better than they seem to be now. For some of the bright spots in the picture are embodied in the reforms in curriculum and in governance now being called for. But the odds are heavy against major reforms in the near future. All institutions have a tremendous capacity for resistance to change — the bigger the institution the greater that capacity. Moreover, education, particularly higher education, is notoriously conservative. Still, my view is from the far side of the generation gap and I may be unduly pessimistic about what the student radicals and reformers can accomplish.

The Faculty

Professionalization of the Disciplines

The overriding characteristic of faculty society, as indicated above, is the increasing professionalization of the disciplines, for which Jencks and Riesman provide such abundant evidence in their book, *The Academic Revolution.*[1] Briefly, what professionalization of the disciplines means is that faculty members more and more identify with their field of study rather than with the institution in which they teach. They are cosmopolitan in the sense that they look to their peers in the disciplines for standards of behavior and achievement, for recognition and rewards, and for communication, the feeling of belonging, of talking the same language.

This one major characteristic of the faculty affects the undergraduate library in a number of ways. First, and most obviously, because recognition in the discipline comes almost exclusively as a result of research and publication, it feeds the ever-growing research orientation of the university and devalues proportionately teachhinr in general and undergraduate teaching in particular.

Second, because the faculty seem to think of achievement in a discipline as virtually equivalent of success in a career, it reinforces an increasing vocationalism and decreasing non-conformist (or independent) intellectualism in the student culture.

Third, it strengthens the department as a power base in the university structure, thus contributing to the fragmentation of centralized power in the university and to the consequent dispersion and weakening of support for centralized programs such as the undergraduate curriculum and for centralized facilities such as the undergraduate library.

And fourth, it underlines the typical professional view of the administration, including the library, as a bureaucracy which is, at best, efficient and unobstrusive or, at worst, a monolithic tyranny to be resisted at almost any cost.

These four aspects of the professionalization of the faculty, thus are clearly related to aspects of the other elements in the academic scene, also with mostly negative implications for the undergraduate library, which are to be considered later on.

But a more positive implication is also at least a possibility. To the extent that identification with a discipline includes acceptance of a common language, a common style of work, and common patterns of communication, understanding of these aspects of the several disciplines may give librarians clues which could open the way to a better relationship with the faculty who work in them.

This is to suggest not that the undergraduate library should be staffed with subject specialists, but rather that all academic librarians and undergraduate librarians in particular, should be especially alert and sensitive to similarities and differences among the disciplines which may have an effect on teaching objectives and methods and on the role of library resources and services in both teaching and in the discipline itself.

at big rsnch places   e.g. in Columbia in Kirk's time

Let me state a few generalizations to illustrate my point. (First, though, I should repeat my earlier warning that these are personal opinions derived from limited experience.):

General Faculty Attitudes

Most faculty members in all disciplines place a high value on "knowing one's subject" and share a corresponding lack of interest in teaching methodology and a common contempt for the "educationists" — a dirty word — who are concerned about learning theory, teaching strategy, behavioral outcomes and the like. Implication: librarians should underplay whatever theoretical expertise they may have in these matters. They should be cautious about too obvious alliances with instructional technologists, media specialists, and so on.

Nevertheless, and despite any disciplinary orientation, most of the faculty are sincerely concerned about their teaching effectiveness. They may be receptive to suggestions and help from the librarian, if they are persuaded that the librarian *really* understands their objectives — what they are driving at — and really has concrete information about students' learning behavior.

Also across disciplines, the faculty share a limited perception of what real understanding and skill in the use of library resources means. In varying degrees, depending on the discipline, they have achieved considerable mastery of the literature of their own respective fields. Below that, at what might be called a general education level of competence, they perceive nothing more complicated or demanding than what is taught in a good high school. Perhaps they are right in this perception, for certainly most library orientation and instruction programs in college duplicate what is covered in good high school programs, merely adding more tools or substituting more scholarly ones.

The implication, then, is that unless librarians can identify the concepts involved in sophisticated use of the library, something above the level of high school or common-sense skills but below the level of the subject specialist's grasp of a particular literature, they will never get much support from the faculty for attempts to provide students with the instruction they seem to need so much.

Blackburn points to certain other attitudes shared by the faculty across disciplines which might also be pertinent here. Librarians, he says, make the faculty feel guilty for failing to get students to use the library and feel humiliated at their own lack of ability to locate materials quickly.[2] This insight underlines the need for tact in presenting the case for or demonstrating the utility of college-level library competence.

Differences Among the Disciplines

A strategy for achieving a working relationship with the teaching faculty calls for understanding, also, of the differences among the several disciplines. If we understand these differences we may be able to decide which fields offer most promise, which faculties should be cultivated. To this end, let me present some notions that might be worth exploring.

If we consider the extent to which each discipline is empirical, in the narrow sense of using data derived from direct observation in a laboratory, through a telescope, in society or "the field," we get one measure of the role of the library in research. At one end of such a scale, the library has little or nothing to contribute to the empirical sciences; at the other end, it is the primary source of "raw" data for the non-empirical fields of literature and history; and in between, it contributes raw and or codified data for semi-empirical or hybrid disciplines such as economics and political science.

Similarly, if we consider the extent to which each discipline is cumulative, with each new discovery building on what has gone before, we get another measure. The cumulative natural sciences depend on the library for information which enables them to build on the work of the past and avoid duplication of effort; for the non-cumulative humanities this library function is much less crucial; and the social sciences again fall somewhere in the middle, since among them there are various overlapping styles of inquiry and each tends to develop new approaches and new evidence dealing with old questions.[3]

A third dimension worth considering might be the extent to which bibliographical expertise in the literature of a field is considered an essential part of the equipment of the professional working in it and is therefore typically required in graduate training. This factor might give us some clue as to the degree to which we might expect the faculty member in a given field to respect the librarian's bibliographical competence in comparison to his own. It is my impression that it explains, for example, the frequent reluctance of the English and history departments to collaborate wholeheartedly in library instructional programs.[4]

And finally, the undergraduate librarian should be particularly concerned with differences among the disciplines with respect to their educational goals and the extent of their interest in students. One study of an "Eastern University with a large and distinguished undergraduate program,"[5] classifies disciplines on their tendencies to stress goals which are "technical" (i.e., proficiency), "moral" (i.e., commitment, values, breadth) and "mixed" (i.e., a little of both) and on whether their interest in students is "high," "medium," or "low." In the resulting two-dimensional, nine-box chart, librarians might well look for allies in those disciplines which express a high interest in students. The significance of the goal categories is not so clear, since library competence might be involved in any or all of them. It seems reasonable to assume, nevertheless, that where library competence is viewed as an important component in technical proficiency, the discipline will wish to maintain control over it and thus be reluctant to collaborate with non-specialist librarians. But where library competence is thought of as a desirable liberalizing attribute of the educated man, the disciplines which stress the "moral" goals are likely to be more amenable to such collaboration.

These four ways of looking at differences among the disciplines can be summarized in the following tentative propositions:

First, the potential contribution of the library is likely to be most clearly recognized in those non-empirical disciplines for which it is a source of "raw" or codi-fied data: literature, history, political science, economics, and, to some extent sociology — and in those cumulative disciplines for which it supplies the essen-tial record of past and present research: all the natural sciences, and, to a much lesser extent, all of the social sciences.

Second, the greatest potential for collaboration between non-specialist librari-ans and teaching faculty for the development of library competence in students lies in those disciplines which do *not* stress bibliographical training as a part of their own advanced or graduate work: the humanities, *except* literature, the social sciences, *except* history and psychology — and in the disciplines which express "medium" or "high" interest in students and, at the same time, are ori-ented toward "moral" and "mixed" goals: as reported these are — (high-moral) economics, history, and fine arts; (high-mixed) geology and social relations; (medium-moral) classics and government; (medium-mixed) biology, anthropol-ogy and English.[6]

Recognizing the fact that this kind of analysis can be applied only in the most grossly general sense, that individual faculty members may differ markedly from their colleagues, and that a kindred spirit is a kindred spirit wherever you find him, we might nevertheless conclude from all this that it might be worthwhile for librarians to cultivate faculty members who work in those fields which have a fairly high *composite* ranking on these four dimensions, namely economics, political science, and the less field-work oriented branches of sociology.

The Student Culture

The GPA Perspective

Turning now to the students, let me begin with a quotation from *Making the Grade,* by Becker, Geer, and Hughes. Describing the attitudes and behavior of undergraduate students with respect to the academic side of college life as char-acterized by a grade point average (GPA) perspective, the authors describe this perspective as follows:

> The GPA perspective takes the rules made by faculty and administration about academic work as the basic reality with which a student must deal. It accepts as the definition of what is important the judgments handed down unilaterally from above and, in so doing, accepts the relationship of subjection between students and University without question. It accepts, of course, the definition embodied in col-lege practice — the definition that makes grades the measure of academic achieve-ment — and not various other definitions offered by University spokesmen from time to time which are not embodied in authoritative practice.
>
> Given this definition of what is important, the GPA perspective indicates various actions appropriate for students: seeking information, working hard, attempting to manipulate faculty in order to get a better grade, organizing for collective action to improve chances of getting a good grade, allocating effort in such a way as to max-

imize the over-all GPA, and so on. In short, students do what they calculate will best enable them to make the grade in what the institutions proffers as the only impersonal, objective, and formally recognized way of making that assessment.[7]

The major point for librarians is in that last sentence. Students will use the library if "they calculate that [doing so] will enable them to make the grade." The obvious implication is that if librarians want to reach the vast majority of undergraduate students, they must work with and through the teaching faculty to ensure that use of the library is a *required, essential* component in course work.

If, moreover, librarians want the library to play a significant educational role in the experience of this majority, if they are not satisfied with merely dispensing required reading, they must try to work out library-related course assignments which call for really complex, really demanding ways of exploiting the organized body of library resources. For the GPA perspective does not mean that students are invariably stimulated to do all the work they can to get *good* grades. Let me quote again:

> In balancing their responsibilities, obligations, and opportunities, students do not underestimate the importance of academic work. They understand and take into account that some minimal level of academic performance is necessary before rewards can be sought in other areas. But they sometimes decide — and this is where their views diverge most from those of the faculty — that they will settle for a lower level of academic achievement than they could expect if they devoted all their effort to academic work, choosing instead to pursue other rewards they also consider important.[8]

Student Sub-Cultures

Another way of looking at the student clientele is in terms of its sub-cultural groupings. One such typology, developed by Martin Trow and Burton Clark, distinguishes among four types, labelled academic, non-conformist, collegiate and vocational.

> These four categories are generated by the combination of two variables: the degree to which students are involved with ideas (much or little), and the extent to which students identify with their college (much or little).
> The students in both the academic and nonconformist subcultures are very much interested in ideas, but members of the former group are highly identified with their college while the latter are not . . . Members of the academic subculture identify with the concerns of faculty about their course work outside of class. There is an attachment to their school as an institution that supports intellectual values and opportunities for learning. On the other hand, the distinctive quality of members of the nonconformist subculture is a rather aggressive nonconformism, a critical detachment from the college they attend and from its faculty, and a generalized hostility to the administration . . .
> The students in the other two subcultures — collegiate and vocational — are not

particularly involved with ideas. Students in the collegiate subculture, while strongly attached and loyal to their college are resistant or indifferent to serious intellectual demands. Their values and activities focus on social life and extra-curricular activities. Students in the vocational subculture are neither intellectually oriented nor particularly attached to or generally involved in their college, which they view as off-the-job training. College is regarded as an organization of courses and credits leading to a diploma and a better job than they could otherwise command.[9]

In considering the implications for our purposes here, of this sort of analysis, we must first note that the undergraduate library is almost exclusively a phenomenon of the very large graduate and research-oriented university. In such a context, we would expect to find that: 1) the collegiate subculture is on the wane and that, in any case, the library would find it hard to reach; 2) the vocational subculture predominates, but that with increasing professionalization of the disciplines and a consequent emphasis on graduate work, the academic subculture is also strong; and 3) both the academic and the vocational subcultures are especially responsive to course and faculty demands, especially concerned with achievement as measured by grades; the former because they genuinely accept the standards of the faculty, the latter because they see adequate grades as necessary credentials to be gathered for eventual certification for a job.

The earlier point about working through the faculty applies to both groups. (Undergraduate librarians should be aware, however, of the possibility that some students in both of these groups, but particularly in the academic subculture, may develop an early attachment to the departmental libraries, if there are such, which serve their respective majors.)

One final point: The nonconformist subculture is a small but interesting and, perhaps, growing minority. Because of its intellectual and aesthetic bent, and because it is less subject to the GPA perspective, the library might well decide that it is the one subculture worth courting directly.

The Student Protest Movement

The lag between research and the actual course of events is nowhere so apparent as in discussion of the student culture. The student protest movement has moved so rapidly, changing direction as it goes, now breaking into factions, later coalescing as a result of dramatic and tragic events, that it is almost impossible to keep up with. In the process it has stimulated floods of print, some few examples of careful and objective analysis, and only a very little empirical research. It has met with more success in its attempt to change the university than one would have thought possible ten years ago, and yet the final outcome of the movement is certainly in doubt.

Nevertheless, one might venture the suggestion that most of the goals of the student movement have significance for the undergraduate library, some of them quite positive. The call for a greater emphasis on teaching instead of research surely portends a more important role for the undergraduate library.

The demand for a share in the power governing the university, as it becomes more sophisticated, may undermine the enormous influence of the graduate departments. This, too, should mean that more attention would be paid to the undergraduate program. The hostility toward bureaucracy in the university may stimulate the library to de-emphasize its own bureaucratic tendencies.[10] Surely these are goals we should support.

The Undergraduate Curriculum

The Standard Curriculum

The familiar elements of the undergraduate curriculum — skills courses, distribution requirements, and major requirements, are common to most universities,[11] and have remained substantially the same for a good many years. A recent study, based on a comparison between descriptions of undergraduate programs in catalogs of 1957 compared with those of 1967, concludes:

> Despite all the talk about innovation, undergraduate curricular requirements, as a whole, have changed remarkably little in ten years. In many cases, the most that could be said of a particular institution was that its curriculum has been renovated — that is, requirements were restated in terms of new patterns of organization and course offerings and updated to recognize the rights of newer disciplines to a place in the sun. One suspects that, in some cases, this latter consideration rather than a real concern for flexibility may have motivated a move from specific course or discipline requirements to broader distribution requirements. In many cases, the minor changes in requirements, amounting to no more than a reshuffling of credits, can only be characterized as tinkering, although one can imagine faculties spending many hours on these pointless decisions.[12]

There has been a marked increase in the number of institutions which report opportunities for individualization in the curriculum.

> Almost one-half or more of the institutions provide advanced placement (85 percent), honors programs (66 percent), independent study (58 percent), seminars (51 percent), and study abroad programs (47 percent). This represents at least twice the number of colleges and universities making these provisions ten years ago.[13]

But since the study does not differentiate between four-year colleges and universities, we do not know how many of the large universities, about 20 percent of the sample, have followed the trend. More important, we have no indication as to the number of students in any of the institutions who can and do take advantage of these opportunities. In the universities we are concerned with here, enrollments are so large that it seems unlikely that any sizable proportion of the undergraduate student body would be involved in such individualized activities.

Thus we are back with the "standard" undergraduate curriculum which is designed to provide first, the general liberal education — with the breadth and depth needed by the "educated man," — second, preparation for citizenship, or more broadly, effective participation in society, and third, training for a job or for admission to advanced professional training. (An additional purpose not proclaimed but real enough, is that of serving as a screening stage through which young people are sorted out into various social and occupational classes.)

Although the ideal of the "educated man" or the cultivated man persists, the time is long past, if there ever was such a time, when there was any real consensus as to what basic knowledge he should have. Some still stress the high culture of western civilization. Others are more concerned with introducing the student to the major problems of our own time. Some want him to acquire the communication and intellectual habits and skills he will need to continue in a life-long learning process. And still others are eclectic, content that if enough hours of breadth and enough hours of depth are required, he will emerge as a reasonable facsimile of the ideal.

As a deliberately pluralistic policy, there would be nothing intrinsically wrong with having the curriculum serve all of these ends, but in most universities the pluralism comes by default, partly as a result of compromise among differing views about the purpose of undergraduate education but mostly through a trade-off process among the departments of the College of Arts and Sciences.

Disciplinary Orientation

Normally the undergraduate curriculum (except in undergraduate professional programs such as business, education, and engineering) is staffed by faculty from this College, each department contributing teachers for the undergraduate offerings in its own discipline. As a group, these teachers have no organizational autonomy nor even identity as an undergraduate faculty. Each is subject to the pressures within his own department — for promotion, tenure, and recognition — to identify with its discipline and particularly with its aspirations for prestige in the graduate school.

This identification feeds the natural tendency of the instructor to regard his undergraduate courses as the foundation for advanced work in the discipline where "real" education begins, rather than as a part of a program of general, liberal education. Often he treats these courses as screening mechanisms, as if they were designed primarily to identify and recruit the most promising candidates for admission to his own graduate field and to weed out those whose aspirations exceed their academic ability. As long as successful completion of an undergraduate major is a qualification for admission to the graduate program in a discipline, this tendency is almost inevitable. But the same major is also expected to provide the "experience in depth" which theory holds to be an essential part of a liberal education, and the introductory courses required for a major in a given discipline are, more often than not, also made distribution requirements for other disciplines and for pre-professional and professional curricula.

In short, any one undergraduate course may be expected to serve three functions: 1) as a contribution to the breadth of knowledge that every educated person should have; 2) as an experience in depth that is thought to be an essential component in a *liberal* education; and 3) as one of a series of certifying steps through which the student must demonstrate his capacity to move up the career ladder into the ranks of those who are qualified to prepare for a place in the "profession" of the discipline. In actuality, the third function is almost always paramount because of the lack of a clear and persuasive rationale for the place of any given course in either the "breadth" or "depth" dimension of liberal education while the certification function is recognizably compatible with the prevailing trend toward professionalization of the disciplines. Furthermore, in the usual organizational structure of the university, the first two functions are "service" functions — services provided by the College of Arts and Sciences to the rest of the university — while only the third is truly "professional." Instructors who teach only undergraduate courses are in a position somewhat comparable to that of librarians who also provide a service function for the teaching faculty.

The University as an Organization

Power and Academic Goals

In the summary of her study of six undergraduate libraries, Braden indicates that establishment of a separate undergraduate library is probably not justified unless "graduate students constitute one-third to one-half of the student body" and until "a collection reaches a million volumes."[14] The significance of these two factors in determining the characteristics of the specific kind of university we are concerned with here is illuminated by a recent study of the relationship between the power structure of the university and its goals.[15] Although there is a general similarity in the power structure of all American universities, the authors found important differences related to a) "graduate emphasis," measured on the basis of the proportion of graduate students,[16] and b) "prestige," for which one measure was number of volumes in the library.[17]

A major conclusion of the study is that power of external forces (funding agencies, alumni, legislatures, and citizens) as compared with that of internal elements (administrative officers, deans, department chairmen, and faculty) is associated with a "service" versus an "elitist" goal orientation.

> At universities whose library holdings are large, the power of the dean of liberal arts, chairmen of departments, and faculty members is considerable. This finding probably reflects the scholarly orientation of these three power-holders and of their consequent demand for good library facilities.
>
> The graduate emphasis of a university is also related to its power structure. As the proportion of graduate students increases, so does the rated power of private agencies. The power of legislators and of the state government, on the other hand, tends to decline, at state universities as well as private ones (where, of course, these

groups have little power to begin with). Moreover, the faculty tends to have more power, relative to other groups, and citizens of the state, less power.[18]

The authors report on the goal orientations of "these three power-holders" as follows:

The goals associated with a powerful dean of liberal arts . . . are the scholarly and elitist goals as opposed to practical and somewhat anti-intellectual goals. The student's intellect, objectivity, knowledgability about great ideas, and scholarly skills are cultivated, pure research is exalted over applied research . . . Admissions policies are selective, graduate work is encouraged at the expense of emphasis on *undergraduate instruction which invariably ranks in the bottom third of goals* (Italics supplied.)

At institutions where chairmen as a group are perceived as having considerable say in decision-making, the goal structure resembles that of universities where deans of liberal arts or of professional schools are powerful . . . The findings for chairmen resemble even more closely the findings for faculty — not surprisingly since chairmen usually regard themselves, and are regarded, as faculty members.

The findings for faculty resemble the findings for chairmen, and . . . these in turn are very similar to the findings for deans of liberal arts and of professional schools . . . The goals pursued are essentially the same . . . At universities where the faculty has considerable power (relative to their power at other universities), low priority is very definitely assigned to such goals as producing a well-rounded student, providing him with the skills and experiences that will facilitate upward mobility, cultivating his taste, and preparing him for citizenship. Similarly, certain support goals are subordinated. Keeping harmony and *emphasizing undergraduate instruction are invariably ranked in the bottom third of goals.*[19] (Italics supplied.)

In their summary, the authors indicate that the administrators and faculty in all kinds of universities, not just the elite, give high priority to the goal of "training students for scholarship, research, and creative endeavour" and that emphasis on undergraduate instruction ranks very low as an actual ("perceived") *and* as a desired ("preferred") goal.[20] However, it is the fact that in the elite universities deans, department chairmen, and faculty have a greater share of the *power* that gives their goal orientation particular significance for our purposes here.

These universities ranking high on any of these measures [research productivity, prestige, or graduate emphasis] manifest an elitist pattern of perceived goals: They emphasize developing the student's intellective and scholarly qualities; they carry on pure research; they see themselves as centers for disseminating ideas and preserving the cultural heritage. With respect to support goals, they stress those aimed at satisfying the desires and needs of the faculty, *they tend to slight undergraduate instruction but to encourage graduate work,* and they demonstrate a concern for position goals having to do with the top quality of the academic program and with prestige.[21] (Italics supplied.)

Organizational Structure

They hire
B. A.'s to do it

Recognizing the fact that those who hold power in the university are fairly unanimous in giving a low priority to undergraduate education (and presumably, to
the undergraduate library which serves it) we may still find it useful to understand the structure through which that power operates. It should be obvious, in
the first place, that the line authority on the university's organization chart —
from the board of trustees through the president, vice presidents, deans and
department chairmen to the individual faculty member — is much less com-
manding than it appears on paper. Boards, in general, carry a large share of
responsibility for raising money; they exercise perfunctory control of the budget
and over high-level promotions and tenure appointments. On whatever other
matters the president brings before them, the trustees usually function in a supportive fashion.[23] The power of the president to determine what is brought
before them is also less significant than one might think, for the faculty, particularly the local faculty "politicians," have various formal and informal avenues
for seeing to it that their views are presented. The president preferring to avoid
confrontation at the board level, rarely makes proposals which a powerful segment of the faculty opposes.

Within the university the president's power is limited because he is subject to a
great many diverse pressures both from lower echelon administrative officers
and from the faculty oligarchy which controls the advisory faculty bodies.[24]
These appear on the organization chart as a hierarchy of departmental committees, college councils, graduate councils, topped by the faculty senate. Despite
their "advisory" label, the power of these bodies is clearly evidenced in the caution with which the wise administrative officer approaches them with reports
and proposals and in their readiness to insist upon a veto power over any proposal for which the remotest claim can be made that it has "educational"
implications.

And yet these official faculty bodies have little effectiveness in a positive direction because they reflect the competition among the departments within the university. For the most important power base within the university is the
department or, as we would infer from the study of goals, the graduate component of the department. There are, of course, external limits on its power: the
total amount of funding for research available from foundations and the government, occasional pressures from legislatures, alumni, and so on. The major limitation, however, is not external at all, but internal. It consists of the competiton
among graduate departments within the university each vying for *its* share of the
budget, *its* voice in determining admissions qualifications, grading policies,
graduation requirements, and recognition of *its* discipline in "distribution" or
general education requirements in the curriculum.[25]

Within the outer limits set by this inter-departmental competition for funds
and for a voice in general policy-making, each department has almost unchallenged control of faculty appointments, tenure and promotion.[26] Through its
power to determine requirements for admission to its graduate program, it

exerts substantial control over the undergraduate curriculum within the university of which it is a part. Furthermore, depending on its national eminence, it may have considerable influence on the undergraduate programs of all those universities and colleges which aspire to that measure of excellence which depends on the mumber of graduates who are accepted by prestigious graduate schools.

Whether as cause or effect, this concentration of significant power in the graduate departments is paralleled in the university at large by fragmentation of power over non-curricular, non-academic matters. There are checks and balances in the general administrative structure as there are in that of any complex bureaucracy where the autonomy of each administrative division is limited by the necessity for coordination with others.

The "Professionally-Oriented" Organization

But the dispersion of effective power among the segments of the university bureaucracy is greater than one finds in other complex organizations of comparable size, such as a corporation or a government agency. One reason for this is that the university falls into the category of organization the sociologists call the "professionally-oriented." In such an organization the sole purpose of the administration is to expedite what the professionals consider the real work of the organization, that which occurs only in the interrelationship between the professional and his clients or, in the university, between the professor and his students. From the viewpoint of the professional, the ideal administrative machinery is one which works economically, efficiently, and as unobtrusively as possible and, for the professor in the university, the library is part of that administration.

Universities are like hospitals in this respect, but they have added stress arising from the fact that the expertise of the professor — at least as teacher — is not so esoteric, not so far beyond a layman's claim to comprehension and competence — and in the professional realm of the university, administrators, again including librarians, are laymen.

In the hospital, the doctor's claim to an authoritative role vis à vis the hospital administration is largely unchallenged; in the university, the professor's claim to authority, by virtue of his knowledge in a specific subject discipline, is similarly unchallenged and probably unchallengeable at the graduate and research level. At the undergraduate level it is challenged, but the challenge is weak, because, as we have seen, in the organizational structure of the university power is generally fragmented and diffused. Neither the administrative hierarchy nor any organized body of the faculty has so far had what it takes to break through the stalemate of indifference created by competition among graduate departments.

But there is hope for change. Not just educationists, but many eminent scholars have long been seriously concerned about the decreasing attention paid to, and the decline in prestige of, teaching, particularly undergraduate teaching. The student protest movement, from Berkeley on, has made it clear that this concern is justified, but more important, in its very excess, it has produced general awareness of the consequences of the trend toward the multiversity. It has forced both administrators and faculty to undertake serious programs of self-examination and reform.[27] (The excesses of the student movement have also, of course, created a public awareness which can easily backfire, as, for example, when a cut in legislative appropriations results in an even more mass approach to undergraduate teaching.)

The Undergraduate Library and the Library System

Organizational Characteristics

The undergraduate library exists as one component in a total university library system. The function of that system in supporting research is immediately recognizable and easily demonstrated which means that inevitably it responds more readily to the demands of the research-oriented establishment than to the weak requirements of the undergraduate program. It shares with the central administration of the university the problem of balancing off the conflicting claims among the research needs of the various departments and professional schools. The undergraduate library, like the undergraduate program as a whole, is scarcely even a contender in this battle.

In contrast with the university administration, however, the university library, as an organization in itself, is not professionally-oriented.[28] Its organization reflects the actual distribution of power, authority and responsibility. This comment is not meant to suggest that the university library system is necessarily or even characteristically administered in an authoritative fashion. It does mean that in library organization — usually for very good reason — there is nothing comparable to the tradition and expectation of decentralized authority or departmental autonomy that one finds in the university organization as a whole.

Moreover, although the undergraduate library may not be far down the hierarchy on the organization chart, the control from above is not nominal but real. Furthermore, its staff is usually not very high in the pecking order. Undergraduate librarians are generalists in a situation which rewards administrators and specialists. They aspire to a teaching role in a community where it is assumed that anybody can teach if he knows his subject. And finally, they are removed from contact with the subject department which, as indicated above, is the major power base of the university.

Undergraduate Library Objectives

In contrast with the crucial value of the library to the research programs of the university, the library needs of the undergraduate program are less clear-cut, less manifest, less obviously essential. Such "objectives" as those identified in Braden's study of six undergraduate libraries are not particularly helpful for the purpose of elucidating any unique function.[29] Most of them are really antidotes to the ills of the large research library — comfortable and attractive quarters and furnishings (in contrast to the scholar's cluttered office or the graduate student's cramped carrel in the stacks), a collection of books carefully selected to fit a liberal, undergraduate program (in contrast to the comprehensive collection of the university), open access to the stacks (in contrast to the labyrinth, whether open or closed stacks, of the main library), centralization (instead of scattering) of materials, simplification (instead of complexity) of bibliographical access.

One of the objectives "To provide services additional to those given in the research library" seems to have resulted in the fact that the undergraduate library sometimes becomes a catch-all for all sorts of special collections and services in the areas of music, art, poetry and so forth. Often these materials and services are unrelated to any curriculum — least of all the undergraduate — but they represent an acknowledgement of cultural enrichment as a general objective of a liberal, undergraduate curriculum and, conveniently, a simultaneous effort to provide for some of the cultural interests of the university community as a whole. One objective listed by Braden is of particular concern in this discussion. It is this: "To attempt to make the library an instructional tool by planning it as a center for instruction in library use to prepare undergraduates for using larger collections." There is little or no solid evidence on the extent to which this objective has been attained. Clearly undergraduate librarians, themselves, are not satisfied with what they have been able to achieve in this area. My major purpose in this paper, of course, is to explain some of the obstacles they face with the hope that a clear understanding of the problems will lead to more effective methods of dealing with them.

more specialized

Operational Problems

Turning from stated objectives to the concrete library needs implied by the character of the undergraduate program, we immediately encounter some of the operational difficulties the undergraduate library faces as part of the university library system. Operationally the university library system is geared toward the scholar's approach to the use of materials. This pattern is partly the result of tradition but it is also in accord with the general research emphasis of a university as a whole. In it the whole organization of library services and bibliographical organization is designed to retrieve for the individual scholar the precise, the unique item he requires. Almost always, as librarians work, they have a mental image of this scholar who will one day need this book, this journal, this bit of information; and all their efforts are bent toward preparing the machinery — including their own knowledge, their own memory store — in such a way that they can extract the single book, the exact issues of a journal, the specific item of information from the vast storehouse which the library is.

The contrasts with the library needs of the undergraduate program are fairly obvious. First, undergraduate library service is a mass service; what the undergraduate needs is not *the* unique item but enough copies of the required readings.[30] Furthermore, the deadlines of the undergraduate student, unlike those of the scholar, are imposed and relatively inflexible; the penalties he faces if he cannot get what he needs when he needs it are very severe.

Second, where variation or choice of reading is permitted, many of the books and journals he can use for a given assignment are virtually interchangeable; he does not require the meticulous bibliographical description which is required to identify each item's uniqueness for the scholar's retrieval.

Third, the "content" of what the undergraduate is expected to learn can come from his teacher, his textbook, or other print and non-print sources — including library materials. It is not clear what these other sources add to the teacher-textbook content nor have we as yet identified with any precision what the library is uniquely or even especially well-prepared to supply. As a specific example, even the term paper, which is the common "individual" assignment in the undergraduate curriculum, is often based on sources which the student somehow ran across while skimming through current magazines or while browsing the paperback racks in the bookstore, or on items suggested by the instructor, by a classmate or by the textbook itself. My frequent personal impression, in fact, is that the better term paper is the product not of an orderly library search but of a marriage between an inquiring, imaginative student mind and sheer serendipity as to sources.

In short, the operational requirements of the undergraduate library are seriously at odds with those of the parent university library system. Many policies and procedures are diametrically opposed to the sort of fine tuning between supply and demand which characterizes the operation of a well-run supermarket — which is the appropriate model for the undergraduate library. We are reluctant to buy duplicates to meet immediate demands, wanting to be assured ahead of time that the demand will be sustained. We jealously guard current issues of periodicals, being inclined to send them off to the bindery at precisely the time their usefulness is greatest because we want to be sure that we have unbroken back files. We rely on a centralized processing department, one in which meticulous bibliographic verification and description of every item must fit the exacting requirements of the scholar, without regard to the cost to the student of the resulting time lag in making materials available.

Advantages and Opportunities

In this section attention so far has been directed exclusively to the negative aspects of the undergraduate library's position in the university library system. The advantages are more obvious: 1) the university library system provides a back-up of resources and services which are available to the undergraduate student so that he is not dependent on the undergraduate library for all his library needs; 2) the undergraduate library collection is likely to be far better than any college library collection of comparable size, because the university can involve a considerably greater range of subject specialists in the process of selection and because, again, the back-up function of the university library reduces the risk which might accrue to a too narrow definition of what is properly "undergraduate;" and 3) a separate undergraduate library building increases the ability of the library administration to resist encroachment on the part of faculty, administrators, departments, and departmental libraries, all of which are always hungry for space.

It is clear, nevertheless, that the undergraduate library has difficulty making the most of its superior collection and physical facilities partly because of its disadvantageous position in the university library system. In its attempt to take on a teaching function it is particularly handicapped, especially in comparison with most four-year college libraries, because it is faced with a massive student body.

Among the trends which might help to remedy this situation are the following:

1.   A call in academic circles for a decentralization of decision-making.[31]
2.   The appearance of a similar sentiment in library literature, at least, and perhaps in practice.[32]
3.   Actual decentralization of the undergraduate program in the form of cluster colleges (Santa Cruz and San Diego) and colleges-within-the-university (Monteith at Wayne State, Charter College at Oakland, Justin Morrill at Michigan State, and the residential college at Michigan).

It must be emphasized that this latter development, the establishment of new colleges within the university, will have no impact on library service to undergraduates unless the university library (or the undergraduate library) makes a point of capitalizing on the opportunity that almost any new program affords. It was disappointing to learn, for example, that the separate college libraries at Santa Cruz are not really libraries at all but reading rooms, that they get neither funds nor staff from the central library. Similarly, it was discouraging to hear that because the new residential colleges at Michigan had no library of its own — the students use the Undergradate Library — the possibility of developing a library *program* for that college was not even seriously considered.

Conclusion

Perspectives on the Undergraduate Library

Before moving on to a proper set of conclusions and recommendations, let me propose four different general perspectives on the undergraduate library:

1.   The undergraduate library is, almost by definition, a phenomenon of the large, research-oriented university. Increase in research activities and in graduate and professional school enrollment produces enormously increased demands on the university library for research materials and services. As a result the

space, the collection, and the services needed for the undergraduate program are simply crowded out. The undergraduate student is, in effect, a displaced person and the undergraduate library is a compensatory measure taken on his behalf. It offers him an efficient and reasonably comfortable refugee camp.

This view, one which might be dubbed "the radical perspective," sees the undergraduate library as essentially one of the symptoms of the ills of the multiversity "system" and of the "sick society" which supports it. Presented in the fashionable heightened "rhetoric" of the dissidents, the picture is both distorted and over-simplified but it has, I think, enough reality in it to make us all uncomfortable.

2.   The reality in the "instrumental" perspective is more easily perceived and much more comfortable to live with. Its language is usually statistical and the view it presents, usually in annual reports, is one of ever-increasing attendance and circulation, longer and longer hours of service, more and more reference questions and so on. The philosophy behind this perspective is well expressed in a statement about the Undergraduate Library of the University of Michigan:

> But for libraries like the UGL, demand can be calculated according to numbers of readers. Given that simplification, the rest follows: The UGL collection is comparatively select because it was created to serve a comparatively select group of readers. The UGL is free to concentrate on problems of number simply because problems of value are relegated to other members of the University community — those who set admission standards, or establish curricula, or determine reading requirements. The UGL is, in short, more clearly instrumental than any other library at the University, and quantifiable standards of efficiency can be more meaningfully applied to it than to any other. The point is worth laboring because both universities and libraries are often called upon to justify operations in terms of working efficiency. The UGL is almost a test case, suggesting that educators and librarians can work with factory-like efficiency, when and if they believe the case is one which safely allows for concentration on numbers.[33]

3.   A third view one might call the "aristocratic" perspective. In this view the undergraduate library provides an environment, materials and services appropriate for general, liberal education, that fundamental learning which marks the "cultivated" man, whatever his professional or social role may be. The reality in this perspective is symbolized by the art galleries, the record collections, the poetry rooms, and so on, which are proudly described as "special services" of the undergraduate library. It is implied in the particular attention given to the physical appearance of the undergraduate library, the preference for carpeting "Because it is quiet and induces an aura of graciousness,"[34] and the provision of attractive lounge areas (although these are often reduced in size or even removed altogether as demand for seating space increases). But most of all it is attested to in book collection policy statements:

> The collection of the Lamont Library at Harvard would "attempt to reach beyond

the curriculum to provide a selection of the best writings of all times and peoples."[35]

The collection of the Uris Library at Cornell would contain "the best of those books which in the judgment of the university faculty are requisite to create a thoroughly informed and cultured modern person."[36]

The Undergraduate Library at the University of Texas "was thought of as an enlarged 'gentleman's library' with books in the arts, letters, and sciences aimed at the level of the layman. Emphasis is on fine biography and history, contemporary *belles lettres,* literary criticism and reliable interpretation of science for the non scientist."[37]

4. The fourth perspective stresses a teaching role for the undergraduate library. Statements on the purpose of the undergraduate library often indicate that the undergraduate student can here, with a smaller and selective collection and a less complex and cumbersome bibliographic apparatus, develop the skills which will enable him later to use the larger and more complicated scholarly library effectively. Some doubters question this ready assumption of transfer of training,[38] however, and there is no research evidence on the point. But in addition, some of these statements use phrases like "instructional tool" or "learning workshops" which suggest something more than or different from mere retrieval skills, that is, the ability to *locate* books and articles and information.

Presumably that "something more" occurs to some extent in the teaching emphasis in undergraduate library reference service, about which we are to hear more later. But the phrases suggest, also, a more general and total involvement in undergraduate education, a role which is well-described in the terms "active service capability" and "the concept of librarian as teacher," which were used in the proposal for this Institute.

Each of these four views offers a different picture of the present state and future prospects of the undergraduate library. From the radical perspective, the undergraduate library symbolizes the system which must be turned around, if not overturned, in the interests of a just and humane society. From the instrumental perspective, the undergraduate library is a product of the same managerial competence and efficiency which has managed to provide abundance and affluence for an astonishing proportion of the American people — despite an ever-increasing population and ever-rising expectations. From the aristocratic perspective, the undergraduate library is the embodiment of the threatened but still vital ideal of a liberal, civilizing education. And from the teaching perspective the undergraduate library epitomizes the fundamental concern of the educator with the *process* of learning.

The teaching perspective is probably the least realistic of the four suggested. But it is also the most challenging. So let us take up the challenge.

Summary and Recommendations

In order to work toward the ideal of the undergraduate library as a teaching instrument, we must begin by developing as clear as possible an understanding of these elements of the academic world which will inevitably play an important part in the outcome of our efforts and by determining to *use* this understanding as a *positive* contribution to the development of an active campaign to achieve our goal. Specifically, with respect to the faculty:

1.   The trend toward professionalization of the disciplines brings along with it a sense of identification with the disciplinary peer group and a corresponding distrust of — and some degree of immunity to — the local administrative hierarchy. We should not attempt to achieve our objectives by way of administrative fiat, but we should use whatever administrative support we can get in seeking access to the faculty. In addition, we should de-emphasize the bureaucratic style of library operations as much as we safely can.

2.   Faculty members are sincerely concerned about their teaching effectiveness and, at the moment, they are feeling guilty because they are under attack for alleged neglect of their teaching duties. We should do our best to capitalize on this situation by making it known, in an aggressive but diplomatic way, that the library and its staff have both the willingness and the capacity to help. We should also support, in any way we can, the efforts of those faculty members who attempt to achieve a redress of the balance between teaching and research on the campus.

3.   Most faculty members know little about learning theory or instructional methodology but their attitude toward these matters is usually one of indifference or contempt. This means that librarians who are knowledgeable in these areas have an important contribution to make but that they must be extremely circumspect in making it.

4.   Faculty members, quite rightly, regard use of the library as a means toward the achievement of their own teaching objectives. We must, therefore, guard against our own tendency to view library use or skill in library use as ends in themselves. (Those who regard, as I do, the ability to use the library effectively, like the ability to write effectively, as one of the attributes of the liberally educated man, must discretely propose this objective as a rather nice bonus that the student can collect incidentally as he strives to attain the instructor's course objectives.)

5.   The faculty has limited understanding of the intellectual processes involved in sophisticated library competence. We must avoid technical, high schoolish programs of instruction in use of the library, developing and using, instead, individual self-teaching devices to convey such how-to-do-it skills to those students who need them, *when* they need them. Since we are far from secure in our own understanding of the intellectual processes in library use, we must also strive to overcome this weakness by attempting constantly to identify and make explicit these processes in our own work.

6.   The potential for active collaboration between the library and the faculty varies from discipline to discipline as well as from individual to individual. We must, therefore, be alert to the possibilities at both levels, deliberately cultivating

the faculty in departments whose fields seem promising and at the same time making the most of every contact with any library-minded professor.

With respect to students:

1.   The single most important influence on the student's academic behavior is the GPA perspective. In order to get the highest payoff for our effort to increase the library's contribution to the educational program, therefore, we must work primarily with and through the faculty.

2.   An important item on the agenda of the student activists, at least of the moderates, is improvement in the quality of undergraduate teaching. We must support these students in this effort. We might, for instance, try to involve the most talented of such students in examining the potential role of the library in excellent teaching and in developing plans to see that this potential is realized.

3.   The student subculture which has been labelled "nonconformist" combines intellectual interests with a rejection of institutional pressures toward the GPA perspective. We should, therefore, explore ways of working directly with students in this category, if possible involving them in plans for making available library activities, materials, and services which meet their interests.

With respect to the undergraduate curriculum:

1.   The most serious obstacle to the development of a coherent and effective undergraduate curriculum for general, liberal education is the power of the competing graduate programs in the disciplines and of the "credentialism" which accompanies it. We must support the efforts of those who recognize this phenomenon and oppose it, participating formally, if possible, informally, if not, in any campus activities concerned with curriculum study and reform.

2.   Another serious obstacle stems from the fact that the undergraduate teaching staff has no identity as such, no claim to autonomy in its work. We should, therefore, make the most of any exceptions to this general rule, establishing relationships with, proposing library programs for, whatever councils, separate colleges, or other administrative entities there may be.

With respect to the university as an organization:

1.   The power structure and goal orientation characteristic of the type of university in which the undergraduate library is likely to occur produce an environment which is hostile to emphasis on undergraduate instruction, as such, but highly favorable to objectives having to do with developing students' intellectual and scholarly skills. In making the case for use of the undergraduate library, therefore, we should stress its relevance to intellectual and scholarly work rather than to undergraduate education or the undergraduate curriculum.

2.   The university is a professionally-oriented complex organization. Understanding the characteristics of this type, we should be neither surprised nor disturbed to recognize that the teaching faculty regard the library as having a "service" function, as playing a supportive, subsidiary part in the educational

program. What is important is not the label placed on our contribution but that it be significant.

3.   Coordination of the tremendous range and variety of library activities necessitates an hierarchical organizational structure for the university library system and a consequent limitation on the autonomy of any individual professional librarian. The resulting disparity between the "academic style" of the professor and the "professional style" of the librarian is an obstacle to the achievement of a colleague relationship. Library policies and procedures, therefore, should be reviewed and revised to the end of giving the individual professional librarian as much authority and responsibility as is practicable without damage to the system as a whole.

With respect to the undergraduate library in the university library system:

1.   The university library system is quite naturally and inevitably responsive primarily to the library requirements of the graduate and research programs of the university. This means that an effort to enhance the contribution of the undergraduate library calls for conscious and deliberate measures to: a) identify in a *positive* way the unique functions of the undergraduate library, b) recruit and/or train librarians for the undergraduate library staff who have the particular qualifications which would enable them to collaborate actively with the teaching faculty (e.g., a commitment to the teaching enterprise, a broad liberal arts background of high quality, and thorough understanding of curriculum design, learning theory, and instructional methods), and c) make certain that this staff has access to the faculty, that it is involved in all levels of planning.

2.   Operations in the university library system are designed to serve the needs and the style of the individual scholar. To the extent that the undergraduate library is obliged to follow this operational pattern, its efficiency in providing necessary mass service may be severely limited. We must develop ways of rationalizing mass library service to undergraduates in cost-efficiency terms, but in doing so we must build into our calculations: a) a better understanding of the differences between the "approach" requirements of the individual and the large group; b) an acceptance of the idea that most of the materials used in undergraduate education are not rare or irreplaceable but expendable — the more they are used up in the learning process the better; and c) recognition of the fact that student time is a crucial element in the cost part of our equations.[39]

3.   The inescapable necessity for mass service in the undergraduate library underlines the validity of what I have called "the instrumental perspective" to such an extent that it threatens to swamp any other view. We must, therefore, distinguish carefully between mass service and the other legitimate undergraduate library functions, make mass service as efficient and economical as possible, and use whatever savings there may be to support these other functions.

None of the recommendations presented above offer much in the way of concrete, practical actions that can be put into effect immediately. But for library administrators and undergraduate librarians who are truly committed to the teaching perspective, they may serve as a useful long-range set of "guidelines for bucking the system."

Notes

1. Christopher Jencks and David Riesman,   *The Academic Revolution* (New York: Doubleday & Company, 1968).

2. Robert T. Blackburn, "College Libraries — Indicated Failures: Some Reasons — and a Possible Remedy," *College and Research Libraries* XXIX (March, 1968): 171-177.

3. Daniel Bell uses the terms "sequential" (natural science), "concentric" (humanities), and "linkage" (social sciences) to describe a parallel distinction among these fields as to the stages of learning they involve. See his *The Reforming of General Education* (New York: Columbia University Press, 1966).

4. The faculty in art and music, unless they are working on historical aspects, are at the other end of this scale. They usually know little about the library or even about the literature of their own field. In my experience, however, they are often reluctant to cooperate with the library because they have so often encountered librarians who tend to recommend biography and criticism to the student when the instructor wants him to experience the work of art directly and personally.

5. Rebecca S. Vreeland and Charles E. Bidwell, "Classifying University Departments: an Approach to the Analysis of Their Effects upon Undergraduates' Values and Attitudes." *Sociology of Education* XXIX (Summer, 1966): 237-254, cited by Kenneth A. Feldman and Theodore M. Newcomb, *The Impact of College on Students,* (San Francisco: Jossey-Bass Inc., 1969), I, 172.

6. Ibid., p. 186.

7. Howard S. Becker, Blanche Geer, and Everett C. Hughes, *Making the Grade: The Academic Side of College Life* (New York: John Wiley and Sons, Inc., 1968), p. 133.

8. Ibid., p. 134.

9. Burton R. Clark and Martin Trow, "The Organizational Context" in *College Peer Groups: Problems and Prospects for Research,* edited by T. M. Newcomb and E. K. Wilson, cited by Feldman and Newcomb, op. cit., pp. 232-33. (Note, however, that this study was first reported on in 1960.)

10. In the mass efficiency of its operations, the undergraduate library is really a symptom of the system that the students are rebelling against, but they have most not yet recognized it as such. We might conclude, therefore, that the undergraduate library should just keep quiet. As one of Braden's guidelines puts it, "Let use of the library develop according to the character of the student body. Do not try to enforce any stringent rules." Irene A. Braden, *The Undergraduate Library* (Chicago: American Library Association), p. 150.

11. "The samness of the undergraduate curriculum among colleges belies the pluralism which is foremost among the official virtues of the system. The pervasiveness of

standard curricular patterns is ample evidence that the processes generating them inhere in the institutional system rather than in each faculty. As well might a common snail imagine it had chosen the pattern on its shell, which is, of course, generic to its kind." Phillip C. Ritterbush, "Adaptive Response within the Institutional System of Higher Education and Research," *Daedalus,* XCIX (Summer, 1970) 656.

12. Paul L. Dressel and Frances H. DeLisle, *Undergraduate Curriculum Trends* (Chicago: American Council on Education, 1969), p. 75.

13. Ibid., p. 44.

14. Braden, op. cit., p. 148.

15. Edward Gross and Paul V. Grambsch, *University Goals and Academic Power* (Washington: American Council on Education, 1968).

16. Ibid., p. 56.

17. Ibid., p. 61.

18. Ibid., p. 114-15.

19. Ibid., pp. 89-96, *passim.*

20. Ibid., p. 109.

21. Ibid., p. 111.

23. In times of trouble and particularly in state institutions, this is often not the case. Clark Kerr remarks: "In the case of the University of California, when the trustees and regents were not under pressure, they thought that they were representing the University. When they were under pressure, a lot of them decided they were representing the public." "Governance of the Universities" *Daedalus,* XCVIII (Fall, 1969), 1104.

24. That this faculty control is oligarchic rather than general is demonstrated in a recent study by T. R. McConnell. His evidence shows that only about ten percent of the faculty are involved in faculty governance. T. R. McConnell, "Campus Governance — Faculty Participation," *The Research Reporter,* The Center for Research and Development in Higher Education, University of California, Berkeley, V, No. 1 (1970). The relationship between this locally powerful faculty oligarchy and strength of the graduate and professional disciplines, which are oriented in a more cosmopolitan direction, is an interesting question on which I have seen no evidence.

25. "Faculty interest in undergraduate teaching has been static by comparison with specialization and social involvement. Our failure to develop a more coherent and educationally effective curriculum reflects the inertia of departmental structure and faculty avoidance of wider perspectives in undergraduate teaching . . . If members of faculties realized that curricula were not really their own corporate creation but lower order resultants of accommodation among departments they might insist upon improvements which would come to reflect their peculiar strengths and widely shared interests." Ritterbush, op. cit., p. 656.

26. Two young graduates of the University of Michigan provide the viewpoint of the student: "The department is a versatile organism. It is a curator of the latest research terminology. It is also a very primitive social system offering an impregnable terri-

torial defense against outsiders, whether they be politicians, administrators, or undergraduates; internally, the department functions as effectively as a Mafia family. The young are kept under control by tight reward-and-sanction mechanisms, such as grades for undergraduates, doctoral puberty rites for graduate students, and tenure for assistant professors. Likewise, the elders of the tribe have built up a series of conventions that foster nonaggressive behavior, despite the fact that Marxists and capitalists may share the same cubicle. For example, personal property such as courses and research, is given sacred sanction; picking on a professor's prized survey course is akin to violating his wife. In making important decisions, departmental councils (normally comprised of elders only) operate on a principle of consensus, whereby the minority never argues so harshly that it can't recant and defer to the majority. In personnel matters, a good department works like a jury to reach unanimity." Roger Rapoport and Laurence J. Kirshbaum, *Is the Library Burning?* (New York: Random House, 1969), pp. 52-53.

27. In addition to the sources cited elsewhere in this paper, these titles are particularly recommended: "The Embattled University," *Daedalus* XCIX (Winter, 1970); Calvin Lee (ed.) *Improving College Teaching* (Washington: American Council on Education); Joseph J. Schwab, *College Curriculum and Student Protest* (Chicago: University of Chicago Press, 1969); Robert Paul Wolff, "The Ideal of the University," *Change,* I (September-October, 1969), 48-72.

28. Library organization, in general, follows the pattern described by Etzioni as characteristic of what he calls the "semi-professions." It is hierarchical and bureaucratic, like that of the business corporation or the army, but in the semi-professions, the top administrators are members of the profession who have climbed the career ladder into the administrative class. Though their duties may be far removed from actual practice of their profession, these administrators are still identified with it. Cf. Amitai Etzioni, *The Semi-Professions and Their Organization: Teachers, Nurses, Social Workers* (New York: Free Press, 1969). In contrast, although university presidents are usually (but not always) former professors and deans and department chairmen invariably are, these positions (except for the presidency) are not regarded in academic circles as the upper rungs in the career ladder of the professoriate. Rather, the man who accepts any administrative position higher than department chairman is seen as one who has left, not to say deserted, his profession.

29. Braden, op. cit., p. 137.

30. Braden refers to the goal of the Uris Library at Cornell with respect to duplication, which was stated in the formula "E plus 1, meaning "enough plus one." Ibid., p. 37. If literally applied, this formula would mean that there would never be a time when there was not one copy remaining on the shelf after all student needs had been satisfied. How many undergraduate libraries even dream of such a happy state?.

31. Cf., for example, Feldman and Newcomb, op. cit., pp. 336-338.

32. Cf. for example, Eldred Smith, "Academic Status for College and University Librarians — Problems and Prospects," *College and Research Libraries* XXXI (January, 1970): 7-13; John H. Moriarity, "Academic in Deed," *College and Research Libraries* XXXI (January, 1970): 14-17.

33. "The Undergraduate Library," *Research News,* Office of Research Administration, University of Michigan, XV (May, 1965), 4.

34. Braden, op. cit., p. 140.

35. Ibid., p. 3.

36. Ibid., p. 101

37. Ibid., p. 124.

38. William S. Dix, "Library Service to Undergraduates: Undergraduate Students Do Not Necessarily Require a Special Facility," *College and Research Libraries* XVII (March, 1956): 148-50.

39. An excellent beginning to the rationalization of library service, one in which the time of the library user is included as a cost factor, is offered by Phillip M. Morse, *Library Effectiveness: A Systems Approach* (Cambridge: M. I. T. Press, 1968).

About the Author

Patricia B. Knapp earned her Ph.D. degree at the University of Chicago. She held various positions at the Chicago Teachers College Library from 1937-1943 and served as a librarian in the USAF from 1943-1945. She was Librarian of George Williams College, 1945-1955; Assistant Professor of Library Science at Rosary College, 1955-1957. In 1957, she became associated with Wayne State University. From 1957-1959, she was Assistant Librarian. From 1959-1965, she was Executive Secretary and Director of the Montieth Library Project, Montieth College, Wayne State University, From 1965 until her death in 1972, she was a member of the faculty of the Department of Library Science at Wayne State. She has published extensively and was honored with the Presidency of the American Association of Library Schools in 1970.

Melvin J. Voigt

The Undergraduate Library: The Collection and Its Selection

Voigt stresses the importance of the collection and then concentrates on the development and use of a selection policy. He also explores the variations in collections. Next, he reviews the methods used in the initial selection of various undergraduate library collections (for comparison, see the Williams and Carpenter articles in Part II and the Cassell article in Part IV). Finally, the maintenance of the collection is discussed.

The Importance of the Collection

Undergraduate libraries do not differ from other libraries in their most important attribute: they could and would not exist without books. Books are the essential ingredient, and thus the critical question in justifying the undergraduate library is whether there is a definable and viable book collection which will be of more value to undergraduate students in meeting the educational objectives of undergraduate education than does the large research library. The existence of an increasing number of undergraduate libraries indicates that librarians have answered this question affirmatively. Some of the other questions which may be asked become less relevant if this question has a positive response. For example, Do the needs of graduate and undergraduate students differ to such a degree that separate libraries for each are justified? or, Are book collections readily divisible into graduate and undergraduate components? As is noted in other papers, there are many other questions which may swing the balance in making a decision to have or not to have an undergraduate library, but factors, such as campus geography, number of students, undergraduate curriculum, and the desirability of special reference services for undergraduates, would probably

SOURCE: From Melvin J. Voigt, "The Undergraduate Library: The Collection and Its Selection," Institute on Training for Service in Undergraduate Libraries, Sponsored by the University Library, University of California at San Diego, August 17-21, 1970. Included by permission of the author.

not carry enough weight unless it is clear that it is possible to create a book collection which will improve the undergraduate's access to the books which are useful to him and which will provide for a large percentage of his library needs.

There has been less concern about dividing graduates and undergraduates, as planners have recognized that a substantial proportion of the use of a good undergraduate library will be from graduate students (unless use is restricted). The possibility of making a sharp division of materials to create an undergraduate component of the collection is not very important for the user if the undergraduate has easy access to the research collection when the smaller library fails to meet his needs.

It is clear that the book collection — its size, selection, and maintenance — is of major importance and that there will be a direct relationship between the care with which it is developed and the success of the library.

The size of the collection raises questions which relate directly to basic considerations in the establishment of an undergraduate library. These questions will be considered in various parts of this presentation. If cost and space factors will not permit a collection large or broad enough to meet the requirements of a given institution, it is likely that a solution other than a separate undergraduate library should be sought.

The Selection Policy

Questions Which Must Be Answered Before a Policy is Formulated

The question which should be considered first in this section is probably that of the necessity for a selection policy or, specifically, for a selection policy statement. This topic, as it relates to libraries generally, was given extensive consideration in last year's UCSD "Institute on Acquisitions Procedures in Academic Libraries." The unanimous conclusion reached by the participants, that formulation and use of a policy statement is essential to an effective acquisitions program, particularly as it relates to specialized projects and programs, indicates the importance of a clear understanding of the objectives of any acquisitions program.

Rolland C. Stewart, in his paper on "The Undergraduate Library Collection,"[1] prepared for the 1969 Institute, emphasized the importance of defining the clientele to be served. Is it "the total undergraduate population irrespective of collegiate affiliation within the university? Undergraduates enrolled in Nursing, Music, Public Administration, Architecture, Engineering? Or undergraduates enrolled in what might be called the 'general education' college?" He goes on to suggest that "the only practical definition to be concerned with relates to courses and not at all to students."[2] But the question of whether the undergraduate library's service should extend to professional schools must be answered, and it is likely that the answer will not be a simple, unqualified "no." Stewart goes on to raise related questions. "Shall the collection satisfy all *courses* to which only undergraduates *are admitted,* or shall it include all courses for which undergraduates *may* enroll?"[3] The fact that in most institutions course offerings at advanced undergraduate levels are open also to graduate students has probably helped lead to the general acceptance of unrestricted use of the undergraduate library. The extent to which graduate students actually use the undergraduate library is a question which cannot be neglected in formulating the collection policy.

The opposite question, the library requirements of the undergraduate beyond the undergraduate library, has a seemingly easy answer in acknowledging and encouraging the use of the research library by undergraduates as a supplement to their own facility. In determining collection policy, the question is not that simple. The "research" concept has become important in undergraduate education and, indeed, far below the college level. Without entering the discussion on the use or misuse of the term, consideration must be given to the fact that the teaching method called "research" increases the requirements for library materials at all levels. Thus it becomes necessary to make a decision on how far the undergraduate library is expected to go in meeting these requirements and at what point the general research library will have to take over. While size of collection will obviously be an important factor in relating the policy to research requirements, it is not the only one; for the makeup of the collection will reflect the degree to which its materials support undergraduate research, and not only by the number of books.

Before a collection statement can be written, there must be consideration of other topics, such as the comparative emphasis on reserved books, on broader curricular requirements, and on noncurricular values, usually expressed in an idealistic phrase, such as "stimulating lifetime reading habits." If professional school requirements are ruled out, the question remains as to how much the collection should do in representing those subjects for the nonprofessional.

Some other questions which must be answered have been considered in other papers and will have been discussed by the group earlier in the week. These include additional aspects on the relation of the collection to the curriculum, the reference collection, and questions of making the collection better meet the needs of culturally and educationally disadvantaged students. A collection policy should be as specific as possible without inhibiting the need for flexibility. It might, for example, state that one-volume "readers" should be included when available, without closing out options for use of judgment in the degree to which these will be supplemented by specific works.

Other questions, which will only be mentioned here but which require answers prior to development of a policy statement, include the following: How large, broad, or intensive should the periodical collection be? What should the policy be on back files of periodicals? On periodical indexes? Basic questions on audio materials — speech, music, taped lectures, and other learning resource materials — must be answered with a good deal more detail than a simple "yes" or "no."

A selection policy, to be useful, must be much more than a definition. To say that an undergraduate library provides a collection of carefully selected books containing the titles all undergraduates should be exposed to, may do, as a broad definition to use in obtaining support, but it has very little value to book selectors as a policy statement.

Dollars and Numbers and the Policy Statement

The first part of this section dealt with fundamental questions related to collection development. A policy statement will not be very useful unless it also takes into account the hard facts of what an institution can and will do in supporting the program. Stewart stated the problem very well in his paper last year. "Assuming that we have groped our way through the *mystique* of defining purposes and have got hold of an ideological tool with which we can create an undergraduate collection, we face the question of money, prospects for more money, and still more money. Paradoxically speaking, the budget is the sire of all selection criteria we might devise. Objectives and the means to achieve them must be commensurate."[4] Determining these numbers and using the dollars effectively will be considered in succeeding sections, but unless the collection policy is based on realistic estimates of dollars available for the original collection and for its maintenance, its value will be greatly diminished.

Dollars can also be expressed quantitatively in what they will provide, and it is to be hoped that the funding agreed upon as realistic for the institution *will* be based on the number of titles considered essential to meet a carefully developed set of objectives. In any case, the collection policy must be realistic in its expectations of the number of titles in the basic collection, the planned rate of growth, the amount of duplication and multiple copies for reserve, the extent of periodical holdings, the size of reference collection, inclusion of audio materials, etc.

Developing and Using a Policy

Previous paragraphs have included most of the ingredients for a policy statement. In addition to covering the purposes and extent and range necessary to implement the purposes, it should spell out the methods of selection development which will be used, including the extent and manner in which faculty and personnel other than the undergraduate library staff will be used. The statement itself should be a document resulting from input from all faculty and staff members who have an interest in the collection's development and maintenance. In the beginning the impetus within the library may come from the director of the library or his assistant. But as soon as possible, the direct responsibility should be assigned to the person who will be responsible for the library. No matter how important the day-to-day activities of planning and operating the library, it would seem highly desirable that the collection should continue to be a major responsibility of the head of the undergraduate library. The whole process of selection for an undergraduate library is an important educational opportunity for the librarian and increases his competency as an interpreter of its collection. One of the most important reasons for a clearly stated collection policy statement is that it will make it possible for the head of the library to carry out the broad responsibilities of management without giving undue time to some of the day-to-day selection decisions which become obvious on the basis of established policy. This statement and the emphasis on a policy statement should not imply that the selector's job is done when the policy statement is written. The last paragraph of the University of Maryland "Selection Philosophy" statement clearly indicates the continuing importance of the selecting process.

> "These guide lines are intended only for general assistance. Each principle should be given consideration and weighed against the others. For example, the aspect of currency in a specific title may be in conflict with completeness or readability. The good judgment of the person recommending the material should put each aspect into proper perspective."[5]

A collection policy statement should be a live document. It should reflect changes in educational programs as they occur and should take into account experience-in-use patterns as they are developed in the library. One might argue that the collection policy should be so simple and so flexible that it should not be formulated and adopted in written form. One suspects however that, when used, this argument is more likely to be a rationalization or an excuse.

The values of a policy statement are many. Selection should, of course, be guided by it. This is especially important when faculty are involved. Faculty opinions on what should be in any library vary greatly, and this is particularly true in an undergraduate library. Experience in the University of California's New Campuses Program, and in refining that selection for *Books for College Libraries,*[6] showed that if faculty members (not all, but many) were allowed to do the choosing without further editing, the imbalance, the areas skipped, and the number of doubtful titles chosen would cause very difficult problems. Faculty members should assist in selection, especially of the basic collection. If they can be involved in the development of the policy statement or, if not, if they work under the guidelines of such a statement, the results will be not only a better collection but also a much smoother road in reaching that objective.

In the next section, questions of variations in collections are considered. Obviously, if the library becomes a "package" identical to other undergraduate libraries, as some suggest may soon happen, a collection policy statement becomes superfluous except to the degree that additions are made to the package. With partial preselection plans and approval systems, a policy statement becomes, if anything, more important. The profile which governs the books coming to the library is, in fact, a part of the policy statement, and the librarian's job of keeping the collection development in line with agreed-on objectives becomes much easier than it would be without the policy's guidance.

Variations in Collections

Until recently, book selection courses in library schools put great emphasis on the librarian's responsibility for the selection of every title to meet the library's requirements and argued strongly against blanket orders, approval plans which allowed for little selection, and package libraries. Now that most of these have become widely practiced, although not wholly accepted, it is necessary to look carefully to determine whether there should be any variation in libraries which have the same broad purposes, such as undergraduate libraries. Certainly there are arguments on both sides, and while the possibility of lower costs in selection and processing is probably the strongest one in favor of uniformity, it is not the only one. The possibilities for greater depth of analysis and for a subject approach geared to undergraduates' needs, to his manner of seeking information, and to the, as yet, poorly understood information processing abilities of the human brain at the college level stage of development, could be greatly improved if this could be done in computer-produced packages. A product with values far beyond the ability of an individual library to produce could be provided. Even with such possibilities, it would seem clear that the collections should be supplemented by additional material fitted to the needs of a specific institution. Orne,[7] in speaking of the collection, makes it sound very easy, requiring less effort than most librarians feel should go into selection. His comment, "The assurance of success with our second factor (the book collection) is now simply a measure of intelligent application, but it is assured," will probably not be argued with if the word "intelligent" is underlined. If the microform libraries being developed today have general acceptance it will be interesting to see whether, by making large increases in the amount of material available, the need for individuality will decrease. It may be that to reach this objective, the collection will have to become so large that, as with the research library today, the library becomes unmanageable for the undergraduate. With greater problems of access, contrasted with the ease with which material can be accepted or rejected when examined on the shelf, the point of exasperated futility may be reached sooner.

Regardless of what may happen, it is clear that there is a good deal of variation in collections today. If one examines the sections on the book collection in each of the chapters dealing with specific undergraduate libraries in Irene Braden's *The Undergraduate Library,*[8] it is clear that while general goals and the selection tools and methods used to reach those goals were similar, there was considerable variation in the resulting collections. Part of this was caused by the availability of duplicates or existing reserve collections. In Cornell's case, a book store was purchased and availability influenced both direction and size of the original collection. Warren Kuhn's report[9] shows that, in size, initial collections varied from 15,000 to 60,000 volumes, present collections from 45,000 to 145,000, and maximums expected ranged from 62,900 to 200,000. It seems doubtful at this time whether there should be any attempt to fix an ideal or standard size for the collection. Orne's recent article[10] is quite specific in what he considers to be the optimum size and comprehensiveness. The size of the institution, availability of research collections and other libraries, the nature of educational programs and methods are among the factors which would appear to govern both the size and nature of the collection.

Circulation studies have indicated that use is concentrated in a smaller proportion of a collection than was generally expected when the first undergraduate libraries were established. Thus an undergraduate library may find it possible to include fewer titles than might have been thought necessary. But this is true only if the selection can produce the titles which make up the actual usage. It was the evidence of usage, together with the experience of the New Campuses Program, which made it possible for UCSD to plan for three undergraduate libraries of 50,000 to 60,000 volumes instead of one library three times as large. It is true that fewer duplicates are involved than in one library serving the same total number of students. But even when one allows for this, the total number of titles is much less than in undergraduate libraries of 150,000 to 200,000 volumes. In the New Campuses Program, where titles were chosen one by one to meet specific requirements of the collection, it was surprising to everyone involved how much depth was provided before the number of titles was reached which had been calculated as "quotas" for most subject fields.

Changes in courses offered to undergraduate students and in teaching methods result in new requirements for libraries. It is difficult to determine how much these changes, particularly the changes in teaching methods affect, or should affect, the collection itself. It can be argued that a good undergraduate collection will be able to meet the students' needs in spite of such changes, as long as the collection is kept up to date and reflects new subject matter which is brought into the curriculum. Many of the early undergraduate collections were made up largely of reserve books. Gradually these were augmented by titles which it was felt the undergraduate should have access to and which were rarely available to him in a closed stack, general circulating library. As teaching methods moved slowly away from dependence on specific readings and reserve books toward allowing students to use materials from a larger collection without prescription, the undergraduate library became a natural solution. Today, with a trend toward allowing the student even more freedom in reaching his educational objectives, it is necessary to question whether the collection again needs to change to reflect this broadened tendency toward allowing the student to find his own way. It is probably true that today's undergraduates need fewer general works in a subject area and more depth than was thought necessary a few years ago.

As is pointed out in other papers, the undergraduate student in an institution with a good undergraduate library tends to use the graduate library more than he did previously. If this greater utilization can be attributed to the undergraduate library in terms of its calling the students attention to materials which he would not otherwise be aware of or in simply making him more aware of the existence and usefulness of libraries generally, it may well be that more attention should be given to consciously developing the collection to further this result and that a means should be found to make the collection itself help bridge the gap between the two libraries. On the other hand, an objective of the library is to provide as much as possible for the undergraduate students' needs. To do this, a principle of selecting good reference works and basic general books in subject areas and then including more specific books indexed or recommended in these more general works, will lead the user into the collection rather than out of it. Probably a good deal of research is needed before we can determine how much should or can be done in changing the basic nature of undergraduate collections to meet these variant objectives.

How Various Collections Were Chosen Initially

The Collection

When selection for the undergraduate library at Harvard began in 1947, there was no previous guide to such a collection which could be used. Since then, the *Lamont Catalogue*[11] the selections for the Michigan Undergraduate Library which became available by purchasing cards or through microfilm, *Books for College Libraries,*[12] and *Choice,*[13] for more recent titles, as well as other lists have become available to assist the selector in developing the undergraduate collection. (See also Carpenter's discussion on the use of the *Lamont Catalogue.*)[14] Since the methods which were used to put together the initial collections at Harvard, Michigan, South Carolina, Indiana, Cornell, and Texas are described in detail in Irene Braden's *The Undergraduate Library,*[15] this paper will not attempt to duplicate that information. In reviewing the development of the original collection for the six institutions surveyed by Braden, one notes that in every case the development of the collection was the responsibility of one individual, whether or not he was expected to become the librarian of the new unit. In each instance there were collections already available which were utilized for the undergraduate collection. At Harvard, there were reserve books and gifts from duplicate collections. At Michigan, study hall libraries and gifts were utilized. At South Carolina, the reserve book collection and two other special duplicating collections were utilized. At Indiana, undergraduate reserve books and the books in several specialized reading rooms were included. At Cornell, there was a departmental library in the Arts and Sciences, and at Texas, materials were taken from what is called the "Resource Collection." After the Michigan list became available it seems to have been used to a greater degree than the *Lamont Catalogue.* There does seem to have been considerable variation in the amount of dependence on such sources as publishers catalogs, reviews in scholarly journals, subject bibliographies in monographs, and listings in *Publishers' Weekly* and other current bibliographical tools. The experience with faculty selection also seems to vary considerably. The experience in these institutions bears out that of others which have not been included in the Braden survey, that faculty can be used up to a point, particularly if they are given something to work with, that is, a copy of the Michigan list or something in card form which they can go through quickly, indicating titles which they feel to be important. As was noted earlier, when faculty are used to develop initial lists, as was attempted at Michigan, the result is usually not very satisfactory. While librarians on the staff of the university library were used to a considerable degree by some of the libraries, it is surprising that more of the selection was not detailed to the subject specialists who must have been available in most of these libraries.

While a number of the universities which pioneered undergraduate libraries attempted to develop basic collections of considerable size by the time the library opened, most of the institutions which have started the development of undergraduate libraries in recent years have begun with very small collections and an accelerated growth pattern over a period of years, with the intent of leveling off when, what are considered ideal collections for their purposes, are attained. This procedure has a disadvantage, particularly if a building is available to house a substantial collection, in that students during the early years are limited to whatever part of the collection may have been obtained up to that time. Thus, while budget considerations may have been the limiting factor in slowing the development of undergraduate libraries, it may be that collections developed in this manner will prove to reflect the needs of the students and educational programs better than those selected *en masse* before opening day. It is interesting to note that in most of the literature which has been published on the development of undergraduate libraries, little attention has been paid to the possibility of students themselves assisting in the selection of a collection for their own use. While it is true that in most cases they will not be able to suggest individual titles which should be purchased, they can be of great value to the undergraduate librarian who is in close touch with student users. This may come primarily through their requests for information, which reference librarians are in the best position to note, but also it may come directly through conscious efforts to encourage them to report on subject areas and types of materials which they need and which are not available to them in the undergraduate library.

At UCSD, because of the initial location of the library and because undergraduate library needs were concentrated in certain areas at the beginning, the collection development began with concentration in certain subject fields and then gradually moved on to other fields as basic collections were completed in the original fields of concentration. If there is a general library close at hand for the undergraduate students to use this may be the best approach, in that the students will have a substantial collection of materials in specific subject areas available within a short period of time, while they can clearly see that in other areas it is essential for them to use a different library. As Robert H. Muller points out,[16] with the aid of both comprehensive and selective tools, it is now possible to compile an initial list of "candidates" to be considered for selection without having to rely largely on nonselective publishers catalogs, bibliographies, booksellers lists, etc.

A major problem in developing any undergraduate library or, for that matter, a basic collection for any new institution is a question of out-of-print books.

Fortunately, from the point of view of availability but perhaps unfortunately from the point of view of price, many of the out-of-print books included in what have become standard lists have been reprinted.

The subject distribution in undergraduate libraries has been remarkably similar. One might conclude from this that the question of what makes up a good undergraduate library has been fairly well determined and that we may be well on the way to package libraries. One can also speculate however that, when it was decided in the published *Lamont Catalogue* that books on literature and language made up 37.5 percent of the total; history, 18.2 percent; books in the social sciences, 17.3 percent; and so on, other libraries accepted these as norms and they became standards to be followed. When the books were selected for the New Campuses Program at the University of California, the Lamont breakdown, not only for large subject areas but for smaller ones as well, was used along with some other sources in estimating how many titles would probably be selected in each of the subject fields identified. While the selectors may, to some degree, have attempted "to fill their quota" and go no further, it was evident early in the selection activity that, given the objectives of basic collections upon which research collections could be built, some subject areas would go well beyond the numbers listed for Lamont and others would fall far short. However, when the totals were added up for broad subject fields, the percentages came fairly close to those for the Lamont Library and those at Michigan as well, as is shown in the table in the preface to *Books for College Libraries*.[17]

Muller[18] lists some of the other problems encountered when carrying out selection, such as determing which are the indispensable classics, where one stops in selecting from the mass of books about an author, how to deal with quantity on a subject when a few items, or perhaps one, stand out far above the others, the question of including works in original languages, and how far one goes in selecting variant translations. While these and many other questions will perplex the selectors of the original collection and those working on maintaining the collection, it is fortunate indeed that every undergraduate library expects to continue adding materials and that, as far as this writer knows, none of them have restricted themselves totally to adding new books. Thus, most persons who are selecting the basic collection for undergraduate libraries today tend to be conservative when questions, such as those noted above, arise with the knowledge, or at least hope, that if experience indicates that a broader selection is necessary, this will be discovered in the use made of the library.

Maintenance of Collections

Decisions on Rate of Growth and Distribution.

Since most undergraduate libraries today are opening with partial collections, with the basic collection to be developed over a period of time, there is a possibility of less guess work in the original selection, as noted earlier. For the purposes of this section, it will be assumed that a basic collection has been established and that we are concerned with the various aspects of maintenance. While most of the growth of the collection will be in terms of newly published books, the need to add older volumes to meet new requirements and changing emphasis within subjects will continue.

There are many factors which go into the question of determining the continuing rate of growth or additions to a collection. Many libraries have followed the lead of the Lamont Library with a policy aiming at having the size of the library remain approximately the same, with the same number of volumes added and discarded each year. It is unlikely that any library will follow such a principle completely. However, where it is an objective, due either to policy or to space limitations, the tendency will be to add fewer volumes than when it is possible to continue adding volumes for a long period of time without restrictions. After the Harvard collection reached a total of 100,000 volumes in 1951, it has had a net growth per year of approximately 3,000 volumes since then and gross growth of just under 6,000 volumes.[19] At Michigan, the undergraduate library had reached 68,000 volumes by 1959 and has had an average net growth of 8,000 volumes per year since then, with the rate of growth dropping only slightly in recent years.[20] The other libraries studied by Irene Braden began with smaller collections and have not been in operation long enough to provide good statistics to determine what their leveling off growth rate might be. Stabliized collections of 150,000 or 200,000 volumes will add more and discard more than ones which have leveled out in the 50,000 to 75,000 volume range. However, it is doubtful that a percentage figure could be substantiated or agreed upon. This question is one that should be related to purposes of the collection and should reflect experience with use. An institution which puts great emphasis on the social sciences or on modern literature will probably need to add more volumes than one which has a greater percentage of use coming from students in history and most fields of literature. Since this is an important question, but with little standardization to date, it is suggested that some time be given to discussion by the group, based on the experience and the plans of the institutions represented.

The last section discussed the question of subject distribution of the original collection. It is rather obvious that the distribution of books added will not be the same as for the original collection. It would be expected that the percentage of books added in the sciences and social sciences would be greater than those percentages in the original collection.

The Budget

Once a growth rate has been determined, the calculation of the budget required for an undergraduate library is probably a good deal easier than for most other parts of the university library. Most of the books will be current, and a large percentage will be published in this country. Thus, statistics of prices, which are generally available, will be applicable. Calculating increases for inflation, year by year, is a good deal simpler than attempting to do this for research collections with large numbers of serials coming from foreign countries and with many out-of-print books with widely fluctuating prices. An undergraduate library will undoubtedly continue to have desiderata lists of books wanted originally which have not been found, as well as books found to be desirable later. Some funding should be reserved to obtain these as they appear, whether from the secondhand market or in the form of reprints.

It is likely that in every undergraduate library there will be pressures for an increasing number of periodicals. Here, the establishment of a policy is particularly important. Unless it is determined whether periodicals will be provided only for current informational purposes, or whether back files of moderate length will be available for a limited *Abridged Reader's Guide to Periodical Literature* type of use, or whether the intent is to provide enough in the way of periodicals to allow students to do many term papers and projects without using the central library, the librarian will be in trouble in making and justifying decisions on individual titles and length of back files. With periodicals and reference works, campus size and distance of the undergraduate library from the research library becomes very important in establishing policy. Once a policy has been determined, it will be a good deal easier to decide whether or not to add a title to the collection and whether back files are required. The policy may need to be made subject by subject as needs will vary, and obviously there will be exceptions. But the librarian and the faculty must be clear on the policy if there is to be any consistency in the collection.

Responsibility for Maintenance

As was indicated earlier, the responsibility for adding to the collection should be assigned to the head of the unit. But he will need all the help he can get. If he depends entirely on his knowledge of books, on his intuition, or even on his personal observations of use, and on conversations with faculty and students, the results will, at best, be spotty. Using reference librarians as part-time bibliographers or selection librarians has become common in many types of libraries. In the undergraduate library the staff working directly with students and faculty should be in a better position to see what is needed and what will be used than any others in or out of the library. But familarity with subjects, authors, and publishing trends is also important. Thus, the selection responsibility should be delegated and spread as widely as possible among those whose knowledge can be useful and who are willing to be guided and restrained by a collection development policy and the realities of budgetary allocations.

Students can be directly useful in addition to their indirect contribution through library use and requests for information. A number of libraries have utilized student committees successfully for general guidance. Others have found that student enthusiasm and knowledge can be especially useful in developing or expanding collections in areas of current concern: minorities, special cultures, political questions, conservation, etc.

Methods of Selection

The more inclusive a library, the easier the job of selection. The undergraduate library, by its special character, complicates the job of selection. The importance or intrinsic value of a candidate for inclusion in the collection may carry less weight than the manner of presentation, the level, and the relevance to specific programs. If an undergraduate library is adding 5,000 volumes per year, the selection of the first 2,500 will be relatively easy. The work of a major writer or an obviously important book in an area of current concern will cause no problems. These books will find their way into the library regardless of the method of selection: from a listing in a trade bibliography, in a review journal, or by inclusion in an approval plan. A surprisingly large part of current acquisitions will be obvious additions. For the remainder, however, the methods of selection are likely to be as varied as the results. Libraries will also vary in their sense of urgency in making new books available as soon as possible after publication. This policy may be the deciding factor in using an approval plan or in making selections on the basis of reviews.

Faculty participation in current selection will be looked on with favor by most librarians, with an immediate qualification that it can rarely be depended on in terms of regularity or consistency. Obviously, books which are wanted for reserve or are included in lists of suggested reading must be obtained (although rarely in the quantities recommended). The success of an undergraduate library has a direct relationship to faculty interest and to the librarian's ability to involve the faculty. Since faculty interest is most likely to be in the collection, it would be foolish not to encourage faculty participation in selection. Yet, experience in libraries generally has been that when the faculty finds that the library staff is able to do a good job in selection, the faculty is happy to turn over the entire process to the library. Thus, there are contradictions which are not easily answered. The experience and views of the participants in the Institute should provide for an interesting discussion of this topic.

Approval plans, as applied to undergraduate libraries, will usually operate either independently of a broader campus plan or as a part of such a plan. If the undergraduate library has the competence one would hope for, the latter system would appear to be superior. To be able to review the totality of American publishing in the fields of interest, with the books in hand, should enable competent librarians to make good selections of a majority of titles added and should result in having the books in use much sooner than by other methods. If the books available for consideration are limited to those a dealer has selected as applicable to the undergraduate library, the librarians will find it difficult to do much more than accept most of the titles, rejecting only the ones which are obviously not suited to his library because of subject emphasis. The doubtful titles from a larger selection can be noted for further consideration when ratings or reviews become available. Making selections from a larger group will also make possible a fast response to new areas of intensive interest on the part of library users.

Selection Tools

If approval plans are not used or if, as is likely, they are supplemented by selections from other sources, the question of selection tools becomes important. For maintenance of collections, published lists which include only books to a certain date and which do not have supplements are obviously of little value. The question, then, is whether current selection tools for the undergraduate library are any different than those for a general library or, more specifically, for a college library. The most obvious source, *Choice,* is intended for the college library, and it would seem reasonable that if it is useful for the college library it is also useful in making selections for the undergraduate library. There may be discussion of its intrinsic value and on how it might best be used in maintaining the undergraduate library. One might suggest that a specialized guide, such as *Books Abroad,* might be of more value to a college library, but others would probably point out that in some institutions the undergraduate library might include more items from *Books Abroad* than would a college library in an institution with limited programs.

There would seem to be little point in listing standard selection tools in this paper. There is little information available on their use by those responsible for the continuing development of undergraduate libraries. A discussion of practical aspects of this topic by participants should be useful.

Notes

1.   Stewart, Rolland C., *The Undergraduate Library Collection.* (Institute on Acquisitions Procedures in Academic Libraries, University of California, San Diego, 1969), 4 p.

2.   Ibid., p. 1.

3.   Ibid., p. 1-2.

4.   Ibid., p. 2.

5.   Maryland, University, *A Selection Philosophy for the Undergraduate Library Collection.* (1968), 3 p.

6.   Voigt, Melvin J. and Treyz, Joseph H., *Books for College Libraries.* (1967), 1056 p.

7.   Orne, Jerrold, "The Undergraduate Library," *Library Journal* 95, (1970) 2230-2233.

8.   Braden, Irene A., *The Undergraduate Library.* (1970), 158 p.

9.   Kuhn, Warren B., "Summary of the Responses to the Warren Kuhn Questionnaire," *UgLi Newsletter* No. 2 (Nov. 1969) p. 5-7.

10. Op. cit.

11. Harvard University, Lamont Library, *Catalogue of the Lamont Library,* (1953), 562 p.

12. Voigt, Melvin J. and Treyz, Joseph H., op. cit.

13. *Choice: Books for College Libraries.* Association of College and Research Libraries, American Library Association. Began publication in 1964.

14. Carpenter, Charles A., "The Lamont Catalogue as a Guide to Book Selection," *College and Research Libraries* 18, (1957) 267-268.

15. Op. cit.

16. Muller, Robert H., "The Undergraduate Library Trend at Large Universities," In *Advances in Librarianship* v. 1 (1970): p. 113-132.

17. Op. cit., p. v.

18. Op. cit.

19. Braden, Irene A., op. cit., p. 17

20. Stewart, Rolland C., op. cit., Appendix B.

About the Author

Melvin J. Voigt has held the positions of: Physics Librarian, University of Michigan, 1935-1942; Librarian and Head of Publications and Research Department, General Mills, Minneapolis, 1942-1946; Librarian and Professor of Library Science, Carnegie Institute of Technology, 1946-1952; Assistant University Librarian, University of California at Berkeley, 1952-1959; and Director of Libraries, Kansas State University, 1959-1960. From 1960 until his retirement in September, 1976, he was University Librarian, University of California at San Diego. He and Joseph Treyz compiled *Books for College Libraries* in 1967.

Billy R. Wilkinson

The Undergraduate Library's Public Service Record: Reference Services

Reference collections, hours of service, and reference staffs in undergraduate libraries are briefly discussed. Then the prevailing philosophy of reference service is presented. The major part of the paper consists of case studies of reference services in two of the leading undergraduate libraries. After presenting the recorded use of reference services at the University of Michigan Undergraduate Library and the Uris Undergraduate Library of Cornell University, samples of questions asked by undergraduates in these two libraries are compared with questions asked by undergraduates at the reference desks of the University's main library during the same weeks and compared with questions asked by students in a liberal arts college library (Lilly Library, Earlham College) during the same autumn semester of 1969.

One of the original justifications for the separate undergraduate library was to provide the same quality of library services as were available for students in a good liberal arts college library. Keyes Metcalf stated the facts plainly:

> A student at Amherst, Williams, Dartmouth, Bowdoin, Oberlin, or one of the better women's colleges has at his or her disposal a much larger and better collection of books than has the Harvard undergraduate.[1]

Going beyond the mere provision of books, Harvie Branscomb, at the dedication of Harvard's Lamont Library in 1949, called for an undergraduate library staff who would give students "much reference direction" and have a "better knowledge of the curriculum of study than librarians generally possess."[2] Bran-

SOURCE: From Billy R. Wilkinson, "The Undergraduate Library's Public Service Record: Reference Services," Institute on Training for Service in Undergraduate Libraries, Sponsored by the University Library, University of California at San Diego, August 17-21, 1970. Included by permission of the author.

scomb suggested "that at last we shall have found a way to bridge the oft discussed gap between class instruction and library service."[3] Over two decades have now passed and a critical look at the reference services of undergraduate libraries is overdue. How have reference librarians used this opportunity afforded by undergraduate libraries?

First, reference collections, hours of service, and reference staffs in undergraduate libraries will be briefly described. Then the prevailing philosophy of reference services will be presented. The major part of the paper will be case studies of reference services in two of the leading undergraduate libraries in the country. After presenting the recorded use of reference services at the University of Michigan Undergraduate Library and at the Uris Library, Cornell University, samples of questions asked by undergraduates in these two undergraduate libraries will be compared with questions asked by undergraduates at the reference desk of the university's main library during the same weeks and with questions asked by students in a liberal arts college library during the same autumn semester of 1969.

Almost all undergraduate libraries have a centralized collection of reference volumes. The J. Henry Meyer Library at Stanford is the major exception with reference alcoves dispersed throughout the building. The number of reference volumes varies from 550 to 4,500.[4] The great majority of reference titles in an undergraduate library duplicate those in the main university library's much larger reference collection. Some undergraduate library planners underestimated the reference titles needed. The University of Michigan Undergraduate Library, for example, found it "necessary to augment the reference collection rapidly [during the first year]. The problem of helping a student halfway to an answer and then referring him to the General Library for additional assistance becomes intolerable in practice if not in theory."[5]

The reference volumes are on open shelves freely accessible to students. There has been little shelving of heavily used items back of the desk as was typical in reference rooms of university libraries. In addition to the usual encyclopedias, indexes, dictionaries, handbooks, and other reference books, the reference collections include pamphlets and other vertical file material. In 1969, the reference collection in the Michigan Undergraduate Library was comprised of 3,549 volumes and 25,077 items in its vertical file. Uris Library had 3,294 reference volumes (1,688 titles) and a smaller amount of vertical file material. During 1968/69, Michigan added 206 reference volumes (150 titles) at a cost of $2,311.55. Some 6,857 items costing $473.94 were added to the vertical file. Cornell added 138 volumes (71 titles) to the Uris Library reference collection in 1968/69, spending $2,862.85.

Both Michigan and Cornell undergraduate libraries offer reference assistance during 76 hours each week (Michigan: 62.8% of the 121 hours open; Cornell: 71% of the 107 hours open). Professional staff members are on duty except for four to six hours weekly when Work-Study Scholars at Michigan (students currently enrolled in the library school who also work in the library) and a senior library assistant at Cornell man the reference desks. Michigan has two reference librarians on duty during 36 of the hours (47.8%); Cornell has one reference librarian at all times. In both libraries, all professionals take turns at the reference desk in addition to having other major responsibilities.

A composite profile of reference librarians in undergraduate libraries would portray a young woman who is in the second or third year of her first professional position. She has done no extensive graduate work in a subject area and usually has an undergraduate humanities major from another institution. One or two staff members have more experience and act as resource persons for the younger staff. In selecting staff for undergraduate libraries, an effort is made to choose librarians "endowed with a great sense of service . . . each of whom is deeply interested in helping students."[6]

The philosophy of reference services for undergraduate students can usually be distilled into one word: teacher. Roberta Keniston, the first Librarian of the University of Michigan Undergraduate Library stated that:

> The reference librarian working with undergraduates serves as adjunct teacher for all departments, acting as interpreter and intermediary between professor and student. He has a unique opportunity to help students expand their intellectual horizons, see relationships between various areas of their studies, appreciate books as a means of intellectual stimulus and growth, clarify their assignments, learn expert use of a library's resources, and become aware of the utility of individual reference works.[7]

Reference librarians in undergraduate libraries have rarely considered themselves to be suppliers of specific information in the manner of special librarians. Undergraduate librarians have conceived of their function as a guide and instructor for students who would learn the ways of libraries and bibliography for future, unassisted use.

Decline in Use of Reference Services

The University of Michigan Undergraduate Library, opened in January, 1958, and the Uris Library, renovated and reopened in September, 1962, have now sustained reference services over a long enough period to be excellent case studies. The recorded use[8] of these two reference services reveals a trend which should be thoroughly investigated.

As is usual at the opening of a new library, the number of brief questions requesting directions and other information is far larger than the quantity of more substantive reference questions. Michigan was no exception. 69% (32,537) of the total questions (46,825) asked in 1958/59 were spot questions;[9] 31% (14,288) were recorded as reference questions.[10] During the next five years, spot questions decreased until an all-time low of 11,610 was reached in 1963/64. In the same period, reference questions increased in number each year until an all-time high of 31,844 was attained in 1963/64. A phenomenal 73% of the total were reference questions while only 27% were spot questions. 1963/64 was a vintage year for the Michigan Undergraduate Library's reference services.

The true vintage has become clearer. A reversal of the previous trend began and has continued. Reference questions decreased in each of the last five years; spot questions increased in four of five years. During the period there was an overall decrease in the total number of questions asked.

By 1968/69 reference questions had returned to slightly under the level set in 1958/59 (Table 1). But more startling is the 55% decrease from the high of 31,844 in 1963/64 to only 14,110 in 1968/69. Reference questions were 61.4% of the total questions asked in 1968/69; spot questions were 38.6%.

Table 1. — Comparison of Questions at Reference Desks of the *Undergraduate Library* and Undergraduate Enrollment, *University of Michigan* [a]

	1958/59	1968/69	Percentage of Increase or Decrease
I. Questions at Reference Desks:			
Spot questions	32,537	22,410	-31.1
Reference questions	14,288	14,110	- 1.2
Total questions	46,825	36,520	-22
II. Student Enrollment:			
Undergraduate Students in			
the College of Literature,			
Science, and the Arts	7,357[b]	12,500[c]	+70

[a]Michigan. University. Library. Undergraduate Library. *Annual Report, Reference Collection and Service.* 1968/69, p.8.
[b]Average representative gross enrollment for Fall and Spring Terms. Data furnished by University of Michigan Statistical Services Office.
[c]Estimated enrollment.

While the reference services have suffered drops of 31.1% in spot questions, 1.2% in reference questions, and 22% in the total number of questions, the undergraduates enrolled in the College of Literature, Science, and the Arts (the primary group of students served by the Undergraduate Library) have increased by 70% (Table 1). During the same eleven years, home loans from the Undergraduate Library have jumped by 117% and total book use has increased by 91%.

On a per capita basis, each L.S.&A. undergraduate asked about two reference questions in 1958/59 and only one reference question each in 1968/69.

Uris Library also had the expected large number of information questions[11] during the first year of operation: 57.4% (3,792) of the total questions (6,609) asked in 1962/63. 42.4% (2,800) were recorded as reference questions. Only 0.2% (17) were the longer search questions. In five of the next six years, information questions decreased with the all-time low of 2,130 occurring in 1968/69. Reference questions grew for two years reaching a high of 3,951 in 1964/65. This was 61.5% of all questions while 2,423 information questions were 37.7% and 46 search questions were 0.7%. However, during three of the four most recent years, reference questions have declined. By 1968/69 reference questions numbered 3,248; still above the level of 1962/63, but 17.7% below 1964/65. In 1968/69 reference questions accounted for 60.3% of the total questions while information questions were 39.5%.

With the Uris Library reference services declining by 18% in total questions (but increasing by 16% in the number of reference questions), the undergraduates enrolled in the College of Arts and Sciences have increased by 10% in the seven years Uris Library has been open (Table 2). During this same period, home loans from the main collection have more than doubled.

Table 2. — Comparison of Questions at Reference Desk of the
Uris Library and Undergraduate Enrollment, Cornell University[a]

	1962/63	1968/69	Percentage of Increase or Decrease
I. Questions at Reference Desk:			
Information and Directional			
questions	3,792	2,130	-43
Reference questions	2,800	3,248	+16
Search questions	17	7	-58
Total questions	6,609	5,385	-18
II. Student Enrollment:			
Undergraduate Students in			
the College of Arts and			
Sciences	2,904[b]	3,207[c]	+10

[a] Cornell University. Library. Uris Library. *Annual Reports.* 1962/63, Appendix I; 1968/69, Appendix I.
[b] Fall Semester, 1962.
[c] As of October 4, 1968.

On a per capita basis, each undergraduate in the College of Arts and Sciences asked only about one reference question in both 1962/63 and 1968/69.

Monitoring of Reference Desks in Undergraduate Libraries

This decline in reference services at both Michigan and Cornell undergraduate libraries prompted my investigation. The first step was to ascertain what actually occurs at their reference desks. The questions asked by undergraduates were monitored for two separate five-day periods during the 1969 fall semester. (Questions asked by graduate students, faculty, and others were not included.) During the hours of 10 A.M.-12 Noon, 1-5 P.M., and 7-9 P.M., Monday through Thursday and 10 A.M.-12 Noon and 1-5 P.M. on Friday, the monitor listened to all questions and recorded each as asked on an individual card. The monitor attempted to be as unobstrusive as possible in order not to create an artificial situation, hinder anyone from approaching the desk or to antagonize patrons. It is believed that this was successfully accomplished.

Definition and sub-categories of questions were developed in advance of the field work. They were based on the United States of American Standards Institute's definition of a "reference question" as "any request for information or aid which requires the use of one or more sources to determine the answer, or which utilizes the professional judgment of the librarian."[12] However, elaborations were made and a time element was added.

The definitions of major types of questions are:

1. Information question: requires brief directional answer from reference librarian who uses no library resources;
2. Reference question: requires use of one or more library resources and less than thirty minutes in obtaining answer;
3. Search question: requires use of several library resources and over thirty minutes but less than one hour in obtaining answer;
4. Problem question: requires use of several library resources and more than one hour in obtaining answer.

To explore more fully the type of substantive question most frequently asked by undergraduate students, reference questions (No. 2 above) are sub-divided into the following categories:

R-1. Bibliographical assistance with the library's own catalogs and holdings;
R-2. Bibliographical assistance with the holdings of other campus libraries;
R-3. Bibliographical verification of material not on campus;
R-4 Retrieval of factual, non-bibliographical information from any source;
R-5. Counseling of students in a reader's advisory capacity (reading guidance);
R-6. Informal personal instruction in use of library or any of its resources;
R-7. Miscellaneous questions not covered by the preceeding six categories.

Tables 3 and 4 show the types of questions asked by undergraduates in the Michigan Undergraduate Library and the Uris Library. The data confirm that only a brief time is spent with each student seeking reference assistance. Two search questions (over 30 minutes) were recorded at Cornell and one problem question (over one hour) occurred at Michigan. Of the 961 reference questions asked at Michigan's Undergraduate Library, only in 19 instances did the librarian spend more than five minutes with the student. At Uris Library the librarian assisted the student for over five minutes in 8 of 230 reference questions. Information questions, which form about one-half of the total questions at Michigan and about 60% at Cornell, are much briefer encounters, often lasting only a few seconds.

Table 3. — Questions Asked by Undergraduates at Reference Desks, *Undergraduate Library, University of Michigan*

Types of Questions	October 6-10, 1969 Number	October 6-10, 1969 Percentage	November 10-14, 1969 Number	November 10-14, 1969 Percentage
Information	502	53.3	479	47.8
Reference:				
R-1	262	27.9	348	34.7
R-2	39	4.2	47	4.6
R-3	---	----	---	----
R-4	91	9.7	75	7.5
R-5	12	1.3	22	2.2
R-6	34	3.6	31	3.1
R-7	---	----	---	----
Sub-total	438	46.7	523	52.1
Search	---	----	---	----
Problem	---	----	1	0.1
Total	940	100	1003	100

Table 4. — Questions Asked by Undergraduates at Reference Desk,
Uris Library, Cornell University

Types of Questions	November 3-7, 1969		December 8-12, 1969	
	Number	Percentage	Number	Percentage
Information	67	40.1	64	32.7
Reference:				
R-1	69	41.4	90	45.9
R-2	6	3.6	7	3.5
R-3	1	0.6	--	----
R-4	18	10.8	30	15.4
R-5	1	0.6	1	0.5
R-6	3	1.7	3	1.5
R-7	1	0.6	--	----
Sub-total	99	59.3	131	66.8
Search	1	0.6	1	0.5
Problem	--	----	--	----
Total	167	100	196	100

Bibliographical assistance with the library's own catalog and holdings (R-1) constitutes the bulk of reference questions. There is very little assistance with holdings of other campus libraries (R-2). In only one instance in 1,191 reference questions was there assistance with non-campus holdings (R-3). Although philosophies of reference service for undergraduates portray the librarian as teacher, little personal instruction is given in the use of the library or any of its resources (R-6). Retrieval of factual, non-bibliographical information (R-4) takes place more often than instruction. Librarians rarely counsel students in a reader's advisory capacity (R-5).

In an attempt to evaluate the calibre of questions and service given, the information questions and R-1 questions were further analyzed. At Michigan 9% of the information questions could be categorized as assistance with physical facilities (location of pencil sharpener, request to borrow pencil, requests for keys or the unlocking of rooms, and similar requests). At Cornell these requests were 45% of the information questions. Other categories of these brief questions (and their percentages of the total information questions) were:

	Michigan Undergraduate Library	Uris Library, Cornell
Requests for location of a particular volume (student had call number and librarian gave directions)	33%	12%
Requests for information or publication (student did not have call number; librarian knew answer without referring to any source or directed student to catalog or reference collection giving no additional help)	12%	18%
Questions concerning services or collections (librarian responded with brief directions or information)	45%	21%

Analyses of the R-1 questions are presented in Tables 5 and 6.

Table 5. — Reference Questions (R-1: Bibliographical Assistance with Library's Own Catalogs and Holdings) asked by Undergraduates at Reference Desks, *Undergraduate Library, University of Michigan*

Sub-categories of R-1 Questions	October 6-10, 1969		November 10-14, 1969	
	Number	Percentage of Total Reference Questions Asked	Number	Percentage of Total Reference Questions Asked
Requests for particular volume or type of volume; librarian gave assistance by:				
Checking list of frequently used reference titles and giving student call number	10	2.2	9	1.7
Charging out heavily used item from drawer of desk or from office	27	6.2	47	8.9

Table 5 — Continued

Sub-categories of R-1 Questions	October 6-10, 1969		November 10-14, 1969	
	Number	Percentage of Total Reference Questions Asked	Number	Percentage of Total Reference Questions Asked
Going to reference shelves and producing particular volume for student who had usually given title or described type	30	6.9	48	9.2
Going to main collection and locating volume which student had been unable to find	20	4.5	11	2.1
Sub-total	87	19.8	115	21.9
Requests for general bibliographical assistance; librarian responded by: Using reference collection or pamphlet file	34	7.8	50	9.6
Assisting student at catalog or record of periodical holdings	104	23.8	116	22.2
Using *Subject Headings Used in . . . the Library of Congress* (or library's own subject headings list for pamphlet file)	10	2.2	15	2.8

Table 5 — Continued

Sub-categories of R-1 Questions	October 6-10, 1969		November 10-14, 1969	
	Number	Percentage of Total Reference Questions Asked	Number	Percentage of Total Reference Questions Asked
Assisting in use of microfilm	17	3.9	39	7.5
Assisting in use of print-out of circulation and reserve charges	10	2.2	13	2.5
Sub-total	175	39.9	233	44.6
Total R-1 Questions	262	59.7	348	66.5
Other Reference Questions (R-2 through R-7)	176	40.2	175	33.4
Total Reference Questions	438	99.9	523	99.9

Table 6. — Reference Questions (R-1: Bibliographical Assistance
with Library's Own Catalogs and Holdings) asked by
Undergraduates at Reference Desk,
Uris Library, Cornell University

Sub-categories of R-1 Questions	November 3-7, 1969		December 8-12, 1969	
	Number	Percentage of Total Reference Questions Asked	Number	Percentage of Total Reference Questions Asked
Requests for particular volume or type of volume; librarian gave assistance by:				
Checking list of frequently used reference titles and giving student call number	--	----	--	----
Charging out heavily used item from drawer of desk or area back of desk	11	11.	4	3.
Going to reference shelves and producing particular volume for student who had usually given title or described type	21	21.	25	19.
Going to main collection and locating volume which student had been unable to find	--	----	9	7.
Sub-total	32	32.	38	29.

Table 6 — Continued

Sub-categories of R-1 Questions	November 3-7, 1969		December 8-12, 1969	
	Number	Percentage of Total Reference Questions Asked	Number	Percentage of Total Reference Questions Asked
Requests for general bibliographical assistance; librarian responded by:				
Using reference collection	16	16.	28	21.
Assisting student at main catalog or serials catalog	19	19.	24	18.
Using *Subject Headings Used in . . . the Library of Congress*	2	2.	--	---
Assisting in use of microforms [a]	--	---	--	---
Assisting in use of circulation records	--	---	--	---
Sub-total	37	37.	52	39.
Total R-1 Questions	69	69.	90	68.
Other Reference Questions (R-2 through R-7)	30	30.	41	31.
Total Reference Questions	99	99.	131	99.

[a]Uris Library has no microforms.

At the Michigan Undergraduate Library, assisting students at the catalog or at the records of periodical holdings constitutes the largest number of reference questions. 55-60% of this assistance is with the records of periodical holdings. Uris reference librarians, who serve considerably fewer students than Michigan, have time to go with students to the reference shelves a greater proportion of the times they are asked reference questions. Assistance at the main or serials catalogs is also a substantial part of Uris reference services.

Use of Reference Services in University Libraries

Undergraduates have available another major reference service at both universities. Have they ceased using the reference services of the undergraduate libraries and begun to ask their questions at the reference deparments of the main university library? To answer this question, another monitor listened to all questions asked at the reference desk of the University of Michigan General Library and of the John M. Olin Library, Cornell University, during the same hours in which their undergraduate libraries were studied. Tables 7 and 8 report the questions asked by undergraduates.

At Michigan during October 6-10, 1969, the Undergraduate Library reference librarians were serving almost 7 times the number of undergraduates as were served by the reference staff in the General Library. During November 10-14, the Undergraduate Library reference librarians served over 5 times as many undergraduates. During the October monitoring, undergraduates asked 21% of the total questions (617) asked at the General Library's reference desk. During the week in November, the undergraduate questions rose to 28% of the total questions (665).

Table 7. — Questions Asked by Undergraduates at Reference Desk,
General Library, University of Michigan

Types of Questions	October 6-10, 1969		November 10-14, 1969	
	Number	Percentage	Number	Percentage
Information	65	48.1	84	44.4
Reference:				
R-1	43	31.9	60	31.8
R-2	--	----	--	----
R-3	3	2.2	5	2.6
R-4	18	13.3	35	18.5
R-5	1	0.7	--	----
R-6	4	3.0	5	2.6
R-7	--	----	--	----
Sub-total	69	51.1	105	55.5
Search	1	0.7	--	----
Problem	--	--	--	----
Total	135	99.9	189	99.9

Table 8. — Questions Asked by Undergraduates at Reference Desks,
John M. Olin Library, Cornell University

Types of Questions	November 3-7, 1969		December 8-12, 1969	
	Number	Percentage	Number	Percentage
Information	42	32.3	56	29.7
Reference:				
R-1	60	46.2	90	47.8
R-2	2	1.5	1	0.5
R-3	1	0.7	5	2.7
R-4	21	16.2	34	18.1
R-5	--	---	--	----
R-6	4	3.0	2	1.1
R-7	--	----	--	----
Sub-total	88	67.6	132	70.2
Search	--	----	--	----
Problem	--	----	--	----
Total	130	99.9	188	99.9

Cornell presents a contrasting situation. The reference librarians in Olin Library answered 130 questions from undergraduates during November 3-7 while the Uris staff members were answering only 167 questions during the same hours. In the December week Olin librarians almost pulled even with the Uris staff (188 questions by undergraduates in Olin; 196 questions in Uris). During the November monitoring, undergraduates asked 23% of the total questions (554) asked at the Olin reference desks. In December the undergraduate questions rose to 34% of the total (548).

Undergraduate Users of Union Catalog

An additional investigation was conducted in both the Michigan General Library and Cornell's Olin Library to test the hypothesis that unassisted use by undergraduates of the union catalog of campus holdings increases use of the main university library and decreases use of the undergraduate library on the same campus. All undergraduates using the union catalog during certain hours of one week were interviewed. Table 9 presents the basic data.

Table 9. — Union Catalog Users in *General Library,*
University of Michigan, and *John M. Olin*
Library, Cornell University

| | Michigan [a] | | Cornell [b] | |
	Number	Percentage	Number	Percentage
Undergraduates Interviewed	474		427	
Undergraduates Refusing Interview	5		---	
Undergraduates Who Had Been Previously Interviewed	33		78	
Total Under-graduate Users	512	28.3	505	32.7
Graduate Students, Faculty, and University Staff (excludes Library Staff)	1,281	70.9	958	62.
Non-University Users (Local Residents; Students and Faculty from Other Institutions)	15	0.8	82	5.3
Total Users of Union Catalog	1,808	100	1,545	100

[a] Interviews conducted during week of September 29-October 3, 1969. Hours on Monday-Thursday were: 10 A.M. - 12 Noon, 1 - 5 P.M., and 7 - 9 P.M. On Friday: 10 A.M. - 12 Noon and 1 - 5 P.M.
[b] Interviews conducted October 27-31, 1969 during the same hours noted above.

In percentages, the undergraduates interviewed were members of the following university classes:

	Michigan (N=474)	Cornell (N=427)
Freshman	16.8%	12.8%
Sophomore	21.7	19.2
Junior	29.7	29.9
Senior	31.6	37.7
Special Unclassified	----	0.2

At Michigan, the undergraduates were from the following schools and colleges:

College of Literature, Science, and the Arts	83.5%
College of Engineering	6.3
School of Education	4.2
College of Architecture and Design	2.1
School of Nursing	1.9
School of Natural Resources	1.1
School of Business Administration	0.4
College of Pharmacy	0.4

Cornell undergraduates were from seven schools and colleges:

College of Arts and Sciences	64.9%
New York State College of Agriculture	11.5
New York State College of Human Ecology	7.2
College of Engineering	7.0
New York State School of Industrial and Labor Relations	4.7
College of Architecture, Art, and Planning	3.7
School of Hotel Administration	0.9

All undergraduates were asked: "Did you use the Undergraduate Library catalog before coming here?" Their responses were:

	Yes	No
Michigan	40.9%	59%
Cornell	24.3	75.6

Those who replied that they had used the Undergraduate Library catalog before coming to the union catalog were then asked: "Why are you now using this main catalog?" The reasons were:

	Michigan (N=205)	Cornell (N = 105)
Undergraduate Library did not have material	46 %	40%
Material in use in Undergraduate Library (out, on reserve, etc.)	32	41
Wanted additional material	16	17
Referred to Union Catalog by Undergraduate reference librarian	1.5	--
Did not use Undergraduate catalog properly	1	--
Wanted different edition	0.5	--
Had wrong citation	0.5	--
Subject headings in Undergraduate catalog not specific enough	0.5	--
Could not find the catalog in Undergraduate Library	----	1

Those who said that they had not used the Undergraduate Library catalog before coming to the union catalog in this particular instance were asked: "Do you usually by-pass the Undergraduate Library catalog and come to the main catalog first?" The responses were:

	Michigan (N=280)	Cornell (N=323)
Yes	65.7%	77.4%
No	23.2	12.4
About half the time, I by-pass it	6.0	7.1
Depends on the material I am seeking	3.9	2.1
Depends on which is closer	0.7	----
Depends on where I want to study	----	0.3
First time in any campus library	0.3	0.6

Undergraduates who affirmed that they usually by-passed the Undergraduate Library catalog were next asked: "Why do you not use the Undergraduate Library catalog first?" Responses were varied:

	Michigan (N=208)	Cornell (N=311)
This is a union catalog listing holdings of all campus libraries	21.6%	32.7%
Most of the university's books are here in the main library	15.8	17.3
I have an Olin Library stack permit[13]	----	14.7
Have found through experience that the Undergraduate Library lacks what I want	19.2	10.6
I like the main university library better	9.1	4.8
I do not like the Undergraduate Library	12.0	3.5
I work here in the main library	0.9	3.5
I use a college or school library first	----	3.2
It depends on the material I am seeking	0.9	2.2
I do not know why	----	1.9
Undergraduate collection is too small	11.5	1.2
Too much is on reserve in the Undergraduate Library	3.8	0.6
My professor sent me here to use union catalog	1.4	0.3
The main library is closer to my living quarters	1.9	0.3
I did not know the Undergraduate Library existed	1.4	0.3
Miscellaneous (ranging from "Help is easier to get in the Olin Library" to "I am interested in a boy who studies here")	----	2.2

The final question posed to all undergraduates using the union catalog was: "If the Undergraduate Library had a catalog like this one which includes holdings of all campus libraries, would you use it there or still come here?"

	Michigan (N=474)	Cornell (N=427)
Still come here	41.7%	47.5%
Use it there [Undergraduate Library]	51.2	35.6
Does not matter to me	1.0	9.1
I do not know	2.7	3.5
Would use whichever is closer	2.5	2.1
Depends on material sought	0.6	1.6

	Michigan (N=208)	Cornell (N=311)
It is unnecessary to duplicate because the Undergraduate Library is so close to main library	----	0.2%
Depends on how noisy the Undergraduate Library is	----	0.2

There seems to be no question that undergraduates, particularly upperclassmen, go in substantial numbers to use the union catalog in the main library. They have entirely by-passed the Undergraduate Library's catalog in most cases (59% at Michigan and 75.6% at Cornell). The major reason given by the undergraduates is the excellent one that the holdings of all campus libraries are included in the union catalog. It would not seem worthwhile to duplicate the union catalog, perhaps in book form, in order to lure the undergraduates back to the Undergraduate Library. Only one-half of the Michigan students interviewed said that they would use a union catalog in the Undergraduate Library while fewer (35.6%) of the Cornell undergraduates would use such a catalog in the Uris Library. Many of the students would continue to go to the main library (41.7% at Michigan; 47.5% at Cornell.) The large number of volumes housed in the main university library is a magnet apparently too strong to be overcome even by the very expensive duplication of the union catalog.

Reference Services at a College Library

Do students receive superior reference services in libraries of liberal arts colleges? Or is this a myth created by our nostalgia for the small, intimate, less complicated world which we imagine these colleges to be? As a case study of a college library's reference services, the Lilly Library at Earlham College, Richmond, Indiana was chosen. You should be immediately warned that this is one of the best college reference services in the country and may not be typical of other college libraries. Supplementing the excellent reference assistance at Earlham is one of the best library instruction programs.[14]

Questions asked by undergraduates at Lilly Library's reference desk were monitored in the same way as previously described. Undergraduate students are the major users. During October 13-17, they accounted for 71% of the total questions (188) with faculty, staff, and others asking 29%. During November 17-21, 83% of the total (195) were undergraduate questions while faculty, staff, and others asked 17%.

Table 10 categorizes the questions asked by undergraduates. Substantive reference questions (84.3% in the first week; 78.5% the second week) overwhelmingly outnumbered the information questions. Requests for bibliographical assistance with the library's catalog and holdings (R-1) were again the major type of questions. R-1 questions comprised 46-50% of all questions at Earlham. In many cases the reference librarians used both the catalog and reference collection to assist students. This was in contrast to the Michigan and Cornell librarians who used one or the other, but rarely use both resources. Earlham librarians also made certain that almost all students were successful in finding the material or the answer being sought. Students were not simply directed to possible sources with no additional assistance. If the librarians had not assisted throughout the entire search, they returned to check the students' progress. The Uris staff followed this procedure to some extent, but the reference librarians at Michigan did not do so in most instances.

Of the 241 reference questions asked by Earlham undergraduates in the two periods, librarians spent more than five minutes with 37 (15.3%) of the questions. For many of these questions, they assisted students for 15-20 minutes. Four search questions were also undertaken for students and two for faculty.

Another difference was noted at Earlham. Librarians approached students in the reference area or at the catalog, not waiting for students to gather courage to ask for help. 34 (14.1%) of the 241 reference questions were initiated by Earlham staff in contrast to only two such instances of 230 questions at Uris Library and four of 961 questions at Michigan's Undergraduate Library. The fact that Earlham librarians know many students naturally contributes to the success of this approach.

Table 10. — Questions Asked by Undergraduates at
Reference Desk, *Lilly Library, Earlham College*

Types of Questions	October 13-17, 1969		November 17-21, 1969	
	Number	Percentage	Number	Percentage
Information	18	13.4	34	20.8
Reference:				
R-1	68	50.8	75	46.1
R-2	--	----	--	----
R-3	4	2.9	11	6.7
R-4	25	18.7	32	19.6
R-5	9	6.7	2	1.2
R-6	6	4.5	8	4.9
R-7	1	0.7	--	----
Sub-total	113	84.3	128	78.5
Search	3	2.2	1	0.6
Problem	--	----	--	----
Total	134	99.9	163	99.9

Conclusion and Summary

The basic conclusion to be drawn from these studies is that we have not taken advantage of the opportunities presented by undergraduate libraries. Michigan and Cornell have not closed the "gap between class instruction and library service." Reference services are of low calibre. Too often the assistance given students is superficial and too brief. Although the reference services have been in a state of decline for several years, there have been almost no attempts to discover why or to make changes from traditional practices.

Some of the reasons for this situation are:

1)   Librarians have a passive, rather than an activist, attitude. They wait for students who know little about libraries to request service. One undergraduate library has officially stated that "it is our responsibility to acquaint students with the library and to offer assistance in its use; it is the student's responsibility to evaluate his library competence and determine the kind of help he will seek. Help is given him according to his expressed need . . . "

2)   Librarians in undergraduate libraries rarely know any students.

3)   There is a total lack of communication between librarians and faculty concerning reference services for their students.

4)   The undergraduate libraries offer very limited and unimaginative instruction programs. Relatively little time, talent, and funds have been spent on orientation for freshmen. When there is some kind of freshmen orientation, advanced students and disadvantaged students are usually ignored. Few attempts have been made to integrate library instruction with course work.

5)   We in universities have used the large number of students as an excuse for our failure to provide good reference services and library instruction programs.

6)   No matter how much we claim to be a profession and a part of the teaching mission of the university, too many of us settle into clerical work which requires little thought.

Continuing to probe staff attitudes for an affect upon reference services, other questions come to mind. They are asked here to show the complexity and subtlety of the situation; definite answers will not be given. Do we expect few requests for assistance from undergraduates, and with this low expectation, unconsciously help keep the requests few in number? Are questions asked by undergraduates so strongly assumed to be easy, unchallenging, and repetitive that this attitude is conveyed to students who oblige by keeping them easy and unchallenging? Do we answer only the tentative and very broad first question asked by a student and then dismiss him without detecting his real need? Do we have preconceived notions of how a question should be asked? And when the student fails to frame the question in this "proper" form, is our answer brief and superficial instead of tentative and probing? Do we in undergraduate libraries consider ourselves to be at the lowest level of reference work in a university library system — serving only third class citizens while reference librarians in the main library and in subject libraries serve the first class (faculty) and second class (graduate students) citizens?

Perhaps the saga of reference services in undergraduate libraries can be summarized by tracing the use of three prepositions — "to," "for," and "with" — in the literautre of librarianship and in the minds of librarians. In the 1950's, university librarians held symposia entitled "Library Service to Undergraduates"[15] and "Library Service to Undergraduate College Students."[16] In discussing reference services, it was always reference services to undergraduate students. In the 1960's, articles began to appear with such titles as "Library Service for Undergraduates."[17] *For* undergraduates is a vast improvement over *to* undergraduates. It is not too much to read into these simple prepositions a change in attitude from paternalism to service. We must, however, go one preposition further in the 1970's. It must be students *with* librarians. If we do not get in touch with students and truly work with them — learning from them and having them learn from us — the last article published on undergraduate libraries will be entitled "Libraries *without* Students."

Notes

1.   Keyes D. Metcalf, "The Undergraduate and the Harvard Library, 1937-1947," *Harvard Library Bulletin* 1 (Autumn, 1947): 289.

2.   Harvie Branscomb, "The Future of Libraries in Academic Institutions, Part III," *Harvard Library Bulletin* 3 (Autumn, 1949): 345.

3.   Ibid.

4.   Warren B. Kuhn, "Undergraduate Libraries in a University," *Library Trends* 18 (October, 1969): 199.

5.   Frederick H. Wagman, "The Undergraduate Library of the University of Michigan," *College and Research Libraries* 20 (May, 1959): 185.

6.   "A New Intellectual Center," *Michigan Alumnus* 64 (December 14, 1957): 151-2.

7.   Michigan. University. Library. Undergraduate Library. "Reference Services to Undergraduates [with] Appendix 1, The Recording of Reference Statistics." [Ann Arbor, n.d.]. (Mimeographed.) Originally appeared as a supplement to the 1957/58 *Annual Report of the Undergraduate Library.*

8.   Statistics in the following section are from: Michigan. University. Library. Undergraduate Library. *Annual Reports.* 1958/59-1968/69; and Cornell University. Library. Uris Library. *Annual Reports.* 1962/63-1968/69.

9.   Spot questions are defined at Michigan as questions asking for information or directions which are "usually very simple, often answerable in a few words plus some directional motions."

10.   Michigan defines reference questions as more substantial questions for which the librarian "explains in some detail the mechanics" of a reference volume, the catalog,

the holdings records of periodicals, or other resources, perhaps going to the shelves or catalog to assist the student.

11. Cornell defines and categorizes questions as: 1.) Information and Direction questions concern "library resources and/or their use. [They are] answered from the personal knowledge of the staff member without consulting any other library resource." 2.) Reference questions are "answered through the use of library resources . . . The source of information used is most frequently one which is obvious to the staff member at the time inquiry is made." Less than 15 minutes is required to answer. 3.) Search questions require "more than 15 minutes to answer and, ordinarily, the use of three or more library resources."

12. United States of America Standards Institute. Sectional Committee Z39 on Standardization in the Field of Library Work and Documentation. *U.S.A. Standards for Library Statistics* (New York: United States of America Standards Institute, 1969), 17.

13. The stacks of the Olin Library, Cornell, are closed to most undergraduates. The University of Michigan General Library stacks are open to all undergraduates.

14. James R. Kennedy. "Integrated Library Instruction," *Library Journal* 95 (April 15, 1970): 1450-3.

15. "Library Service to Undergraduates: A Symposium," *College and Research Libraries* 14 (July, 1953): 266-75.

16. "Library Service to Undergraduate College Students," *College and Research Libraries* 17 (March, 1956): 143-55.

17. M.W. Moss, "Library Service for Undergraduates," in *The Provision and Use of Library and Documentation Services,* ed. W. L. Saunders ("International Series of Monographs in Library and Information Science," Vol. 4. Oxford: Pergamon Press, 1966), 85-113.

About the Author

After service in several positions at the Louis Round Wilson Library, University of North Carolina, Chapel Hill, and 25 Head, Catawba County Library, Newton, North Carolina, Billy R. Wilkinson was appointed Goldwin Smith Librarian at Cornell University in 1959. He was then designated as Undergraduate Librarian in 1961 and was in charge of the Uris Undergraduate Library from its opening in September, 1962 until 1967 when he became a doctoral student. He received his doctorate from the Columbia University School of Library Service in 1971. From 1971-1977, he was Staff Relations Officer at The New York Public Library. He is now Associate University Librarian at the University of Illinois at Chicago Circle.

Part VII.

Institute on the Undergraduate Environment, 1971: Continuing Explorations Among Students, Librarians & Faculty

Part VII: Introduction

If the UgLi "movement" came of age in La Jolla, California at the Institute for Service in Undergraduate Libraries in August, 1970, it was greatly nurtured by another, much larger gathering of the faithful the next summer. A Pre-Conference Institute entitled "Librarians Confront the Undergraduate Environment" was sponsored by the University Libraries Section of the Association of College and Research Libraries and held June 18-19, 1971 in Dallas, Texas. John R. Haak chaired the conference which featured major papers by four eminent California educators. Paul Heist, Research Psychologist and Professor of Education, University of California at Berkeley, presented the first paper on "students in the 70s — Caught in the Academic Maelstrom." James Davis, College Librarian, University of California at Los Angeles, vividly portrayed undergraduate librarians in "Coping — An UgLi Way of Life." James Gibbs, Dean of Undergraduate Studies, Stanford University, spoke on "The University's Response to the Need for Change in Undergraduate Education." Then Joseph Gusfield, Professor of Sociology and Chairman, Department of Sociology, University of California at San Diego, reviewed the "Attitudes of University Faculty Toward the Need for Change in Undergraduate Education."

The papers by Heist, Davis, and Gusfield are published in their entirety for the first time on the following pages by permission of each author and by special permission of the University Libraries Section of the Association of College and Research Libraries.

Paul Heist

Students in the 70s—
Caught in the
Academic Maelstrom

An expert in the sociology of higher education
reviews the several major themes in higher education during the 1950s and 1960s. He observes that
during the period 1966-1970 students had a "significantly different orientation to the future than
one would expect in our generally affluent society." They "were not highly interested in vocational positions" and "seemingly refused to think
about their education as preparation for or entrance into the established remunerative ways of
life." Heist then discusses in great detail data
gathered for three years on the first-year class at
the University of California, Berkeley. The studies
detect "increasing seriousness of many, in their
expressed desires, aspirations and expectations
towards greater emphasis on future goals and career preparation." Data on the freshmen students
of 1971 are compared in selected areas to freshmen enrolling at Berkeley during the previous
twelve years.

The field of higher education in the United States has had an interesting, if not
somewhat dramatic, history since the end of World War II. A faster pace of
changing developments and the earliest attempts at introducing innovations into
numerous aspects of the system began some years before 1960. Following that
date, however, we witnessed a stepped-up transition with an increasing innovative fervor spreading to numerous campuses across the country. The decade of
the sixties culminated in more trouble and turbulence for a greater variety of our

SOURCE: From Paul Heist, "Students in the 70s — Caught in the Academic Maelstrom," Librarians Confront the Undergraduate Environment, a Pre-Conference Institute Sponsored by the University Libraries Section, the Association of College and
Research Libraries, American Library Association, Dallas, Texas, June 18-19, 1971.
Included by permissions of the author and the University Libraries Section, Association
of College and Research Libraries.

universities and colleges than we had ever witnessed before in the history of education.

The series of events of these last two decades has had several interesting strands or themes. One of the earliest of such was initiated by the entrance to college of thousands of mature war veterans, largely financed by federal funds, and who introduced new considerations to the whole area of public and private education. A second strand was evident in the gradually increasing funds, also from federal sources, released for a great many purposes within academic realms. Another strand began with the Supreme Court decision in 1954, soon abetted by the peaceful sit-ins of black students in the South and the campaigns led by Martin Luther King and others.

An additional historical strand beginning during the 1950s, and unbeknown to most of us at the time, was the political activity, mostly constructive, of small groups of students in scattered colleges and universities across the nation. Most of these students were of liberal commitment and given over to activity which often grew out of a critical but progressive stance. Perhaps for the first time, there were a number of concentrated clusters of students of liberal inclination in higher education settings. In the California Bay Area, for example, campus political activity became organized after the mid-fifties in the semblance of two student groups known as SLATE and FOCUS. Both of these groups had strong "representation" in the anti-HUAC demonstration in 1960. The first example bordering on violence which occurred in the Bay Area was an effort of the Establishment, (to use the students' label) and not an effort by the students — the occasion when students were washed out of the Hall of Justice in San Francisco.

Since the mid-fifties a small minority of politically active students have come and gone on the Berkeley campus. Many contributed to the development of a liberal student movement some years before the days of the Free Speech Movement. During the same period, the thrust of the black liberation cause had moved out of the South, chiefly via the efforts of the Southern Christian Leadership Conference, the Congress of Racial Equality, and the Student Non-Violent Coordinating Committee. The activity of these three national groups, at that time often encompassing blacks and whites, was the antecedent by several years to any seriously aggresive protest by black citizens and also antecedent to later moves to establish special minority programs on major campuses across the nation.

One major development, chiefly for and by white students, in the early 1960s was the spreading phenomena of the Students for a Democratic Society. However, the persistence of a campaign over many weeks on the Berkeley campus, under the guise of the Free Speech Movement, served to give new impetus and direction to what had already come to be referred to as a national student movement.

The Free Speech Movement in 1964 is now seen as the kick-off event, whether accurately or not, for a whole series of non-violent and violent protests and demonstrations throughout the nation. Student activities of this nature, witnessed in every region of the nation and addressed to a host of grievances, continued through the recent spring of 1971. However, we learned to live with these events with a certain amount of ease. Many will remember when we first faced up to a variety of demonstrations, either by experiencing them on other campuses or on the local campus. We now seem to have a certain amount of equanimity about accepting this aspect of our social history which seemed quite foreign and wholly unanticipated in the first decade following World War II.

The fluctuating concerns about the Vietnam War, the unwelcome draft, racial inequalities, and unresolved social problems have served as a fuel for widespread flames of confrontations between students, institutions, police and militia. The seemingly unending conflicts, as well as the concomitant changes of the 1960s in such things as the styles of life, the songs, the dress, and the new mores of high school and college students, all tended to widen the normal credibility gap between large proportions of students and various segments of the older generation. However, it appears that the protests of the last decade have not resulted in *general* changes in the course of higher education in the seventies or, it may be that the total portent is yet to be deciphered and yet to be understood. There are still some among the Berkeley faculty who retain the hope that the gains of the last decade will have a major pay-off and that we have yet to witness the significance in our institutions.

Another major strand of history in the educational world of the past twenty years is the aforementioned theme of innovation, observed mostly in attempts here and there at devising new structural units and revising curricula. Innovative developments, varying greatly from state to state and one section of country to another, were inter-woven with a tremendous and continuous growth of postwar higher education; the latter was witnessed in the number of new institutions, the increase in buildings and facilities, the expanding enrollment, and the addition of many more persons on the faculty, administrative staffs, library staffs, and in non-academic positions.

This theme or strand directed towards change, i.e., institutional innovations, did not become prominent however, until after 1960. The major thrust actually reached a level of recognized fruition after 1967. In fact, some of the institutions resulting from these efforts to improve or change education were so recent in construction as to have their programs jeopardized by the mild economic recession of the early seventies (1971-1972). Others that were already established, or that seem well established, were similarly plagued by the first budgetary cuts of that period.

The sequence of this trend towards some innovative efforts has evolved in line with the stages or levels of intensity of student activism. Although the planning and construction of a number of new institutions with revised curricula preceded the major period of student activism, the planning and developing of most new residential and cluster colleges appear to be related to the persistence and severity of demonstrations and certain major manifestations of unrest and discontent. In other words, if one looks at the history of the situation closely, some of the student criticism and concern may be credited with having given impetus, if not direction, to some of the significant innovations across the nation. At least, some of the attempts at serious redress appear to have been made in response to the critical student voice heard between 1964 and 1969.

The total potency and results of this movement to modify and change education in specific settings, including program revision, representation in governance and construction of new colleges, is somewhat difficult to assess at this time. Among those who have taken a close look at the history of innovation and the actual functioning of new institutions and programs, some experts are quite skeptical of what has been accomplished and question whether the isolated structural and program renovations have led to any greater effectiveness in teaching-learning situations.[1] As already concluded above, no significant changes have been effected across the nation.

On the positive side, however, a number of the colleges in the variety of new institutions are still very much caught up with the excitement and the enthusiasm of the changed directions and experimentation. There is as yet no reason to believe that the overall impact of the attempts at innovation will not have positive aftereffects, thus providing a basis for future decisions and planning regarding additional redesigned, experimental programs. There is some reason to believe that, while the new programs per se may not provide a significant basis for continuation as far as the faculty are concerned, the caliber and motivation of the student clientele in a number of those institutions may save the day.

One final strand in this brief history of recent education could be described as more a product of the events of the sixties than as an interactive aspect of an extended historical sequence. However, as observed today, the lives and behavior of numerous young people may be seen appropriately as links in a recent chain of social dynamics and as interrelated with earlier events. The thinking of at least a large minority of modern students seems to be related to that of the earliest protesting individuals and groups of the post-war period such as the SDS leaders who were active during the 1950s and the early 1960s. These early leaders, and the students that followed them, started by questioning and challenging the institutions of education.

The focus referred to here is the particular thinking and behavior of many current high school and college students, but the theme is a little difficult to describe. Acknowledging and emphasizing that students are *never* all of a kind, attention nevertheless is being drawn to some common characteristics that have been repeatedly but recently (1971-1972) observed by researchers, administrators, and teachers.[2] Along these lines, it was especially interesting for several of us in recent weeks to talk with junior high and high school principals from schools in three major cities in the West: Seattle, Berkeley, and Oakland. These high school administrators and leaders were identifying certain traits of behavior in many high school youths of today which had been noted also in numerous undergraduate and graduate students on various college campuses.

One particular characteristic may be described as a significantly different orientation to the future than one would expect in our generally affluent society and of most students of the same age some years ago. For several years (1966-

1970), it had been observed that many undergraduate and graduate students were not highly interested in *vocational* positions, as we tend to define and cluster occupations. They seemingly refused to think about their education as preparation for or entrance into the established remunerative ways of life. Numerous graduate students we have encountered in the Division of Higher Education, and in several other departments, at Berkeley were speaking more and more about becoming change agents and working in coordinative, but risk-taking assignments, often rejecting the more traditional and certified pathways to security. They were talking less like young disciplinarians of earlier periods and more like persons seeking some new quest and a better future for themselves — and perhaps for all of us. Among undergraduates, the majority were looking for subject areas and relationships that would permit meaningful learning experiences, explorations of self, and explorations of one's role in the scheme of things.

Many students in this period of the late sixties did not desire to be pinned down to the specifics of a definite job and increasingly spoke of an unstructured existence or a general social service assignment. The sentiments of the entrants of the early seventies are found to be rather similar to this, as will be indicated in the following remarks. We have had a pocketful of surprising stories from recent years from extremely capable, intelligent young people who are doing exactly this — seeking a more unstructured future.

The secondary school administrators mentioned above were describing similar changes in the aspirations of a large number of high school students. These administrators observed the changes in the general attitudes of students toward learning, in their refusal to become involved in vocational planning, and in a general ethos to "hang loose" and reject many of the adult or traditional emphases of the school system. These occupational thrusts, typifying what many more students were, and are still, seeking and expecting in the present period, could not be readily accommodated by the established teachers and programs in the existing systems.

A related phenomenon to the changing attitudes and new cultural mores of the younger generation is the increasing mobility of thousands of adolescents and post-adolescents. For some years, we observed rapidly growing numbers of young people starting off on the highways and by-ways of the world with the means and comforts of their existence strapped to their backs. This modern transiency, now somewhat lessened, appeared to be closely related to the growing numbers who were dropping out of the formal channels of education. Presumably, many will return to education, but many of them say they will never go back. The motivation of many of such youth on the move was more a matter of escape and a reaction to boredom, frustration, and unhappiness than a case of a joyful quest for adventure and knowledge about the world.

Reverting for a moment to consider these changing orientations of modern youth, as one of several historical themes (or strands) having their origins in the questioning and protesting of earlier generations, there are some important implications to be considered by educators. Much time and attention must be given to creating and providing living-learning experiences, starting in junior high school or perhaps earlier, which permit the younger generation to relate to, understand, and work with the problems of this society. The learning experiences, whether within traditional schools or outside them, must provide for constructive and significant ties between preparation for and the reality of meaningful existence. In short, the real world and the students' futures cannot be left out of the curriculum any longer.

Needless to add, this tremendous task is not likely to be accomplished without fundamental changes in the underlying values and practices of the total society. The implications for learning at advanced level of education are equally important. However, focusing on such implications will be put aside for the moment to take a closer look at a variety of data on one sample of college students, in an attempt to substantiate or broaden the considerations already introduced.

University Students of the Seventies

A specific look at a large sample of young Americans is made possible through a study of a first-year class at the University of California at Berkeley. Entering students have been surveyed for three years now, but the data employed here comes only from the most recent class (1971). Recent studies on other university campuses indicate the data could be taken from Santa Barbara, UCLA, or Davis, and we would find the story to be quite the same. When the data from the freshmen students at Berkeley are reviewed in the context of such other studies, as well in the context of several previous surveys of entering Berkeley students during the 1960s, we have the opportunity to see some changes and trends in the goals and thinking of college students during the years of student unrest. Using this option, the description of the recent entrants, students enrolling in 1971, will be followed by a second look at them in comparison to a couple of entering classes of the previous decade.

To put some of the data in context, it should be explained that the California high school graduates who enter the University of California represent approximately the top 12 per cent on the criterion of grade achievement. Consequently, they are far from a random sampling of California youth, at least in the way of achievement at the secondary school level. However, on many other characteristics, from aptitude to a variety of behaviorisms, they seem to represent the typical diversity of American youth, at least in the western states.

In drawing from the data for the 1971 freshmen, the following areas will be included in these brief descriptions: home and school background, plans for present and future education, preferred campus activities, attitudes towards education, student activism and social problems, and attitudes about political issures and ethical matters.

Also in the way of background, it is of interest that the Berkeley entrants came from all sections of the state of California. This happens to be more true of Berkeley than of other campuses perhaps because of its more central location or perhaps for historical reasons—the University of Berkeley being an older and more widely known campus. Approximately 65 percent of the students are from homes within a 50 mile radius of the campus, leaving 35 percent to be distributed across the rest of the state and the U.S. These entrants attended high school in communities of all sizes; however, the majority of the students are from cities of 50,000 or larger. They are mostly "big high school" youth.

According to the reports by the students, the parents of approximately two thirds of the students place great emphasis on getting grades, while only a third of the students tended to enjoy or admitted being challenged by academic competition. Less than 25 percent of the students were very active in high school in either student government or political and social action groups; 40 percent did not involve themselves *in any way* in student government or in political and social action groups.

It is of interest that, considering their high grade achievements (B average or higher) in high school, 60 percent did not participate in literary clubs, debate, dramatic clubs, activities in music or other performing arts, nor in hobbies or special interest groups. As an aside here, the role of the arts in our educational system has been a matter of concern for some years, with a number of researchers wondering to what extent our school systems honor or respect the esthetic aspect of our lives and to what extent our schools are successful in educating our youth to becoming involved in music, the graphic arts, or the literary world. Here in the case of University of California entrants, we have a very select sample of high school achievers, and the majority of them have not participated in these kinds of activities. The implications are of particular significance, both for the lack of this source of satisfaction in the lives of a great many people and in confirmation of the known fact that these aspects of our culture are nourished and maintained by a relatively small minority.

As a final point regarding their pre-college education, over 60 percent of both men and women were "fairly" to "very" satisfied with their high school experiences. This degree of satisfaction is in line with their general achievement and success, but it might also be sort of a social desirability response, with some tendency to report what is expected rather than really revealing their sentiments. One might expect these bright and capable students to be the most critical and the most unhappy of high school graduates, but a majority of them said that they were satisfied or very satisfied with their experiences.

Considering the homes and families of these modern youth, very briefly, a large majority — over two thirds — were found to have parents who professed an affiliation with one of the three major Hebraic-Christian faiths (Catholic, Protestant, or Jewish). Within the political sphere, eighty percent of the parents were affiliated or sympathetic with either the Democratic or Republican Party, with only six percent of the parents identified as independent and one percent as socialist or radical.

In contrast, only 36 percent of the students acknowledged belief and participation in one of the three major religious faiths, only a little over half the percentage of their parents. In fact, 60 percent of these entering freshmen declared themselves as non-religious within the Hebraic-Christian frame of reference.

In the political sphere, only seven percent of the students defined their thinking as conservative with about 40 percent declaring themselves liberal or very liberal at this stage in their lives. Only eight percent claimed to be radical or anarchistic in their political thinking. Another eight percent identified themselves as definitely non-political. Again, these figures are in contrast to those of the parents who were affiliating with and behaving as part of the established two-party system.

Some efforts were made to determine the students' attitudes and preferences as related to their behavior and activity during the college years. Only a proportion of these results will be reviewed here to aid in this general description. For example, a majority of students said that they would prefer to be involved in off campus political activities, as compared to student government. The majority said that inter-collegiate athletics are not important to them, and also preferred that athletics not be emphasized in the school which they attended. (There is a mild trend along these lines in our society; quite a bit has been written about the de-emphasis of major college sports, and apparently many students in the early seventies are subscribing to it.)

A majority of 55 percent to 60 percent would prefer an institution where there would be no fraternities or sororities. Over 70 percent indicated that they preferred a publicly supported (tax funds) college. More than that, given their choice of an ideal place to go to school, a majority would choose a public college, rather than a private, liberal arts college. They also wanted to enroll in institutions which had graduate and professional schools in the same complex. They desired that much emphasis be given to independent study, with classes predominantly of the seminar-discussion type and curricular programs emphasizing experimentation. The preferences indicated in this last sentence do (did) not typify the opportunities for them on the Berkeley campus.

The majority of the students considered the grading of courses as necessary evil. About the same proportion had a preference for a "pass" or "fail" form of evaluation instead of the use of letter grades. But perhaps more surprising for 17 year old students is that 77 percent were in favor of student participation in decisions regarding content, organization, and reorganization of courses. The same percentage (77) thought they ought to be or should be involved in the design of the courses they were taking.

The students' chief interests and preferences in the way of on-campus activity was another matter of concern. They were asked to indicate to what extent various activities were anticipated as important sources of satisfaction. The three activities which large numbers believed would bring the greatest satisfaction were: a) self discovery experiences leading to an understanding of one's self (69%); b) pursuing one's own outside interests and being honest to them; and c) rapping with fellow students. Most students also subscribed to two attitudinal statements which support a rather high commitment to one's own education: a) "The primary purpose of college is to explore new ideas, to become involved in learning and develop broad scholarly interest, and to find satisfaction in the world of ideas," and b) "When a subject really interests me, I don't like to be under constraints by any formal classroom restriction or a classroom assignment." In academia we seem to have difficulty understanding or respecting some of these desires. More and more frequently, at least in the very recent years, students would like to pursue and study some subjects or topics along the lines of their own inclinations.

A continuing concern for political activism was shown in the students' responses to a number of items; for example 80 percent thought that student activity, whether directed toward academic institutions or toward political and social problems, had had good results. About half of the 80 percent expressed a recognition that the activity at times had gotten out of hand, but they were still supporting it. When asked more specifically what they thought of the goals and methods of radical student activism in recent years, almost 75 percent either strongly approved the goals or approved them with minor reservations. However, almost two thirds *disapproved* of aggressive methods of the radical students. Another question concerned confrontation tactics per se. Only 16 percent subscribed to physical confrontation, violence, or the destruction of property as essential to effect social change. But, 16 percent is a significant minority proportion in a large student body, when it comes to giving leadership to protest activities. The largest proportion (44%) were in favor of non-violent protest and demonstration as the only feasible way to get results, while 30 percent went for a softer role, preferring peaceful petitioning and open communications as a means of getting results.

Still another means was provided by the survey instrument to get at aspects of the students' orientation towards dealing with social problems or effecting change. When asked about their interest in taking part in certain agencies or programs, over 50 percent responded that they would like to take part in either the Peace Corps or VISTA. Forty-eight percent would also like to become involved in community organizing for social action and to deal with social problems. Many more students, in their first and second year, are entering activities in the Berkeley community which are directed towards helping students in the public schools, working with minority groups, dealing with the politics of the city, or helping with the communications between the police force and the institutions. Sixty-three percent either have or would like to participate in a tutoring program for minority children; 76 percent have or would like to do volunteer work in the area of ecological problems; and over 40 percent would like to help in a drug treatment clinic.

With all this expressed concern for the righting of wrongs and becoming involved in causes, one might wonder what are the views of these entering students towards the immediate and long range future. In response to a question about their views and feelings concerning the present American society as a whole, including our system of government and status of business and industry, 60 percent reported (previous to Watergate) that they were pessimistic or very pessimistic about the future of our society, with ten percent indicating an uncertainty about the direction and the future of our society. Only three percent admitted to being very optimistic.

The entering students were also asked about the requirements which they would see as the most important in any future job. For the most part, men and women ignored the security status and high income criteria and, in order, most often designated one of the following: a) opportunity to be helpful to others and useful to society; b) opportunity to use their special abilities and talents, especially in service to others; and c) the privilege to be creative and original in whatever they pursued. Admittedly, data such as these can be looked at with a jaundiced eye or taken with a grain of salt; perhaps students have simply talked themselves into thinking that they should be involved with the problems of society. However, there are other evidences for the validity of the data. For example, the graduate students now enrolled in higher education at Berkeley are a whole new breed; the majority are younger, they are more intelligent, they are more energetic, more committed, more troublesome (in their readiness to address the *status quo*), and definitely oriented toward doing something with their doctorates in higher education which will lead to change, provide new directions, and will involve our institutions with the problems of society.

The perspective of these entering students can be rounded out by examining one other area — their political and social attitudes. The selection of only a small number of attitude statements will convey the general picture. In the political sphere, 75 percent are opposed to the investigation of the political beliefs of college and university faculty by legislative committees. This reminds one of the students who protested against the investigative HUAC committee of a decade ago. Eighty percent believed that any person who advocates unpopular beliefs or ideas should be allowed to speak to students, and 62 percent believe that members of the Communist party should be allowed to teach in colleges, but with another 21 percent indicating that they do not know what they believe on this controversial question of long standing.

In the area of ethical/social questions, 92 percent think that college students are mature enough to have the freedom to make personal decisions about premarital sex relations. Eighty-three percent believe that birth control pills should be available from campus health services, and 90 percent believe students who enter college are mature enough to make personal decisions about the use of alcohol. The reader may be reminded that concerns which today are such a matter of course to us — the use of the pill and the changed sexual mores — were *not* part of our culture only ten years ago. These attitudes and practices represent a very rapid shift in our society; likewise, the concerns of students have changed radically. Already these things seem quite commonplace, but less than two decades ago they were major considerations on many college campuses.

Comparative Data from the Sixties

The freshmen students of 1971, just described, may be better understood in context with other students who enrolled on the Berkeley campus during the previous twelve years.[3] This supplementary analysis will be limited to a few selected areas. Starting with religion, we find a rather large change over 11 years, shifting from a majority of 70 percent of the 1959 students who affiliated with and professed a faith in one of the three major Hebraic-Christian religions to a minority in 1971 of almost half the size (36%) — a very significant shift in the course of the years. In the late 1950s, analysts of social-cultural trends were speaking of a resurgence of religion and a return to the church, a trend which they believed developed gradually following the termination of World War II. In a variety of studies conducted previous to 1960 at the Center for the Study of Higher Education, the data from a sample of colleges across the nation generally confirmed that there was such an increase in religious beliefs and practices. However, by 1965, the trend had been reversed, with a number of research findings suggesting that organized religion was playing a decreasing role in the value system of the young people. For the 1966 freshmen at Berkeley, the percentage reporting affiliation and participation in those same major religions had dropped to a little over 50 percent; and the majority of others who indicated no religious preferences declared themselves to be agnostic or atheist. This was the first time that such a large number of "non-religious" persons were noted on the Berkeley campus.

Resorting to some other reference data of the late 1950s, it had been shown that a large number of students at places such as Reed and Antioch Colleges, or in a few schools in the Ivy League country, declared themselves to be atheists or agnostics. The chief reason for such proportions may be the kind of clientele who come to these schools. Colleges like Reed and Antioch attract fairly high proportions of Jewish youth and numerous young people from families who profess an affiliation with the American Friends or the Unitarians. The parents in these families frequently have been "using" these liberal religions as stepping stones to rejecting their religious practices entirely. Fifteen years ago, at Reed College 60 percent of the entering students claimed to be agnostics; this was not the case in public institutions.

The statistics regarding the decreasing role of religion for an increasing majority demand some interpretation. There is substantial reason to believe that the students of the early seventies are more interested than their counterparts of previous years in matters of social morality and in ethical-humanistic questions. In other words, very many are not really *non-religious,* in the best sense of the term, although they are opposed to dogmatic faiths, the imposing of external belief systems, and the restrictions of an orthodox philosophy. There was also considerable evidence that from 1966 to 1971 more and more students were turning to *other* forms of religion, such as faiths or belief systems from India and the Orient, or other expressions of the spiritual, the mystical, and the esthetic. In the words of one social scientist: "The inner world replaces the outer world in many of our students, meditation is replacing prayer, the here and now replaces the hereafter, drugs replace the sacraments and the avant garde has claimed religion as its own."

Moving to politics, the available data are not directly comparable across the years, but results over the eleven or twelve years are somewhat similar to the religious situation, in that the proportion of students affiliating with the major political organizations decreased rather drastically over the years. However, the total proportion of parents belonging to the two parties had changed only a little — approximately 90 percent in 1959 to 80 percent in 1971.

From the *students'* standpoint, we seem to have some evidence of what is often referred to as the generation gap. In 1959, approximately 75 percent of Berkeley entrants were expressing a *willingness* to align themselves with one of the two major parties in our nation. This 75 percent dropped to 61 percent by 1966 and to less than 40 percent for the recent class — thus from 75 percent to 40 percent in about a decade. Along with a decrease of student interest in affiliating with either of the major parties, large differences developed in the ratio of the numbers who *described* themselves as Democratic or Republican. In 1959, 44 percent, the largest proportion, opted for the Republican party. This decreased to 22 percent in 1966 and to less than 12 percent in 1970. In 1966 only three percent classified themselves as non-political; this changed to eight percent in 1970. Within the context of generally similar home backgrounds, the recent entrants, at the age of seventeen, have established a significantly greater degree of autonomy from both the religious and political affiliation of their parents.

In essence, the major student swing has been from a majority professing conservatism in their political outlook in 1959 to a reversal of a similar proportion now claiming a liberalism of commitment. With this change from more widespread conservatism, there has been a greater amount of political activity on the Berkeley campus in dealing with issues and problems which have overtones of being clearly political or social. However, in describing what was taking place fairly recently (in 1970-71) on the Berkeley campus, one might ask: Is the University now just a place of apathy and acquiescence, for the most part, with "activism" limited to a few minor episodes? Or, are the students directing their energies, commitments, and their attention to other forms of political and non-political activity? According to the data, the answer lies with a definite "yes" for the latter.

Turning to one other area in this brief, over-the-years survey of students — their intellectual disposition or orientation — we find again that the student body is changing, although considerably less in the proportions which can be categorized. Since 1959, the university recruitment/admission process has resulted in a significantly smaller proportion of entering students who may be described as non-intellectual (i.e., not highly motivated or not intrinsically interested in learning). However, the 33 percent of non-intellectual students enrolling in 1971, as compared to 49 percent in 1959, still represents a very sizeable number of students for the faculty to consider in the teaching/learning process. This one-third of the students cannot be described as eager or ready learners, and they do not represent potential young scholars, notwithstanding their record and good grades. The faculty at Berkeley, and on the rest of the University campuses, prefers to believe that these students with lesser academic inclinations are not so numerous. At the other end of the continuum, those high in intellectual orientation are present on campus in only a little greater proportion than they were in 1959; the shift is only from 13 percent to 19 percent. The University seems to be admitting a larger concentration of near-average American youth, albeit they represent the top 12 percent of high school graduates. We are seeing a larger concentration in the middle, a lesser number at the bottom and not much change at the top, in terms of non-intellectual disposition. In the way of comparison, these proportions of 13 percent to 19 percent with a high intellectual disposition would compare to approximately 28 percent at Antioch College, 35 to 40 percent at Swarthmore, and 60 percent at Reed. Students with strong intellectual commitments are highly concentrated in some schools, but the distribution of high school graduates to a large campus like the University of California, a selective institution, does not result in a large proportion of students with intense interests in learning.

The story to be taken from these proportions just reviewed is that this large University, and the faculty, is faced with a major challenge in accommodating the diversity of the students. Both the intellectual and non-intellectual students sit together in the same classrooms. Both expect to learn and be prepared for dissimilar future occupations and professions and both "types" have to be respected as potential learners.

Summary and Implications

In reviewing selected characteristics of several entering freshman classes at Berkeley, over a period of eleven years, we found that the more recent entrants (early seventies) have a changed concern for values, social issues, and religious and ethical questions. For the most part, these students were not interested in formalized or institutional religion. In general, they seem to reject, or at least increasingly question, any institutionalized or traditionally systematized basis for their values and thinking. In other words, many tend to be more in disagreement with the institutionalized aspects of our society than those students of a decade ago.

These more recent students are also more sophisticated when compared to the earlier students. They are more released from their sub-cultural heritages, exhibit greater independence of judgment, and are generally pessimistic about the future of our society. They show a greater concern for social problems and expect more from their education in terms of relevance to the issues of our society.

Although not reported above, the results of a recent research project demonstrated that the students also came to Berkeley with enthusiasm, high expectations, and desire. Later, after two years on campus, there was still a great deal of enthusiasm shown by the majority in a large sample. It was very encouraging to see that most hadn't become disillusioned in spite of the fact that a class of 200 students was the smallest educational experience in which they had been involved. Quite a few had sat in classrooms with as many as 1,000 other students.

What are possible implications to be taken from these data? The first, more a challenge than an implication, derives from the matter of change per se. We asked in the sixties whether the faculty, the librarians, the staff in student personnel services, and the administrators (the establishment of the institution) could or would stand up to the challenge of the changing student body. The question is still appropriate in the seventies; the students in our society (junior high, high school, and college levels) have been a continuously changing population. Most of them are aware of this and know that they think differently and share different values than their counterparts did 10 years ago; their behavior is different and often more questionable, and they resort to activities and relationships which more and more parents have had difficulty accepting. At the same time, in the early years of this decade, we found that the current college entrants — in many ways the product of the sixties — have very often "helped" their parents to new and different orientations. Along with such a new development, however, a great many of the students are entering the University with serious aspirations and goals, though not genuinely academic concerns.

In iteration, these new, changed and changing students of the early seventies — more different from their parents in beliefs and political attitudes than students of a decade and more ago, but simultaneously more instrumental (individually and via the pervading youth culture) in changing some of their parents' orientations and attitudes — were entering the university with serious aspirations and definite expectations. But these aspirations and expectations, manifested by increasing numbers, were focused more on the ends and not the means of an education, on occupational and professional goals rather than on the content and substance of the curriculum and the satisfactions of learning experiences.

This greater emphasis on the application of a college education, admittedly always the case for a proportion of students, but now seemingly an increasing contradiction or reaction to the major inclinations of students during the sixties, had an interesting and somewhat disturbing concomitant. Along with the increasing numbers acknowledging the importance of future goals and vocational aspirations, many admitting to less or lessening interests in continuing or advanced education — seemingly somewhat paradoxical to the expressed seriousness of goals and aspirations. Some observers of the college world and the general post high school youth culture have spoken of a trend along these lines. If such actually exists, whether witnessed after high school, after two years of college or following a B.A. degree, the beginning of such behavior can be traced back to the late sixties.

During those last years of protest and on-campus demonstrations, especially with little real change resulting on most campuses, many young people began to question the merit of college degrees or the value of the educational experiences, and the number enrolling but then dropping out was very much on the upswing at the turn of the decade. One very visible aspect of such a trend was the ever-growing number of young people taking to the road with a pack on their back, or joining the Peace Corps or Vista. Surveys conducted on samples of such people revealed that many were drop-outs or at least had not completed work for a college degree, and an amazing number declared that they had no intentions of returning to finish work for a degree.

Whatever the reality of any such general trends and tendencies, numerous students of uncertain goals, purposes and directions were among those enrolling on the Berkeley campus in the Fall of 1969 through 1972. However, most apparent in the *data* of these entering classes — regarding the academic sphere — was the increasing seriousness of many in their expressed desires, aspirations and expectations, and the obvious shift on the part of both men and women towards greater emphasis on future goals and career preparation. Since these shifts represented significant differences, indicating an undergraduate student body, or at least an increasing proportion, of dissimilar motivation to the student bodies of a few years earlier, it appeared appropriate to ask about the possible effect, if any, on the teaching-learning environment and the essence of the challenge to the instructional staff.

This conjecture (above) is intended to be more than rhetorical, but judging by the general response of the Berkeley faculty to a major report of a few years earlier,[4] the faculty might be the last to seek to understand the changing composition of the entering student body, to ask about students' needs and interests, or to respond to any recommendations about new emphases in the way of curricular experiences or changes in instructional techniques.

It is fairly safe to surmise that the majority of faculty members in the mass of educational institutions tend to use the same methods and procedures that they did in the early sixties and the late sixties. Faculty become well practiced and established in certain ways and tend not to behave very differently over the years, nor to become involved in experimental programs. The students could be a completely new breed, but this fact could go very much unnoticed in a predominantly academic culture where minimal, if any, attention or respect is given to the different characteristics of the learners. Even the best of college teachers operate out of the context and content of their disciplines, and too infrequently do they think of their work as teaching *students per se* or assisting individuals to learn. They are given to thinking about and dealing with a class as a group, while focusing chiefly on course content and seldom on the orientations and varying perceptual processes of the learners.

Not being very sanguine about effective changes in the teaching-learning situations in the general undergraduate curricula of the majority of U.S. institutions, how does one address or challenge the traditional academic settings to prevent having a majority of students become lost in an almost meaningless maelstrom of course after course, only a few of which tend to be provocative of new ideas and new directions, only some of which are meaningfully related to the recognized practicalities of the post-college years.

It has already been acknowledged that a great many of the recent attempts at innovation have either not accomplished their major objectives or have failed, for the most part, to represent a real break with traditional practices.

It is possible that the vast majority of innovations were too highly dependent on only the teaching efforts of regular faculty members — many of whom probably haven't been able to carry through on the essential execution of non-traditional or innovative procedures. The programs that have succeeded, such as those accomplishing intended objectives — probably with a special (often self-selected) student clientele — appear to be the result of a combination of con-tributive factors. In such instances, the inadequacy of any single aspect of the program might well have been counteracted by a number of other sources of strength. Such is the explanation of the continuing success of several new or resi-dential colleges found in quite different settings.

These observations serve as reminders of the assessed success of a couple of honors programs which were evaluated in the early sixties. The actual curricula were not different from many another program, but the special provisions and services which had been arranged by the institutional library proved to be an extraordinary component of both programs. The staff, services and actual use of the library had been made an integral and functional aspect of the curriculum and the instruction, rather than just an adjunct service or a facility to be used on demand.

The above illustration has been employed to introduce the idea of program complexity and the importance of multiple contributors, in contrast to seeing a program, or the curriculum, as the responsibility of *only* the regular instruction-al staff. Besides the more intimate involvement of libraries and the contribution of library staffs, there are other examples of expanded programs. A few institu-tions have supplemented or rounded out their innovative programs by changing the setting for teaching and learning, such as dormitory facilities or off-campus agencies, or through positions of employment and so-called field study experi-ences. In other institutions, teams (two or more) of teachers from diverse disci-plines have served as a vital constituent to effect change in the teaching-learning situation.

Perhaps most recently staff from the segments of student personnel programs (e.g., counselors and the directors of housing programs) have taken or been assigned roles that permitted a shift from outside the actual curriculum to direct and more immediate participation within. In several community college settings, to cite one type of change, personnel staff and/or counselors have been distrib-uted and housed within the quarters of curricular subdivisions, rather than all being placed in centralized facilities, thus providing more direct and immediate access to their services. Such a shift in one institution has led to the counselors being available and utilized by both students and faculty, with a much larger number of both segments becoming acquainted and working with a counselor largely due to sheer proximity.

In conclusion, and at the risk of triteness and over-simplicity, there appears to be genuine merit in considering and responding to student bodies, their diversity at any one time and their changes over time, by resorting to diversity of approaches and procedures in recognition of the multiplicity of human charac-teristics and motivation, and by subscribing to a policy and practice of flexibility in viewing and planning for each and every class and teaching-learning situation. Beyond that, instructional faculty may have to expand their perception and understanding of the total context of student lives and student learning, with a willingness to examine and explore all facets — namely facilities and available services — that may be instrumental to an optimal learning situation for the great variety of students encountered.

Notes

1. Martin, W.B., *Conformity: Standards and Change in Higher Education,* (San Francisco: Jossey-Bass, 1969). Gaff, Jerry G., *The Cluster College,* (San Francisco: Jossey-Bass, 1970).

2. Much of the data to be reported or utilized in this article was drawn from several research projects under the direction of the author at the Center for Research and Development in Higher Education and the Project for Research in Undergraduate Education.

3. Some of this information is drawn from the following report: Jako, K., *The Berkeley Students of the Sixties* (Berkeley: Project for Research in Undergraduate Education, 1970).

4. Select Committee on Education, *Education at Berkeley,* (Berkeley: University of California, 1966).

About the Author

Paul Heist taught at Oregon State University from 1950-1956. He received his Ph.D. degree in 1956 and joined the faculty of the University of California at Berkeley where he is Research Psychologist and Professor of Education in the Division of Higher Education of the School of Education. In 1971, he became Chairman of the Division. From 1956-1970, he was on the staff of the Center for the Study of Higher Education. Since 1969, he has directed the research project on undergraduate education.

James Davis

Coping —
An UgLi Way of Life

The author takes the role of champion of active
undergraduate librarianship. He first discusses
UgLis in general and then presents comparative
statistical data on eight UgLis to explain why
these libraries have been forced to cope in more
ways than nearly any other kind of library. Finally, he gives many examples of library-tested methods of coping which were designed by masters of
the art, the undergraduate librarians.

A friend of mine maintains that no good deed goes unpunished, and my being
here today convinces me that there's something in that statement. At last year's
ACRL session in Detroit, Billy Wilkinson talked about the failure of undergraduate reference service to involve itself meaningfully in the undergraduate scene;
Kenneth Toombs described the demise of the South Carolina UgLi; and Norah
Jones discussed active undergraduate librarianship with specific reference to her
own institution. This panel was followed in August by an Institute, "Training
for Service in Undergraduate Libraries," held at the University of California,
San Diego. For most of the 31 participants, the Institute was almost a mystic
experience, and many of us got an idea of how Saul must have felt when he got
the Word on the way to Damascus. After the Institute, I was happy to participate in planning this preconference, and be in a position to see that we would
continue proselytizing recruits to active librarianship in undergraduate libraries.
Unfortunately, I was outnumbered when we were making the arrangements for
this part of the program and, after all my selfless good will, now find myself
scheduled to talk with you about library service in UgLis.

The message that finally came through in San Diego is that we exist to give
active, rather than passive, service; that we must anticipate as well as reflect student needs, and that all our functions and activities should be coordinated to

SOURCE: From James Davis, "Coping — An UgLi Way of Life," Librarians Confront
the Undergraduate Environment, A Pre-Conference Institute Sponsored by the University Libraries Section, the Association of College and Research Libraries, American
Library Association, Dallas, Texas, June 18-19, 1971. Included by permissions of the
author and the University Libraries Section, Association of College and Research
Libraries.

this service. This may sound simplistic; many of you have been aware of this purpose for years, but for me it was a revelation, and it's in my new role as a champion of active undergraduate librarianship that I will discuss coping. I would like first to talk about UgLis in general, and then present some statistical information which will help to explain why UgLis have been forced to cope in more ways, and to a greater degree, than nearly any other kind of library. Finally, I will try to describe some library-tested methods of coping, devised by master of this art, UgLi librarians.

To start out, some general, personal comments on undergraduate libraries may prove interesting, if not helpful. Irene Braden Hoadley, in her dissertation, *The Undergraduate Library,* stated that six ways undergraduate libraries were to differ from traditional university libraries were by:

1. Providing open access to the collection to avoid the difficulties of the closed-stack system,
2. Centralizing and simplifying services to the undergraduate,
3. Providing a collection of carefully selected books,
4. Attempting to make the library an instructional tool by planning it as a center for instruction in library use to prepare undergraduates for using larger collections,
5. Providing services additional to those given by the research collection,
6. Constructing a building with the undergraduate's habits of use in mind.

And, of course, her basic criterion was that the libraries she discussed be housed in a separate building. I submit that most of these would be critical factors in the planning of any library if the word "user" were substituted for "undergraduate." In point of fact, it seems to me that the criteria which most specifically apply to UgLis are responsible for their most serious problems and have caused the great need for UgLis to cope.

To consider her six points:

Open access to books: I don't believe anyone would deny any reader ready access to library materials. I'd like to believe that the concept of open stacks is becoming more accepted, indeed prevalent. For example, both Northwestern and UCLA have recently opened their research collections to all comers; other libraries, including the University of Washington, have had open stacks for years.

Centralized and simplified services: Decentralization is one of the prevailing ills of libraries today. Perhaps it's an inevitable result of growth, but it's a very real problem, one that is not lessened by the apparent joy we take in obfuscating service through activities and jargon that seem designed more to satisfy librarians than to assist users. This point of simplified services would serve as a rationale for the limited size of the staff so frequently encountered in UgLis.

Centers for instruction in library use and Buildings with undergraduate's habits of use in mind. No librarian would deny these as important aspects of his library, whether it's a school, academic, public, or even special one.

A collection of carefully selected books: I do not believe it should be a unique feature of UgLis that their collections be carefully selected. If this is a euphemism for keeping the collections limited in size, let's admit it.

Additional services: Here's a real booby-trap, and it's often worked to our disadvantage. Although the book collections generally duplicate significant works in the research library, unique services such as audio facilities, meeting rooms and art exhibitions are projected for UgLis. These extra attractions (as well as the existence of multiple copies and reliable editions) serve to lure in non-undergraduates. In at least one UgLi, more than 20% of the use of its general collection is by graduate students and faculty.

These criteria, with the exception of "a carefully selected duplicate collection of books" should be applicable to any academic library; that they are listed would indicate that the staff of many large university libraries had been neglecting their undergraduate students in favor of their user-elite, the graduate students and faculty. Rather than change the academic *status quo* by challenging this emphasis and reminding their librarians that the Library Bill of Rights proposes equal library service for all, university libraries hit upon the idea of isolating undergraduates in what might be considered specially designed or adapted ghettos with small "selective" collections of books and minimal staffs. That UgLis and their numerically inadequate staffs have burst forth with as many innovative programs as they have, must be regarded as a feat comparable to the RAF's during the Battle of Britain: Never have so few done so much with so little for so many.

Let's see how all this has worked out in practice. I have used Mrs. Hoadley's six separately housed UgLis as a basis for these comparisons and have current information from four of them. (One additional UgLi submitted data but, since it is no longer in a separate building, I did not include it; the sixth UgLi has been discontinued.) To these basic four, I added libraries that had been activated by the end of 1966 and had been housed in a separate building by the end of 1969; six candidates were identified. Two of these were eliminated, one because of the small size of its collection (25,000 volumes in 1969), and one because of its unique organization (it has three branch libraries). The list, then, consists of the UgLis at Harvard, Michigan, Cornell, Texas, UCLA, Stanford, North Carolina, and Illinois.

I'd like to discuss these grand old undergraduate libraries, giving the latest statistical material available, and then mention ways they are trying to overcome, compensate for, and cope with these figures. These figures, which report through June 30, 1970, are taken from the forthcoming issue of the *UgLi Newsletter.* (I believe it's significant that an undergraduate librarian, John Haak, edits, publishes, and distributes this very useful serial with no assistance from any organized library association. If any of you are not familiar with the *Newsletter,* I commend it to you.)

After this buildup, here are some statistics I'd like you to consider. They will, I think, make clear the demands made on UgLis and explain why we have had to find ways of coping. I would like to point out that the lowest (or highest) actual figures reported did not necessarily produce the lowest (or highest) percentages and, in the interests of protecting us all, I will name only the UgLi at the top of each category.

As of a year ago, these libraries served undergraduate enrollments ranging from 5,670 to 28,722 at Texas; the ratio of undergraduates to graduates was generally close to the rule of thumb and at least one-third of the total enrollment should be graduate before establishment of an UgLi is considered. The basic adjusted budget for library materials (books, serials, film, etc.) of these libraries goes from a low of $20,974 to a high at Illinois of $100,000. This represents from 1.93% to Illinois' 7.44% of the university library's total book budget and allows an expenditure per undergraduate of from $1.88 to $10.70 at Stanford. By the end of June, 1970, the book collections in these libraries ranged from a low of 64,343 volumes to 166,525 at Harvard, with the books per undergraduate ratio going from 2.53 to 29.37 (Harvard). Books charged from these collections ranged from 160,233 to 515,513 at Michigan, representing a use per title by undergraduates of from 10.97 to 56.17 (that high being at Harvard). If total numerical use of the collections were considered, including use within the building, Texas would lead us all with a circulation of more than a million (38.38 uses per volume by undergraduates).

This represents fairly solid use. Let's see how the staffing pattern supports this demand for assistance. Total size of UgLi staff, excluding student assistants, goes from a low of 14.5 FTE to 29.75 at Michigan. This works out from a low of 5.12% of the total library staff to a high at Stanford of 10.11%. Breaking this down, there are from 3 librarians at one UgLi to 9 at Michigan, representing from 1.77% to 9.24% of the librarians on that campus, with Stanford having the highest percentage. And there are from 10 to 20.75 non-professionals working in UgLis (Michigan has the most) which goes from a low of 5.17% of that part of the staff to 11.76% at Texas.

Reference is a good indication of how effective a library has been in communicating its willingness to help, and here I believe UgLis have a record of which they can really be proud. Assistance is offered by librarians at least 64 hours each week, and at Michigan the figure is 119 hours each week. One UgLi doesn't have a reference desk as such; the staff there serves as floorwalkers and seeks out students to help. The number of questions asked of reference librarians, when recorded, was highest at UCLA where 56,994 contacts were made last year.

High as many of these figures are, none of them is very impressive when you consider that we're serving the largest single group on our respective campuses; I do feel that they bear out my premise that UgLi librarians are the RAF of the library world. Recently I was talking to a member of our library administration and said that I felt they were getting more and better returns on their allocations to us than on nearly any other service the library offers, and would like to discuss why I feel this is so. Although we're undersupported as many library services are, and although undergraduates have been victims of benign neglect for so long, they are grateful for anything that is done for them. But more than that, a concern for and interest in their activities is essential and that is how we've become "where it's at" in academic libraries. Because of the poor ratio of librar-

ians and materials to undergraduates and the heavy use these students make of
UgLis and their services, we've had to cut corners and improvise often with little
notice. In short, we've had to cope and after this extended preamble, I'll try to
get to how we do it. I should mention that not all the examples I'll be mentioning
have originated at the eight libraries included in the previous statistical exposé.

I'm going to work from the outside in, from the building, past services such as
reference and exhibits, through collections (including serials and audio), to the
heart of the UgLi; its staff. I hope that you may find some procedures that you
will feel worth considering for implementation in your own libraries.

UgLi buildings should be used, not thought of as some sort of static,
unchanging set for *Sleeping Beauty*. Shortly after we moved into new quarters,
students began moving chairs and tables around and every week we'd move
them back in place. After some time we figured the hell with it — let them move
the stuff where they want and eventually everything will be properly placed.
They still move the furniture, but we're all happier now.

Too many buildings are considered ends in themselves, rather than an area in
which to provide a warm atmosphere and friendly service. This is a good example of goal displacement, and John Haak's article in the May 1, 1971 issue of
Library Journal covered the topic very nicely. Design elements are pointless
unless they serve a useful purpose. If a pillar is in a visible or prominent place,
why not put a sign on it. Just make sure the sign is legible from at least ten feet
away. One UgLi had psychedelic signs made pointing out its service points, and
I'm sure the students immediately felt that that library was theirs. This sort of
rapport is what we should all be working to foster.

One new UgLi arranged with the campus museum to display 19 large modern
paintings which the museum was unable to exhibit. They are scattered throughout the building and have engendered a great deal of interest — a favorite pas-
time of students (and perhaps staff) is to retitle certain of these works. Another
UgLi is beginning to negotiate with its Art Department to show students' paintings in the library after the annual group student show.

Last year, one UgLi found the sight of its bulletin boards depressing, so they
went to remnant shops, found brightly patterned fabrics, and stapled them over
the cork board. The result is a lively, unconventional effect that more libraries
might consider.

One unstatisticized UgLi has recently instituted its so-called "Liberated Bathroom." They were given a part of a building with no toilets available to the public or staff, so they gerrymandered their walls to encompass what had formerly
been a men's toilet. The door to the facility has been labelled "Bathroom" and
it's heavily used, even though its clientele is occasionally disconcerted. An internal lock was installed, and this has seemed to simplify matters for the more
modest individuals using this essential service.

Reference service would be very much more difficult without encyclopedias,
but buying them is frustrating because they're out of date before they've been
purchased. One UgLi has an arrangement with the main reference department
whereby each unit pays for half a subscription each year to major encyclopedias,

in this case the *Americana, Britannica, Collier's,* and *World Book.* In even years one unit gets two of the sets, odd years the other two, and vice versa. Another UgLi modifies this two-year plan by working it on a four-year cycle, though both units share equally the cost of each set.

At least one university library is presented annually with a set of an encyclopedia by the grateful publisher in partial recompense for the use its researchers make of that library. Members of the reference department of that library decided that the new set belongs in the UgLi because it would be used more by undergraduates than by their own clientele.

Acquiring major sets of reference works can be prohibitive, but an approach worth considering is to coordinate efforts with a library school, if one is near by. One UgLi has sets of *NUC,* the BM and BN catalogs as a result of joint requests, and is now receiving the Mansell *Pre-1956 Imprints* catalog. Use of these sets is in no way limited to the library school students; staff use them constantly, and students who are preparing bibliographies are delighted to find such things exist.

In the early 1960's, the Berkeley and Los Angeles campuses of the University of California had their card catalogs photocopied and these copies bound; each UgLi was presented with a copy of the set for its campus, and both libraries use the sets constantly. One UgLi librarian has said that knowing where a book is is nearly as good as having it, and while that may be overstating the case, these printed catalogs are of inestimable value for determining holdings to a specific date, for nailing down local applications of subject headings, and for making referrals to other libraries on the campus. Good reference service, particularly in UgLis, includes making knowledgeable referrals to other resources. This would be immensely more difficult in these UgLis without the catalog of the main collection.

The Rand McNally *Commercial Atlas* is a good example of an expensive annual publication that every UgLi should have. One subscribes to it on alternate years. Another accepts the cast-off copy from the reference department when that department has received the new edition. This procedure should work fairly well until the new census figures are incorporated into a new volume. This same UgLi accepts the outdated Jane publications *(All the World's Aircraft, . . . Ships,* &c.) for which there is some demand, though not enough to justify the huge financial outlay that would be required to purchase each volume as it is issued.

Other reference materials seem to be taking a bigger piece of the action each year. A standard ploy is to have orders prepared toward the end of the year for reference and other books and hope that money may become available from other funds. Granted, this was more successful in more affluent times, but one UgLi did get its sets of *Espasa* and *Italiana* that way, and there's always the hope that other library units may not have been as conscientious in using up — or oversubscribing — their allocations. At least one UgLi is hoping to pick up the new atlases of Israel and the United States this way, and last month another UgLi was given an additional 25% increase in its original allocation for ordering books this year. Bibliographic checking on these orders has been suspended on the theory that it's better to get an extra copy of some worthwhile titles quickly than to be thorough and get only one.

Exhibits are often considered peripheral UgLi responsibilities, but some libraries maintain interesting ones without too much effort. One UgLi provided cases and let a local group of Armenian students assemble a collection of handicrafts and photographs to show how these crafts influenced the architecture of Armenia. Another exhibit was prepared by the student Bahai'i group to commemorate a holiday, and a third was a combined Christmas/Channukah production that was assembled from objects the staff had had on hand for years.

Cooperative exhibits have been done: one UgLi, utilizing a faculty member who was working on the products of a company that designed decorated cloth bindings, displayed examples for a month; later it was shown at another UgLi. One year an UgLi provided the only recognition on its campus of National Library Week and an exhibit containing motion picture stills of library scenes. This UgLi is still trying to locate more photographs, but will be happy to lend the ones it has (about 20) to any library that is interested in borrowing them.

Another UgLi has a case in which a campus museum arranges regular exhibits of artifacts from all times and places; these have been very interesting and students have enjoyed inspecting them. One UgLi contacted a camera bug and offered to show any of his photographs that he'd like to exhibit. As a result of this, they have been contacted by many camera men and women anxious to display 20-35 examples of their choice work.

One UgLi was in desperate need of an exhibit and had a brainstorm. Using Chase's *Calendar*, White's *Conspectus, et al*, they compiled a list of events in a given month — such occasions as National Bowling Month, the International Pancake Race, and Charles Dickens' birthday — and ran down objects in the community to illustrate each. The exhibit included Aldine, Bodoni, and Elzevier books, corrected galley proofs, and photographs from the library, a can of sauerkraut, reproductions of paintings from the art library's clipping file, commemorative postage stamps, 40 or 50 miscellaneous items connected only by that month's importance to each. Captions naming the event and the objects represented were typed, the whole thing put in cases, and produced the most enthusiastically received exhibit in that UgLi's history. The exhibit reflected the Ugli's entire scope of activities and covered many other library services on that campus.

Exhibits should relate to the present as well as to the past, and one UgLi was delighted with the offer of students from the library school on that campus to assemble an exhibit on an upcoming presidential election. The students selected the books, ordered them, urged them through cataloging, prepared a brochure, and mounted the exhibit. Everyone, from the Dean of the School to the undergraduate students was very pleased with the results of the project.

Pamphlet collections can provide good exhibit material. One UgLi arranged for pamphlet covers to be xeroxed on colored stock and mounted the copies on bulletin boards along with clippings from newspapers. Recently, the exhibit included simultaneous displays of material on the SST, the draft, the university's current budget crisis, VD, and various liberation groups. Each board contained a note that stated that more information was available in the pamphlet file. Students did inquire.

Suggestion boxes are familiar to everyone, but not all libraries utilize them fully. This is unfortunate, because they can be fantastically successful. Some libraries send letters in response to any inquiry that's signed; others use notebooks for questions (and later answers). One of the most interesting arrangements is also one of the most dangerous. One UgLi decided to have such a service with every comment posted in a central location along with its response. Responses are retyped on a p slip to limit the length of the explanation, rationalization, or comment and there is generally a gaggle of students — and staff — reading them after they've been posted. More than 150 questions were received in the first couple of months and raised matters that had been swept under various rugs for years: problems like coeds being chased across campus, complaints about outdoor rock concerts that disturbed the studious, requests for books, suggestions for improving service and even an occasional compliment. Admitting that the system can err has had a salutory effect; the openness of showing the criticisms as well as the bouquets seems to have been good for the morale of the staff as well as of the students. The bonus has been faster solutions to many problems than could have been accomplished through regular library channels.

Developing a book collection for an UgLi is difficult. Two varying schools of thought exist, one that it should be a "best" collection, the other that it should reflect the needs and interests of the undergraduates at that specific school. The two philosophies are not mutually exclusive and most UgLis represent some sort of compromise. Because of different courses of study on campuses that have UgLis, each collection should uniquely reflect and support those educational programs. Methods of accomplishing this seem to differ, and greater or lesser attention is paid to cribs such as *Books for College Libraries* and *Choice*. One UgLi does very little book selection as such, depending upon purchases for reserve use to provide the depth and scope that the collection needs. A former librarian there maintains that this procedure works very well, and I've no reason to criticize this approach for it certainly frees the staff for other activities. Through student recommendations, they can get materials from bio-chemical warfare to macrame. This same library has a good-sized collection of periodicals to supplement its books and believes it's worth spending nearly 20% of its budget for these serials.

There is general agreement that the UgLi book collection should be a duplicate one — or largely so — of titles in the university library. One real advantage to maintenance of the duplicate status of cataloged material in the collection is that faculty then have no reason to exercise their *droit du seigneur* and keep UgLi materials out beyond the standard loan period; they can use the research collection for that.

One persistent problem is the assignment of responsibility for assuring that the material the UgLi needs is indeed duplicate. This usually falls on the UgLi staff, with the result that they often serve as collection developers for the research library. But the problem of who pays for the research copy is frequently a knotty one. One UgLi prepares two orders, one charged to its own funds and one for the order department to fund any way it can. This is certainly faster — and more efficient — than for the UgLi to locate an accommodating fund on its own. Occasionally it is impossible to arrange for duplication. One UgLi discovered it needed a subscription to the *Ladies' Home Journal* which is indexed in the *Readers' Guide*. It was argued that the library was getting an example of a women's magazine and didn't need the *Journal*. The UgLi finally decided "Damn the duplication policy" and ordered it. The *Ladies' Home Journal*, which is now being read literally to pieces, is still the unique copy on that campus.

The optimum size of an UgLi book collection should still be negotiable. As new programs are instituted, whole new areas need to be developed; certainly in this time of increasing experimentation with independent study, UgLis need to represent a breadth and diversity of books not imagined when they were first established. (This may sound not unlike arguments proposed by other academic libraries, but it's particularly true, I believe, in the case of UgLis.) Optimum size was originally thought of as somewhere around 100,000 volumes; one UgLi now has room for about 250,000 volumes and has no reservations about reaching that figure.

Earlier various ways were mentioned as being used by some UgLis trying to eke out book money for reference materials. One UgLi has been equally imaginative in augmenting its basic book allocation. Through personal contact with faculty members, the UgLi librarian has convinced some to order duplicate copies from their departmental book funds and to have those books cataloged to the UgLi. Each of these orders is routed to the librarian for approval before it is placed, and the program has been moderately successful. Another UgLi was approached by a departmental book chairman who volunteered to do the same sort of thing; his offer has been temporarily refused by the library administration.

Getting enough copies of books for reserve use is often a problem, though one UgLi reported that it had no trouble obtaining the material it needed. One reserve service buys no copies of books needed for reserve if the request is received after the first day of the quarter. Another UgLi orders no books for reserve on a rush basis after the second week of the term. In both cases, it is felt that the books would arrive too late to do much good and they prefer to channel the energy of processing personnel to the term that lies ahead. Eventually the books for which late requests were submitted do arrive; they are put in the general collection until such time as the reserve request is resuscitated. One of these reserve rooms has also arranged with a local book store to notify the store that an official order is on its way from the Main Library's acquisition department. The reserve staff types an extra copy of the official order form and it's delivered by a member of the staff who is passing by the store. A week or ten days lapse before the official order arrives; this lead time is very useful, both for the UgLi and the store. Another UgLi provides posters to be displayed on bulletin boards in academic departments. The poster simply states (in capital letters) the deadline for getting reserve lists to the UgLi, and has proven to be very successful in helping faculty to plan ahead.

Processing, revising, and reproducing reserve lists is a time consuming activity. Automation is possible in some libraries, but the reserve staff of one technology-resistant university library produce their reserve lists on 3 x 5 catalog cards, one entry per card. These cards are photocopied as many times as necessary; usually copies are made for a course list, for the reserve author catalog, and for the instructor. Additions and deletions are simple, and the typed set of originals is kept and can be reproduced again whenever the class is offered.

Materials available for students to use, either in the reserve room or at the reference desk in UgLis shouldn't be limited to books, or even the usual non-book forms. Included in UgLis right now are such diverse items as a sheep's skull and a slide rule. Kleenex, staples, paper clips, and punches are also readily at hand. This kind of pragmatic assistance is basic, simple to offer, and priceless for the appreciation it produces.

One UgLi started a new book shelf stocked with paperbacks; it's reportedly very successful, and certainly it's relatively inexpensive to operate. The librarian has an arrangement with a local book store to have a copy of every new, interesting title set aside and every week the librarian visits the store and selects from those new publications the ones he wants. Another UgLi is more traditional in that it tries to keep most of its new book collection a hard cover one, but the librarian there also makes weekly excursions to a local book store to select items from stock. The staff of that store is extremely helpful and points out titles not yet reviewed or advertised that might have been overlooked. That new book shelf is the most popular one on its campus. As a personal aside, I'd like to say that I feel book reviews in the local underground papers and Judy Serebnick's "Contemporary Scene" section of *LJ* seem to be the most consistently useful guides to new material.

Another method of coping and cooperation occurred recently when the head of one UgLi contacted another to determine how that second library worked up its new book collection. Copies of statements were sent off and these documents were subsequently forwarded to a third UgLi and helped that librarian to formulate the new book policies and procedures there.

The several campuses of the University of California are connected by its tie line, a telephone arrangement that allows one campus to call another without charge. This has been a boon to the UgLis at San Diego, Los Angeles, and Berkeley, for it simplifies the consultation that is vital to the continuing activities of these three libraries as well as to the University system. It has also facilitated the transfer of a student assistant from the UgLi at one campus to another UgLi for one quarter when she found she needed some courses her own school did not offer. This was very satisfactory, both for the UgLis and the student, and she's now one of the best student assistants ever seen at either UgLi.

Serials is an area where there seems to be less unanimity among UgLis. Titles-currently-received range from 100 to 976 at UCLA, a figure that's 22% more than that of the next highest UgLi. At at least one UgLi the serials are the most heavily used part of the collection, or at least the most voraciously consumed, judging from the rate of loss and mutilation. Backfiles are usually incomplete, but most UgLis try to go back to at least 1950. Many feel keenly the lack of film holdings and appear interested in following Earlham College's lead in converting bound volumes to film. One UgLi has compiled a union list of the periodical titles included in the major Wilson indexes, showing the holdings of the UgLi and other campus libraries and including the local public library's listings when there is no campus copy. This service is appreciated nearly as much as the provision of sample copies of new periodicals for students to look at and evaluate.

Filling in backfiles and missing issues is a time consuming and frustrating exercise and most UgLis simply don't have the budget to go at this in a serious way. One UgLi librarian is alerted by the local gift division and stops by donors' homes after work to fill in missing issues. This UgLi also has made a standing offer to accept any duplicate issues of periodicals that come into the library. These are used in exchange for needed periodicals with a local dealer. It takes time and effort to institute such an arrangement, but it's better than spending money. The library staff contributes old issues of personal magazines at many campuses; one UgLi manages to get discarded issues from local beauty parlors, though they've no idea how that got started.

One UgLi binds many of its sets and sends those volumes to the main library, keeping only the current issues of many titles in the UgLi. Another UgLi has convinced its main library that certain periodical titles are research material only after they are bound, and gets the current copies of those titles and later binds them for the research library. They feel this reduces the need for some duplicate titles, broadens the scope of their browsing collection, and decreases the need for shelving space for bound periodicals. A ploy used at another campus is to charge subscriptions for a second binding copy to the library's replacement fund on the theory that it's less fuss to automatically order a second copy of titles subject to higher replacement rates. Other campuses don't accept this argument, but one UgLi has talked the main library into sending the second binding copies of several periodicals to the UgLi for browsing until they are ready for binding.

Newspapers are another area in which particularly interesting methods of coping are used. All but one UgLi receive papers, from 6 to Michigan's 32 titles. At one campus, several groups of foreign students subscribe to home newspapers and place them in the UgLi for convenient access. Another UgLi contacted the newspapers in towns from which they had heavy undergraduate enrollment and solicited free subscriptions. This *chuzpah* worked quite productively. I should point out that the newspaper area seems a good place to keep copies of local underground papers and other publications in newspaper format. Judging from UCLA, interest in the Los Angeles *Free Press,* the Berkeley *Daily Californian,* and *Rolling Stone* is somewhat greater than in the *Washington Post.*

Most of the eight UgLis under discussion have audio material in their collections; many others have recordings available and I expect that there are as many ways of organizing an audio service as there are audio services. I'll discuss only one particularly interesting one. Since its students were to have no access to the actual recordings, there was no need to classify the material beyond an identification number. All energies were spent on describing the collection, which was to be essentially one of spoken recordings. This UgLi felt LC did an inadequate job of analyzing recordings, and the library has made title analytics for every selection on every record in its collection. (It's interesting to note that LC is now beginning to give contents notes in its phonodisc cataloging.) This UgLi also noted the role played by each member of the cast who was listed. The staff believed strongly that the recordings were an extension of the book collection and created form cards for all authors and for long literary pieces included in the audio collection. These cards were interfiled in its public catalog. Now any student looking for poetry of Keats or a copy of *Major Barbara* finds a card stating that a recorded version of the work is available and can be heard as well as read. Incidentally, this UgLi liked the form card idea so well that it converted the subject headings of its pamphlets to LC and put form cards into the catalog indicating which subjects were included in the pamphlet collection. Use of pamphlets jumped 50% the year that was done.

The area of staffing is really the most critical matter involving UgLis: weak collections, poorly planned buildings, unsympathetic faculty-student relations, can be relatively unimportant if the staff of the library is actively interested in the undergraduate and his work. These librarians must appreciate that the students they are working with — and for — have enormous potential for accomplishing significant changes. If libraries (and librarians) are to participate in this process, they must come to be accepted as an essential part of the students' lives. The old belief that staff must be young in order to relate to undergraduates is nonsense. I frequently feel that the idea of getting young (read "inexperienced") staff is simply a gambit to keep overhead down. Whatever it is, it's a tragic miscalculation, for if there is any part of an academic library that requires flexible, unflappable, intelligent, and knowledgeable staff, it's in the kaleidoscopic milieu of the UgLi. Age is more a matter of mental attitude than a chronological fact, and I am still surprised to find people only recently out of school who seem ready for retirement. The average age of the librarians at one UgLi is 35 (individuals range from their early 20's to late 50's), and I understand that they have little difficulty working with alternate hordes of undergraduates, high school students, and faculty. The idea that the UgLi was to provide initial professional experience for its staff, who would then move on to more important work, was soon discarded; the professional experience of these same UgLi librarians averages 9.5 years.

Earlier, I mentioned some figures which showed that no UgLi has more than nine librarians. The ratio of undergraduates to UgLi librarians ranges from a low of 776 at Stanford to a high of 8,099 students per UgLi librarian. Against this appalling differential, several UgLis have found the same solution — library school students. Ranging from four, each working 12 to 17 hours, through five at 30 hours to 10 working 20 hours each, these students staff the reference desk during evening and weekend hours, perform bibliographic checking, and supervise student assistants; they perform, in short, as librarians. It's significant that at two schools these Library Associates, or Graduate Assistants as they are called, are paid from the academic salary roll. I'm sure that any UgLi that has utilized this manpower would find it extremely difficult to continue its service and processing programs without them. (The same might be said for use of work-study students; one UgLi happily has been able to create jobs for as many as five student assistants as a result of this program.)

A variation on this theme occurred when library school students asked if they might be able to work at a reference point in connection with their advanced reference course work. The UgLi librarian was approached and enthusiastically agreed, even though the UgLi reference staff was less than half the size of the main reference department. During the final term of reference study, 42 students each worked at the UgLi reference desk one or two hours a week and assisted behind the scenes for an additional hour weekly. The good will and practical experience the UgLi provided these neophyte colleagues was very valuable, both to the students and the staff.

Another successful approach has been to use part-time librarians. The reference staff of one UgLi has four of them and soon will have six half-timers instead of three full-time librarians. This gives them greater flexibility in staffing, with more bodies on hand during the peak hours of the day. One of these part-timers works every Saturday and thus reduces friction in that painful ritual of rotating schedules and compensatory time off.

Last year one UgLi proposed an exchange of reference staff with the main branch. A schedule was developed and one UgLi librarian worked a couple of hours a day for a week at the main reference desk while a counterpart was at the UgLi reference point. The following week, two others traded hours. This worked out very well; each group became more sympathetic about — and interested in — the work of the other.

Recently, the library at one campus granted its Assistant UgLi Librarian a year's leave to be an "interlibrary loan" to the University of California, Berkeley, which was in the countdown year before opening its own UgLi. My understanding is that this was an extremely successful arrangement for both UgLis — the new one had the advantage of an old UgLi hand to assist in making final arrangements, and the established one got back a librarian with recharged batteries and a fresh perspective. Marc Gittelsohn, the Moffit Librarian at the University of California, Berkeley, strongly recommends a procedure of this sort to any university planning to open an UgLi. The librarian who was exchanged found his working sabbatical a stimulating and enjoyable experience.

Shortly after I became a librarian, I was told that there was no good librarian who wasn't a five o'clock drinker. I later discovered that 40 hours a week is inadequate to accomplish all of that which needs to be done. I'm pleased to report other librarians acknowledge this point. The reference staff at one UgLi meets after work at least once a month to discuss matters for which there's not been time during the day. An agenda is posted on the door to the office, and everyone lists items they want to have considered. Chicken or pizza to go are obtained and washed down with an inoffensive domestic vintage; the librarians are able to meet without interruptions, yell at each other, and to determine procedures they wish to implement. All of this is on their own time, but they feel it's been time well spent.

Increasingly the idea of the librarian as subject specialist has gained acceptance as the proper direction for academic librarians to aim for. This is just another example of the collective inferiority complex librarians have, and I disagree with this direction particularly in respect to UgLi librarians. One UgLi has specified for some years that the most important quality it requires in its staff is broad general knowledge. A knowledge in depth tends to create tunnel vision, and UgLi librarians, especially, need CinemaScope. The ability to hop gracefully and skillfully from one topic to another is critical, most particularly in UgLis; the flexibility of approach is essential. I can't help feeling that the vogue for demanding subject specialization for many librarians is just another example of academic inflation. The library — all libraries — should be a haven for renaissance men and women as well as for specialists.

The concept of the teacher-librarian has gained increasing respectability of late. Generally speaking, however, I doubt that librarians will ever be allowed to do much more than prepare an occasional bibliographic lecture. I feel we have much more potential for achievement by working parallel with the teaching staff than by trying to infiltrate them. On one campus an extremely successful course in bibliography and library use has been established. It's taught by librarians and the feedback from students is uniformly favorable about the content, if not always the presentation. A self-directed, self-paced program of library instruction has been tried by one of our eight UgLis with the special admissions of minority students on its campus and has proved to be by far the most successful part of that program. It has been adapted by other libraries, and plans are under way to offer the program in connection with required pre-major courses in several departments at the originating campus. This, it seems to me, is the direction we should take; it certainly produces more returns on our efforts.

A less conventional but even more profitable approach is to cultivate the faculty socially. One UgLi librarian drinks regularly with an active member of the local faculty, conducting informal seminars on library service between rounds, and has developed a mutually beneficial grapevine. Another UgLi librarian plays volleyball with students during noon hours and chamber music with faculty in the evening. Tending bar for various library and campus festivities and membership in the local faculty club can also provide good entrees.

Related to the matter of staff is the problem many universities establishing UgLis seem to create when they design and construct a new UgLi facility and *then* look for an UgLi librarian to run it. Some universities avoid this by appointing an administrative officer charged with responsibility for library services for undergraduates, but this is quite rare. It seems only fair that the person who is to be responsible for an UgLi should be in on the planning of a new facility, and that that person's decisions should carry the ultimate ones. The idea of importing an alien to run a new UgLi, a person who is not familiar with that campus and the particular interests and hangups of the undergraduates there, tends seriously to negate the initial effectiveness of the service.

An example of the pride in our work with undergraduates that's so important occurred recently when two UgLi librarians, while visiting the main branch, were discussing a candidate for the vacant position as head of the UgLi. "Why would anyone want to come here?" asked an eavesdropping main librarian. "He's not coming 'here,' " responded one of the UgLi librarians, "he's coming to the Undergraduate Library!"

I'll provide this final example as a means of summing up. One UgLi librarian listed for me a number of ways her UgLi copes, and then concluded, "Actually, we hardly have time for extra services. We are so involved in giving the most students the most of the essential services, [that] it is hard to spread ourselves around, but we try. I am not complaining. [The] Undergraduate [Library] has been treated fairly here; we probably have the 'best deal' on the campus. The difficulty is our school is growing too large." I believe this statement explains why the UgLi art of coping has been so highly developed, and helps to explain why UgLis are the most exciting, frustrating library service being offered today.

About the Author

From 1961-1970, James Davis was Head, Reference Section, College Library, University of California at Los Angeles. An expert coper, he was on leave during 1969-1970 from UCLA to assist in the planning and preparation for the opening of the Moffitt Undergraduate Library, University of California at Berkeley. He then succeeded Norah E. Jones as College Librarian at UCLA in 1971. Beginning in 1971, he was on the staff of the UCLA School of Library Service and has more recently assisted with public relations and exhibition assignments in the Univeristy Librarian's Office at UCLA.

Joseph Gusfield

Attitudes of University Faculty Toward the Need for Change in Undergraduate Education

Sociologist Gusfield reviews the "golden age of faculty power" and expertly outlines the professionalization and specialization of faculty which has become overwhelmingly dominant in recent years, and the accompanying decline of student power. He predicts that in the future there will be a "diminishing teacher evaluation of the students and increasing student evaluation of teachers" with a greater "emphasis and concern with local questions." He also wonders about the "shift away from lecturing and reading and more towards the visual and experiential activities" and the implications for libraries. He observes that the "library has represented culture because faculty members have a high culture of book learning. However, we live in a world where increasingly the culture — popular and immediate culture — is not always book learning."

(The following is presented as spoken with a few minor changes. It was prepared as a lecture and presented in this form from limited notes and an outline. The author apologizes for his lack of time to prepare a written form for this publication, recognizing full well that the spoken and the written word are different media. Impossible dullness in one is clarity in the other; wit and verve in one is rambling banality in the other. Respect for the written word is, after all, the cornerstone of librarianship.)

SOURCE: From Joseph Gusfield, "Attitudes of University Faculty Toward the Need for Change in Undergraduate Education," Librarians Confront the Undergraduate Environment, a Pre-Conference Institute Sponsored by the University Libraries Section, the Association of College and Research Libraries, Dallas, Texas, June 18-19, 1971. Included by permissions of the author and the University Libraries Section, Association of College and Research Libraries.

There is something incestuous about studying faculty but, despite that taboo, I have tried over the years to keep a reasonable amount of equanimity and objectivity, both of which are rather hard to do.

Sociologists are always talking about what was, or what is going to be. They tend to see a world in which things are continuously changing. So to talk about faculty and about students presents a much more difficult issue today than it may have a few years ago.

Despite the variety of 2,000 or so colleges and universities that we have in the United States, it was at one time possible to make statements that seemed to summarize what was dominant. This has become harder and harder so that in much of what follows I am less concerned with the faculty than I am with what the faculty has been, what it may be today, and what it is likely to become tomorrow. It has always been impossible to talk about faculty without talking about students. Students are the job or the business of teachers. I do not say it is our only business, but it is a business. It is also an education.

In emphasizing change, I am going to look ahead and try to see what may be the future relationship between faculty and students. In this sense, I am again functioning as the sociologist who sees his world as one that is in motion. There is the story that after Adam and Eve had been ordered out of the Garden of Eden, Eve, in good wifely fashion, was berating Adam for having put them in this kind of situation. Where were they going to live? How were they going to make a living? Where were they going to get clothes? Adam, after listening to this for sometime, finally turned to Eve and said, "But after all, my dear, we are living in a period of transition." And so we are.

When John Haak asked me to speak and when Pat Knapp first broached the idea to me, both of them said to talk about the faculty and let it be known that you are not necessarily going to say things that have direct or immediate application to libraries. I have tried to do that and I have tried to be as useless as possible, or as "irrelevant" as the term would be today. However, I found that I could not fulfill their request because in so many ways there was a relationship between faculty as they have been and the library. There are also possible relationships for the future or possible non-relationships.

I want to point my remarks toward three tenses: the past, the present, the future. I will begin with what faculty today have now begun to call "the golden age of faculty power" or the "age of the professoriate." This is a way of looking at faculty and professoring as a job, that is, as a category of work which has certain kinds of characteristics.

Some of the things which I have to say may be somewhat familiar to you from your experience. The job of professoring has gone through immense changes throughout the history of American colleges and universities. From about 1915, which marked the development of the American Association of University Professors, to World War II (and especially post-World War II period, which I now see coming to a close), there has been a rather steady growth and increase in the general power and position of college professors within universities and in relationship to their students. This power is in turn related to and results in a cohesive sense of group identity and relationship.

Much of this has grown up around the notion of professionalization. I do not want to get into the question of defining a profession. A student working on his doctoral dissertation now has had enough trouble trying to define a profession. Suffice it to say that what has happened in faculty life over the past 25 to 50 years has been a growing tendency to identify one's work with some particular speciality and with some group of people who are involved in that same speciality.

I always have to fill out applications which ask for my occupation. I just renewed my passport and again they asked for my occupation. I stop and ask myself — Am I a college professor? Well, that is a very broad area which includes professors of dairy production, professors of Greek and Latin, professors of sociology, professors of library science. It is a generic term and covers all kinds of professoring. On the other hand, I will sometimes introduce myself as a college professor, but am more likely to describe myself as a sociologist. Many college professors are more likely to describe themselves by their specific groups.

This again does not indicate that I am a college teacher and I am a little loath to deny that because there is still an ambivalence left over from my ill spent youth. So I compromise and write down "Professor of Sociology." The shift from being a member of an institution to being someone identified with a particular speciality has been a very important one.

I am now talking about that "golden age" of professionalization when to be a college professor meant to occupy a specialty, to have been trained in that specialty, to have all the indicia of it (especially the Ph.D.). Indeed, one is not born into academic life until one has a Ph.D. It is more than the trade union card; it is the basic sense of identity. In fact, we even fall into thinking of a young person as a person who does not have a Ph.D. and a mature person as a person who does have a Ph.D. This, in turn, means a degree of professionalization and a way of maintaining control over who can call himself a sociologist and who can not. This power is a great hallmark of a profession; it also means that the audiences to which one becomes attentive are those whom you see across college and university lines in your discipline.

Each year I go to the American Sociological Association meetings, the Pacific Sociological Association meetings, and other regional meetings. Just as you are here renewing your identity as librarians, I constantly renew my identity as a sociologist. People know each other now in terms of what are their common, specialized knowledges. They find their careers within that. In studies of people who lose their careers (for example, engineers who become business executives, chemists who become business executives, even sociologists who become college presidents), acute problems are often discovered. The questions are: "What am I?" and "Where do I belong?" Engineers have had dreams in which they can no longer operate a slide rule. Freudians may interpret it as they wish, but sociologists tend to interpret it in terms of career identity.

During this golden age, when one related to a particular audience of one's colleagues there was the development of a national audience. So too, there was a development of a career which is itself oriented towards that audience. By a career, I mean a movement in and through stages and steps. Obviously, academic life and faculties in general have for a long time had rather formalistic careers. One moves from being a teaching assistant to instructor, to an assistant professor, to associate professor, and ultimately one reaches Nirvana by becoming a full professor. It is a set of stages. In the professionalized version of academic life, one also moves away from one's institution. Your position, your career must consequently depend upon that national audience because you move from place to place.

Joan Gideon, the novelist, has a wonderful essay that appeared in *Life* a few years ago called "A Generation not for Barricades." In it, she tried to describe the 1950s, particularly her life as an undergraduate in the early 1950s in Berkeley. She remarks that one visualizes his or her future as "being at college near a good beach." Her essay somehow expresses a concept of success or a notion of a career which is aimed at something not necessarily wedded to a specific institution. It is this aspect of faculty life that I am emphasizing.

This golden age has also carried with it considerable power. I know that faculty are always claiming that they are really the weaker part of the university, but anyone who looks at American universities historically will recognize the postwar period as the golden age of faculty power — an age in which the power of the administrator and the power of students were extraordinarily limited. It has been an age in which faculty were able effectively to limit greatly the aims, policies, and ideas that came from administrators and trustees.

A student came to me a couple of months ago and asked, "Is the Academic Senate of the University of California a good device for governing?" and I said, "My God, no. It's major purpose is *not* to govern." If you examine what it is that academic senates do, you will find, in the main, that they try to keep their own autonomy. The autonomy of the full professor and the department in a situation where professionalization is so great has become considerable. The plan of organization for universities into departments built around specialties and the development of professorial autonomy are consequently part of this age of considerable power.

The power of the faculty vis-à-vis the student has also been very great. If you look at the history of American colleges and universities, students have frequently had a great deal of power. (They have also frequently protested and been violent over issues.) However, when I discuss the power of the faculty vis-à-vis the student, I mean that the faculty member does not have to pay much attention to the student and the student has to pay a lot of attention to the faculty. This was not the milieu from 1880-1890 until World War II. At many times, students did ignore their professors. They did what they wished to do, informally defining their standards of work as they wished, and utilizing standards of informal pressures.

Students were also able to do something else. They were able to leave. American universities went through a great crisis around the turn of the century precisely because students were leaving. They were not coming to college. They did not view it as very important or relevant.

But after World War II, college began to become important. So too, the faculty became more important because they set the ground rules of work, grades, and assignments — the stuff with which students had to cope and to which they had to adapt their lives. This has meant a move towards undergraduate education modeled on graduate education.

What is it that the student must know? He must know disciplines. What is it that the faculty teach? They teach disciplines in which they have a degree of professional expertise. To go outside of the discipline is to lose that which is part of one's identity. And so the post-war period has been a period of faculty power in which students have had to take the faculty seriously. Someone a few years ago described what was happening on American campuses as "creeping asceticism." This is the necessity for students to be serious, to work hard, and to consider their study important to their lives and careers.

Professionalization has a tendency to move one away from the immediate audience and has divorced the faculty from students and their pressures. When students ask for personal relationships between faculty and students, they are saying that they have no way of controlling this monster who walks in like a surgeon two hours a week to a class of 250 students, gives his lecture, and departs. They have no way of limiting his impact on their lives because they have none of those relationships by which and through which people control each other.

At the same time that all this professionalization has been going on, faculty have also appeared as something else. The faculty, especially the liberal arts undergraduate faculty and the faculty in the traditional sciences, the social sciences, the humanities, and the more generalized disciplines, have also appeared as intellectuals. Part of my problem in knowing whether I am a college professor or a sociologist is the ambivalence between professionalization and intellectuality. There is the notion of a person who represents a particular kind of culture — the culture of the educated man. In other words, there is the culture of the sociologist and there is the culture of the educated man. The two sometimes come together, but not always.

The educated man knows no bounds in terms of discipline. "Nothing human shall be alien unto me." No graduate student is ever taught this; instead he is taught what he should know and know thoroughly and that he should not talk about other things of which he knows very little. But in undergraduate education, the encounter between student and teacher has involved this kind of high culture. Therefore, the ambivalence about over-professionalization has occurred. This is not the first decade in which teachers have whipped themselves over the fact that they do not quite know whether they are research specialists or instructors of the young.

The conflict has always been the same. Perhaps this is my theme. At different times, the balance gets tipped in different directions. These two aspects of the faculty have been important aspects of a college education. Particularly in the liberal arts, the faculty are the custodians and bearers of this great gift of high culture, the gift that constitutes a continuity between Aristotle and ourselves, or as I have tried to indicate, between Adam and Eve and ourselves. Professionalization has also been of great importance.

If professionalization and specialization have been dominant in recent years, it has been a function of several factors. One, of course, is the market. It has been one of the paradoxes of our recent period of academic history that the demand for teaching caused by the great growth in the number of undergraduate students has created the good market position of professors, which in turn has enabled them to pay greater attention to research. They have been sought after. They have been wined and dined and courted — almost as football players used to be sought in another age. This good market in turn bolstered the power that they have had vis-à-vis the administration and the students. Research has become something viewed as immensely important by society. Various agencies, private foundations, and the government stood ready to finance and to subsidize research, often in very general terms, so that it was often possible for professors to do what they wanted to do. The professors were able to get someone to pay for the research and found that by virtue of the research, their positions on the market increased rather than decreased.

Further, the power of the faculty has also rested on the sheer specialization of knowledge. It is a fact that particular areas of knowledge become deeper and deeper and harder and harder for everyone to know everything about them. The Renaissance man was left behind at the time of the Renaissance. One cannot consequently be a member of the Board of Trustees and hope to know enough about sociology and Greek and organic chemistry to be able to make intelligent judgements about the future of those fields or the nature of whom to hire and whom not to hire. This means that there is a great amount of autonomy by the faculty.

The days are past when, as was true in the late 19th century in some parts of the United States, a man could be a college president at the same time as he taught geology, natural science, philosophy, Greek, and Latin. Well into the twentieth century, Texas had a number of colleges where one man did all the teaching. This is less and less possible. As you know, sometimes faculty complain "How can I teach undergraduates a course in English literature? I am a specialist in the early 17th century and you are asking me now to talk about novels written in the 1920s. That's not my field".

These elements have had a great deal to do with the shift towards specialization and the resulting power and autonomy of the faculty. By and large, it has been a pretty good life. It has certainly been a life which has brought me more income and more power than I thought possible in the days when I was a graduate student. Then, we looked forward to shabby gentility. Someone put it very nicely a few years ago in a discussion of the professoriate by referring to the American faculty under the general phrase of "the leisure of the theory classes."

The culture of the student and the power of the student vis-à-vis the faculty have been enormously weakened. If one looks at the history of American colleges in the 1920s, and even well into the 1930s, the cohesiveness of student groups is easily recognized. The very model of the fraternity and the sorority suggested to students that they had a considerable amount of autonomy over their daily lives and a considerable capacity to ignore what it was that their faculty had wished them to do in the way of assignments. Much of what happened in this later golden age of faculty power has weakened this student culture, reduced its cohesiveness and its capacity to lead its own life. Around the turn of the century when colleges began to pick up a bit in enrollment, one of the great motifs was to go to college for the friends that you would make. In other words, the important thing was not the curriculum; it was the extracurriculum. Thus, you went to college not so much for the classes or for the "dear ol' Dean" or for musty old Professor Gusfield, but for the friends that you would make, the lasting associations, the business contacts. C. Michael Otten has published a history of the University of California at Berkeley in terms of faculty and student relationships — formal and informal relationships and how decisions are made about student housing and other aspects of student life that underscores this description.

Student culture has been weakened in this recent age of faculty power. For one thing, as universities got larger and larger, student bodies became heterogeneous. They were composed not only of male and female students, but of people from a variety of social and intellectual backgrounds. There was not a generation of college students who were the first of their family to be in college; there were also second and third generation students who came from a variety of places and were going to a variety of places — those who were going back to their hometowns after getting degrees in a profession such as law or medicine to practice near their families and those who saw their roots and careers outward. The degree of specialization increased and fragmented enormously. Several years ago, I counted 105 different departments and 89 institutes at the University of California at Berkeley. This means an enormous fragmentation of the concept of a student. In a small upstate college in New York in 1954, I had students do a methodological study of fraternities on the campus, i.e., the different cultures in them, who belonged to them. All students, whether they belonged to a fraternity or not, knew one fraternity from another. They knew that this was the place where the "jocks" lived and this is where the rich kids lived. My students mapped and patterned the whole thing. In 1955, I went to teach at the University of Illinois, which by today's standards was then comparatively small with only 19,000 students. I attempted to have my students do the same study of fraternities and thought that it was bound to work because the University of Illinois had more fraternities and sororities than any other campus in the country. I discovered, however, that at least half of the students did not know one fraternity from another. They lived in different groups and different pockets. This, in turn, weakened the capacity of students vis-à-vis the faculty.

The market function of college operated the same way. As colleges become important, it was not easy to drop out of college. Every once in awhile people say to me — "What is the matter with these kids? In my day, it was a privilege to go to college. If they don't like it, why don't we get rid of them?" I try to explain to them that college may have been a privilege once, but that now it is an obligation and a right. Indeed, our laws are moving increasingly in that direction — to indicate that going to public universities is a right and therefore, the rules under which students are expelled are to be scrutinized by the courts. Students will quickly tell you that they are in college as a necessity to stay out of the draft or to get a career. Consequently, its importance has risen enormously and that in turn has underwritten the power of the faculty.

What I have been describing is not ancient history, but let's call it medieval history. It is a world that may return sometime in the future. It is the world I wish would return in the future because it was a good one from a number of viewpoints. It was also a bad one from other viewpoints. But it was a "golden age" for faculty.

When we discuss the careers and orientations of faculty as departmental, specialized, and oriented towards a national audience, we are making the distinction between cosmopolitans and locals. Local people are oriented towards their institution. They are part of that institution. They are concerned with that institution and its members. This means that, to some extent, they are not oriented towards a national or cosmopolitan audience. The intellectual in his orientation is, of course, oriented towards a larger outward society, but he is somewhat different from the professional.

The cosmopolitan sees the institution only as a way station (he is going somewhere else) or as a place to hang his hat. Faculty like to make a distinction between their work and other things. They say "Now that the semester is over, I can get busy with my work." This is a bit like the old cry of the British Naval officer to the men, waking them up in the morning, "Wakey, Wakey, Rise and shine. You've had your time, now I'll have mine." The important distinction, in short, is that scholarship and specialization are centrally important and while teaching exists, it is either to be seen in relation to one's specialty or is to be seen as something not as important to your career because, after all, your career lies in a national audience. The advancement within your institution, as well as your general advancement in life, will not depend very heavily upon teaching. It is a local concern.

We are all familiar with much of this in one way or another. It has involved the down-grading of the extracurriculum — those aspects of student life which are unrelated to the classroom. It means that the internal growth of a student becomes subsidiary and subordinate, not as important. We want to put it in old terms: we are not concerned in the university with building character. The building of moral character has disappeared. A number of years ago I was in a symposium in a small college with the Dean of Women and the question was "Women's Place in the Modern World". The Dean said "I don't know about women's place in the modern world, but on this campus women's place is in the dormitories at 11 o'clock at night." This concern is no longer present.

It is very interesting to find that only a few faculty in a large modern university have ever been in a dormitory, know what students eat for lunch, have any concern about it, or even care. Perhaps they should not care; I am not sure they should. But it is clear that they do not care and to that extent, the student extra-curriculum has been enormously downgraded in importance and in power.

Let us turn away from this distinction between local and cosmopolitan audiences. Turn away from the past and get some view of the present. One could begin by saying, "Students are revolting." Somebody would respond "Ah, yes, aren't they?" I do not have to recite the events of the past few years on college campuses. They are all too familiar to everyone. I do not wish to get involved in an analysis of why it happened or what the relationship is to education. However, the consequences of the fall-out from that period are quite great. Certainly, one of the things that has happened is a retipping of the balance. I should not say tipping, but should rather call it a new balance between faculty power and student power. With the rise of student power, faculty now become concerned. Whether they are concerned for ideological reasons, for moral reasons, for political reasons, or for personal reasons, is unimportant for the moment. But they are concerned and they must ask themselves constantly: What will the students do? What are they thinking? How do they feel?

Some years ago, before the advent of student protest, a group at Cornell extensively surveyed American college students and published *What College Students Think* in 1960. Unfortunately, they were dead wrong. They may have been right for the late 1950s when the data were collected, but by the time it was published, the reported passivity of students vis-à-vis politics, and even internal issues, had begun to wane.

The rise of student power has meant, as the sociologist Irving Louis Horowitz puts it, "the development of students as a class." What he means by this is not that they are freshmen or sophomores, but that students have begun to think of themselves as a specific and cohesive group — not just the students at Goucher or Haverford, or the University of California at San Diego — but students as a total group, as having something in common, as having sets of interests, and organization.

Indeed, one is startled at how much intermobility exists of a horizontal nature among students — the extent of transfers and moving around. I became very curious about this in my last year of teaching at the University of Illinois and I always asked my class, "How many of you have ever been to Berkeley?" There was always a hand raised. He or she (and it was usually both) had made the great pilgrimage to the mecca of student revolt. This means that the degree of communication and the extensiveness of similar events have made students conscious of themselves as a class. Television has helped in this communication. While the events following the Cambodian invasion did not occur on every campus in the United States, they did occur on a great many campuses. Someone recently pointed out that this past year (1970-1971) contained the number of demonstrations, riots, sit-ins, and strikes which eight or ten years ago would have been front page news. To many of us, it seemed a year of calm and passivity on college campuses. Dr. James Gibbs (Dean of Undergraduate Studies at Stanford University) would well know that not all universities have been so calm and peaceful in this past year. Stanford has stood out as a shining example of the opposite.

We have become used to student power and to student organization. Insofar as students view themselves as a class, they increasingly come to recognize, as Karl Marx would say, that their true natural enemies are the faculty. Much of student revolt over the past decade has been far more political than it has been educational. It has been oriented towards national and political issues. We are now obviously moving into a period of time when we are increasingly seeing educational issues as basic student concerns.

At the same time that students emerge as a class, we have also with us the generation gap, the youth culture, the extraordinary shifts in styles of life which are associated with youth versus age — whatever terms you wish to use. These shifts in styles of life have carried many things with them — a greater emphasis on the emotive and the experiential, a greater emphasis upon the non-intellective rather than on the intellective. Science is suspect. Its technology has brought about war. I do not want to make more of it than is there but learning and intellect are somewhat suspect in having shut off certain aspects of life. Therefore, commitment becomes crucial and important.

Some years ago I published a book on the American Temperance Movement, an interest of mine in American reform politics. A student of mine who has read it berated me. He said, "You didn't tell us how you felt about it." Indeed, I had not intended to tell him how I felt about it. I did not think it pertinent and I still don't think it pertinent. He, however, was saying, "I want to know how you feel."

Occasionally, I get angry at classes and launch into a kind of sermonistic preaching. Then students come up and say, "Gee, that was great." I ask, "What was great about it?" The responses are, "It has a sense of you as a person. It had a sense of someone who had feeling about something." You cannot underestimate this. It is part of the phenomena that tends to legitimize the criticism of the intellect and to give feeling and emotion a stronger place. It gives experience a stronger place. These things become important because the younger faculty have been associated with it. Increasingly, the student of today is the faculty member of tomorrow.

The recent survey by the Carnegie Commission of 35,000 faculty in the United States reveals the enormous gap that now exists between the young faculty and the older faculty. They do not think the same; they do not see life the same — not only on national political issues, but especially on what we would call "local issues" that have to do with students, such as student participation, student power, the character of the curriculum or the non-curriculum. The response and reaction towards student power by young faculty is one of acceptance and approval.

Much of what I am saying may be summed up by indicating that what seems to me to be taking place is a push among a number of students, particularly the middle class and upper-middle class students who have become most identified with student revolt, in the direction of the Psycho-Social Moratorium, as Eric Erikson some years ago called it.

There has always been this ambivalence about college. Is it a place where you can train for something? Is it a place where you are supposed to be made into a particular kind of something — an agronomist or a sociologist? Or is it a place and a period of time in which you seek your identity? I gather that Paul Heist (see his paper) was saying that some of his recent survey material indicates this greater preoccupation of students with the identity search, the push for wanting to know who they are, for wanting to use the period of college education as a time of experiment and self-understanding or self-awareness.

This means that what faculty have been doing in the past runs completely counter to these kinds of feelings and concerns. However, the push towards equality among students and faculty grows apace. In a period when student power is increasing, it has several elements that deal with the basic problem of the authority of the faculty in the classroom. One of these is the whole question of what criteria do we use in hiring and promoting faculty? Here the emphasis upon teachers is one way of stating the problem. Students want greater attention to the local institution and greater attention to teaching as such. They do not care if a faculty member has a Nobel Prize unless he is there at 9 o'clock in the morning saying things that are interesting.

In 1963, I had lunch with a couple of my wife's cousins. Both had degrees in engineering from Berkeley. They were living in Los Angeles and they were disturbed about the education of their children, particularly elementary and high school education. They asked, "How many hours a week do you teach?" I then taught eight hours a week, which among my circle of full professors was a rather large amount. "Eight hours a week. Gee, I work 40 hours a week," they said. I responded, "Well, you must understand there is a lot of preparation, a lot of committee meetings, a lot of research. I do work hard. Most people of a professional status in this society put in much more than a 40 hour week." But they said, "Eight hours, we should do something to increase the amount of teaching." I said, "Look, you people graduated from the University of California at Berkeley and it is very proud of the number of Nobel Prize winners that it has. If you ask these men to teach eight hours a week, they will quit and go to some other place that will offer them much more in the way of free time." They looked at me and said, "We don't care. If they don't teach, we don't give a damn what awards they have. They shouldn't be in the university." That was 1963 and two people who had come through the same institution.

This push towards localization is very much a part of the student orientation towards education. I am beginning to ask in effect what is the fall-out of the student revolt in relation to issues that have to do with faculty authority and faculty power. I am beginning to answer that there is a movement in a direction of readjusting the balance. It is a movement which also means an enormous amount of generational conflict within the faculty. You begin to see this as faculty discuss the interview of a new man for the department. Someone in some kind of circumlocution said, "What about his politics?" I said, "I never asked about his politics. I don't know whether he is a monarchist or . . .". The faculty member responds, "That's not what we mean. How does he feel about students? That's the crucial question." And indeed this generational conflict means that an enormous polarization is going on among faculty. It is harder and harder to talk about *the* faculty. On crucial issues such as the rise of the student power, they are polarized. It makes the more resistant faculty even more resistant because they must now articulate, clarify, and determine. They must make judgments. They can no longer take for granted the things that used to be taken for granted. It used to be taken for granted that if you made assignments, most of the students would not do all of them, but would do a fair share of them, enough to pass the examination. That is what would have happened in the past. Now, the students will argue over the question of assignment and turn it into a matter of reform or participation.

I have been talking about the present. Let me discuss the shape of things to come. Will conflict continue? I will stick my neck out and predict that conflict will continue. It will continue, not so much because sources of discontent necessarily continue, but because students and faculty have now developed themselves as conflict groups.

They now define situations as ones about which conflict is possible. In the past, they were defining them in opposite fashion. To this extent, students have come into being as part of a whole general trend of American life toward participation. At any rate, those who in the past have not participated formally, are now participating. This shift means that a number of issues now become joined. We are certainly moving towards a diminishing teacher evaluation of students and increasing student evaluation of teachers. I do not think that it will reach the time when teachers may be flunked by their students, but certainly the increasing emphasis upon the evaluation of the teacher is a check in the balance of power. It also means that increasingly throughout American colleges and universities there will be an emphasis and concern with local questions.

Concern with students will be thought necessary in order to make legitimate career possibilities and concerns. This means a greater push toward the local. Indeed, one impact of less emphasis upon research is to take away a faculty member's attractiveness in the market and consequently make it more necessary for him to be concerned with what happens in his local institution.

But there are several other things, one of which is television. One of the aspects of the emphasis upon the emotive and the experiential is to make the visual, and the immediate experience more important. If there is one thing which the faculty has stood for and considered to be important to the higher culture and to a college educated man, it is books. I suggest that the book is now no longer the major weapon of the faculty. At least, books are now not as effective a tool as was true in the past.

The shift away from lecturing and reading and more towards the visual and experiential activities is something about which we do not know a great deal. But there is a movement away from books as a basic source of teaching. I am not sure what this means for libraries, but it is not something about which libraries in their present type of construction can feel very sanguine.

The library has represented culture because faculty members have a high culture of book learning. However, we live in a world where increasingly the culture — popular and immediate culture — is not always book learning. There has been a great increase in the use of paperback books, but television, radio, and movies make for a very different quality in people's awareness and information sources.

A similar trend is involved in the push towards greater student control of assignments. There is a push towards independent studies and towards interdisciplinary activities. Independent studies are the carving out by students of that which is meaningful for them as individuals. Once again, the psycho-social moratorium — in order to be freer to do that which is for them interesting. I do not want to get into the question of whether this is good pedagogically or not, but it makes very different sources of learning.

To some extent, it may mean that students will demand of libraries that the libraries help them in pulling things together. Or it may mean the movement away from reading towards experience. A student came to me several months ago and wanted to do an independent study project which consisted of taking children to the zoo. He said that what he would be doing would help his own self development since he would learn about children and he would grow by teaching children about animals. Whatever you may want to say about this particular incident, it should be pointed out that the student did not mention anything about writing a paper or doing any reading about child psychology. This was just what he did not want to do; he wanted the experience that comes from taking children to the zoo, not the intellectual reflection.

These moves towards independent studies, the carving out of programs, and a pass-fail grading system mean a shift away from the faculty as the determiners of content. It is a movement in the direction of much greater student concern with self-development and with a wide variety of learning sources. I do not know whether something new has happened to students in terms of their own inward psychology, but what has happened is the enormous increase in student power which has the political capacity for moving colleges and universities toward independent study programs.

It has not happened all over. Out of the heterogeneity of universities, we are developing, more sharply than in the past, two very distinct kinds of students. They have existed in the past, but the development is now increasing. With the admission of large numbers of minorities, there are students who have a serious orientation towards college — serious in the classical American sense of needing the education skills that the education institutions will give them. The other kind of students are the ones I have been discussing — those who moved in many elements of student revolt and who have now become concerned with reforming and changing the content of their education.

Peter Berger has written about what he calls the "blueing of America," not the "greening of America." He means that there is a tendency for the middle-class and upper middle-class student to want to get out of the mobility race, to raise his children so that they appreciate flowers, not success. At the same time, the children of blue collar workers are intent on moving up. Berger thinks that in the future, there may be an enormous circulation of elites. I hope he is right. At any rate, one must recognize that different groups are wanting or doing different kinds of things. This polarization will mean that certain kinds of educational reforms may be more pertinent for the student who can afford to see his college as a place for identity, for having his identity crisis, for self-awareness, and for individual choice. Other kinds of educational reforms will concern the student who tends to see college as a vehicle to move up, to gain particular skills, as having utility.

I have not yet said anything about what, I think, is the growing and important issue that begins to emerge: namely, why go to college? Much of what I have been discussing has been a way of saying that in the past students may have gone to college for its extracurriculum or sometimes they went for moral character. In the last golden age of faculty power, they went in order to learn what it is that the faculty does in their leisure time when they are not teaching. If you begin now to say let us have done with the era of professionalization and be done with teaching undergraduates as if they were all going to be future doctoral students, we then begin to ask what is it that we are to convey. Is it the higher culture which constitutes the educated man? What is this? And what are the implications in a society when mass communications tend to constitute a very large amount of what we call "our culture?" If that is to be the case, what then are we to teach?

A Columbia University economist, Ivar Berg, has written a fascinating book, *Education and Jobs, the Great Training Robbery*. His thesis is that college education has never had the technological importance that we have given to it. We just do not need that many college educated students for this level of technology. During the great depression of the 1930's, there was a want ad: "Office boys wanted. $25 a week. Only Phi Beta Kappas need apply." In other words, if more people go to college than is necessary for the technology, we will have college graduates in the most menial of jobs.

The two departments which have the largest number of majors in the United States at an undergraduate level are history and English literature. They produce about 20,000 B.A.s in history and about 20,000 B.A.s in English literature each year. If this country were to use all those historians and literary critics you can imagine the much bigger mess in which we would be. In short, you would ask yourself what is this education for. That is a central philosophical and intellectual question we must face.

One answer — the answer of the cynic — is that it gets the kids off the streets. They would be in the labor market if they were not in college. Recent studies on the unemployment of youth show that a phenomenal number are without jobs. You must ask: Do we have something for young people to do in our society? Or do they go to college because we do not know what else to do with them? If this is the case, then we raise very pertinently the question of faculty power diminishing and student power beginning to increase. What do I have to say to the student who wants to learn how to take children to the zoo which is better than what he wishes to do? What can I say to him that constitutes an educational structure?

I have my answers, but they are my answers. I do not know how much they are shared. Increasingly, when you pull away the graduate training and the discipline criteria, you are left with the fundamental philosophical question. What should education mean? It is not easy to say that it means economic virtue. It, however, does mean that as a matter of certification; you have to have a diploma. It is hard to say what one should get out of the college experience. A degree is something that is good to have, but why? We now face an issue that we have avoided for a long period of time because the faculties had enough power to make their definitions stick.

One now begins to see that it is a very different world than the one I moved into after I achieved Valhalla and got a Ph.D. The golden age is gone. On the one hand, people say it is a more challenging world, one full of great possibilities, a more interesting and exciting world than the one from which we have just come.

On the other hand, there is the remark made by the prisoner who was being hung in one of those great British festivals of the 18th century. All the crowds had come and brought their lunch to see the hanging. He was asked how he felt. He looked around at the cheering crowd as the noose was put around his neck and said, "Well, you know, if it weren't for the honor of it all, I would just as soon skip the whole thing."

About the Author

Joseph R. Gusfield received his Ph.D. degree from the University of Chicago in 1954. From 1947-1949, he was an assistant in the social sciences at the University of Chicago and then from 1949-1951, he was an instructor. From 1951-1955, he was Assistant Professor of Sociology at Hobart and William Smith Colleges. In 1955, he was appointed to the faculty of the University of Illinois, Champaign-Urbana. During 1962-1963, he was Fulbright Lecturer at Patna University, India. He then became Professor and Chairman of the Department of Sociology at the University of California, San Diego.

Part VIII.

A Critical Overview of Undergraduate Libraries

Part VIII: Introduction

As John R. Haak told the librarians attending the August, 1970 Institute on Training for Service in Undergraduate Libraries at the University of California, San Diego: " . . . the day finally dawns when the issue of the undergraduate library's effectiveness is raised, and the honeymoon is over."[1]

The preceding Parts VI and VII were the beginnings of evaluation of the undergraduate library. This final section brings together additional evaluations and critiques.

In addition to the two institutes which have been previously reviewed, a much earlier gathering of American and English librarians discussed common problems in library service for undergraduate students. In September, 1964, a deputation from the Association of Research Libraries met with the (British) Standing Conference of National and University Libraries in Hull, England. B.S. Page, Librarian of the Brotherton Library, University of Leeds, began by reading a paper on "Library Provision for Undergraduates in England" and Stephen A. McCarthy, Director of Libraries at Cornell University, spoke on "Library Provision for Undergraduates in the United States." Both papers are reprinted here.

Other individuals also began contributing substantial papers to the growing literature on undergraduate libraries, and the interested reader may want to pursue the following:

M.W. Moss, University Library, University of Keele, was the author of a major paper, "Library Service for Undergraduates," published in 1966 in *The Provision and Use of Library and Documentation Services,* edited by W. L. Saunders in the International Series of Monographs in Library and Information Science, volume 4.

Elizabeth Mills analyzed three undergraduate libraries — Lamont, Michigan and UCLA — and speculated on their futures in her article "The Separate Undergraduate Library," which was published in 1968.[2]

Many chroniclers of undergraduate libraries devoted themselves to tangible data such as architectural plans, seating, selection, audio equipment, and numbers of volumes circulated. Irene A. Braden also began to probe into the services of undergraduate libraries and attempted to evaluate them. Her dissertation was accepted in 1967 at the University of Michigan, but was not published until 1970.[3]

Robert H. Muller, then at the University of Michigan, discussed "The Under-graduate Library Trend at Large Universities" in *Advances in Librarianship,* vol. 1, edited by Melvin J. Voigt, in 1970.[4] Muller furnishes very detailed information on staff and salary costs, costs of operation, size of book space, and number of seats. He and Paula de Vaux compiled a selective bibiliography on undergraduate libraries which appears at the end of the paper.

Jerrold Orne, University Librarian, University of North Carolina, Chapel Hill, contributed "The Undergraduate Library," which also appeared in 1970.

The Director of Libraries, York University, Toronto, and formerly Acting Librarian of the Lamont Library at Harvard during the 1960-1961 academic year, Thomas F. O'Connell, argued in his 1970 article in the *Canadian Library Journal*[6] "that the undergraduate library is not necessarily the best answer to the problem of bigness" in a modern university library system.

During the same year, Redmond A. Burke wrote "The Separately Housed Undergraduate Library Versus the University Library" which appeared in *College and Research Libraries.*[7] He offered as an alternative to the undergraduate library "the bold assertion that a knowledge of the university library and its bibliographical operations and skill in making total use of it constitute a major discipline in the total curriculum. Each department could assume an obligation to develop this art of library knowledge and skill in its area."[8]

Of these seven contributions to the growing literature on undergraduate libraries, only the Moss paper and the concluding chapter from Braden's book are reprinted in this volume.

If 1970 seemed a vintage year for publication of articles concerning undergraduate libraries, 1971 was also significant because the entire May 1, 1971 issue of *Library Journal* was devoted to this special library. The issue contained:

1) a revision of John R. Haak's paper on goals and their determination and displacement which he presented at the Institute on Training for Service in Undergraduate Libraries (See Part VI for Haak's original paper;

2) Billy R. Wilkinson's adaption of his paper delivered at the July 1970 meeting of the University Libraries Section of the Association of College and Research Libraries at the Detroit Conference of the American Library Association (The original paper, "Are We Fooling Ourselves About Undergraduate Libraries?" is included below);

3) Karen Horny's "Building Northwestern's Core";

4) and a picture essay on "Barnard's Alternative Library."

In the issue's editorial entitled "Undergraduate Specialists," John Berry III writes that "we are seeing the development of yet another specialty within our profession — undergraduate librarianship."[9] He hopes that they will "provide a truly specialist service to that very special undergraduate clientele."[10]

These undergraduate specialists had surely understood the long article in the form of a letter to the 1969 readers of the *Wilson Library Bulletin* by Rick Kean which he entitled "Finding People Who Feel Alienated and Alone in Their Best Impulses and Most Honest Perceptions and Telling Them They're Not Crazy."[11] He seemed to be writing for many, if not all, undergraduate students when he concluded his "letter" with these paragraphs:

> I also have only a little to say about libraries. I have spent more time in Yale University's Sterling Memorial Library writing this article than I have spent there in the past three years. It was not an altogether unpleasant experience.
>
> When I think of libraries, I think of social theater. I think not so much of the massive problems of acquisition, categorization, storage, and retrieval, which must be very much at the heart of your professional concerns, but rather of the formats for learning that libraries present, the potentials for interaction they allow.
>
> I want to leave you with the flash I first had about libraries as I began to think about writing this article. The problem with libraries as I see them is that they seem to allow only two categories of behavior. If you know what you want, you can go in and get some help. If you don't know what you want, but just about anything will do, you can go in and quietly browse. If you find yourself somewhere in the middle — in that noisy, confused, irascible, fitty, and starty stage where you think you've got an idea but you're not quite sure you can explain it and that's not it but maybe this sounds right I'm not sure though and WOW — then to go to a librarian for help is often to feel you've committed an antisocial act. That's the one that puts me — and I think my generation — in a bind.
>
> I hope this has been helpful to you. I know it has for me. It has also been very difficult to write (it is now early in the morning of the third day past my deadline). I feel good about it — trying to tell you what I think by recreating the experience. It has opened a new dimension. I think I'll begin keeping a diary.
>
> Love, Peace and Liberation,
Rick Kean
New Haven
July 18, 1969[12]

More recently, Ellen Hull Keever, Reference Department, University of Alabama Libraries, has asked critical questions about these special libraries in her "Reassessment of the Undergraduate Library: A Personal Critique" which was published in 1973 in *The Southeastern Librarian*.[13] Her critique is reprinted as the final paper of the *Reader*.

James Davis, another perceptive contributor to both the undergraduate library movement and its literature (See Part VII for his "Coping — An UgLi Way of Life") has also recently published "The Changing Role of the Undergraduate Library in Universities" in *New Dimensions for Academic Library Service,* edited by E. J. Josey.[14] Davis concludes his paper with these words: "Undergraduate libraries are not a nostrum for many of the ills presently besetting academic libraries. Many undergraduate libraries have needlessly been established as unrealistic solutions to problems unrelated to service for undergraduate students. But judiciously conceived and properly supported, both administratively and fiscally, they can infuse all components of the community of an academic library with a new spirit of enthusiasm and interest."[15]

In 1978, Henry W. Wingate, University of Virginia, has asked a critical question in his "The Undergraduate Library: Is It Obsolete?" in the January issue of *College and Research Libraries*.[16]

Thus the undergraduate library saga, which began in 1608 with Thomas James who tried to talk Sir James Bodley into a separate library at Oxford for the "yonguer sort," or in 1907 with the establishment of the Columbia College Study in a classroom building on the Columbia University Morningside Heights Campus, or in 1949 with the opening of the Lamont Library in Harvard Yard, continues. The latest issue of the *UgLi Newsletter*[17] quite matter-of-factly states that there are "thirty-seven operating undergraduate libraries in the United States and Canada."[18] This *Reader* has been concerned with these special academic libraries and the staff members in them who serve the undergraduate clientele on university campuses.

Notes

1. John R. Haak, "Goal Determination and the Undergraduate Library," Institute on Training for Service in Undergraduate Libraries, Sponsored by the University Library, University of California at San Diego, August 17-21, 1970, p. 3.

2. Elizabeth Mills, "The Separate Undergraduate Library," *College and Research Libraries* 29 (March, 1968): pp. 144-156.

3. Irene A. Braden, *The Undergraduate Library* (Chicago: American Library Association, 1970).

4. Robert H. Muller, "The Undergraduate Library Trend at Large Universities," *Advances in Librarianship* Vol. 1, Edited by Melvin J. Voigt (New York: Academic Press, 1970), pp. 113-132.

5. Jerrold Orne, "The Undergraduate Library," *Library Journal* 95 (June 15, 1970): pp. 2230-2233.

6. Thomas F. O'Connell, "Undergraduate Library?" *Canadian Library Journal* 27 (July-August, 1970): pp. 278-282.

7. Redmond A. Burke, "The Separately Housed Undergraduate Library Versus the University Library," *College and Research Libraries* 31 (November, 1970): pp. 399-402.

8. Ibid., p. 402.

9. John Berry III, "Undergraduate Specialists," *Library Journal* 96 (May 1, 1971): p. 1551.

10. Ibid.

11. Rick Kean, "Finding People Who Feel Alienated and Alone in Their Best Impulses and Most Honest Perceptions and Telling Them They're Not Crazy," *Wilson Library Bulletin* 44 (September, 1969): pp. 36-44.

12. Ibid., p. 44.

13. Ellen Hull Keever, "Reassessment of the Undergraduate Library: A Personal Critique," *The Southeastern Librarian* 23 (Spring, 1973): pp. 24-30.

14. James Davis, "The Changing Role of the Undergraduate Library in Universities," *New Dimensions for Academic Library Service,* Edited by E. J. Josey (Metuchen, N.J.: Scarecrow Press, 1975).

15. Ibid., p. 73.

16. Henry W. Wingate, "The Undergraduate Library: Is It Obsolete?" *College and Research Libraries,* 29 (January, 1978): pp. 29-33.

17. *UgLi Newsletter* No. 10, December, 1976.

18. Ibid., p. 1.

B. S. Page

Library Provisions for Undergraduates in England

In September, 1964, a group of library directors from the Association of Research Libraries met with members of the (British) Standing Conference of National and University Libraries in Hull, England to discuss common problems. Among other matters, those attending discussed library service for the undergraduate students. This paper and the one following by Stephen A. McCarthy were presented to express the English and American approaches to the matter. Page concludes that the success of the separate undergraduate library depends on two things: ". . . it must be inviting and stimulating as a building, and it must have a special staff ready to interpret it to the undergraduate not as a substitute for the main library but as an extension of it designed for his special benefit."

"Library provision for undergraduates" I shall take to mean, first, book buying in relation to undergraduates, and secondly, administrative arrangements for the undergraduate in the library. I ought perhaps to state that the British point of view which I am about to present would appear slightly to the left of center if orthodoxy were measured, as it could very reasonably be measured, by the recent SCONUL submission to the University Grants Committee, Committee on Libraries — a document which I have naturally kept in mind as a standard and to which I shall appeal from time to time:[1] the divergence, in so far as it is significant, doubtless owes something to the fact that I am at present occupied with planning a separate undergraduate library building for the University of Leeds — a building which will, to the best of my knowledge, be the first of its kind to be opened in this country since 1939.

The year 1939 is a good year in which to begin. In or about that year the following sentence was written by a distinguished British university librarian: "It may be safely asserted that it is the aim of most university librarians to devote

SOURCE: From B. S. Page, "Library Provision for Undergraduates in England," *College and Research Libraries* 26 (May, 1965), pp. 212-222. Reprinted by permission of the author.

the minimum of expenditure to purchases which are only of interest to under-graduates in preparing for examinations, and to apply the great bulk of available funds to the acquisition of books and periodicals of a kind which assist research in as many fields as possible." The case would be stated rather differently now — less bluntly but still, I think, with a recognizable undertone of impatience; thus the SCONUL document says: "This Conference would wish to stress the fact that every extra copy of a students' textbook acquired by the library means one less additional work purchased by the library." The competing claims of research needs and undergraduate study needs are indeed acutely felt in our uni-versity libraries partly because library budgets are still grossly inadequate and partly because the British student has traditionally been expected to equip him-self with the books essential for his course of study. In the last quarter of a cen-tury the student population has grown enormously (almost fourfold in my own university), the student himself is more insistent on his claims, and the appeal of self-help is noticeably less prominent in society at large. Whatever we may think of these tendencies, it seems hardly likely that we can influence them, and most university librarians would now accordingly take the view that they were called upon to duplicate — by which of course I mean "obtain multiple copies of" — a considerable number of students' textbooks and recommended books of one kind or another. They would, however, still wish to assume that there was a nucleus of essential books which the student bought for himself.

Most students do in fact buy at least a modest number of books — this has been shown by several recent investigations — and those students who are sup-ported at the university by a state or local authority grant receive as part of this grant a sum of £30 a year for books, instruments, and materials, though nothing at all is done officially to ensure that the sum is used for the purpose intended. The SCONUL document says that "in some university libraries an attempt is made to encourage students to buy their textbooks by providing only reference copies of the books which students should buy for themselves." The difficulty in applying such an arrangement is to know precisely what are the books which students should buy for themselves; and therefore what is urgently needed is that members of the teaching staff should be persuaded always to indicate clearly both to their students and to the library which items on their reading lists they consider that the student should own and which he should obtain from the library. More interest in and more planning of students' reading by members of the teaching staff, and earlier and more continous cooperation between them and the library would obviate much wastage of money and effort; the library would know in general where and when the demand would be greatest, and in a particular case could decide whether to acquire additional copies or temporarily restrict the circulation of existing copies. Admittedly the library may itself be at fault in not doing more to organize this cooperation. In the meantime some uni-versity libraries are reducing the tension of which I spoke earlier — the tension between research needs and study needs — by having separate funds for the duplication of students' books and also by harnessing the departmental library in the cause of providing more copies for an ever-increasing student body.

I now turn to my other main topic — the undergraduate in the library. It is a part of an undergraduate's education to find his way about a large collection of books: few university librarians would, I imagine, dissent in principle from this statement. Is the inference then that the undergraduate has only to be let loose in a large library to find his reward unaided? Quite frankly, I used to think that it was. I now see two difficulties: first, a university library is normally designed for research as well as for undergraduate study, and a time comes when the number of undergraduate readers is so large as seriously to impede the use of the main collections and main services by the research scholar. The undergraduate takes over the reading room, and if he is allowed, takes over the stack; he appropriates (not unreasonably from his point of view) any accommodation within sight. The Yale University librarian's report for 1959 says — "We are continuing to look for, and adopt, measures which will care for both the undergraduate's need for a quiet place to study and the research scholar's need for ready access to our books and manuscripts and a quiet and orderly place in which to use them." My second difficulty is this: some students have the sort of intellectual curiosity which will enable them or rather compel them to make themselves at home in a large collection of books (these people of course are nature's librarians or researchers or both): but do most students really react in this way to a library of (to take a relatively low figure) half a million volumes? Do they not need a *point d'appui,* and do they not need also somebody strategically placed to give them guidance and stimulus?

If these two difficulties are genuine, there seems to be an undeniable case for having in a library of sufficient size with a student clientele of sufficient size a separate division for undergraduates. (Mr. Bowyer in his admirable article in the *Journal of Documentation*[2] says "a separate service," but I think that up to this point at least we should be in general agreement.) Separation does not of course mean segregation, and there is no thought of confining the undergraduate to a part of the library. On the other hand, as I have already intimated, one of the principal duties of the special staff of the undergraduate division would be to refer the undergraduate to the main collections. The SCONUL document warns of the danger that in "small undergraduate collections" the students will not venture outside their limits. But the less good student, whatever the library organization, will hardly venture even outside the limits of his prescribed reading unless he is actively encouraged to do so, and is he more likely to be encouraged in a functionally undifferentiated library or in one which provides a special service for his needs? The best student may be hampered by having to look for his material in two places, but no library can be so organized as to avoid this necessity altogether (even if it were desirable that it should). As to the size of the undergraduate collection, opinions differ. It has been said that a smaller collection, by showing its limitations, is better calculated to send the student elsewhere. It has also been said that a standard collection applicable to all libraries could be worked out by analyzing the demands of students in a particular library (this of course has a beguiling suggestion of economy, but suggestions of economy are in this context to be regarded with suspicion). My own belief is that standardization is not advisable (each library should build up its stock to meet its own conditions), that too small a collection looks dry and unappetizing and that there should be elbow room for browsing; if pressed to be more explicit, I should postulate that the size of the undergraduate collection should be adequate to give the undergraduate *qua* student an intelligible and attractive conspectus of the literature of each subject covered by the cirriculum. I say "the undergraduate *qua* student" because of course the undergraduate is or ought to be for part of his time an apprentice in research and for this purpose will clearly need to make use of the main collections.

Lastly — what is perhaps the most controversial issue — is a separate building desirable? I should doubt whether "desirable" is the right word. If the undergraduate division could be suitably planned in the main university library building, this might well be ideal. Separate buildings have usually, perhaps always, been the result of a space problem in the main library. Yet it would seem possible to make a very sizeable virtue out of this necessity. Clearly the undergraduate library must be near the main library and must communicate with it as directly and as comfortably as possible. Granted this, your separate building could have an appeal of its own: the undergraduate might come to have toward it "a proprietary feeling" (this is Mr. Wagman's[3] phrase) and might enter it more readily and more hopefully than if he approached it through the doors of the main library. With more students coming to our universities every year — many of them a different type of student not so much dedicated to the pursuit of knowledge in a specialized field as concerned with continuing their education for a further three years — the undergraduate library could conceivably be a powerful instrument in adapting the traditional values of a university to the needs of a new society. That of course is a large question, and outside my scope. The success of the separate undergraduate library from the practical point of view would depend very largely on two things: it must be inviting and stimulating as a building, and it must have a special staff ready to interpret it to the undergraduate not as a substitute for the main library but as an extension of it designed for his special benefit.

Notes

1. In 1963 the University Grants Committee appointed a committee "to consider the most effective and economical arrangements for meeting the needs of the universities and the colleges of Advanced Technology and Central Institutions for books and periodicals . . . " SCONUL in common with other professional bodies received from this committee a questionnaire covering most aspects of university librarianship, and its detailed reply to this questionnaire is the document referred to. This document is unpublished, but the brief quotations (which are included here by permission) are self-explanatory.

2. T. H. Bowyer, "Considerations on Book Provision for Undergraduates in British University Libraries," *Journal of Documentation* 19 (1963): 151-67.

3.   Mr. Frederick Wagman, Director of Libraries, University of Michigan, Ann Arbor.

About the Author

Bertram Samuel Page was educated at King Charles I School, Kidderminster and at the University of Birmingham. From 1931-1936, he was an Assistant Librarian and Sub-Librarian at the University of Birmingham. In 1935, he was a Rockefeller Fellow. From 1936-1947, he served as Librarian of King's College, Newcastle-upon-Tyne. In 1947, he was appointed University Librarian and Keeper of the Brotherton Collection, University Library, University of Leeds.

Stephen A. McCarthy

Library Provision for Undergraduates in the United States

For the occasion of this paper, see the abstract for the preceeding article by B. S. Page. McCarthy reviews briefly the historical background of undergraduate library service in the United States and points out that the separate undergraduate library has been only one approach to such service. He concludes that each institution must carefully "analyze its own needs and adopt or devise the best solution it can support."

Prior to World War II the common pattern of library organization and service in most American universities provided a central, general library which served faculty members, graduate students, and undergraduates. In most institutions there was also a system of departmental and college or school libraries which varied greatly in size and extent from institution to institution. Within the central library most of the services were common services; that is, they were intended to serve any member of the community who might have occasion to use them. In addition to the common core of services, there were certain services, such as interlibrary loan and rare books and manuscripts, which were primarily intended for and used by graduate students and faculty members; and there were other services, notably the reserve service, of which the heaviest use was made by undergraduates. In some relatively few institutions there were rather more specialized provisions for undergraduates. These might take the form of special reading rooms either within the central building or elsewhere which undertook to concentrate for convenient use by undergraduates those materials which were most frequently used. In some institutions these were perhaps not much more than a special reserve collection, but there were instances as at Columbia and

SOURCE: From Stephen A. McCarthy, "Library Provision for Undergraduates in the United States," *College and Research Libraries* 26 (May, 1965), pp. 222-224. Reprinted by permission of the author.

352

Chicago, where the college library included a small reference collection and supplementary and background reading material. Although there were these relatively few instances of special provision for undergraduates, it was generally true that the undergraduate found his library collection and services in the central library and as a part of the principal services of that library.

A major change in library service to undergraduates occurred with the opening of the Lamont library at Harvard in January 1949. The construction of a separate building designed to meet the particular needs of undergraduates and housing a collection chosen with the particular needs of undergraduates as the principal criterion of selection constituted a new and more positive attempt to provide high quality library service to undergraduates. Important as the Lamont library was in improving library service to undergraduates at Harvard, it seems probable that it may prove to have been even more important because of the new pattern of central library service which it established. In the years since 1949, in a number of universities, the provision of a separate building, either through new construction or through remodeling, to serve as the undergraduate or college library has occurred. Plans announced or under discussion in still other institutions indicate that the next ten years will see the creation of additional undergraduate or college libraries. Thus in a period of roughly twenty-five years, the single central library will have been replaced in a group of American universities by a two building central library, one of which will be especially devoted to service to undergraduates.

It should be immediately noted that although the separate undergraduate or college library has been adopted as the pattern of library service in a group of institutions, it has either not been considered or it has been rejected by others which provide central library service to the university community in a single building.

The separate undergraduate library has been regarded as a means of improving library service to undergraduates by giving them their own special facilities, a book and periodical collection chosen to meet their needs and a staff interested in providing library service to young college students. At the same time, the general or research library has been enabled to direct its attention and services primarily to the needs of graduate students and faculty and thus, it is assumed, has been able to provide improved service to these elements in the university community. Since both libraries are open to all students and faculty who wish or need to use them, no barrier is created by the division. Instead, it is hoped that use is facilitated by the nature of the collections and services and that easy transitions from one library to the other can be made as need arises.

Undergraduate libraries commonly are open-shelf libraries, with a series of reading rooms, group study rooms, alcoves and carrels, and facilities for typing, the use of microforms, and audiovisual materials. The organization tends to follow the traditional lines of circulation, reference, and reserve with modest provisions for periodicals and documents. In such buildings relatively little staff work space is required as acquisition and processing are normally carried on as part of the central operation.

In stocking the Lamont library, Harvard used a combination of library staff and faculty to select the volumes which comprised the basic collection. The published catalog of this collection has served as a guide in the formation of subsequent undergraduate collections with varying degrees of reliance. The shelflist of the undergraduate library at the University of Michigan has also been used as a guide. In most institutions that have formed undergraduate collections the effort has been made to enlist the assistance of the faculty in choosing the titles to be included.

The size of the collections in the undergraduate libraries has ranged from twenty to twenty-five thousand titles up to forty thousand and from thirty-five to fifty thousand volumes. The expressed intention has been that these collections would not exceed one hundred thousand volumes or one hundred twenty-five thousand volumes. When this size is reached, it is planned that the collections will be weeded and thus kept at an approximately stable figure.

Up to this point it has not been noted that in each institution that has provided an undergraduate library there was serious need of additional library space. The undergraduate library has provided some of the needed space. The plan once adopted can be rationalized as a good, or a superior, means of rendering library service to undergraduates. It can be that. Approached in another way it can be argued that when book collections and the number of readers to be served become very large, it is desirable to break up the collections and the readers into smaller, more manageable units. The undergraduate library is one plausible way of making such a division. It is also apparent that for a given institution this device may provide an economical solution to a difficult capital funding problem. Regardless of the rationalization or explanation one may prefer to use, it seems likely that as enrollments continue to increase and as book collections continue to grow the separate undergraduate library will provide an attractive and useful form of decentralization of the central library service for many large institutions.

It should be clear, however, that not all American university librarians regard the undergraduate library as the best means of serving undergraduates. Direct expodure to a large book collection, not one especially selected for him, is considered a valuable educational experience for the undergraduate. This is best provided in a single central library in which undergraduates have access to the stacks.

Another approach, perhaps a new type, is exemplified in the new Notre Dame library in which the first two floors constitute the college library and the research library is housed in a tower stack. The college library is conceived as serving a broader function than service to undergraduates — it serves the entire university community with an openshelf collection of the more commonly used books. The user goes to the research stack when he requires less frequently used material. *Jrs & Srs resented, early, being kept out of the tower*

The experience of American university libraries in their growth and expansion *and were let go freely with a passcard signed by a teacher. The first 2 floors were ½ study area — with tables & carrels.*

indicates that there are various ways of providing library service to undergraduates and that in the varying circumstances in which institutions find themselves it is important for each institution to analyze its own needs and adopt or devise the best solution it can support.

About the Author

Stephen A. McCarthy earned his Ph.D. in library science at the Graduate School of the University of Chicago in 1941. He was Assistant Director from 1937-1941, Associate Director from 1941-1942, and Director from 1942-1944 at the University of Nebraska Library. In 1944, he was appointed Assistant Director of Libraries at Columbia University and served until 1946 when he was named Director of Libraries at Cornell University. In 1967, he became Executive Director of the Association of Research Libraries in Washington, D. C. and served until his recent retirement. He was a Fulbright Lecturer and Consultant during 1953-1954 in Egypt and has surveyed or consulted on numerous library projects, collections, and buildings.

M. W. Moss

Library Service for
Undergraduates

A British librarian places the undergraduate
library as developed in the United States in
perspective in relation to the broader context of
library service to the university community. He
also considers the various arguments defending
and opposing the establishment of the separate
undergraduate library. He concludes with a
review of possible future trends in undergraduate
library service in Great Britain against the background of planned expansion within British universities.

The separate undergraduate library has come to be widely accepted in America
as a principle of university librarianship, and new libraries of this kind are being
planned every year. The universities of Indiana, Chicago and Illinois, for example, are proposing to accept this solution to their library space problems and
other universities are considering it. Indeed, in preparing for the predicted peak
enrollments of 1970, some American universities are even contemplating the
development of separate campuses for undergraduates, each with its own
library.

Library provision on this scale is still a long way off in Britain, but interest in
undergraduate libraries is particularly relevant at the present time and likely to
become even more so if the present rate of expansion continues. Moreover, in
the autumn of 1964 the first effects of the post-war bulge began to be felt in the
universities. Allowing for differences in administrative and teaching methods,
much can be learned from American experiment and experience with this and
other types of library, and information could be extremely valuable for university libraries in this country, since a good deal of what applies to the American
university situation today could well be applicable here within the next 10 years
or so.

Library service for undergraduate students is a complex subject with very wide

SOURCE: From M. W. Moss, "Library Service for Undergraduates," in *The Provision
and Use of Library and Documentation Services,* edited by W. L. Saunders, International
Series of Monographs in Library and Information Science, Vol. 4 (Oxford: Pergamon
Press, 1966): pp. 85-113. Reprinted by permission of the publisher.

implications. The present study represents an attempt to place the undergraduate library in perspective in relation to the broader context of library service to the university community in general. This necessitates discussion of some of the origins of its development and its characteristics as typified by several such libraries which are already very well established in the United States. In addition to these general observations some consideration will be given to the various arguments generally adopted in order to defend or to oppose this type of library, as the case may be. Finally, possible future trends in undergraduate library service in Great Britain will be briefly reviewed against the background of the planned expansion of universities which is now well under way in this country.

The writer would like to express his thanks to the staff of the Sheffield and Liverpool University Libraries for obtaining useful material that was not readily available.

Some General Considerations on Undergraduate Library Service

The establishment of the separate undergraduate library within the last 20 years is the outcome of a variety of factors, some of which are particularly pertinent to the American university and college scene, but probably the most important of these is a long and growing awareness of the neglect of student needs in terms of book provision and library service in general. Since its first appearance on the American scene in the form of the Lamont Library at Harvard, the separate undergraduate library has come to represent,however controversially, a belief on the part of some librarians at least that the undergraduate reader has special needs of his own which can only be met satisfactorily with special facilities and a positive attempt to improve library service to this type of reader by providing the facilities which are thought to be necessary.

However, Harvard's Lamont Library, although perhaps the ultimate in undergraduate provision, is only one form of a service which over the years has been open to a diversity of interpretations, usually based on the size and scope of the institution concerned and the funds available. It is a tribute to Harvard that it was the first among the great American universities to attack this problem and that it did so, not under the pressure of increased enrollment, and not because circumstances forced it, but because it wished to improve library service to undergraduates despite the increasing demands of scholarship. It should be remembered in this connection that at Harvard the graduate students outnumber the undergraduates and that the Widener Library and the many branch libraries offer far more by way of library facilities than is available at most universities to serve much larger student bodies.

Thus Harvard was a pioneer in this respect and it was the Lamont gift that made it possible for not just a separate room but a separate building to be created. In the main, the American universities which followed Harvard's example in establishing a separate undergraduate library seem to have done so first and foremost under the pressures of local needs and circumstances rather than of any obligation to the student body, although it is those very needs and circumstances which have helped a good deal in focusing so much thoughtful attention on the problems of undergraduate library provision. These circumstances naturally vary considerably from institution to institution and it is not surprising, therefore, that even when one bears in mind that financial resources too are not very evenly distributed, librarians themselves have adopted a variety of solutions to what many now regard as the same basic problem.

In consequence, as is not uncommon, much of the theory of undergraduate library service has tended to follow rather than precede the practice and some of it has little or no bearing on current developments. It is difficult, therefore, to speak of a concept in relation to undergraduate library service in any but the broadest terms. In addition to the evidence of different approaches to the problem, the matter is further complicated by the fact that many teaching staff and a number of university librarians have grave doubts as to the wisdom of making special separate provision for undergraduate students, whether on one floor in the main library or in a completely separate building.[1] These librarians and university teachers feel that the work each is trying to carry out for the benefit of the undergraduate would be seriously hampered if special provision were made for the students, that the separation of students into graduate and undergraduate is a formal, institutional issue, and that the use of libraries should be independent of the status of the student. There is also apparent the fear that the student would lose much of the value that comes with the complete facilities of the main collection. These are all valid objections which warrant examination and will be discussed at a later stage.

Two brief examples may serve here to indicate different approaches to the problem of serving a large student population. The construction of the Michigan Library in 1958 with a bookstock of about 100,000 volumes represents one attempt to meet the special needs of the undergraduate. Here a separate building with a carefully selected student collection is provided. The construction of the Fondren Library at the Rice Institute in Texas several years earlier represents an entirely different approach to the problem, dictated, of course, by entirely different local circumstances. At Rice all library holdings, comprising some half million volumes, have been housed in a single building and no distinction whatever is made between undergraduate and research collections. Both of these decisions were made deliberately after considerable study of the needs of the different institutions.

In Great Britain there is nothing at present of the nature or scope of the Michigan Undergraduate Library, for example, but separate undergraduate reading rooms exist at Glasgow, Liverpool and Oxford, and the undergraduate reading room equipped with a good working collection and housed within the main library building is becoming increasingly common. These are all rather extreme examples and the comparison between British and American undergraduate provision is hardly a fair one, but in spite of the tendency to work out the problem in terms of the unique needs of each institution, some consideration of the modern university and the practices and experience of its library may help to provide certain common denominators of value in assessing the nature and purpose of the undergraduate library as it is known today.

Discussion of the advisability of special libraries for undergraduates appears earlier in the literature of librarianship than one might suppose. As long ago as 1608 when Thomas James was appointed to Bodley's Library, he suggested the establishment of an undergraduate library to help the younger students. But Sir Thomas Bodley was opposed to the idea, and in a letter to James he pointed out that another keeper would be needed and that books used by the younger students might also be required by the more senior students at times. He concluded by saying that he believed there was much to be said against such a library.[2] The matter rested there for many years until the Radcliffe Camera, the building near the Bodleian which it had occupied since 1749, was finally attached to the Bodleian itself as an undergraduate reading room.

In the seventeenth and eighteenth centuries when there was only a handful of universities in Britain, the chief duty of librarians seems to have been the preservation of the scholarly collections from theft or loss, and the emphasis in the university library was very much on advanced study and research, since this was the gauge by which a university and its library had come to be judged. This marked emphasis upon research and conservation as being the prime functions of the university library persists to the present day, and not only affects the service offered by the university library but also makes no allowance for the social revolution which has taken place in British universities since the end of the last war. Even with the establishment of a number of provincial universities in the late nineteenth and early twentieth centuries, the history of British university librarianship is marked by constant underestimating of rate of growth and student numbers in terms of library buildings, and by little or no allowance for different and changing patterns of university teaching and library use. A major result of this failure to keep pace with educational developments is the general inadequacy today of university library buildings, book collections and service to readers. Only now with the growing awareness of present and long-standing deficiencies and the very real possibility that in the near future a re-examination of commonly accepted ideas and attitudes will be called for are steps gradually being taken to remedy the shortcomings apparent at all levels of university library service, and particularly at the all-important undergraduate level.

In the United States, although university teaching, administrative methods and student habits are different in some ways from those in Britain, many of the problems which have been and are being resolved there are results of the pressures of conditions and needs which this country's university libraries also will probably have to face in the not-too-distant future. Not the least of American university problems is the accommodation of rapidly increasing student numbers and the maintenance of a good library service for them, in addition to meeting the considerable demands of teaching staff and graduate students. This dilemma has been a familiar one to American university librarians for many years, and it is the undergraduate library which has been one of their most important means of attempting to resolve it. To some extent, therefore, since Britain has at present nothing in the order of a Lamont or Michigan student library, we must rely upon the practical experience of foreign precedent with certain reservations, and the full significance of the undergraduate library is perhaps best appreciated in the broad American context. If one can speak of a concept in relation to the development of the undergraduate library, the Americans have at least interpreted that concept in their own way according to their circumstances and have translated it into practical terms during the past 15 years.

American university libraries remained small until well into the nineteenth century, but have developed rapidly since then, particularly during the last 30 years. They have sought means of providing for research within the main library and space within the library for teaching and research to be carried out in close connection with books. A new library for the Johns Hopkins University in Baltimore, opened in 1914, is regarded by many as the starting point of modern university library planning since it was the first real attempt to elaborate a plan in accordance with the functions of the library. It provided a series of rooms for teaching departments adjacent to the stack on each side and communicating with its appropriate sections, and a general reading room across the end of the stack and also in direct communication with it. A year later, in 1915, Harvard opened its Widener Library which was the first to provide "carrels" or study cubicles in the stack itself. A large number of American university libraries were built in the following 15 years or so and the various principles of planning which gradually emerged form a good deal of experimental design included the segregation in a "reserved reading room" of large numbers of junior students doing their prescribed reading.

In Britain during the 1930's a number of universities had undergraduate reading rooms which were usually merely a room set aside for students who were carrying out their own reading but not consulting library books, as, for example, at Bedford College, London. Generally speaking, these rooms were housed in the main library building, though at Oxford and Glasgow they were separate, and while some contained a "general collection" or a "small selection of current books", others contained no books whatsoever and the student was more or less left to his own devices. If such collections were provided they were thought of almost entirely in terms of prescribed reading material or "the most wanted books". Moreover, librarians came to realize that a large number of these students using their libraries did not consult the books on the shelves but came only for their own study because they had nowhere else to go where they could read their notes or their own books, and this encouraged some librarians to provide reading rooms without any books, not only to cater for this type of student use of library facilities, but also as a means of preserving the hard-pressed library itself very much more for those who needed it for advanced study and research. This development is quite understandable in the circumstances, for if the undergraduate was not permitted to enter the stacks and made no use of any books available to him, there was little or nothing to justify his presence in the library in terms of the limited approach to library service for undergraduates at this time. In the United States, too, the provision of separate rooms or halls for undergraduate reading, although sometimes stocked with a reasonable number of books and placed in close proximity to the appropriate teaching departments for the convenience of users, was still largely a concession to neglected students and a means by which heavily burdened university libraries, greatly in need of extension, could find some measure of relief from the sheer pressure of student numbers.

Some idea of the approach adopted by librarians to student library service and their concept of the function of the university library can be obtained from the following statement which was contributed to a report on a survey of libraries made by the Library Association during the years 1936 to 1937. "It is not the librarian's primary function to cater for the needs of those who do not wish to use his collections, although, as has already been indicated, some so-called 'reference rooms' are tending to become mere reading rooms."[3]

However, if this seems an oversimplification of the state of undergraduate library service before, and indeed after, the last war, it must be remembered that even those librarians who were keenly aware of the need to improve their service to students were greatly compromised not only by their very definite obligations to the university, its teaching staff and graduate students for building as good a research collection as possible, but also by the constant stringency of financial resources which made even these important obligations virtually impossible to carry out to the full.

On the realization by the Americans during the 1930's that university libraries were favouring their senior classes of users with such devices as closed stacks, carrels, extended borrowing privileges for seniors and often small specialized branch libraries with restricted use, all at the expense of the intellectual development of the average undergraduate, some attempt was made to redress the balance by establishing browsing rooms, various types of better-stocked reading rooms, and also reserved reading rooms containing multiple copies of a few thousand books in very heavy demand which could be borrowed for a very short period only or not removed from the library at all. While representing a step in the right direction, it could hardly be said, however, that these devices represented an adequate effort to provide good overall library service to the undergraduate student body.

But clearly the university has an obligation to offer its undergraduate students the opportunity of acquiring a sound education. They usually comprise by far the largest section of the university's population, and after all, they are the potential graduate students and teaching staff as well as the future professional and civic leaders of the community. As one American librarian put it a few years ago: "A university which recognizes no obligation to these students is dishonest in accepting their money and their time."[4] As has already been said, the excellence of a university library has traditionally been measured by the strength of its research collections, and by the early 1950's many American librarians were ready to admit that this emphasis upon the acquisition of materials necessary for research was one of the major contributory factors in the neglect of the needs of the undergraduate over the years. The small American college library, realistically aware that it could not attempt to provide research material, in concentrating upon the best possible integration of the library with the academic programme of its institution was in fact fulfilling its responsibilities to the undergraduate much more successfully in many cases than the more renowned library of the larger university. Moreover, the lack of adequate library facilities, together with large student enrollments, gradually lead to the lecture-plus-textbook method of teaching and to the development of an examination system that determines the manner in which students study. Students quickly learn that the best way to study for the type of examination papers set is to confine one's reading to the assignments and to do the reading shortly before the examination. This causes library use to be largely confined to a few titles and to a few days in the term. Study of attendance records in American university reserve rooms has shown this practice to be extremely widespread.[5]

Large lecture classes breed impersonal student-teaching staff relations and seem to make students liable to resist the efforts of the faculty to teach. Lecturers are sometimes heard to complain that the vast majority of their students have no interest in learning and have declined in quality. Others recognize the unwillingness of the student to learn, but attribute this to the failure of the university to offer an interesting and demanding curriculum rather than to lack of ability in the student. In many cases the scepticism of the lecturer towards his students may be met by a growing scepticism on their part towards his lecturing ability and recommended reading, and the university librarian will very swiftly become aware of the resulting strain and conflict.

As a result of this highly unsatisfactory state of affairs, university libraries and instruction methods became the focus of keen attention among university librarians, and serious efforts began to be made to take into account the teaching as well as the research needs of the university, the aim being to make possible the fuller use of the library as a tool for instruction. This concept of the university library has been widely held in America for many years, and in some ways the undergraduate library is esentially an extension of it, but most British university libraries are only just beginning to feel that it is a function within their sphere of influence.

In America the increasing occupation with the teaching function of the library and the attempt to balance the trend in intensive specialization by introducing more general material of the kind associated with liberal arts studies led to the establishment or improvement of undergraduate reading room collections, browsing rooms, reference service and the general availability of books themselves. The problems of undergraduate library service were now arising essentially from the inclusion of the libraries' mass instructional and special research services in a single building. Most of the older and larger American university libraries were fixed architecturally and could not often overcome the limitations of their design. Thus, at a time when the ratio of number of readers per book was rising at a faster rate than ever before, libraries were finding it extremely difficult to enlarge central libraries sufficiently to handle these students.

In addition to main buildings being physically inadequate for satisfactory service to both undergraduate and research student, there was a growing feeling that a number of other characteristics of the large university library were totally unsuited to the needs of the undergraduate reader. These characteristics merit some consideration here since the awareness of them has exerted considerable influence upon the nature and scope of the undergraduate library itself.

The first feature of the university library which is regarded as being unable to function efficiently in relation to the undergraduate user is the sheer bulk of the book collection. This is not so applicable to British universities at present, but in America there are at least twenty-five universities with a bookstock in excess of 1 million volumes and almost as many more with a stock of half to three-quarters of a million volumes. Many librarians believe that it is no service to the undergraduate student with a problem to solve or an essay to write, particularly to the first-year student, to turn him loose among a huge collection which, in any case, consists largely of research materials. They argue that his needs are best met with a collection of material prescribed by lecturers together with a good selection of standard works and alternative treatises to cover his supplementary needs, maintaining that to offer anything much larger at this stage probably confuses and daunts rather than helps him, especially if, as is all too frequently the case, he has come up from a school which had no library worth the name, and from a home where books and reading were not regarded as an integral part of life. This latter point may be a very significant one in view of the very wide variety of social backgrounds from which today's students come when entering university. Moreover, there is some evidence, in British universities at least, that students' first experience of the library is a mildly traumatic one and that they tend to be overawed by its resources.[6] Equally, it may be argued that if freshmen find the university library "intimidating" when they first enter and attempt to use it, it may be not so much the library's size but rather their inability to find their way about and exploit its resources which is responsible, in which case the answer would seem to lie in librarians and teaching staff co-operating more closely in educating students in the use of the library.

Another feature of the large university library, considered to make it unsuitable for undergraduate use and allied to the one just mentioned, lies in the nature of the book collection itself. It is characteristically a research collection, and as such it contains a far greater variety of books on every subject than any undergraduate could possibly have been accustomed to previously through his school and public library. Some of these books are by competent authors and some are not. Some are general treatments of a subject and some are intensive studies of a highly specialized aspect of a field of knowledge. Some are authoritative and lasting statements, while others may already have been superseded by numerous other titles, all of which have been collected by the library in the interests of scholarship. A great many items have no immediate historical, literary, critical or synthesizing value but have been acquired as the raw materials for future research, and the reasons for their presence in the collection may be fully appreciated only by the scholar or librarian.

Furthermore, teaching staff today cannot afford to build personal collections, as they did a generation ago, and quite naturally lean heavily on the library for their book and journal needs. Expansion in student numbers entails a corresponding increase in the numbers of staff, and as each newly appointed member of staff brings with him his own special research interest, which must be catered for both retrospectively and currently, the cumulative burden upon the library's book funds becomes extremely severe. It is also maintained that while inter-library lending causes the research student to suffer constant frustrations and delays in obtaining required material, so, too, does the practice of permitting large numbers of undergraduates to have direct access to the stacks and to borrow from them. Evidence of the extent to which this is true is extremely difficult to come by, but the increasing emphasis laid upon independent investigation by undergraduates, especially in their final year, and the growing distinction, particularly in America, between research and non-research degrees for graduate students is resulting not only in the undergraduate using more graduate books, but the graduate using more undergraduate books.

However, in spite of these basic problems it may be argued on educational grounds that the freshman should be educated to use a large research collection from the start of his university career, not only so that should he eventually decide to undertake research he will be reasonably well equipped to handle the library's full resources, but also so that he might develop during these undergraduate years a sound sense of judgement in collating the investigations of others and in the weighing up of opinion.[7]

Leonard Jolley conveys the importance of this experience very clearly in the following words: "Perhaps the most important lesson the student can take away from his university career is to have learned to treat books not as sources of authority but as instruments to think with and this is a lesson which cannot be imparted in the lecture theatre but must be slowly and painfully acquired by daily toil in the library."[8]

Another characteristic of the large university library likely to discourage rather than encourage its use by undergraduates is the nature of the catalogue. As this provides the key to these huge and varied collections, it may of necessity be so large and so complex that it simply serves to hamper the students' efficient use of the collections. A number of surveys of library use by undergraduates carried out in British universities, for example, show a marked reluctance on the part of students to use the catalogue except as a last resort, and a general tendency for them to rely on a sense of location and to go directly to the shelves to search for what they require.

This unsystematic and time-wasting method of approach caused the Lamont Undergraduate Library to decide from the beginning to reduce bibliographical detail in its catalogues to a minimum so as not to form a barrier between student and books.

A further feature of the university library likely to deter undergraduates and which is far more relevant to the American situation at present than to the British, where a good deal of scope for development exists, is the question of reference staff. Qualified advisory staff, who normally might be expected to help the undergraduate overcome some of the difficulties already named, may be so occupied in meeting the demands of the graduate students and teaching staff that undergraduate needs are either ignored or given cursory attention. Also, the kind of staff assembled for research library purposes is not necessarily the kind of staff that can work most effectively with younger students. At Harvard, before the establishment of the Lamont Library, it was found that undergraduates, on the one hand, and graduates and teaching staff, on the other, were all competing in the Widener Library for reference service and that it was invariably the case that the student or teacher engaged on research monopolized the service at the expense of the undergraduate. In consequence, care was taken to ensure a readily available reference service for undergraduates when the Lamont Library was planned.[9] The real function of such a service is to assist the self educator, to train the student to train himself, and the staff must always be available to give assistance to the student at each successive stage towards the full bibliographical control of his subject.

Finally, considerations of size both in terms of holdings and of student numbers usually make it expedient for the large university library to close its stacks to undergraduates, thus depriving them of free access to books. Similar considerations frequently lead, particularly in the United States, to the establishment of reserve book rooms and other devices that may not be educationally satisfactory. In the past, if the stack has been open at all to readers, it has in the main been for the research worker on account of the obvious advantages of enabling him to work in close proximity to his material. The stack was thus considered the place of study for the research worker, and it was argued that while stack books were available to all who applied for them, indiscriminate access to the shelves would simply defeat its own ends in a large university. However, since the Second World War almost all the newer British and American university library buildings have provided open stacks, and some of the older libraries, such as Northwestern in the United States, have opened theirs. The chief argument for this practice is the belief in the widening of the student's academic interests resulting from browsing and direct contact with books and in the discouraging of his heavy reliance upon textbooks and prescribed reading for his work. This ready accessibility of books to students was one of the main objectives in setting up the Lamont Library and was assured by the basic plan of the building with its open alcove-type stacks standing between the entrances and the reading areas.[10] Shelving the majority of required reading on open shelves has the advantage of enabling undergraduates to help themselves, and shelving these books with the rest of the collection has the added advantage of continuously acquainting the student with other books on the same subject. In such circumstances browsing among books should become a part of the daily student routine and this leads to scanning books that catch the eye, and thus the reading habit is launched.

Given, of course, that national libraries must maintain closed stacks, the arguments against open stacks in university libraries apply mainly to those with huge and valuable research collections such as the Bodleian Library, though open stacks have several practical implications which should not be overlooked. For instance, there is the inevitable cost of keeping shelves in order, the possibility of annoyance to research workers with carrels in the stack, and the obvious disadvantages of reliance on the classification system as a guide to resources. Local conditions, methods of administration, physical facilities and the habits of students are elements that must also be considered in this question. Nevertheless, in discussing this same problem over 20 years ago, a British university and college library manual probably arrived at the most reasonable conclusion when it stated:

> If once it is established that the open stack benefits many (and probably most) readers while handicapping none, the administrative drawbacks can hardly be considered important. It is true that books will be frequently misplaced and that from time to time large moves will have to be undertaken but these objections apply hardly less to reading rooms, and must in any case be outweighed by the interests of readers.[11]

The Undergraduate Library

The various difficulties, already discussed, which are encountered by the average undergraduate student when he attempts to use a university library of even moderate size are frequently used as the basis of arguments in favour of the undergraduate library, whether comprising an entire floor of the main library or a completely separate building, and correspondingly they have influenced, perhaps dictated, the general conception of such a library. They are, however, largely practical considerations related to the contention that in some situations the problem of providing adequate physical facilities for library service to undergraduate students may be solved most efficiently and even economically by a separate building. On the whole the larger, older and poorly designed or inflexible library buildings are the ones which tend to find themselves in this predicament. Both shelf space and reading space are at a premium, and efficient library service to the student community becomes increasingly difficult, if not impossible, to maintain as demands upon stock and library staff grow progressively heavier. Because limited funds often make it impossible to buy multiple copies of books, to give them shelf space and to provide adequate reading space for the students, the teaching staff have no option but to rely more and more on textbooks for the course work. At Michigan, for example, before the opening of its undergraduate library in 1958, this kind of situation made it quite possible for a student to spend 4 years as an undergraduate at the university without once entering the general library building.[12]

The other justification for special provision for undergraduates is more theoretical and relates to the role of the library and the librarian in the education of the undergraduate student. If the latter seems more difficult to defend, the cause may be an unconscious, perhaps even conscious, diffidence on the part of librarians regarding their own importance for the educational process. However, as one American librarian has written: "A university education should awaken a student's curiosity and train his mind to enable him to continue educating himself throughout his lifetime. If the habit of reading is to be acquired at university then every opportunity in that direction must be made attractive. In this the library can exert leadership."[13]

The inadequacies of existing library facilities can also have a serious effect on the service provided for graduates and teaching staff, since if undergraduates turn to specialized departmental libraries for their needs, these libraries, which are frequently designed almost wholly for the convenience of research workers, immediately have a divided function. In any case, the idea of providing a series of scattered undergraduate departmental reading rooms is usually rejected on the grounds that none of them would contain an adequate collection or provide satisfactory service for its users and that the cost of setting up such a network would go far towards paying for a much more effective library for undergraduate use. When the Lamont Library was still in the planning stage, Keyes Metcalf stated that one of its main objectives was "To concentrate as far as is practicable the library service for undergraduates in a central location",[14] the general idea being that by concentrating the books and other materials needed by the undergraduates in one building, by providing as many copies of each book as are needed, and by employing an energetic staff to work intelligently with both faculty and students, it should be possible to bring the library in closer contact with the students' course work and the interests aroused in the lecture room, and to induce the students to give more attention to books that exercise the intellect and the imagination. Such a library with its accent entirely upon service to undergraduates would afford teaching staff much greater freedom in shaping their courses as they should, and also serve as an intellectual centre for the undergraduate student body.

Although it may seem to be a means of transforming necessity into virtue, the undergraduate library represents a positive and painstaking effort to correct the various deficiencies in library service to students which have become painfully apparent over the years. It means a library building specifically planned and administered to be of maximum benefit to undergraduate students, based on the premises that the library should be as important as the lecturer in undergraduate education, the one complementing the other, and that any undergraduate may realize his potentiality for developing a life-long interest in reading good books and in continued self-education long after his university career is over if the library assists him and makes the whole process attractive. The undergraduate library thus seeks to introduce the student to books, to lead him to form good reading habits, to assist him with his set work and to teach him really to use the library to the full.

The siting and planning of the undergraduate library will, of course, vary a good deal from university to university, and are largely governed by local circumstances, but one or two general remarks may be made on these aspects. While existing buildings may make it impossible for the undergraduate library to be the geographical centre of the university, it should certainly be the intellectual centre of the undergraduate community and be sited as strategically as possible in relation to the various teaching departments, particularly those of the humanities and social sciences which are likely to use it the most by the very nature of their work and its heavy reliance upon books rather than equipment. It is also desirable that the undergraduate library building is located in close proximity to the main university library, since it is generally agreed that the undergraduate should not be restricted to his own library, and it is hoped that his experience in the undergraduate library will encourage him to make advantageous use of the research collections. He should be welcomed at all branches of the university library system when he has a serious purpose in using them. Likewise, the proximity of the undergraduate library to the main research library has distinct advantages for scholars and teaching staff. At Lamont, for instance, periodicals are not allowed to leave the building and they are frequently consulted by scholars who find that the required volumes from the Widener Research Library are out on loan. The same applies to much of the apparently "standard" material at Lamont since its collection is far more than a student textbook collection. This overlapping of use between the undergraduate and main libraries, while obviously highly desirable in theory, could well produce numerous practical difficulties including serious interference with the essential function of each of the two libraries, so careful planning is needed to reduce such interference to a minimum and to strike a reasonable balance between the two.

The actual planning of the undergraduate library building will again vary according to existing conditions and the preferences of the librarian concerned as developments in the United States have shown, but there do seem to exist a number of important factors which should be taken into account in any situation. In these days of unparalleled growth of universities, declared as national policy, the first essential of any library building is flexibility. Modular planning can achieve this to a surprising degree allowing for expansion both outwards and upwards, for any necessary internal re-arrangements and for any modifications caused by shift of emphasis in the teaching pattern of the university. The internal layout of book stacks, study facilities and services will of course largely depend upon the planning of the librarian in conjunction with the architect. However, in recent years library building, planning and equipment have come to revolve around readers whose claims for materials and services are becoming increasingly heavy and varied. For instance, the proportion of the student population for which it is thought desirable to provide seats has tended to rise[15] and the allowance of square feet per person desirable in reading areas has gone up, especially where informal arrangement is intended. At the same time, it is generally agreed that access to collections must be easier than before. These standards have suggested larger capacities, and, more significantly, they seek to put users close to the materials they require. The guiding force behind all this spaciousness, comfort, ample study space and ease of access is the desire to encourage students to examine and use their study material at will, and, where desired, in consultation with their instructors or with librarians. As the idea has spread, great reading rooms have tended to become outmoded in favour of study cubicles and reading alcoves distributed throughout the book stacks, and reference departments have tended to be divorced from those that remain, while reserve book sections too have assumed less importance.

This stress upon availability of materials is reflected by the fact that the second main objective of Lamont, as seen by Keyes Metcalf, was simply "to make books readily accessible to the students".[16] This was achieved in Lamont's case by the basic plan of the building which provides an alcove-type stack through the centre, open on one side to the major reading areas and on the other to the entrances, the reference room and special collections. Users of the library, almost as often as they enter, move from one room to another, or leave, can hardly avoid passing through corridors or alcoves lined with books. Availability implies not only open shelves but a minimization of all other barriers between readers and books. In the context of the undergraduate library, enormous catalogues such as those used in the great research libraries are invaluable keys for scholars, but are necessarily so complex that they are deemed discouraging and time-consuming barriers to undergraduates, and at Lamont, Minnesota and New Mexico the catalogue is small in physical proportions and the cataloguing itself is kept to a minimum. Moreover, facilities are provided for by-passing it wherever possible in the form of visible indexes of reserved books, annotated copies of reading lists and at Lamont a simplified classification system based upon Dewey.

The general problem of reserve books exists in most academic libraries but is particularly relevant to the undergraduate library. Every undergraduate library will have to keep a certain number of heavily used books on reserve, but this number should be kept to an absolute minimum and as many books as possible shelved with the main open-shelf collection. Close cooperation between teaching and library staff in deciding which books to reserve and for how long should help to assure fuller use and circulation of the general collection. In order for the library to function smoothly in relation to student assignments, it is important for it to have in good time lists of required course readings, and if these are provided early enough, the library is in a position to obtain titles not already owned, to procure additional copies, or to replace those which may be lost or missing.

Changing objectives of the university, or at least changing methods of achieving these, have offered the library an increasingly significant place in the education of the undergraduate. This has not been primarily because of the development of courses in general education, with their aim to provide a broad and common intellectual experience at the university level, but rather because of the efforts to engage students actively in learning for themselves. Lectures, textbooks and examinations have been supplemented by methods of challenging students to take a larger share in their education.

If sensitivity and reflection and the ability to analyze and to judge are to be fostered at university, both lecturer and student must turn to books that encourage them to think and to feel for themselves. They must investigate primary and secondary sources where originality of thought and expression may be encountered.

This emphasis upon undergraduates' use of books other than textbooks makes the reserve collection totally inadequate for them. In America, and increasingly in Britain, the library has been and seems likely to continue to be primarily responsible for providing the duplicates necessary in courses that do not rely on textbooks and anthologies but seek to take the student to original works in as close to the original form as possible. This has brought about the expansion of student collections in both size and scope.

The undergraduate library should hold books on open shelves in sufficient quantity to reflect the entire undergraduate curriculum, including books of general interest.[17] Books, here interpreted in the widest sense, preferably should be brought together not by format and process but by content and idea to serve groups of related departments of instruction. The collection of the undergraduate library is formed to meet most of the needs of the undergraduate student and usually comprises an extensive open-shelf collection of reserve books, collateral readings, the main periodicals in each field, bibliographies, reference works, and a careful selection of books for general cultural and recreational reading which is often housed separately. It has been suggested that the collection be "an ideal collection roughly comparable to the library of a truly cultivated man", with its own simplified catalogue, its own librarian and its own reading area.

The University of Michigan, for example, intends to build up its undergraduate collection to somewhere between 100,000 and 150,000 volumes, allowing for necessary duplication and then to maintain it at that level with careful and systematic weeding.[18] It is important that such a collection should never be considered as completed. Special funds must always be available for continued experimentation with new books to fill gaps, to replace obsolete or unsuitable material, to add better translations, better editions, and more up-to-date secondary works, and, in general, to effect changes according to the pattern and emphasis of the teaching programme. The available reading must not be fixed or restricted in any way if courses and teaching staff are to remain vigorous and stimulating. As has already been said, the bulk of the collection should be readily accessible to students with only specially assigned books on very heavy demand placed on overnight reserve to enable them to circulate as widely as possible in a limited period.

Another important feature of the undergraduate library is the reference service. Intelligent and sympathetic reference staff are a great asset in such a library since their efforts are focused on a definite clientele, with whose projects and problems they can become familiar. Reference advice can suggest where and how to find works on one's subject and what books and articles may possibly be helpful, but not usually, one would think, exactly what to read, as this is duplicating the effort of the teaching staff. It is not so much finding facts and answering questions for inquirers which is the primary task, although many such queries have to be answered, but the reference staff should aim through the inquiries made to educate the student to help himself. To this end a substantial collection of bibliographies and reference books is required on the open shelves, where they are accessible to both staff and students. It is important for this collection to be as comprehensive as possible since, as the Director of the University of Michigan Library has said: "The problem of helping a student halfway to an answer and then referring him to the General Library for additional assistance becomes intolerable in practice if not in theory."[19] The opening of the Lamont Library at Harvard made reference service more readily available to undergraduates than it had been in the Widener Library where faculty members, visiting scholars and graduate students tended to monopolize it. After the library had been subjected to 12 months' use it was noticed that there had been a gradual but distinct rise in the number and quality of reference questions and the rise has continued steadily since then. It is hoped that this will continue as students develop the habit of turning to librarians for bibliographical help.[20]

Careful introduction of freshmen to the library is particularly important, as are introductions to the layout of the stacks and of the reserves as well as to the catalogue, circulation practices and reference shelves. The professional librarian is constantly astonished to find how ignorant most students and many teachers are of the means of acquiring the knowledge they require. The process of finding things out demands skills which have to be taught and this must be pointed out. Thus the introduction of the student to the library is not something which is done once and for all. It is a continuous process which may well last beyond the student's university career and which becomes the more obviously valuable the longer it is carried on. These services are in accord with the general educational policy of encouraging students from the beginning to know and to use good books.

In spite of the difficulties and costs, the reason for having an undergraduate collection and library service, whether in the main library or completely separate, is the furtherance of student self-education and the university should recognize the relevant services as a necessary charge upon it for making possible the kind of education that it believes in and promises to offer. Undergraduates are no longer simply pupils, and the possibilities for intellectual initiative should not be postponed to the graduate stage or even to the final undergraduate year. Independent investigation (rather than research) by undergraduates is becoming increasingly common in both British and American universities, whether for a paper in an advanced course, for a special project or reading course, or as a requirement for an honours degree, and this is intended to further some of the main ends as seminar discussion based on challenging reading materials. In a more specialized and individual way it should encourage critically responsible inquiry and the capacity through analysis to formulate and to support conclusions. Such investigation must necessarily relate to a particular topic, usually in a special departmental field, and this reinforces the demands upon the undergraduate collection. As well as the fairly standard material already discussed, it is useful therefore to have a few of the leading specialized journals on hand for occasional articles, and, more important, for book reviews and bibliographical surveys. The student should become at least familiar with what these are and how they can serve both in exploratory reading in a field and in specific inquiry. It is unlikely that even the largest undergraduate collection by present standards would be able to cater for all the needs of the student engaged upon this kind of independent investigation and so he must be permitted to make use of the much greater resources of the main research library whenever the occasion demands. This is the case, for instance, at the Michigan, Lamont and Columbia undergraduate libraries.

The wide and consistent use of imaginative and thought-provoking books as instruments of education should, it is hoped, direct the interest of undergraduates beyond the completion of the assignment. If curricular and library services encourage first-hand acquaintance with creative and scholarly works through group discussion and individual inquiry and through open shelves and convenient arrangements for reading in and out of the library, librarian and teaching staff should anticipate, if these things are being well done, not only an increase in ability to read perceptively and discriminatingly but also curiosity and enjoyment in reading and in having books to read.[21]

In addition to the undergraduate library's provision of books and other material for curricular and general background reading purposes, the ease of access to its stacks, the facilities for overnight loan and reference inquiries, and ample reading space, devices for the encouragement of extra-curricular reading are also becoming an accepted library responsibility, especially in the United States. Such reading is usually housed in what is known as the "browsing room" with shelves of standard and recent literature, or in lounge-like comfort in a wing of a regular reading room with strategically placed shelves for new accessions or for a rental collection of contemporary fiction, drama, poetry and essays, for example. Conveniently placed shelves or stands for current journals or attractive and accessible periodical rooms may also further casual reading and the pursuit of special interests. Undergraduate reading of one kind or another may be encouraged to some extent by the smallest detail that makes any reader more comfortable and may be discouraged at least slightly by the mildest annoyance or smallest inconvenience. Hence the growing emphasis in recent years upon lighting, air conditioning, the use of colour and library furniture. Other features of the undergraduate library which are designed for the comfort and convenience of readers and which warrant serious consideration when such a library is being planned are typing cubicles, smoking areas and refreshment facilities.

Books are the staple of libraries, but more than books may be expected of them. Now that courses in the history and interpretative analysis of art and music are becoming common, attention is being given to provision for the first-hand acquaintance of students with works of the visual arts and music. Lamont, for instance, provides a number of special rooms where facilities for listening to music, poetry and drama related to various courses are made available. The Michigan Undergraduate Library includes a small multi-purpose room equipped with 200 stacking chairs, motion picture projectors, and public address system for use by the students for lectures, discussion groups, the showing of films, or "for any affair which concerns undergraduates and the library."[22] Librarians are by no means unanimously of the opinion that it is desirable to provide such rooms in a library, but a very reasonable case may be made out for these facilities as valuable adjuncts to the teaching programme, and if they are to be provided, it is perhaps preferable to centralize them as part of the general service to students in the undergraduate library where the appropriate reading materials are available. However, it may still be argued that libraries, on the one hand, and art and music departments, on the other, are natural alternatives and perhaps rivals for this responsibility, particularly if no special library for undergraduates exists.

The initiative of the librarian is needed to assist or encourage the teaching staff to make the library the center of study and of educational resources, at least in the humanities and social sciences. (A special problem is presented in the natural sciences by the power of laboratories to draw books away from the central library into departmental or special libraries.) He can certainly collaborate with lecturers in improving the book collections by making suggestions of purchases that will give better balance between areas in a field or will further a department's long-range plans for source materials or standard sets, for example.

Considerable tact may also be required to lead teaching staff and curriculum towards more reliance on the library and less on textbooks. The university librarian has more immediate acquaintance with the students' use of the collections than have most of the academic staff; but of greater importance for his influence is the rapport that he has established through his work with the library committee and with individual members of the teaching staff. He is clearly in a stronger position if he is a member of the various faculty committees, and stronger still if he does some teaching, though this rarely seems the case.

The presence of the undergraduate library on the campus has a number of other implications, most of which seem to be borne out by American experience at least. The most important and perhaps most obvious of these is its direct effect upon the students and teaching staff for whom it is intended. Without in any way curtailing the undergraduate's access to the great research collections, state universities like Colorado, Florida State, Michigan, Nebraska, New Mexico, Oklahoma and the municipal University of Cincinnati have shown that carefully selected and attractively housed undergraduate libraries have not only increased support for lecture-room instruction but have stimulated considerable voluntary reading, and in connection with the latter a revival of "lists of books every college graduate should have read" before receiving his degree is making its presence felt on the campus. Twelve months after it opened the Lamont Library reported that while borrowings from the main research library dropped only slightly during that period, the total for the research and undergraduate libraries combined was 37,000 volumes greater than the research library's figure for 1948 when Lamont was not yet available. Overnight borrowings for reserved books increased by almost 20% and undergraduate use of books within the library also increased substantially.[23] Centralization, because it brings greater convenience, undoubtedly contributed to these and other results as did the availability of books and the improvement of the book stock by increased duplication of heavily used titles. This duplication made it possible to restrict to closed shelves, which are behind the issue desks in Lamont, fewer reserved books than ever before. Closed reserves can probably never be abolished completely, but they can be reduced in number still further when student enrollments eventually become more steady and as more of the books that are needed come back into print.

Writing on the Michigan Undergraduate Library a few years ago, Dr. Wagman reported considerable increases in library use by students and in the amount of material read in the library and borrowed for home reading since its opening at the beginning of 1958. Analysis of the circulation for home use indicated that 37.7% represented voluntary reading and 62.3% was course-related. Further analysis of the course-related reading revealed that a very large part of this also was not required but apparently stimulated by the course work. Dr. Wagman continues:

> Other less measurable effects of the new library are noteworthy. It has definitely become the hub of undergraduate activity on the campus. Its central location has made it possible for the students to spend the hours between classes reading in the library and thousands of them do so. Many students are now using the library who confess that hitherto they had preferred the movies to the study halls and had rarely or never ventured into the General Library. Obviously, also, the undergraduates are reading a great many more good books than before and under the guidance of the reference staff, short-handed as it is, are learning how to use a library catalog, indices, bibliographies, and other reference works. Psychologically, the effect of this library on the students has been extremely gratifying.[24]

It was feared that free access to the reserve books would result in their rapid disappearance and, in fact, 1% of the total bookstock did disappear during one spring term, but since new regulations have been brought in regarding theft and mutilation of books, there are indications that book losses have decreased.

The vast majority of the teaching staff at Michigan understood the potential value of the new library before it was completed and it is now becoming apparent that their interest in using the library as an aid to their teaching has begun to exceed the library's ability to keep up. In short, as Dr. Wagman says, "Both building and staff have proved to be much too small."[25]

Another implication of the undergraduate library, stemming from the fact that it enables all student services to be centralized in one location, is the economies made possible by such special facilities. When Lamont was being planned it was claimed that costs were lower because simpler and cheaper cataloguing could be used for undergraduate books; undergraduates use an expendable type of book and by not mixing these with the less expendable type certain losses could be avoided; the library is in smaller units and expansion can be made without as much danger of over-expansion; and the type of service differs enough for staff differentiation to be a good idea. Taken as general statements these claims seem rather arbitrary and questionable, but when applied to a specific situation there appears to be a good deal of truth in them. Special undergraduate provision should also mean much easier communication with students and teaching staff and, in giving students some sense of independence and a proprietary feeling towards the library, should provide the type of personal library service which can be found where there is not the overwhelming pressure upon limited resources and staff which is likely to exist in a large university library system. Required seminars and final year dissertations for honours students undoubtedly result in more concentrated use of library materials, and any shift from the textbook method of instruction invariably puts additional demands upon the library.

Finally, the establishment of a separate undergraduate library does relieve demand upon central and departmental libraries and helps to release them for purposes of research. In his address at a Conference on the Place of the Library in the University, held in March 1949, Keyes Metcalf stated in order of importance the three premises on which the Lamont Library was planned. First, "The undergraduates will make more and better use of a library designed expressly for them", and then the practical considerations, "That this was the best way to relieve the pressure in the Widener building and make unneccessary a new central building; and that if the pressure were relieved, the Widener Library Building would become a more satisfactory research center than it has been in the past."[26]

Since the opening of Michigan's Undergraduate Library, its General Library and branch libraries have come to be used predominantly by graduate students and the teaching staff, as was anticipated. The stacks of the General Library have been opened to all and it also is now, for the most part, an open-shelf library. Graduate students are working in the General Library and the branches in much greater number than ever before, and it has become possible to adapt much of the space formerly employed for undergraduate reading rooms to special uses. The Reference Department and the branch librarians have more time to spend on service to teaching staff and graduate students and on bibliographic enterprises. It has also been possible to curtail the staff of the Circulation Department in the General Library despite the fact that circulation of books from that collection has not decreased.[27]

Little or no mention has been made so far of the existence of any opposition to the idea of the separate undergraduate library, and although the case in favour of such a library seems overwhelming and has, indeed, been argued far more frequently than the case against it, a number of valid objections have been raised from time to time and the subject has remained a lively and mildly controversial one. There are both librarians and teachers who remain unconvinced of the educational value of a separate facility for students, although almost all those who are familiar with the Lamont Library think it a successful operation. They argue, as stated earlier, that in principle there should not be a division into a scholars' library and a students' library, that the separation of students into graduate and undergraduate is purely arbitrary and a formal, institutional issue, and that the use of libraries should be independent of the status of the student. Recognition of this last point has led almost all American universities with an undergraduate library on the campus to permit and to encourage undergraduates to use the main research library for material which their own library does not possess.

It is also pointed out[28] that if good undergraduate libraries are provided, a large percentage of students may never seek to use the general library and will be the poorer for it. There are some students who will one day be university teachers and there are others whose way of life may lie in other directions but who are not content with books selected for them, who like to look into sources and test statements, who are interested in other matters than their course of study, and these should be allowed freedom to browse among the mass of the main library, the miscellaneous treasures perhaps collected over many generations and by many divers interests. There is no means of selecting such students from the general body of students and there is certainly no validity in the separation of students for the pass or the honours degree. While one may meet this point by maintaining that, in any case, the really keen students will always make the necessary effort to use the general library, the fact remains that opposition to the separate undergraduate library is largely based on the contention that students may be led to believe that its book collection represents everything that they need to read.

A further argument against the undergraduate library arises from the recognition that the characteristics of the large university library have positive as well as negative values for the undergraduate users of its collections and services. The positive values are seen in the greater abundance and variety of the book collections and the fact that the service staff usually includes a number of subject specialists who, taken together, will have both a broader range and a greater depth of bibliographical knowledge than the relatively small staff of the undergraduate library.

When attempting to arrive at policy decisions regarding undergraduate library users, librarians may have been asking the questions in relation to the capacities or abilities of the student and not in relation to his educational needs. Thus, it is suggested that the university librarian must ask, not can the student use our library facilities, but should the undergraduate students be able to use our library? If this is so, the student is still in the unsatisfactory position of experiencing difficulty in using the library, but the university librarian will be less concerned with changing his library to match undergraduate capacities and will devote himself rather to attempts to bring the students' abilities up to the level of the library and its services. In order to achieve this, it is argued, a broader and more basic method of library instruction is needed to give the student an understanding of the library as a social agency and to enable him to grasp the means by which knowledge is recorded and arranged in the library as well as practical knowledge of the working of the catalogue and the use of reference tools and bibliographies. This type of instruction would require a special series of lectures which might be made an integral part of the courses the student will take during his university career, as present methods of instruction in library use are very often too narrowly conceived and executed.[29]

Doubt has also been cast on the various devices employed by librarians in an attempt to encourage the reading habit and the love of books in students to enable them to read more widely and more profitably. It is argued that since the habit of reading and the love of books are attitudes and a preference for books and reading the exercise of a sense of values, of the establishment of which very little is known, it is safe to assume that they flow far more frequently from the home and other early influences, and from persons or groups of persons than they do from books or collections of books. Hence it is held that these qualities which librarians try so hard to instil are already in the student when he arrives at the university or that they are developed, where they are developed at all, from influences received in the lecture room, the department and the hall of residence.

To accept this position is not necessarily to say that the library should not consciously play a part in stimulating an interest in books and in reading. It does suggest, however, that the librarian as a person may be far more influential than the luxuriously furnished reading rooms and the invitingly arranged shelves. The Librarian of Princeton University may well have had this point in mind when he wrote some years ago:

> I really suspect that the range of performance between different systems of organization — unified collection, divisional plan, special undergraduate collection, or what you will — is considerably less than the difference in performance caused by a host of other factors, and further that we are talking solemn nonsense when we pretend that there is much science at work in the selection of any form of arrangement.[30]

And this in turn suggests that the chief librarian might put his money into staff rather than into special undergraduate collections. These staff would need to be competent, interested people, sufficiently numerous to have time to work with undergraduates and sufficiently learned to make the association fruitful. Librarians who take this line of argument believe it unwise to divorce undergraduate facilities physically from the university library itself. While they may concede that in some situations it may be necessary or expedient to create separate facilities and a separate collection, they feel that the student has so much to gain by being required to use a large collection that they regard a separate, selected library as a poor second choice. Even those who approve of the Lamont Library and its large collection point out that the Harvard undergraduate must still use the other Harvard libraries on occasion and wonder whether he should not be trained for such use from the very beginning of his university career.

Other librarians who agree that undergraduates merit a special type of library service and form a sufficiently homogeneous group to lend themselves to a separate service question the need to house it in a separate building and cite such universities as Yale, Chicago, Duke, Texas, Illinois and UCLA where the main library building is utilized for the undergraduate collection. In addition to cost, of course, this is largely a matter of existing accommodation and the size of the student population, factors which have in fact compelled Chicago and Illinois to start planning separate undergraduate libraries, while UCLA has built a new research library and is adapting the original library building to services for undergraduates.

The stage is being reached where even small universities are being obliged to plan ahead and allow for rapidly increasing student enrollments up to at least 1970. Writing in 1953, William Dix, Librarian of the Rice Institute in Texas, speaking from his experience of this institution with its 1500 students including some 200 graduates and a post-war library containing about 225,000 books, could see no reason for making any special provision for undergraduates in such a situation.[31] He felt that with a little care and planning there was no reason for the undergraduate to become lost in working with a unified collection numbering not more than half a million volumes, and in the circumstances his policy seems justified, though it does not take future development into account. Until recent years only the larger libraries were being caught out by rising student numbers but the pressure is now being felt among the smaller universities with smaller libraries and similar problems are having to be faced.

Arising from the fear that the student would lose much of the value that comes with the complete facilities of the main collection is the argument that he needs the intellectual stimulation of an unselected collection and that the closer one comes to establishing for undergraduates the library setting a researcher needs, the better. Dix, following this line of argument, writes:

> In principle we feel that the undergraduate should be constantly confronted by books a little beyond his grasp, that we are not concerned primarily with his finding specific books but with instructing him to learn to think, to use the library, and to grow intellectually.[32]

Thus it is argued that when the student goes to the shelves of the main collection for a particular elementary book he finds there also the major standard works on the same subject.[33] Even if some of these are written in a language which he does not read or are accounts of original research which he cannot understand, he at least becomes aware of their existence, and if he is of the material from which scholars are made, there is just a possibility that he might be led gradually to more advanced material. Such an effect, it is claimed, cannot be produced if the undergraduate works entirely with a few basic books which have been placed on reserve, or if he works entirely with a small collection supposedly within his grasp.

Furthermore, it is not only stimulating for an alert student to find books slightly beyond his grasp, but it is also good for him perhaps to see graduate students and teaching staff working at the same table and in the same part of the building on problems like his, except more advanced. This argument seems to be on less certain ground and is based on the assumption that research workers and undergraduates are not segregated within the main library. In any case, the alleged benefit for the undergraduate resulting from working in company with graduates and teaching staff seems at best elusive and remote and unlikely to apply generally.

The argument for teaching students to use a research collection of moderate size in smaller institutions may be strengthened by the fact that, with the exception of Michigan, Harvard and a few other universities with large undergraduate libraries and substantial financial resources for stocking them, limited budgets have resulted in many of the smaller universities in America providing less than satisfactory book collections for their students. Indeed, some seem little better than the small reading room and reserve book collections which were a common form of service to undergraduates long before the principle of the undergraduate library came to be generally accepted.

It seems very dubious whether undergraduate library provision on this scale is worth providing at all and it may well be preferable in such cases for all available funds to be devoted to the building up of the general collection to a level of size and comprehensiveness satisfactory for both research scholars and undergraduates. In addition to helping to maintain the quality of library service offered, centralization of facilities also serves to keep administrative problems to a minimum. The librarian may find it difficult not only to justify the setting up of such small collections for undergraduates but also to agree to suggestions, sometimes made by teaching staff, to reduce the library from 50,000 to 10,000 volumes, for example, in order to prevent the students from being confused over which books they should select.[34] This practice seems to be a complete negation of the role of librarians and teaching staff in setting up good working collections for the purpose of extensive undergraduate reading and in encouraging students to make intelligent use of these collections.

The validity of the various criticisms made will largely depend upon the nature of the individual undergraduate library and the system of which it forms a part. What is important is the size and scope of its collections, the quality of service offered to its users and the extent to which both library and teaching staff are successful in finding all the true readers and potential readers in the undergraduate population and in ensuring that these students obtain the books they want and have the opportunity to discuss these books, to broaden their reading and to grow intellectually to the limits of their natural capacity.

Conclusion

Thus, although a comparatively recent phenomenon in higher education in America, the undergraduate library has been in the making for many years. Indeed, it appears that as early as 1765, the Harvard College Records referred to the need for separate library facilities for undergraduates.[35] In Britain, too, as has already been mentioned, reference was made to a similar need at Oxford when Bodley was librarian, and Oxford was in fact the first university in this country to make special provision for undergraduates in the form of the Radcliffe Camera. But with the exception of Glasgow where a Reading Room for junior undergraduates was opened in 1939 with a collection of 13,000 volumes on closed reserve and seats for 530 readers,[36] special library provision for undergraduates has been of a most limited kind. This is partially explained by the fact that British universities have not been considered large enough to warrant a separate collection for undergraduates, but inadequate service has been largely due to the constant stringency of financial resources which has dogged university libraries in this country for many years and given them a poor basis for expansion.

Early awareness of the existence of a problem in relation to undergraduates and the university library was assured in the United States by the extremely rapid development of many of its university libraries after the turn of the century together with a swiftly growing student population. The increasingly unsatisfactory nature of library service and facilities led to much thought being given to the problem and the wide variety of attempted solutions culminated in the Lamont Library at Harvard, the planning of which by Keyes Metcalf and his colleagues began in the late thirties. The opening of the Lamont Library had a considerable influence on American librarianship and efforts began to be made to make the library the focal point of study, and to develop the library staff's educational role in the university. It is this concept of the university library as an educational force, a teaching instrument as the Americans call it, which has been one of the major distinctions between university librarianship in Britain and the United States. Even at the present time some British universities may not aspire to this concept of library service, feeling that it is out of their sphere of influence, and some would perhaps question whether it was an advance at all.

However, there comes a point when libraries reach a size where they are so difficult to use that only the most persevering reader can really get what he wants. It is at this point that it becomes apparent that the library must not only provide in an efficient manner the services that make books available, but must give its readers some help in searching for what they require.

As well as a greater range of instruction in library use, however, the growing influx of students to the universities may also call for a student reference service with suitable collections and fully trained staff. This has long been an accepted part of the function of the American university library, but in Britain lack of staff and a general reluctance on the part of students to approach those available has made for an almost non-existent reference service in our university libraries. A certain amount of bibliographical help is given, of course, but this appears to be mainly to research students and teaching staff.

The older and larger universities may soon have to give serious thought to the advisability of establishing separate undergraduate libraries. Some have already committed themselves in one way or another. In January 1964 Liverpool University opened a new Arts Reading Room with shelving for 60,000 volumes and seating for 460 readers. It is intended primarily for undergraduates, and houses what were previously the departmental collections of social science, geography and history. Several universities, including Manchester, Liverpool and Birmingham, have set aside capital sums for the purchase of multiple copies of standard material, and a number of other universities such as Keele and Reading contain special undergraduate collections of prescribed texts within the main library. However, one of the most interesting developments in this respect on the British university scene at present is the proposed undergraduate library at Leeds.[37]

At the moment the Brotherton Building is in need of considerable enlargement for increased reading room facilities, administrative offices and an enlarged bookstack, but as it is very much hemmed in by other departments, there is no possibility of providing any substantial enlargement without first demolishing some of the surrounding buildings. One of the proposals of the University of Leeds Development Plan is to establish a separate undergraduate library containing 30,000 to 50,000 books and seats for about 800 students. The building of such a library has the advantage of being able to start without having to wait for the demolition of active departmental buildings, as the architects point out. It would also, of course, relieve much of the pressure on the main Brotherton Library which could then become the principal research library of the university. It is hoped to complete the new library at Leeds in the late sixties.

Other universities may well follow suit, particularly under the pressures of the still more rapid expansions that are asked for in the next few years. The Robbins Report on Higher Education recommends a target of 350,000 university places by 1980-1,[38] and the pattern of service suitable for a student population of 5000 is not necessarily the best for 10,000, which is the figure now being aimed at by the 1970's, by many of the larger civic universities. An important consequence of all this activity is the genuine interest which is being awakened in American experiment and experience, especially in such well-established buildings as those at Harvard and Michigan.

The present problems of undergraduate students in terms of library service and the possible solutions for the future are two of the most important questions facing any university with inadequate undergraduate provision, since their solution will help considerably in planning for other library facilities. In his description of the steps which led to the decision to build an undergraduate library at Michigan, Dr. Wagman listed some of the reasons which were present in the Harvard situation. He also wrote: "Relatively few of the larger universities are blessed with library facilities adequate to meet the demands of present student bodies, and the problem of providing meaningful service to undergraduate students is likely to yield, ten years from now, to the more pressing problem of how to provide any service at all for the entire group."[39]

Notes

1. See, for example, Tauber, M. F., et al., *The Columbia University Libraries; The College Library and the Undergraduate Library Problem at Columbia* (Columbia University Press: 1958), pp. 152-60.

2. Wheeler, G. W., ed., *Letters of Sir Thomas Bodley to Thomas James* (Oxford: Clarendon Press, 1926), p. 183.

3. McColvin, L. R., ed., *A Survey of Libraries. Reports on a Survey Made by the Library Association During 1936-1937* (London: Library Association, 1938), p. 414.

4. Lundy, F.A., "The Divisional Plan Library." *College and Research Libraries,* 17 (1956): 145.

5. Hurt, P., *The University Library and Undergraduate Instruction* (Berkeley: University of California Press, 1936), pp. 24-7.

6. In the survey at Southampton University 19% of the sample admitted to finding the library intimidating at first and 48% mildly intimidating. See Line, M. B., "Student Attitudes to the University Library . . . " *J. Docum.,* 19 (1963).

7. It is disturbing to find it taken for granted in a recent discussion that the young research worker begins "by spending considerable time and energy learning library technique which he should have learnt as an undergraduate." Sharpe, L. J., *Information Methods of Research Workers in the Social Science* (London: Library Association, 1961), p. 20.

8. Jolley, L., "The Function of the University Library," *J. Docum.,* 18 (1962): 136.

9. Haviland, M. C., "The Reference Function of the Lamont Library," *Harvard Library Bulletin,* 3 (1949): 297.

10. Shepley, H. R., "The Lamont Library. I. Design," *Harvard Library Bulletin,* 3 (1949): 24.

11. Woledge, G., and Page, B. S., eds., *A Manual of University and College Library Practice,* (London: Library Association, 1940), p. 54.

12. Wagman, F. H., "The Case for the Separate Undergraduate Library," *College and Research Libraries,* 17 (1956): 153.

13. Lundy, F. A., "The Divisional Plan Library," *College and Research Libraries,* 17 (1956): 145.

14. Metcalf, Keyes D., "The Undergraduate and the Harvard Library, 1937-1947," *Harvard Library Bulletin,* 1 (1947): 305.

15. Lamont, opened as long ago as 1949, provided seats for three of every eight undergraduates.

16. Metcalf, op. cit., p. 305.

17. American undergraduate library collections vary enormously in size from 12,000 volumes at Minnesota to some 150,000 volumes at Michigan. Lamont's collection numbers about 100,000 volumes but these represent only 39,000 titles.

18. Wagman, F. H., "The Undergraduate Library of the University of Michigan," *College and Research Libraries,* 20 (1959): 184.

19. Ibid., p. 185.

20. McNiff, P. J., and Williams, E. E., "Lamont Library: The First Year," *Harvard Library Bulletin,* 4 (1950): 207.

21. Arragon, R. F., "The Relationship Between the Library and Collegiate Objectives," *Library Quarterly,* 20 (1954): 284.

22. Wagman, op. cit., p. 185.

23. McNiff and Williams, op. cit., p. 205.

24. Wagman, F. H., "The Undergraduate Library of the University of Michigan," *College and Research Libraries,* 20 (1959): 179.

25. Ibid.

26. *The Place of the Library in a University: A Conference Held at Harvard University, 30-31 March 1949* (Cambridge: Harvard University Library, 1950), p. 42.

27. Wagman, op. cit., p. 188.

28. Sharp, L. W., "What Do We Look For in a University Library?" (London: Library Association, *Proceedings of the Annual Conference 1955),* pp. 31-2.

29. Gwynn, S. E., "The Liberal Arts Function of the University Library," *Library Quarterly,* 24 (1954): 313.

30. Dix, W. S., "Undergraduates Do Not Neccessarily Require a Special Facility," *College and Research Libraries,* 17 (1956): 150.

31. Dix, W. S., "Undergraduate Libraries," *College and Research Libraries,* 14 (1953): 271.

32. Ibid.

33. The larger and better undergraduate libraries are attempting to achieve this range of choice.

34. Govan, J. F., "This Is, Indeed, the Heart of the Matter," *College and Research Libraries,* 23 (1962): 470.

35. McNiff, P. J., "Lamont Library, Harvard College," *College and Research Libraries,* 14 (1953): 269.

36. *Library Association Record,* 41 (1939): 522.

37. *University of Leeds Development Plan . . . ,* prepared by Chamberlin, Powell and Bon, Architects, April 1960. The University, Leeds, 1960, pp. 26, 55-6.

38. Committee on Higher Education, *Higher Education: Report of the Committee Appointed by the Prime Minister Under the Chairmanship of Lord Robbins 1961-63,* Cmnd. 2154, October 1963, pp. 151-2.

39. Wagman, F. H., "The Case for the Separate Undergraduate Library," *College and Research Libraries,* 17 (1956): 151.

About the Author

M. W. Moss received his Bachelor of Arts degree from the University of Liverpool. He is an Assistant Librarian at the University Library, University of Keele, Keele, Staffordshire, England.

Irene A. Braden

Conclusions

In 1965 and 1966 the author probed into the services of undergraduate libraries and attempted to
evaluate them. This is the first substantial and
critical survey conducted. In her study of the
undergraduate libraries at Harvard, Michigan,
South Carolina, Indiana, Cornell, and Texas, she
included reference services, reserve books, special
services, technical services, and instruction in
library use as well as the building and its
collection. The following is her concluding summary chapter from the volume which was published by the American Library Association in
1970. She states that she has not developed a
definitive plan to follow in establishing or not
establishing an undergraduate library, but she
does list fourteen guidelines as suggestions for
institutions considering such a course.

The separately housed undergraduate library was proposed to accomplish several objectives to improve service to the undergraduate student in the large university. These objectives were:

To construct a building with the undergraduate's habits of use in mind

To furnish a collection of carefully selected books containing the titles to
which all undergraduates should be exposed as part of their liberal education, as well as to house the reserve book collection

To provide open access to the collection in order to avoid the problems
encountered by the student in using a large research collection

To provide services additional to those given in the research library

SOURCE: From Irene A Braden, "Conclusions," in her *The Undergraduate Library*,
ACRL Monograph No. 31 (Chicago: American Library Association, 1970), pp. 137-150.
Reprinted by permission of the publisher.

To attempt to make the library an instructional tool by planning it as a center for instruction in library use to prepare undergraduates for using larger collections

To centralize and simplify services to the undergraduate.

The several libraries will be compared with regard to their individual treatment of these problems, as well as with regard to the reasons for the establishment of each; the buildings; the book collections; services; the staffing of each; and the results in terms of student use. Following these comparisons, an attempt will be made to suggest guidelines, arising out of the experience of these six institutions, that may be helpful for other universities considering the establishment of an undergraduate library.

Background

The reasons for establishing undergraduate libraries were strikingly similar, although all of the reasons given above were not subscribed to at each library. Space shortage for books and for readers was a primary consideration at Harvard, Michigan, South Carolina, and Cornell; Harvard, Michigan, Indiana, Cornell, and Texas stressed difficulty of access to books because of closed stacks and scattered facilities. Michigan and Texas wanted to broaden the students' education by encouraging good reading habits. Michigan's decision was also influenced by its commitment to a system of divisional libraries. South Carolina was concerned with providing adequate physical facilities for the undergraduate. At Indiana, the increasing enrollment was a factor in providing more space. At Texas, the undergraduate library was part of an overall accelerated library program.

This should indicate, then, that two reasons — shortage of space for books and/or readers and ease of access — were the prime factors. However, it would be difficult to state that any of the five objectives was not actually a part of the overall plan of each of these universities. For instance although the Undergraduate Library at Texas was proposed as part of an accelerated library program with emphasis on the program's educational advantages, there was also the need to provide space for readers even if it was not expressly stated. To say that one reason dominated the thought at any one of these institutions would be doing it an injustice. Any new program is motivated by many ideas. The differences are the result of local conditions.

Building

One of the characteristics which was supposed to distinguish the separately housed undergraduate library from a general university library was that the building would be planned with the habits of the undergraduate in mind. The architectural design most favored is a modular building, consisting of large reading areas, some special-purpose rooms, and small reading rooms. The open modular building is more functional and less expensive to build, but it is not the only type of building that makes an effective undergraduate library, as the Uris Library at Cornell illustrates. The modular plan was used at Harvard, Michigan, South Carolina, and Texas, where new buildings were constructed. At Cornell and Indiana, old buildings were adapted to new purposes so that a modular arrangement was not possible.

A central location either in the classroom area or close to the residential area is considered the best location, depending on the pattern of library use. If use is known to be heavier during the day, a central campus location seems more desirable. However, if use is heavier in the evening, a location near the dormitories seems preferable. With the exception of South Carolina, all of the libraries are in a central location. South Carolina considered a location near the dormitory area more suitable to the needs of their students. Besides the educational consideration, the availability of a site has to be considered, although this is not a serious problem unless a central campus location is desired. Unless the dormitories are all in one area, problems are encountered in placing the undergraduate library near the dormitory area.

The interior arrangement of the building should place the reader in proximity to books, but it should not intermingle books and readers because of the distraction caused by persons looking for books. The arrangement of books in the center of the floor with seating on either side has been the favored arrangement. Lamont's interior arrangement was basically one of books in the center with reading areas on either side (South Carolina and Texas use the same basic plan). Such an arrangement forces the student to pass books to reach most of the seats in the building. Michigan arranged its bookstacks in two rows with seating placed between and at both sides. The bookstacks at Michigan have since been rearranged in one stack area in the center of the room with standard 3-foot aisles. The rearrangement seems to be more satisfactory from the viewpoint of maximum space utilization. Because of the physical arrangement of the buildings at Cornell and Indiana, this arrangement could not be utilized. Cornell shelves most of its books in a traditional stack area, while Indiana located the books around the edges of three reading areas.

The question of whether these undergraduate library buildings achieve the aims envisaged for them can only be answered in part. In providing a building that would serve the needs of the undergraduate student, the results at Harvard, Michigan, South Carolina, and Cornell are good. The diversity afforded by the physical nature of the Uris Library differs sharply from the simplicity of the Lamont Library and the undergraduate libraries at Michigan and South Carolina. The Uris Library provides a veritable maze which seems to delight the students. From the viewpoint of the students, the Undergraduate Library at Texas is functional, but from the viewpoint of the staff, the building has shortcomings. The building is not well planned in that related staff functions are scattered.

Enclosing the area around the reserve desk would decrease the noise in the first floor reading area. With the exception of Indiana, one error in planning the undergraduate libraries is a lack of sufficient staff work space. Obviously, the volume of work was not anticipated. Staffs increased as the work in the circulation and reserve departments increased. As a result, compromises to convert work space have had to be made. The results have not always been convenient or satisfactory, but sometimes it was all that could be done.

Besides not having enough work space, staff facilities have tended to be too widely scattered over the building, resulting in a waste of staff time. Centralization of these facilities would have resulted in a more efficient operation. This is true in all of the undergraduate libraries except South Carolina and, to some extent, Indiana. At Texas, the problem is especially unfortunate. The Catalog Department is not on the same floor as the card catalog, and the acquisition librarian is on still another floor. Staff lockers are so inconveniently placed that they are not used.

Surprisingly, only in two instances—at Michigan and at Indiana—are the buildings considered much too small. At Indiana, nothing could be done about the size of the building, because an old building (not even a library building) was adapted for use as the undergraduate library. The Undergraduate Library at Indiana provides seating for only about 8 percent of its undergraduates. Indiana is now faced with the problem of adapting the building as the demands on it increase. Little can be done about the physical facilities until the completion of the new library. Because of the experience with the Undergraduate Library in its present quarters, two things were learned about the old building which are being incorporated in the new building. Wide corridors and wide entrances to enable the students to get in and out quickly are considered important to prevent queueing. To help the student identify books new to the library, a new-book room is being placed near the entrance to the new library. In effect, the room is to be a browsing room, although the whole library actually constitutes a browsing collection.

At Michigan, it was known when the building was planned that it was going to be too small, but there was insufficient money to make it larger. When the whole building is given over to the Undergraduate Library, some of the problem will be alleviated. In a state-supported institution where the enrollment is not kept at a constant figure, little can be done to meet the demands that ever increasing enrollments create for seating and books.

Although many of the things that were learned from planning and operating the undergraduate library building were unique to that institution, each library seemed to benefit from the mistakes of its predecessors. This can be seen in two particular instances. The alcoves in the Lamont Library were too small. As it is, they now accommodate one reader. If they had been 3 feet larger, each could easily have seated four readers. South Carolina has the same basic interior arrangement, but the alcoves were made large enough to accommodate five to eight readers. In planning the group study rooms for the Michigan Undergraduate Library, a miscalculation was made about the size. They were made to accommodate six persons, but it was not often that six persons wanted to study together. As a result, two or three persons will use a room, leaving the remainder of the seats unused. When the Undergraduate Library at Texas was built, the group study rooms were made to accommodate four persons, which has proven more satisfactory.

Some of the building features which proved unsatisfactory were not the result of bad planning, but were unavoidable. At Indiana, there were too many entrances and exits; there was no elevator or book lift; the building was badly ventilated; and the physical layout of the building did not permit a satisfactory arrangement of functions. Cornell, where an old building was also used, was faced with some unavoidable limitations. Because of the layout of the building, the circulation desk and the main entrance to the stacks are located in the largest reading room, thereby concentrating the heaviest traffic in one area. To alleviate this problem somewhat, the reserve desk was separated from the circulation desk, which has caused some duplication of effort and staff.

At Michigan, some features, such as the entrance, had to be planned as they are because of the site. The main entrance on the narrow side of the building is undesirable, because a student has to walk through the whole building to get to the back. The entrance would have been more satisfactory on the long axis of the building, but the site did not allow this. The arrangement of the entrance inside the building was well planned, but it had to be altered and made awkward because of changes made by the fire marshall. As it is, students enter to the far right of the entrance and then have to turn back into the lobby. Because the checkout stations had to be relocated to conform to the decisions of a new fire marshall, the lobby is not large enough to disperse the traffic quickly and effectively.

The other mistakes made at the various undergraduate libraries were small things, some of which were easily remedied and some of which cannot be corrected. South Carolina discovered two small faults with its building. First, no provision was made for ventilation when the air conditioning is out of order. Second, carpeting should not have been placed in front of the circulation desk because of the heavy wear.

At Texas, the faults in planning cannot be easily changed. Although Texas planned the group study rooms to be the right size, the typing rooms are too large. The outside book return, which is located on the west side of the building, empties into the office of the reserve librarian. The elevators are so situated that it is inconvenient to move books from the circulation desk to another floor. It is necessary to go from the circulation area through a door into the reserve area, through another door into the reading area, and then through another door into the lobby where the elevators are located. However, most of the insights gained from working in these buildings show that the shortcomings of the buildings are not serious.

As far as furnishings are concerned, certain features have been considered successful in these libraries. Carpeting is preferred because it is quiet and induces an aura of graciousness which the students respect. Only South Carolina installed carpeting when its building was built. Cornell installed carpeting in parts of the library in December, 1965, and Indiana carpeted lobbies and stairways to help diminish noise. Michigan and Texas considered carpeting in planning their libraries but rejected the idea because of the initial cost. The Lamont Library was built before carpeting was seriously considered as a floor covering for libraries.

A minimum of 50 footcandles is sufficient for lighting. Seventy footcandles seems to be the upper limit necessary for good lighting. Each of the libraries meets the minimum requirements. (This information is unavailable for Indiana.)

Variety in seating is desirable. Individual seats should constitute the majority of seating; lounge furniture should constitute only about 5 percent, with the remainder of the seats at tables seating no more than four readers. Round tables have not been considered desirable. Indiana, Cornell, and Texas provided only a small amount of lounge furniture. Indiana and Cornell feature seating at small tables, and Texas uses large divided-top tables. Generally, it has been concluded that students prefer individual seating because of the privacy it affords. The preferred seating is the individual carrel or the divided-top tables which provide the same effect. Lounge furniture is considered less functional because of the lack of writing area and because students tend to make themselves too comfortable. The small amount of lounge furniture at Michigan (only recently reduced), Cornell, Indiana, and Texas seem to bear out this point. Harvard has stated that experience has shown that less lounge furniutre would be more efficient. Only at South Carolina is the large amount of lounge furniture not questioned because of student preferences and use of the facilities.

The most functional and economical type of seating is provided by large tables with dividers that seat from four to sixteen persons. The best use is made of available space, allowing more seating in an area without crowding. The least economical, but one of the most popular types of seating, is the group study room accommodating four readers.

Although more individual seating was placed in the Lamont Library than had previously been placed in any library (about 44 percent of the study seats), it is still not enough. If lounge chairs are included as individual seating, each undergraduate library has provided more than half (in fact almost two thirds) of its seating in individual seats. There are two exceptions. Indiana has only a few individual seats. At Texas, the amount depends on whether or not the divided-top tables are considered individual seating.

Some of the librarians advocate light-colored furniture, rather than dark, in order to prevent eyestrain. There is some disagreement on this point, but the facts indicate that eyestrain can be caused by the shift from light to dark surfaces. However, most agree that dark furniture is aesthetically more pleasing than light furniture. Because of its better wearing quality, plastic-upholstered furniture is recommended over that with fabric covering. It is also easier to maintain. Harvard has some leather-covered lounge furniture. Michigan, Indiana, and Cornell have used plastic materials for their chairs and settees. Overall, they have proven satisfactory. South Carolina began with fabric-covered lounge furniture, but the fabric has already begun to wear and is now being replaced with plastic fabrics. Texas has fabric-covered chairs but is not completely satisfied with them, because they become dirty quickly. As additional furniture is added, plastic-covered chairs are being acquired.

Book Collection

The undergraduate library was to furnish a collection of carefully selected books to which all undergraduates should be exposed as part of their liberal education; it was also to house the reserve-book collection for undergraduates. One of the first questions about the undergraduate library is the validity of further decentralization of the book collection. Unfortunately, the patterns of research and instruction do not necessarily correspond with book classification or with department or college organization. There are overlapping and constant change in the disciplines and their patterns of research. Decentralization scatters the book collection over the campus and inconveniences students as cross disciplinary study becomes prevalent. If an undergraduate library means that more books are being removed from existing collections to be segregated for use by undergraduates, then the idea of the undergraduate library is ineffective. However, the book collections of these undergraduate libraries were not taken from existing collections but are largely duplicate collections of books found elsewhere in the university library system. The success of this duplication depends, in part, on the affluence of the institution — the extent to which it can afford to duplicate titles. If it is necessary to transfer materials, other segments of the clientele are inconvenienced at the expense of the undergraduate.

The manner in which the several collections were formed was basically the same. Harvard began by developing criteria for the collection. Using bibliographic sources, local lists, and faculty recommendations, a master card file was compiled and submitted to the faculty for final selection. Michigan compiled a master card file using the Lamont list as a basis and supplementing it with other bibliographic tools, interviews with the faculty, reading lists, etc. Faculty members were hired to work on the project and buying trips undertaken to obtain out-of-print materials. At South Carolina, the collection was selected by the director of libraries, with six bibliographic tools providing the basis for the collection. Indiana began with the Michigan list, consulted with faculty, and made a buying trip for some materials. Cornell began with the Michigan list and a desiderata file compiled by the librarian. The stock of a bookstore was purchased and much of the material added to the collection. Texas also based its collection on the Michigan shelf list. Desiderata lists for materials of local interest were compiled by faculty members.

Progress has been made in serving the liberal education needs of the undergraduates. Harvard indicates that it has succeeded in building a collection which satisfies the needs of its undergraduates. However, this might be questioned since use of the collection has been decreasing. Michigan proposed to meet the needs of the undergraduates in the College of Literature, Science, and the Arts. It feels that it has met the needs of the underclassman in that college, but it makes no real attempt to satisfy the needs of the upperclassman in any schools or colleges of the university. South Carolina recognizes that it has not yet come to the point of satisfying the needs of its undergraduates since the undergraduate library attempts to serve all undergraduates (with the exception of those in professional curricula and those served by department libraries). Indiana made an effort to develop a general collection (below the extensive research level) by purchasing in many areas beyond the confines of the arts college. The collection at Cornell also provides books for exploration, recreation, and stimulation besides those supporting the instructional program. Texas attempts to meet the needs of students enrolled in courses in the College of Arts and Sciences, while also including materials in specialized areas where there is more interest on the layman's level.

To better serve the needs of undergraduates, undergraduate libraries allowed more open access than a general university library usually does. Harvard pioneered in opening the total collection to its clientele, but after one semester, it had to place reserve books in a closed area. The Undergraduate Library at Michigan provides more open access than any other undergraduate library, since most of its reserve books are on the open shelf. South Carolina, Indiana, Cornell, and Texas all provide a like amount of open access — the general collection and some reserve books are on the open shelves. Although some of the libraries experimented with more extensive open access, they found that the students abused the privilege. The demands placed on some books are so heavy that students often panic and steal or hide books, depriving all others of the books' use.

A selective collection seems to be better for most undergraduates. Some students profit from having access to a large research collection, but more undergraduates seem to be confused than helped. A selective collection with open access appears to offer the student opportunities for enrichment, discovery and entertainment, voluntary reading, and required reading. Each undergraduate library provides a selective collection. However, it must be noted that there is no conclusive evidence that the students have actually profited from this except in terms of use of the collection.

The book collection of the undergraduate library should be in a constant state of flux. No particular copy need be a permanent inclusion in the collection, although some titles, which are part of a basic liberal education, should always be there. Some mistakes are made in purchasing and eventually the books have to be removed from the collection. Others lose their relevance or become outdated. The collection should change and grow with the curriculum. Unfortunately, little of this has been accomplished. Only at Cornell and Harvard have weeding programs been carried on. At all the undergraduate libraries, worn-out, missing, or lost books have been withdrawn and replaced when feasible. Most of the collections have changed as they have grown, by emphasizing different areas or collecting in previously neglected subjects.

Most of the undergraduate libraries have an insufficient budget to develop their collection in the most desirable way. However, this is not true everywhere. Harvard considers its book budget sufficient (usually the full amount is not spent) for the needs of its students. South Carolina does not want a larger book budget, because it wants to retain the small, selective character of the collection, although the present collection is not large enough. Texas considers its budget sufficient, but the size of the collection needs to be increased. Until 1965, Michigan considered its budget inadequate. The size of the collection, however, is adequate. Both Indiana and Cornell feel the need for more money and more books. Both are relatively new libraries and have not had the time or the money to build collections in depth or quantity.

Duplication of heavily used reserve titles and general-collection titles is necessary. Indiana, Texas, and Cornell indicate they need more duplication to meet the demands of the students. Harvard and Michigan have liberal duplication policies which meet most needs. South Carolina has purposely limited extensive duplication in order to provide more titles instead of more copies.

Some of the undergraduate libraries have experienced the problem of a few departments buying most of the books and spending more than their "fair share" of the book budget (none of the undergraduate libraries allocate specific amounts of money to academic departments). This has been true at Michigan where four departments purchased 62 percent of all reserve books. South Carolina has experienced this same problem but to a lesser degree. At Indiana, Cornell, and Texas, a few academic departments show more interest than the average department. This interest results in scattered strengths in the collection.

Some miscalculations were made in not providing sufficient periodical files. Ten-year back files, which were usually provided, were not sufficient to meet the needs of the students. Harvard and Michigan did not have a stated cut-off date and provided more extensive holdings. South Carolina provides no periodicals except for current unbound issues. Indiana, Cornell, and Texas followed the ten-year policy with some exceptions: complete runs of important titles were provided, and some holdings began with the date of the library's opening.

Faculty participation aided in building all the undergraduate collections. In no case, however, were the results completely satisfactory because of a lack of interest and enthusiasm. Harvard, Michigan, and Cornell made large-scale attempts to solicit faculty cooperation but the results were uneven. Texas and Indiana did not make such an extensive drive, but, again, the results were mixed. South Carolina received little help from the faculty in developing its collection. Close work with the faculty in continued collection development is advantageous. All of the libraries have achieved this in varying degrees. However, cooperation varies as the faculty changes and as interest in the library rises or wanes. There is too much variation from year to year and school to school to make any valid conclusions.

In most of the undergraduate libraries, the reserve-book collection is an extension of the general collection. These are the books directly supporting the instructional program. The reserve collections at all the undergraduate libraries consist of required reading for undergraduate courses. In addition, some under-graduate libraries (Indiana and Cornell) include supplemental or recommended books as reserve materials.

Services

An important point in considering the establishment of an undergraduate library is the kind of service given to the undergraduate student in the existing library. When the library administration becomes aware of the service the undergraduate is receiving and discovers it is not what it should be, it looks for a way to improve it. Service to the undergraduate is usually influenced by the size of the collection and the nature of the enrollment.

Service to graduate students and faculty necessarily interferes with that to undergraduates. The undergraduate needs a place to sit, a collection to use, and someone to direct his use of the library. The staff of a general library is more ori-ented to serving research needs than it is to teaching the undergraduate how to use the library, which is the kind of help he needs.

Reference service in an undergraduate library has two distinct characteristics: first, most questions are of a less complicated nature, and second, reference serv-ice tends to be in terms of teaching students how to use the library rather than of assisting in bibliographic searching. Each of the undergraduate libraries, with the exception of Lamont and South Carolina, offers similar service both in qual-ity and quantity. The situation at South Carolina is somewhat different in that it does not maintain a reference desk because of the size of the staff. Reference service at the Lamont Library is provided only during the day by a nonprofes-sional. There has not been much demand for reference service because of the ease with which a student can find what he wants.

The reserve systems used in these undergraduate libraries are similar, with one notable exception. Harvard, South Carolina, Indiana, Cornell, and Texas basic-ally adhere to a closed-reserve collection made up of reserve books not current-ly being used (a reserve book does not become part of the general collection). South Carolina has been able to prove that reserve books need not exist in great multitudes. By close work with the faculty, closed-reserve books have been reduced to a bare minimum. Only those titles for which there is extensive demand for a short period of time are on closed reserve. Cornell retains most of its reserve collection in a closed-stack arrangement, but some books are placed on open reserve. Indiana also maintains a two-part reserve system. Most of the collection is on closed reserve, but an open-reserve reading room is also provid-ed. At Texas, all reserve books, with the exception of three-day and some "Buil-ding Use Only" books, are on closed reserve. The books on the open shelves are placed in their sequential location in each class. The one exception to the basic closed-reserve system is at Michigan. Only a small part of the reserve collection is on closed reserve; most reserved titles are on the open shelves in their sequen-tial location with special markings to indicate they are reserve books. Unfortunately, student abuse has caused the near collapse of the system. Although Michigan's open-reserve system is educationally desirable, there are practical limitations — mainly the hiding and stealing of books made easier with an open reserve system.

For circulation control, South Carolina, Indiana, and Cornell use the McBee Keysort circulation system, which has met the needs of their operations. Michigan and Texas use the system developed at Michigan, which is a two-part form, both parts of which are retained and filed (one by call number and the other by transaction number). In both libraries, thought is being given to another system because of the increased volume of circulation. Lamont uses its own circulation system and considers it suited to its needs.

The special services found in the undergraduate libraries are not actually necessary to the functioning of the library, but they are important for making the undergraduate library something more than a depository for books. Special services are part of the concept of the "cultural center" and part of the distinguishing features of the undergraduate library.

All the undergraduate libraries except South Carolina have special services. South Carolina did not include any because of lack of staff and funds. Harvard, Michigan, Cornell, and Texas have audio facilities. The inclusion of these facilities was usually determined by the availability or the absence of other campus facilities. Indiana is adding audio service to its undergraduate library. South Carolina is the only undergraduate library which does not have typing facilities. Harvard and Indiana provide only space, but Michigan, Cornell, and Texas have rental typewriters. Harvard has a poetry room and a separate collection of modern fiction. Michigan has a student lounge which enables the student to have a cup of coffee without leaving the building, an auditorium or multipurpose room for meetings, and a print study gallery.

The special services differ among the libraries because of different concepts of what an undergrdauate library should be, local conditions, and financial considerations. Since there is little agreement on the role of an undergraduate library, various interpretations have produced different effects. Local conditions have played an important part in some features of the undergraduate library. The presence of audio facilities on the campus may exclude their need in the undergraduate library. The same is true for any other feature. Financial considerations also help determine the extent of extra facilities to be located in the undergraduate library. A stringent budget might eliminate some facilities considered useful.

The undergraduate library has provided a means of simplifying and centralizing services that could be concentrated in one place to advantage. Use was simplified by the provision of open stacks and the elimination of unnecessary procedures in obtaining books. The layout of the buildings, interspersing books and readers, added to the ease of use. Centralization was achieved by bringing together books and services in one building and by providing the means whereby the undergraduate could be given more attention and the type of service he needs. The smallness of the undergraduate library also contributes to its simplicity. All of the undergraduate libraries adhered to these principles. South Carolina, however, was unwilling to accept completely the principle of simplification, because it felt that would discourage students from learning how to use a more complex library system.

It is the responsibility of the university not only to teach the student how to use the library but also to teach him what constitutes a good library. Many undergraduates come to college with little library training, and it should be part of their education to get this training at the university. The undergraduate does not easily learn this in the general university library nor is he usually able to get the individual type of service he needs.

There are two views on how students should approach the book collection. One advocates finding the book from the shelf, while the other advocates access through the card catalog. Students usually approach the book collection through the card catalog, because they are seeking a particular title. However, once they go to the shelves, they may find other books equally suited to their purpose. Since the book collection of the undergraduate library serves as the laboratory for the liberal arts student, the library affords the student the opportunity to sample the wealth of knowledge found in books, whether he finds it through the card catalog or by browsing.

The type of instruction in use of the library varies from formal classroom lectures to informal instruction given at the reference desk. Harvard has given instruction only on an individual basis when a student asks for help. At Michigan, the Undergraduate Library is considered a "training library," and the reference librarians are considered teachers instructing students in library use and stimulating them to go beyond required reading. South Carolina considers teaching the student to use the library the weakest point in its operation, simply because there is insufficient staff. Indiana provides instruction in library use through the reference staff and by tours. In conjunction with the English departments at Cornell and at Michigan, library orientation lectures are given to all freshmen each fall. In addition, the reference staff helps individual students in learning how to use the library. Texas also provides classroom instruction in library use, but participation is on a voluntary basis so that most instruction is provided when it is individually requested.

Staff

The staff serves the student more as teachers than as mere dispensers of facts, and guides the student in his use of the library and his selection of books. The staff must be able to adapt readily to new situations and be flexible enough to meet the constant demands and pressures which manifest themselves. The staff has to be interested in working with people and able to communicate with the undergraduate student. A system of assigning the staff reference duty, book selection, and the responsibility of one area has proven satisfactory at Michigan,

Cornell, Indiana, and Texas (at Texas and Indiana most book selection is done by the acquisition librarian).

Table 1. — Comparison of Enrollment, Total Book Use,
and Attendance in the Six Undergraduate Libraries Surveyed

	HARVARD			MICHIGAN			SOUTH CAROLINA		
	Enroll.[b]	T.B.U.[d]	Attend.[c]	Enroll.	T.B.U.	Attend.	Enroll.	T.B.U.	Attend.
1948-49[a]	5,464	81,766							
1949-50	5,043	151,873							
1950-51	4,649	159,086							
1951-52	4,439	152,798							
1952-53	4,433	148,908							
1953-54	4,356	351,783							
1954-55	4,448	359,284							
1955-56	4,470	336,652							
1956-57	4,463	298,102							
1957-58	4,472	328,270							
1958-59	[c]	329,549		7,357	481,512	1,457,441			
1959-60	4,542	349,965		7,355	644,956	1,556,227	4,273	30,909	113,012
1960-61	4,596	368,699		7,669	665,946	1,548,837	4,882	37,799	130,901
1961-62	4,764	363,299		8,268	713,034	1,731,283	5,163	44,506	147,276
1962-63	4,728	370,061		8,402	842,670	1,807,896	5,443	53,380	132,743
1963-64	4,719	317,663		8,779	973,301	1,883,083	5,689	57,431	188,363
1964-65	4,785	339,170		9,536	1,023,084	1,969,935	6,244	67,451	220,649

	INDIANA			CORNELL			TEXAS		
	Enroll.[c]	T.B.U.	Attend.[c]	Enroll.	T.B.U.	Attend.	Enroll.	T.B.U.	Attend.
1948-49									
1949-50									
1950-51									
1951-52									
1952-53									
1953-54									
1954-55									
1955-56									
1956-57									
1957-58									
1958-59									
1959-60									
1960-61									
1961-62		47,361							
1962-63		144,101		2,902	189,560	705,251			
1963-64		187,930		3,028	217,306	758,331	8,954	423,475	1,473,048
1964-65		241,370		3,069	239,873	752,583	9,746	732,259	1,769,560

[a] Figures for a partial year—not used in figuring percentages.
[b] Undergraduate enrollment for the fall semester of the academic year.
[c] Figures not available.
[d] Total book use.

Library Use

Throughout this paper it has been asserted that more extensive use is being made of the library. Is this really true or does it just seem that way because enrollments are increasing (Table 1)? Without a comparison of the same figures before the advent of the undergraduate library, the real implication (if there is one) is not evident. In each case, the percent of increase of total book use and attendance has been greater than the percent of increase in enrollment. The increase in total book use has been the most spectacular (Table 1). In the three older undergraduate libraries, it has exceeded 100 percent, while the three other undergraduate libraries should reach or exceed that point in a like period of time.

There are some interesting comparisons in library use. Total book use has increased as follows (for the period the library has been open): Harvard, 123 percent; Michigan, 112 percent; South Carolina, 118 percent; Indiana, 67 percent; Cornell, 26 percent; Texas, 71 percent (Table 1). Attendance (where the figures are available) has not risen as sharply: Michigan, 35 percent; South Carolina, 95 percent; Cornell, 6 percent; Texas, 20 percent. These figures seem to indicate that the students who use the library make extensive use of its facilities. The slower rise in attendance may also be attributed to the building's being used to capacity. It seems that attendance has risen faster in the newer libraries than the older ones, which verifies the need that these libraries serve.

Why are more students using the library? One reason is new teaching methods. Many instructors are abandoning the lecture and textbook method of instruction and emphasizing independent study. As more instructors adopt the "teaching with books" method, more student use of the library follows.

The real question is which comes first — curriculum changes or an undergraduate library. At some institutions, the nature of the curriculum — more emphasis on honors programs, independent work, etc. — creates a need that cannot always be satisfactorily met in the large university library. In other instances, the presence of an undergraduate library with its expanded facilities may make it possible for instructors to do more "teaching with books" than they had done in the past, because the library situation made such practices impractical. There does not seem to be much doubt — at least among undergraduate librarians and library administrators at institutions where there are undergraduate libraries — that instructors are making more extensive use of the library in their instructional programs.

Undergraduate libraries, however, also serve in large part simply as study halls. Depending on the nature of the parent institution, the amount may vary anywhere from 50 to 90 percent of the undergraduate library's use, depending on how one defines "study hall use" of the library. If it is limited strictly to studying from a student's own books and notes, then the percentage of use would be lower than the figures given above. However, if study hall use includes reading reserve books, the above figures are probably pretty accurate.

Another problem in connection with study hall use is that any one user does not usually come to the library to use it only as a study hall or to use only library materials. His reason in coming may be two-fold, or he may come only to study from his own books but be enticed to use library materials once he is there. This is basically the reason that a study hall "barn" would not suffice as a place to study, because it offers none of the intellectual advantages of a library.

Undergraduate libraries are often used as study halls because in many cases it is the only place where the undergraduate can satisfactorily study. Dormitories and apartments are often crowded and noisy and do not offer good study conditions. Another cause for the high percentage of study hall usage of undergraduate libraries is the increasing academic pressures placed on students. A third factor is the changing nature of student bodies. Students are now more serious, perhaps because of the keen competition they face to get into college and to remain there.

Use of the library presents a peculiar situation at the Lamont Library. When the building first opened, Harvard undergraduates used the library heavily. But after a few years, general book circulation began to decline, reserve-book use declined, and fewer people seemed to come to the library. At the same time, there was also a reduction in professional staff — from eight professionals in 1949 to two in 1965. There is a definite possibility of a correlation between the reduction in staff and the decline in use of the library, because it seems natural that as service declined, use would decline (of course, the opposite may be true, but the whole pattern of development at other schools seems to contradict this). Another factor affecting use of the Lamont Library is the restriction on Radcliffe girls in using the library. Perhaps it is time to reexamine this policy, because a change would surely increase the use of the library, not only by adding a new clientele but by enticing some Harvard undergraduates back to Lamont.

At Michigan, an instructional program in the use of the library for the undergraduate student would allow the student to make more effective use of the library, but the number of students is so large that no satisfactory solution has been found. South Carolina wants to increase the effectiveness of the library by finding a way to communicate with the students and by giving the student personal help in teaching him to use the library.

Some of the undergraduate libraries have been confronted with another kind of library use—student socializing in the library. Students find they need a break from studying and get it by visiting with other students. If the students do not have a place to go in the library for this purpose, they talk in the reading areas, which is distracting and annoying to the students who are trying to study. When many students are gathered in one place, it is logical that it also serves as a social meeting place. Although some of the undergraduate libraries are faced with this problem — mainly Cornell, Indiana, and Michigan — it apparently does not exist at the others. The library is, of course, a natural meeting place for students. Some students go to the library for the sole purpose of being seen and to see who is there. There is really no way to avoid this, nor is it undesirable for the undergraduate library to serve as a meeting place so long as the social function does not interfere with the real purpose of the library.

Effective use of the library seems to revolve around having enough books and providing service to the student. Without a sufficient book collection, the needs of the undergraduate student cannot be satisfied. But, if there is not a staff to guide the student in his use of the collection, then the needs of the undergraduate are not being met, and the library does not serve its real purpose.

Summary

Now that the establishment of an undergraduate library has succeeded at several institutions, the idea is considered by some as a cure for any library problem that a university library may face. The undergraduate library, however, seems necessary only when the enrollment becomes too heterogeneous to be served in one building and by one staff. When the student body contains many undergraduates and a large percentage of graduate students in addition to a significant faculty group, the distinct service which the undergraduate library affords is a partial answer to the problem. Undergraduate libraries remove the undergraduate from the research library, allowing him better service in his own library, while meeting the needs of the graduate students and faculty members in a more satisfactory way in the research library.

Enrollment at the six institutions which now have undergraduate libraries varied greatly when they opened their undergraduate libraries (Table 1). The total enrollment is not as important, however, as is the percentage of students who are undergraduates. Even so, the figures do not reveal any pattern which other schools might use as a rule of thumb. However, the ratio of graduate students to undergraduates has to be considered. If the enrollment is 90 percent undergraduate, a separate undergraduate library is unnecessary, because the main library is basically an undergraduate library by nature of the enrollment. When graduate students constitute one third to one half of the student body, an undergraduate library is a feasible answer to solving the university's library problem.

Neither is there a definite formula to follow in regard to the size of the main library collection. When a collection reaches a million volumes, few libraries maintain open stacks to provide the undergraduate with access to the collection so that he can make full use of it. When the book collection reaches this point, some sort of division of the library becomes desirable. Whether a vertical division as represented by undergraduate libraries or a horizontal one as reflected in the divisional plan is made depends on many factors. Of course, there is always the opposing viewpoint that the student should be exposed to the total library collection to allow him to select his own books.

The nature of the main library building — its physical layout and structure — helps determine the feasibility of a separate undergraduate library building. If the main library building is one that can be adapted to meet the needs of the undergraduate as well as those of graduate students and faculty, there is no need for a separate undergraduate library. But, if the present building cannot be made to provide for the needs of the undergraduate for seating, access to books, and service, another solution has to be found. Or, if the use to which it is being put makes the building unadaptable to the needs of the undergraduate, it is not desirable to attempt a renovation. The solution may be an undergraduate collection in a separate reading room in one wing of the building or on one floor of the building. It may be as simple as opening the stacks to the undergraduate. But, if the problem is basically one of not enough space for seating due to increasing enrollments, another answer usually has to be found. There is always the possibility of enlarging the building, but it may be easier and less expensive to build a new building.

Although some universities consider the idea of a separate undergraduate library desirable, they reject it because they think the cost of the operation is too high. The undergraduate library is costly in terms of duplication of staff and books, but it is cheap in terms of operation when compared with similar service in a general university library. It is more expensive than offering no special service for the undergraduate, but it is inexpensive in terms of supplying a needed service.

In summary, the feasibility of building a separate undergraduate library varies with the situation at each institution. The size of the student body, the size of the book collection, the kind of service available for the undergraduate student, the building situation, and the curriculum needs are all facets of the problem. Just because Harvard has one, every institution of that size does not necessarily need an undergraduate library. Neither do the undergraduate libraries at Cornell, Michigan, Indiana, Texas, or South Carolina imply any definite trend. In each case, the decision to have an undergraduate library was the answer to a particular problem at a particular institution.

Even though no definitive plan to follow in establishing an undergraduate library has emerged from this study, the fourteen following guidelines are suggested for institutions considering an undergraduate library:

1. Determine the philosophy of library services to be followed.

2. Prepare a written program stating the objectives of library development and translate these objectives into space requirements based upon the size of the student body and the curriculum. Also indicate such factors as type of building, size of staff, kinds of furnishings and equipment, and service functions.

3. Obtain the services of a library consultant.

4. Secure the needed financial support.

5. Select a building site suitable for the students' needs. It is advantageous to be near the main library building because of limitations of the undergraduate library book collection.

6. Decide on the building design (assuming a new, separate building). Choose a design which satisfies current needs but is also flexible enough to provide for future needs (a modular construction is most

satisfactory). The size of the building depends on the size and nature of the enrollment to be served. Plan the facilities and services to be contained in the building. Set up the specifications and correlate the functions and their relationships. Plan the traffic patterns for best utilization.

7. Special features of the building should include group study rooms (seating no more than four readers), a special-purpose room or small auditorium (for meetings, classes, movies, etc.) if not available elsewhere, typing facilities, photocopying facilities, a student lounge or informal area where students can gather, talk, and relax.

8. Plan seating for at least 30 percent of the enrollment, with about 75 percent being individual seats (lounge chairs, individual carrels, or tables with eggcrate dividers) and the remainder at tables for four.

9. Choose carpeting for a floor covering, if possible (vinyl or rubber tile is satisfactory but noisy).

10. Provide sufficient work space and office space for the staff and a staff lounge. The offices and work space are best centralized in one area.

11. Begin the development of the book collection by using a basic list (such as that of the University of Michigan Undergraduate Library); expand it in areas of strength and delete materials not considered necessary. The collection should contain frequently used materials and general reference tools. The collection should contain books, periodicals (complete runs of heavily used titles and limited runs of the remainder — usually about ten-year back files), pamphlets, and audio materials. The collection should contain a basic liberal arts core of books, but it need not be a well-rounded collection. The collection should reflect the curriculum and interests of the students being served. Selection should be based on working needs with little regard to other university library holdings. The collection probably need not exceed 75,000 titles in 200,000 volumes, because it then ceases to be selective in character.

12. Plan public service areas as close to each other as possible, especially circulation and reserve. Provide reference service daily until 10:00 P.M. and on weekends. The circulation system should entail as little work of the patron as possible and allow quick return of books to the shelves. Reserve books should be easily available (as many on open shelves as feasible).

13. Plan for a sufficient number of staff, both professional and nonprofessional. The staff should be responsible for one area, in addition to doing reference work and book selection. Consider a young staff, although this is not necessary.

14. Let use of the library develop according to the character of the student body. Do not try to enforce any stringent rules.

The undergraduate library was created because of a recognition that the undergraduate student body was being neglected due to emphasis on service to graduate students and faculty. It was the intention of those creating these special facilities to produce a new type of library on the university campus, different from the general university library in both collections and services. This study has attempted to outline the development of the several individual libraries and to point out the similarities and differences in their operations. It is the judgment of the present researcher that the undergraduate library has provided a more efficient and satisfactory service to the undergraduate — and has at the same time improved the service of the central library to graduate students and faculty by relieving the central collection of undergraduate service. This method of providing expanded and improved library service has blazed a new path on the frontier of library service — one which many more libraries will eventually follow.

About the Author

Irene Braden Hoadley received her doctorate in library science from the University of Michigan in 1967. She has held the following positions: Cataloger, Sam Houston State Teachers College Library, 1961-62; Head, Circulation Department, Kansas State University Library, 1962-1964; Graduate Assistant, Department of Library Science, University of Michigan, 1964-1966; Librarian for General Administration and Research, Ohio State University Library, 1967-1974; Director of Libraries, Texas A. and M. University, 1974- .

Billy R. Wilkinson

Are We Fooling Ourselves About Undergraduate Libraries?

The development of the separate undergraduate library on the university campus is traced briefly. The following services are then discussed: the undergraduate library as a study hall, social center, reserve book dispenser, browsing collection, listening facility, and visual materials center. Reference services were also originally analyzed in this paper; however, Wilkinson's paper "The Undergraduate Library's Public Service Record: Reference Services" in Part VI has a detailed examination. An attempt is made to evaluate each as to its success or failure. The tentative evaluations range from "complete successes" as study hall and as social center to a summary that "reference services are of low calibre; too often the assistance given students is superficial and too brief" based on an extensive survey of reference questions asked at the desks and a detailed analysis of the reference services of two undergraduate libraries (Cornell and Michigan) and two liberal arts college libraries (Earlham and Swarthmore).

The development of the separate undergraduate library on the university campus is briefly traced and the services offered by the libraries are then discussed. An attempt is made to evaluate these services as to their success or failure.

An undergraduate library is defined as a separate library building on a university campus designed especially for undergraduates and which has as its purpose a full range of services for these university students; it may attempt to serve all undergraduates, but it is particularly concerned with the students in the College of Arts and Sciences, the General College, or whatever this part of the university is called.

To set the stage for the past twenty years when the Lamont Library at Harvard

SOURCE: From Billy R. Wilkinson, "Are We Fooling Ourselves About Undergraduate Libraries?" Paper delivered at the meeting of the University Libraries Section of the Association of College and Research Libraries, American Library Association Conference, Detroit, July, 1970. Included by permission of the author. Later published as "A Screaming Success as Study Halls," *Library Journal* 96 (May 1, 1971) pp. 1567-1571.

and many other undergraduate libraries sprang up on American campuses, two antecedents of undergraduate libraries are of interest — the first in England and the second in this country.

Frederick Wagman, the Director of the University of Michigan Library, has traced the development of undergraduate libraries back to 1608 in England when Thomas James was head of Bodley's Library at Oxford.[1] James proposed the establishment of an undergraduate library to help the younger students, but Sir Thomas Bodley would have no part of it and dismissed the proposal in a letter to James. Bodley wrote:

> Your deuise for a librarie for the yonguer sort, will have many great exceptions . . . there must be a keepre ordeined for that place. And where you mention the yonguer sort, I knowe what books should be bought for them, but the elder as well (as) the yonguer, may have often occasion to looke upon them . . . In effect, to my understanding there is muche to be saide against it . . .[2]

There was so "much to be said against it" that for the next 299 years, no American university actually tried, on any significant scale, a separate undergraduate library for its students. Then, at the beginning of this century, Columbia University created the Columbia College Study.

James H. Canfield, Librarian of Columbia University, wrote in his 1907 Report to the President that

> the establishment of the College Study — undoubtedly the best lighted, best ventilated, and most commodious reading room on the campus — is an excellent illustration of our desire to help undergraduates to help themselves, our constant effort to develop in the student self-reliance in the selection and use of books. It also enabled us to test the theory which is not new, but which thus far has never been put into actual practice. That is, that a collection of not to exceed 6,000 volumes, carefully selected and kept fresh and up-to-date in every sense of the word, is sufficient to meet all the ordinary demands of the undergraduates of the average college. This has been given just a half year's trial, and the result is entirely satisfactory.[3]

After reading of the virtues of Columbia College Study as extolled by Canfield, the present day undergraduate libraries do not seem so pioneering. To borrow a phrase from the musical *Guys and Dolls,* the Columbia College Library is "the oldest, established, permanent, floating" undergraduate library on the campus of an American University.

These two excursions into the past show that separate undergraduate libraries are not a new concept in university library service. However, the real period of accelerated development of the undergraduate library began only twenty years ago in 1949 with the opening of the Lamont Library at Harvard. The early planning, the actual design, the functions and an evaluation after the first years of the Lamont Library are all well documented in the literature. In fact, the Lamont Library is probably one of the most documented events in the history of

American libraries. Keyes Metcalf and the other librarians associated with Lamont, perhaps sensing the importance of what they were doing, took time to record it. Refer to many articles in the *Harvard Library Bulletin* for details.[4]

The following summary of the total Harvard situation is necessary to give an understanding of the Lamont Library.

Metcalf became Librarian at Harvard in 1937. By that time, the Widener Library, which had been opened in 1915, was regarded as "cold, impersonal, and even unfriendly," to quote one observer. It was also full. Metcalf's first decision was whether or not to plan on the construction of a new central library for the university. He has written that "the conservative thing to do"[5] would have been to build a new central library. But the cost was prohibitive — an estimated $10,000,000. No suitable site in a central location was another objection. A third and equally important deterrent was that a building of the size needed would be so large as to be unwieldly from the standpoint of service. The idea of a new central library was given up, and plans for expansion were developed along the following lines.

A study of Harvard's library disclosed that more space was needed for books, staff and readers. Two other problems required attention. There were no adequate quarters in Widener for valuable collections of rare books and manuscripts, and no way had been found for providing proper facilities and services for undergraduates in a building where the pressure for service for researchers was so great. Undergraduates had to use a catalog containing millions of cards and, it was thought, could not be given direct access to the main book collection.[6]

With these needs and disadvantages in mind, plans were developed for four new units to house parts of the Harvard Library. The first would store less-used books; the second would satisfactorily house and service the rare books and manuscripts; the third would provide underground stacks in Harvard Yard, connected to Widener by tunnel; and the fourth would give undergraduates separate library facilities. The Houghton Library for rare books and manuscripts became a reality in 1942. The New England Deposit Library was also opened in 1942 for the storage of less-used books.

Thus, it is clear that the Lamont Library was not an isolated event, but part of a four-pronged solution to the problems facing Harvard.

Lamont was planned on three suppositions:

1. That undergraduates will make more and better use of a library designed expressly for them;
2. That this was the best way to relieve the pressure in the Widener building and make unnecessary a new central library building; and
3. That if that pressure were relieved, the Widener Library building would become a more satisfactory research center than it had been in the past.[7]

In planning the Lamont Library, the Harvard staff and architects wanted it to be:

> conveniently located and inviting of access . . . on one of the main undergraduate traffic routes, and there should be no flights of stairs to climb to the entrance or monumental vestibules or foyers to traverse before coming to the books. Once within the Library, the student should find the entire book collection as accessible as possible.[8]

It is generally acknowledged that Lamont met these requirements.

Thus in the late 1940s, Mother Harvard had started something — in fact, she greatly influenced several ideas which are still very much with us in the world of university libraries. Separate undergraduate libraries, separate buildings for rare books and manuscripts, storage libraries, and underground libraries all got this early boost from Harvard. Indiana with its Lilly Library, Yale with the Beinecke Library, and Kansas with the Spencer Library are other very famous examples of separate rare book libraries. Several libraries are now going underground — the best illustration is the new Undergraduate Library at the University of Illinois — built under the quad to avoid shading a sacred experimental corn plot on the campus. There are also many examples of storage libraries, such as the ones at the University of Michigan and Princeton.

But the idea of a separate undergraduate library got the biggest boost of all by the building of the Lamont Library at Harvard. Even though university librarians were keenly interested in this separate approach to library service for undergraduates, no other university built a separate undergraduate library during the next 9 years. The University of Minnesota did open its Freshman-Sophomore Library in 1952 in a classroom building. Then in 1958, the University of Michigan opened its Undergraduate Library and during the following years new and separate libraries were erected at South Carolina, Texas, North Carolina at Chapel Hill, Stanford, Ohio State, Penn State, Tennessee, and Illinois. At present [1970], new buildings are being planned or are under construction at Wisconsin, California at Berkeley, Oklahoma, Washington, Marryland, Massachusetts, and British Columbia.

There has evolved another approach to the separate undergraduate library — that of building a new research library and then renovating the old main library into an undergraduate library. In 1962, Cornell was the first university to do this. UCLA and Michigan State have also taken this route, and currently Duke, Hawaii and Emory are remodeling their original library buildings. Nebraska has remodeled part of a university building for its undergraduate library. If anyone has been counting, this all adds up to 24 separate undergraduate libraries and several have probably been missed. There are also many undergraduate libraries which occupy extensive quarters in the central university library. Indiana University, which had a separate undergraduate library, has recently built a new university library which features undergraduate services in one section of a three-part building.

For additional details on this library phenomenon of the 1960s, refer to the writings of Irene Braden,[9] Warren Kuhn,[10] Elizabeth Mills,[11] Robert Muller,[12] and Jerrold Orne.[13]

So much for the historical background. There is a current rage for undergraduate libraries; many millions of dollars have been spent on them. The buildings are there or they are rising. The book collections are there or they are being assembled.

The big questions are: What do we have? Are undergraduate students getting decent service in these libraries?

In an attempt to answer these questions, I have divided what happens in undergraduate libraries into seven functions or services. These are:

1. The undergraduate library as a study hall — students coming to the library with their own books and using them exclusively.

2. As a social center — students meeting and talking with other students. One librarian has called it "face time" — you get your face seen and see other faces. The library is a perfect place for this.

3. As the reserve book dispenser — books segregated onto special shelves at the request of professors.

4. As a browsing collection — the main collection with open-access for all students — there is just no such thing as a closed stack in any undergraduate library which I have seen.

5. As listening facility — audio rooms or listening rooms — the equipment plus records and tapes of music and spoken arts.

6. As visual materials center — films, filmstrips, pictures, paintings, prints, etc.

7. And as a center for reference services — the assistance given students by librarians — what happens at the reference desk or in an encounter between student and librarian.

How do undergraduate libraries rate? Have they been a success or failure in these seven areas? You are warned that the following comments are generalizations and that naturally there are exceptions.

All undergraduate libraries have been a screaming success as study halls. The Undergraduate Library of the University of Michigan may be the smash hit of all time; the attendance in that library during 1968/69 was 1,899,000. This is 8,000 to 10,000 students per day. The New York Public Library at 42nd Street does not have as many users each day. Studies have shown at Michigan and elsewhere that from 40% to 65% of those in the library are studying their own materials. Thus, the major function is a study hall.

Undergraduate libraries are also highly successful as social centers. Perhaps here is where the phrase "a screaming success" should have been used. If this is doubted, just go to one of them around 9 o'clock on any night (except Saturday, that is). Some librarians resisted this function but they were fighting human nature and lost. Luckily, carpeting and other acoustical treatments have helped tremendously in keeping the study hall from being taken over by the social center.

So far, undergraduate libraries chalk up two complete successes which have one great advantage: the students are there. They do not have to be pulled in off the campus. They are there.

But what else happens?

The Reserve desk is probably the busiest service point in the entire building. In 1968/69 Michigan had 50,000 volumes and 10,000 periodical articles on closed reserve with a total circulation of 276,000. There are many librarians, however, who question whether a booming reserve book business equals good teaching in a university. Studies at Cornell and elsewhere have shown that 40% or more of the volumes on reserve are deadwood and are not used. A healthy sign has been detected at several undergraduate libraries where the number of volumes requested for reserve by faculty has been whittled down by strong librarians. But it is appalling to read that one university is planning shelving space for 65,000 reserve volumes in its undergraduate library now under construction. In case one wishes to cite the thousands of students as an excuse for so many reserve books, another example of the abuse of reserve services may be given where there is *no* excuse: a college library has 8,000 volumes on closed reserve and another 10,000 volumes on open shelf reserve. It has only 1,114 students and is in a new $3,000,000 library with completely open stacks.

What is to be said here? Success or failure? If the number of volumes on reserve is gradually being decreased each year, it may be more of a success than if the librarians are still gently receiving long, out-of-date lists from lazy, unconcerned faculty and laboriously processing the volumes to hide them away so that no one uses them. That submissive attitude perpetuates stagnant service.

Do the undergraduates use the freely accessible main collections which have been selected for them? The answer is yes, and it seems to be getting better each year. Cornell with over 85,000 volumes in its Uris Library has experienced an increase in use with each passing year. Michigan with 155,000 volumes had a home circulation of 245,000 in 1968/69. Many thousands more are used in the building.

Perhaps one of the most worrisome aspects of undergraduate libraries has been the selection of this basic collection for undergraduate use. The Lamont catalog was published and served as a basis for some of the selection. Then, the Michigan shelf-list was made available, and now *Books for College Libraries,* developed in California, is used. There is not enough space to go into this aspect. Suffice it to say that the selection processes have been very detailed and elaborate with the involvement of both faculty and librarians. A great deal of time and energy has been spent on selecting individual titles for the collections. They are good, small collections. But we must realize that they will never come close to satisfying all the needs of undergraduates. The collections may now contain titles that students and faculty never use.

Almost every undergraduate library has some equipment for listening to records and tapes. The extent of this audio service varies greatly. Music and spoken arts recordings make up the collection at Michigan; only spoken arts recordings are in the Cornell Listening Rooms. At Stanford the language laboratory, consisting of four classrooms and an audio-control center, occupies about one-fourth of the ground floor, but the laboratory is not administered by the library. Have these audio facilities been a success or failure? At Cornell, the number of listeners increased each of the first four years of operation, but has drastically declined each of the last three years. My evaluation is that the reasons for this deteriorating situation at Cornell are a lack of communication with appropriate faculty members by librarians concerning the record collection and also a lack of communication with students. Since the abandonment of the freshman orientation lectures several years ago, most Cornell students do not even know of the existence of the collection.

Going from the audio to the visual is painfully easy. University libraries barely know that films exist. They have done little or absolutely nothing with films. A complete failure is the mark for most undergraduate libraries.

Reference services, the final aspect of undergraduate libraries to be considered, are critically investigated in Wilkinson's article, "The Undergraduate Library's Public Service Record: Reference Services" in Part VI of this *Reader.*

As you see I have some reservations about undergraduate libraries. I believe that the job has been only half done in the first twenty years. Good study space and small collections have been provided. Most of the time, energy and money has been spent in these areas. The same effort, or even greater effort, must be put into reference and other services — and the advertising of these services. I would recommend that one of the places to start in this task is with the faculty. Faculty members are a key to successful and meaningful use of an academic library. Unless they know and respect how much a librarian can assist students, the great potential of undergraduate libraries will never be realized. But first, last and always, librarians must get intimately involved with students. We can no longer sit comfortably at our reference desks waiting for something to happen. I used to think that I was a hopelessly romantic dreamer, but I now know that this mix of students, faculty, and librarians can be attained. It exists at the Lilly Library of Earlham College. Evan Farber, James Kennedy, and the other Earlham librarians give superb reference service and have an excellent library instruction program. They know and work intimately with the students and faculty.

The times cry out for every undergraduate library to become as good as the Earlham College Library. Instructional methods are gradually shifting from textbooks, reserve books and lectures to independent study, seminars and reading courses. Today's students resent the monolithic and impersonal character of universities. As Fay Blake reported on a paper given by C. R. Haywood at a conference on the Library-College movement:

Paternalistic, impersonal, undemocratic academic libraries are hung up on their own efficiency and develop acquisitions and reference departments which are neither student-oriented or student-determined . . . . To the undergraduate it must often appear that mechanization has become the library's raison d'être, and that the ultimate goal of the academic library is to narrow human contacts to the last possible minimum. When the institution as a whole adopts such an impersonal bureaucratic stance, the student demonstrates. When the library follows suit, he is more likely simply to avoid it — so far, at least.[14]

My experience on university campuses strongly confirms this. As we interviewed students using the union catalogs, several of them wanted to talk to us. They were not so much interested in talking about the library as they were in discussing the university. What they said can be summed up in one sentence: "The University doesn't give a damn about its undergraduates."

American universities in the 1970s must either get out of undergraduate education or they must do a much better job than was done in the 1960s. If universities want to flourish as centers of undergraduate education, let us start with undergraduate libraries fulfilling their promise.

Notes

1. Frederick H. Wagman, "The Case for the Separate Undergraduate Library," *College and Research Libraries* 17 (March, 1956): 150.

2. Sir Thomas Bodley, *Letters of Sir Thomas Bodley to Thomas James,* ed. by G. W. Wheeler (Oxford: Clarendon Press, 1926), p. 18

3. Columbia University. Library. *Report of the Librarian.* 1906/07.

4. Keyes D. Metcalf, "The Lamont Library, Part II, Function," *Harvard Library Bulletin* 3 (Winter, 1949): 12-30; Morrison C. Haviland, "The Reference Function of the Lamont Library," *Harvard Library Bulletin* 3 (Spring, 1949): 297-9; Philip J. McNiff, "The Charging System of the Lamont Library," *Harvard Library Bulletin* 3 (Spring, 1949): 438-40; Philip J. McNiff and Edwin E. Williams, "Lamont Library: the First Year," *Harvard Library Bulletin* 4 (Spring, 1950): 203-12; Richard O. Pautzsch, "The Classification Scheme for the Lamont Library," *Harvard Library Bulletin* 4 (Winter, 1950): 126-7; Henry R. Shepley, "The Lamont Library, Part I, Design," *Harvard Library Bulletin* 3 (Winter, 1949): 5-11; and Edwin E. Williams, "The Selection of Books for Lamont," *Harvard Library Bulletin* 3 (Autumn, 1949): 386-94.

5. Keyes D. Metcalf, "Harvard Faces Its Library Problems," *Harvard Library Bulletin* 3 (Spring, 1949): 185.

6. Ibid., 185-6.

7. Ibid., 187.

8. Shepley, 5.

9. Irene A. Braden, *The Undergraduate Library* "ACRL Monographs," No. 31, (Chicago: American Library Association, 1970).

10. Warren B. Kuhn, "Undergraduate Libraries in a University," *Library Trends* 18 (October, 1969): 188-209.

11. Elizabeth Mills, "The Separate Undergraduate Library," *College and Research Libraries* 29 (March, 1968): 144-56.

12. Robert H. Muller, "The Undergraduate Library Trend at Large Universities," in *Advances in Librarianship,* ed. by Melvin J. Voigt (New York: Academic Press, 1970) I, 113-32.

13. Jerrold Orne, "The Undergraduate Library," *Library Journal* 95 (June 15, 1970): 2230-3.

14. Fay Blake, "The Library-College Movement Dying of Old Age at Thirty: A Personal View," *Wilson Library Bulletin* 44 (January, 1970): 558-9.

About the Author

After service in several positions at the Louis Round Wilson Library, University of North Carolina, Chapel Hill, and as Head, Catawba County Library, Newton, North Carolina, Billy R. Wilkinson was appointed Goldwin Smith Librarian at Cornell University in 1959. He was then designated as Undergraduate Librarian in 1961 and was in charge of the Uris Undergraduate Library from its opening in September, 1962 until 1967 when he became a doctoral student. He received his doctorate from the Columbia University School of Library Service in 1971. From 1971-1977, he was Staff Relations Officer at The New York Public Library. He is now Associate University Librarian at the University of Illinois at Chicago Circle.

Ellen Hull Keever

Reassessment of the Undergraduate Library: A Personal Critique

After a brief review of the undergraduate library
movement, the author lists the "eleven existent
undergraduate libraries which are being abandoned for diverse reasons." She also reports on a
survey which she conducted among undergraduate librarians as to their preference of three
options (1. the separately housed building, 2. the
one-building collection, or 3. the segmented building with separate towers for undergraduate and
research use). She generalizes "that the decision to
establish an undergraduate collection must inevitably be a local matter, dependent upon many variables . . . Perhaps multiplicity, rather than
uniformity, of response to the problems of the
research library may be tomorrow's trend."

The first half of the twentieth century witnessed the tremendous growth of the
research library in America, an expansion which spawned fresh problems of its
own. Crowded conditions, competition with graduate students and faculty
members for service, frustration born of time lost securing materials, often led
the younger student to see himself a second-class citizen in the library and
prompted what may be termed the undergraduate library reaction. In a number
of American universities the single central library was replaced by the two
building concept: the research library *plus* a building specifically designed with
undergraduate needs in mind.[1] Indeed, up until the late 1960's the initial impetus
of the undergraduate library movement appeared to have thrust the trend into
an established pattern. Undergraduate libraries proliferated;[2] librarians reported
a harmonious period of development. Compatibility between expressed goals
and brick-and-mortar reality was complacently assumed. Recent cut-backs in

SOURCE: From Ellen Hull Keever, "Reassessment of the Undergraduate Library: A
Personal Critique," *The Southeastern Librarian* 23 (Spring, 1973) pp. 24-30. Reprinted by
permission of the author.

federal funds and current tendencies in university education, however, have caused an apparent reassessment. The rationale underlying the establishment of the undergraduate library is being reviewed, and the objectives of such a library are being re-evaluated.

As the Lamont Library at Harvard (1949) was the genesis of the new movement, it is interesting to note the primarily functional and pragmatic premises underlying its establishment: (1) that undergraduates would make more and better use of a library designed expressly for them; (2) that this would be the best way to relieve the pressure in the Widener building (the research library) and make unnecessary a new central library building; and (3) that if that pressure were relieved, the Widener Library building would become a more satisfactory research center than it has been in the past.[3]

As the undergraduate library movement gained momentum, responses were multiform and imaginative. But as the count of institutions having either a separately housed or in-building collection multiplied, the reasons for their existence underwent change. Increasingly the more practical functions (e.g., study hall, reserve book dispenser, reliever of critical space shortage in the central building) were less discussed. Now the focus of concern was on the special provision of service to undergraduates in terms of an instructional approach to the learning of library skills, voluntary collateral reading inspired by the nature of the collection itself, a diversity of resources, including the audiovisual, of which the highly selective collection became the visible symbol. A distinct philosophy of the undergraduate library was evolving, based upon the assumption that undergraduates had clearly defined needs to which one could minister.[4] It is this rationale, predicated upon a dichotomy between undergraduate and graduate student-faculty interest with which a significant number of undergraduate librarians feel increasingly ill-at-ease.[5]

Some librarians feel that the distinction between graduate and undergraduate needs is becoming increasingly obsolete. The departure from the textbook/lecture norm, the overlap between advanced undergraduate and graduate courses, and the trend toward increased undergraduate study of an independent character, blur the standard categorization of students. Wide agreement may now be found with Thomas J. O'Connell's statement that "new students come to our universities in many stages of preparedness" so that it is impossible today to view them "as a whole and distinguishable segment of our academic society."[6] The same librarians who doubt the possibility of clearly defined undergraduate characteristics also indicate uncertainty as to whether the concept of the separate undergraduate library possesses viability. Not all undergraduate librarians are wavering, however. It would appear that in large universities with strong graduate programs, a commitment to the undergraduate library concept is still strong. Where research is a lesser factor, in institutions where undergraduates make up at least eighty percent of the total university population, criticism is more vociferous.[7] It is beyond surmise that there are significant misgivings among undergraduate librarians today, and that, more often than not, those who have substantial skepticism are located where the research orientation is not paramount.

Eleven existent undergraduate libraries are being abandoned for diverse reasons. South Carolina reports that the Cooper Undergraduate Library will be abolished in 1974, a science library to occupy the present building.[8] Pennsylvania abandoned its undergraduate library about three years ago because, in conjunction with the main service area, it proved too noisy, and the concept of voluntary collateral reading, overly optismistic.[9] In planning their new library building at the University of Cincinnati the committee rejected the concept of a separate undergraduate library because of the trend toward increased undergraduate learning of an independent character.[10] Exigencies of budget have forced integration of main and undergraduate collections at Syracuse[11] and Cleveland State Universities.[12] A letter from Stephen R. Salmon, Director of Libraries at the University of Houston, indicates that rather than making books easier to find, the separate undergraduate collection within the same building had the reverse effect.[13] Accordingly, undergraduate books have been returned to the general collection. Miami University, Oxford, Ohio, has abolished its separately housed undergraduate library, because "Miami University is primarily an undergraduate institution," and "our graduate population, according to projected plans, will be carefully controlled."[14] An additional reason cited was that the concept was inappropriate to a library situation where there are only a quarter of a million volumes. Initial plans called for the $20,000,000 building of New York University to have a lower-floor undergraduate library under the same roof with its graduate library. Now, Dean of Libraries George Winchester Stone, Jr. reports there will be no separate undergraduate facility in their new library which will come on line in June, 1973.[15] At Wayne State University there were plans in 1970 ultimately to convert the present main library into an undergraduate library, but their librarian reports those plans "remain in an embryonic state, and there are no prospects for tangible progress at this time."[16] Other places where the undergraduate library is being phased out are Boston University and Texas A&M. Several other institutions are questioning the validity of their undergraduate library premises.

Another interesting phenomenon is the extent to which librarians would like an alternate architectural response to their present situation. Of twenty-eight respondents who were asked if they preferred (1) the separately housed building, (2) the one-building collection, or (3) the segmented building with separate towers for undergraduate and research use, a majority preferred what they did not have. Of those thirteen located within a central building, six would rather be in a segmented building, while seven preferred a separate situation. Fifteen of those in separate structures replied. Of these, three would rather be in segmented buildings, three would opt for a one-building, integrated collection, while nine are content. Allowing for the fact that the grass is always greener elsewhere, to what extent does this unsettled state of affairs bespeak a search for answers to problems that are other than building-ralated?

A critical question as to the justification of the undergraduate library has been whether it is possible to garner a definable, highly select collection of books which one could label "undergraduate." Highly esteemed librarians have deemed the collection the essential characteristic of the undergraduate library. Melvin J. Voigt reported from the University of California at San Diego's Institute on Acquisitions Procedures in Academic Libraries that "formulation and use of a policy statement is essential to an effective acquisitions program."[17] In light of the collection's crucial significance, it is ironic that twenty-four of thirty-two respondents disclaimed any written selection policy whatsoever; only two such written policies were in fact turned up, one from Michigan, and one from Alabama. Twenty-seven, as opposed to five, librarians felt that in an undergraduate library books could be more carefully selected with undergraduate needs in mind, but when queried as to the degree to which this goal has been actualized in practice, twelve librarians expressed frustration. It is of related significance that the overwhelming predilection for a tool to aid in the current selection process is *Choice*. All but six respondents gave it first priority. The critical question is whether the influence of *Choice* might be overweening in determining the shape of tomorrow's collections. Will those collections have an appearance of pre-packaged uniformity? At any rate, if book selection is of the essence in the undergraduate library, the goal of rigorous selectivity awaits full effectuation.

Another concern comes with the matter of weeding. In an era of mercurial expansion of knowledge, when changing conditions often render the most current information obsolete, it is essential to the viability of a collection that it be freed of its out-of-date books. Without the elimination of material that has lost its relevance, the collection will lose its essential purpose: to be sharply pertinent to student needs. Yet only seven of thirty-two respondents report a regular weeding program in their libraries.

In perhaps no area is there such considerable uncertainty as that of determination of the optimum size of the collection. Whereas there seemed to be some agreement that threshold adequacy for a basic collection should be around 35,000 titles, respondents reported their desired maximum ceilings as follows:

Projected Size (Volumes)	Actual Size (Volumes)
50,000	
Duke	16,000
Southern Calif., Los Angeles	43,576
Miami (Fla.)	58,000
Oklahoma	15,000
60,000	
Florida State	27,629
University of Calif., San Diego	31,677
70,000	
Alabama	35,000

Projected Size (Volumes)	Actual Size (Volumes)
80,000	
Leeds	N/A
Alberta	70,500
100,000-125,000	
Colorado	60,000
Cornell	93,375
Indiana	80,000
North Carolina	70,500
150,000-175,000	
University of Calif., Berkeley	N/A
Illinois	101,027
Kent State	26,000
Michigan State	112,000
Southern Illinois	155,000
Virginia	Planning stage
200,000	
University of British Columbia	120,181
University of Calif., Los Angeles	143,576
Maryland	100,000
Michigan	172,733

A number of librarians not only question that library skills learned in the undergraduate library transfer to the research-oriented library, but also make pedagogical quarrel with the sort of approach which suggests that undergraduates should not use the total resources of the university library. William S. Dix, now University Librarian at Princeton, when Librarian at Rice Institute in 1953, raised the question of whether it was desirable to make special provision for the undergraduate in smaller university libraries of less than half a million volumes, but he was for that time an iconoclast. Now his voice has been joined by others, some of whom would take exception to the half-million demarcation.[18] This intellectual stance sees the student with academic initiative delimited by a smaller collection as deprived, the frankly average student as spoon-fed.

Today there is absence of assurance that the undergraduate library is the prescriptive answer to problems of severe space shortage and inaccessibility of materials for undergraduates. Although no one doubts the undergraduate library to be one valid response to the huge research complex which is the twentieth-century multiversity, there is an increasing uncertainty about structuring such a library when the total library collection is modest, the graduate program less strongly research-oriented, the proportion of undergraduates to graduates as much as four to one. Certainly the more idealistic objectives of the undergraduate library are not on all counts chimerical; the well-documented increase in circulation at Cornell, Michigan, and South Carolina, among other institutions, clearly relates to the removal of barriers between students and books. Undergraduate libraries have been triumphantly successful at Harvard, Michigan, Illinois, and elsewhere. One could nevertheless generalize that the decision to establish an undergraduate collection must inevitably be a local matter, dependent upon many variables, such as geography, other components of the total library system, the size and nature of a student body. Perhaps multiplicity, rather than uniformity, of response to the problems of the monolithic structure of the research library may be tomorrow's trend.

One cannot, however, pay no regard to significant unrest which surfaces and demands a hearing. The pertinent question has to do with the interpretation to be made of this vacillation in commitment on the part of some undergraduate librarians. Is it because administrators and legislators have denied librarians funds to implement programs based on worthy ideals? Were those ideals so visionary as to lack the potency to effect demonstrable change in the institution which is the library? Or is there a revolution in college education unalterably leading to a reversal of the present regime, which will in time reduce regularly scheduled lectures, call upon the student for more and more independent study, and finally render the undergraduate library, predicated upon definable undergraduate needs, obsolete?

Notes

1. For important treatments of the historical development of the undergraduate library movement, the reader is referred to Warren B. Kuhn, "Undergraduate Libraries in a University," *Library Trends* 18: (Oct., 1969), 188-209 or Elizabeth Mills, "The Separate Undergraduate Library," *College and Research Libraries* 29 (March, 1968): 144-56. A more recent study is that of Robert H. Muller, whose article "The Undergraduate Library Trends at Large Universiities," appeared in *Advances in Librarianship*, Vol. I, ed. by Melvin J. Voigt, (New York: Academic Press, 1970.)

2. Initial separately-housed libraries were at Harvard, University of Michigan, University of South Carolina, Indiana University, Cornell University, University of North Carolina, University of Texas, University of Illinois, Stanford University, and University of Nebraska. For current listings of the forty-five undergraduate libraries which are a) separately housed, or b) housed within the same building as the Main Library, see Tables I and II.

3. Keyes D. Metcalf. "Harvard Faces Its Library Problems." *Harvard Library Bulletin* 3 (Autumn, 1949): 187.

4. The clearest exposition of the intangible goals of the undergraduate library was made by Irene Braden in *The Undergraduate Library*. (Chicago: American Library Association, 1970.) The statement of these goals has received wide acceptance.

5. The attitudes of ninety-eight librarians of undergraduate libraries were solicited in a questionnaire distributed by this writer in June, 1972. Responses came from seventy-five librarians, thirty-two of whom completed questionnaires. Forty-three, however, opted for the written response in letter-form rather than the completed

questionnaire. Some responded to most, though not to every, question. When dealing with specific issues in this paper, I have tried in each instance to indicate the size of my sample in terms of the responses received to that particular question. Finally, in the list of institutions presented in tabular form, I have included the names of certain undergraduate libraries from which I received no response. In these instances my data are derived from the November, 1971, Statistical Issue of the *U.G.L.I. Newsletter.*

6.   Thomas J. O'Connell. "Undergraduate Library?" *Canadian Library Journal* 28, (July, 1970): 278-79.

7.   In all but four instances, the libraries who expressed a continuing approval of the undergraduate library concept were in universities where at least one out of three of all students was on a graduate level.

8.   University of South Carolina, Columbia. (Reply to questionnaire) June, 1972.

9.   Rudolf Hirsch. Letter dated May 30, 1972.

10.   Bruce Kauffman. Letter dated May 31, 1972.

11.   Warren N. Boes. Letter dated June 22, 1972.

12.   L. Dolores Ryan. Letter dated May 30, 1972.

13.   Stephen R. Salmon. Letter dated May 30, 1972.

14.   Charles D. Churchwell. Letter dated July 10, 1972.

15.   George Winchester Stone, Jr. Letter dated June 13, 1972.

16.   Robert T. Grozier. Letter dated May 31, 1972.

17.   Melvin J. Voigt. "The Undergraduate Library; the Collection and Its Selection." Mimeographed paper presented during the Institute in Training for Service in Undergraduate Libraries, sponsored by the University Library, University of California, San Diego, August 17-21, 1970, 2.

18.   Eminent among librarians with this point of view are Stuart Forth (Kentucky), Charles Churchwell (Miami University), Rodney Waldron (Oregon State), Bruce Kauffman (Pennsylvania), and of course, William S. Dix (Princeton).

About the Author

Ellen Hull Keever is Reference Librarian, University of Alabama Libraries, University of Alabama.

University library	Volumes in undergraduate library	Budget for undergraduate library	Enrollment	
			Undergraduate	Graduate
1) Alberta (Canada)	70,141	$173,284.75	6,331	1,969
2) California, Berkeley	N/A	361,754.00	19,000	8,000
3) California, Los Angeles	143,576	350,290.76	17,248	10,524
4) California, San Diego	31,677	87,616.00	5,000	1,000
5) Cornell	96,375	218,295.51	10,000	4,000
6) Emory	N/A	N/A	4,591[4] (1967)	752[4] (1967)
7) Florida	N/A	N/A	16,500	6,700
8) Harvard	166,525 (69/70)[3]	N/A	5,670[3]	1,300[3]
9) Hawaii	78,285	233,900.00	16,229	4,696
10) Illinois (Urbana campus)	101,027	218,318.00	24,558	9,460
11) Leeds (England)[1]	N/A	N/A	7,500[1]	2,500[1]
12) Maryland[2]	100,000[5]	-----	29,866[4]	5,821[4]
13) Michigan	172,733	278,462.00	23,440	10,835
14) Minnesota	20,254	35,938.00	36,956[4] (1966)	7,120[4] (1966)
15) Nebraska	19,000 (69/70)[3]	N/A	15,965[3]	3,653[3]
16) North Carolina	70,500	138,200.00	12,300	5,800
17) Ohio State	N/A	N/A	31,825	6,368
18) Pennsylvania State	59,655[3]	N/A	21,000[3]	4,000[3]
19) South Carolina[5]	55,142	15,000.00	12,000	4,000
20) Stanford	87,551 (69/70)[3]	N/A	6,221[3]	5,319[3]
21) Tennessee	155,000	306,820.00	18,321	4,353
22) Texas	112,831 (69/70)[3]	N/A	28,772[3]	6,956[3]
23) Washington	105,449 (69/70)[3]	33,815.00	26,158[3]	6,571[3]
24) Wisconsin	N/A	N/A	21,805[4]	8,222[4]

Unless otherwise indicated by footnote, data are derived from questionnaire mailed in June, 1972.
1. Will occupy separate building when construction is complete. Due to open September, 1974.
2. These figures are for a projected opening day collection. This library is in its planning stage only.
3. This data derived from November 1971 Statistical Issue of the *U.G.L.I. Newsletter* and represents 69/70 data.
4. This data derived from *American Universities and Colleges*, 10th edition. Washington: American Council on Education, 1968.
5. To be abolished in 1974.

Table 2 — Undergraduate Libraries Located in Main Library Building (June, 1972)

University library	Volumes in undergraduate library	Budget for undergraduate library	Enrollment	
			Undergraduate	Graduate
1) Bowling Green State	N/A	N/A	10,315[4]	952[4]
2) British Columbia	120,181	$99,000.00	18,127	2,810
3) Colorado	60,000 (Est.)[3]	61,651.00[3]	16,789[3]	3,672[3]
4) Southern California	43,576	52,700.00	9,627	9,257
5) Duke	16,000	72,000.00	6,000	2,000
6) Florida State	27,629	38,428.00	13,099	3,104
7) Southern Illinois	40,000	N/A	17,000	5,000
8) Indiana	80,000 (Est.)[1]	150,000.00	22,000	8,000
9) Iowa	35,000[1]	N/A	17,755[4]	4,491[4]
10) Iowa State University	9,500	61,000.00	17,500	2,300
11) Kent State (Ohio)	26,000	23,624.00	19,200	2,500
12) Maryland	100,000[1]	N/A	24,000[4]	10,000[4]
13) Massachusetts	N/A	N/A	13,679[4]	2,514[4]
14) Miami (Fla.)	58,000	N/A	12,318	2,600
15) Michigan State	112,000	196,500.00	32,000	8,000
16) Missouri (Columbia)	16,300	37,000.00	16,400	5,600
17) Northwestern University	33,000	121,901.64	6,607	2,748
18) Oklahoma	15,000	30,304.00	12,684	2,659
19) Pittsburg	N/A	N/A	4,616[4]	1,419[4]
20) Virginia[2]	N/A	N/A	9,290	2,826

Unless otherwise indicated by footnote, data are derived from questionnaire mailed in June, 1972.
1. Plans to have an Opening Day Collection of this number of volumes.
2. Presently an in-building collection in the early stages. Plans call for a separate building.
3. This data derived from November, 1971 Statistical Issue of the *U.G. L.I. Newsletter* and represents 69/70 data.
4. This data derived from *American Universities and Colleges*, 10th edition. Washington: American Council on Education, 1968.

General Reading List

Books

Bergen, Dan, and Duryea, E.D., eds. *Libraries and the College Climate of Learning*. Syracuse: Program in Higher Education of the School of Education and the School of Library Science, Syracuse University, 1964.

Braden, Irene A. *The Undergraduate Library*. ACRL Monographs, No. 31. Chicago: American Library Association, 1970.

Cornell. University Library. *The Cornell Library Conference. Papers Read at the Dedication of the Central Libraries, October, 1962*. Ithaca: Cornell University Library, 1964.

Indiana. University Library. *The Undergraduate and the Library*. Bloomington: Indiana University Libraries, 1965.

Knapp, Patricia B. *College Teaching and the College Library*. ACRL Monographs, No. 23. Chicago: American Library Association, Association of College and Research Libraries, 1959.

———. *The Monteith College Library Experiment*. In collaboration with Carol E. Ballingall and Gilbert E. Donahue, with the assistance of Grace E. Dawson. New York: Scarecrow Press, 1966.

Shores, Louis. *Origins of the American College Library, 1638-1800*. Contributions to Education, George Peabody College for Teachers, No. 134. Nashville: George Peabody College for Teachers, 1934.

———; Jordan, Robert; and Harvey, John, eds. *The Library-College: Contributions for American Higher Education at the Jamestown College Workshop, 1965*. Drexel Library School Series, No. 16. Philadelphia: Drexel Press, 1966.

Periodical Articles and Essays in Monographs

Arragon, R.F. "The Relationship Between the Library and Collegiate Objectives." *Library Quarterly*, 24 (October, 1954): 284-95.

Blackburn, Robert T. "College Libraries — Indicated Failures: Some Reasons — and a Possible Remedy." *College and Research Libraries,* 24 (May, 1968): 171-77.

Blake, Fay M. "The Library-College Movement Dying of Old Age at Thirty: A Personal View." *Wilson Library Bulletin,* 44 (January, 1970): 557-60.

Braden, Irene A. "The Separately Housed Undergraduate Library." *College and Research Libraries,* 29 (July, 1968): 281-84.

Branscomb, Harvie. "The Future of Libraries in Academic Institutions, Part III." *Harvard Library Bulletin,* 3 (Autumn, 1949): 338-46.

"Built for the Undergraduates: New Library Seats 1,905." *Illinois Alumni News,* 48 (October, 1969): 1, 3.

Burke, Redmond A. "The Separately Housed Undergraduate Library Versus the University Library." *College and Research Libraries,* 31 (November, 1970): 399-402.

Cantor, Enid A. "The Cornell Library Complex." *Cornell Daily Sun* (Ithaca), October 10, 1962.

———. "The Old Becoming the New Undergraduate Library." *Cornell Daily Sun* (Ithaca), March 14, 1962.

Carpenter, Charles A. "The Lamont Catalog as a Guide to Book Selection." *College and Research Libraries,* 18 (July, 1957): 267-68, 302.

Cassell, Jean. "The University of Texas Undergraduate Library Collection." *Texas Library Journal,* 39 (Winter, 1963): 123-26.

Coney, Donald. "The Future of Libraries in Academic Institutions, Part I." *Harvard Library Bulletin,* 3 (Autumn, 1949): 327-31.

"Conference on the Place of the Library in a University." *Harvard Library Bulletin,* 3 (Spring, 1949): 305.

Cook, J. J. "Increased Seating in the Undergraduate Library: A Study in Effective Space Utilization." *Case Studies in Systems Analysis in a University Library.* Edited by Barton R. Burkhalter. Metuchen, New Jersey: Scarecrow Press, 1968.

Deale, H. Vail, ed. *Trends in College Librarianship.* Vol. 18, No. 1 of *Library Trends.* Urbana: University of Illinois Graduate School of Library Science, July, 1969.

"The Dedication of the Lamont Library." *Harvard Library Bulletin,* 3 (Spring, 1949): 304-5.

Dix, William S. "Library Service to Undergraduate College Students, A Symposium: Undergraduates Do Not Necessarily Require a Special Facility." *College and Research Libraries,* 17 (March, 1956): 148-50.

————. "Library Service to Undergraduates: A Symposium: Undergraduate Libraries." *College and Research Libraries,* 14 (July, 1953): 271-72.

Elkins, Kimball C. "Foreshadowings of Lamont: Student Proposals in the Nineteenth Century." *Harvard Library Bulletin,* 8 (Winter, 1954): 41-53.

Finzi, John C. "The University Libraries Section" [Report on Symposium entitled "The Undergraduate Library: A Time for Assessment"]. *Library of Congress Information Bulletin,* Appendix 2, 29 (Aug. 6, 1970): A83-85.

Gittelsohn, Marc. "Progress Report on the Moffitt Undergraduate Library, University of California at Berkeley." *UGLI Newsletter,* 2 (November, 1969): 1-4.

Golter, Robert. "The Afro-American Collection, Meyer Memorial Library, Stanford University." *UGLI Newsletter,* 2 (November, 1969): 4-5.

Gore, Daniel. "Anachronistic Wizard: The College Reference Librarian." *Library Journal,* 89 (April 15, 1964): 1688-92.

————. "The Mismanagement of College Libraries: A View from the Inside." *AAUP Bulletin,* 52 (March, 1966): 46-51.

Govan, James F. "Collegiate Education: Past and Present." *Library Trends,* 18 (July, 1969): 13-28.

————. "This Is, Indeed, the Heart of the Matter." *College and Research Libraries,* 23 (November, 1962): 467-72.

Gwynn, Stanley E. "The Liberal Arts Function of the University Library." *Library Quarterly,* 24 (October, 1954): 311-21.

————. "Library Service to Undergraduates, a Symposium: The College Library at the University of Chicago." *College and Research* Libraries, 14 (July, 1953): 267-68.

Haak, John R. "Goal Determination." *Library Journal,* 96 (May 1, 1971): 1573-78.

————. "Report on the Meeting of Undergraduate Librarians at A.L.A." *UGLI Newsletter,* 1 (July, 1969): 1-3.

[Haak, John R.] "A Listing of Documents Received Concerning Undergraduate Libraries." *UGLI Newsletter,* 2 (November, 1969): 10-16.

Haro, Robert P. "College Libraries for Students." *Library Journal,* 94 (June 1, 1969): 2207-8.

Haviland, Morrison C. "The Reference Function of the Lamont Library." *Harvard Library Bulletin,* 3 (Spring, 1949): 297-99.

Hinchliff, William. "Ivory Tower Ghettoes." *Library Journal,* 94 (November 1, 1969): 3971-74.

Horney, Karen. "Building Northwestern's Core." *Library Journal,* 96 (May 1, 1971): 1580-83.

Jones, Frank N. "Libraries of the Harvard Houses." *Harvard Library Bulletin,* 2 (Autumn, 1948): 362-77.

Jones, Norah E. "The UCLA Experience: An Undergraduate Library — for Undergraduates!" *Wilson Library Bulletin,* 45 (February, 1971): 584-90.

Jordan, Robert T. "The 'Library-College,' a Merging of Library and Classroom." *Libraries and the College Climate of Learning.* Edited by Dan Bergen and E.D. Duryea. Syracuse: Program in Higher Education of the School of Education and the School of Library Science, Syracuse University, 1964.

Kean, Rick. "Finding People Who Feel Alienated and Alone in their Best Impulses and Most Honest Perceptions and Telling Them They're Not Crazy." *Wilson Library Bulletin,* 44 (September, 1969): 36-44.

Keast, William Rea. "The True University of These Days Is a Collection of Books." Cornell University Library. *The Cornell Library Conference, Papers Read at the Dedication of the Central Libraries, October, 1962.* Ithaca: Cornell University Library, 1964: 41-50.

Kells, H. R., and Stewart, C. T. "Summary of the Working Sessions; Conference on the Cluster College Concept." *Journal of Higher Education,* 38 (October, 1967): 359-63.

Keniston, Roberta. "Circulation Gains at Michigan." *Library Journal.* 83 (December 1, 1958): 3357-59.

———. "The University of Michigan Undergraduate Library." *Michigan Librarian,* 25 (June, 1959): 24-25.

Kennedy, James R. "Integrated Library Instruction." *Library Journal,* 95 (April 15, 1970): 1450-53.

———. "Library Instruction." *GLCA* [Great Lakes Colleges Association] *Librarians' Newsletter,* 1 (December, 1966): 1-2.

———. "Library Service in Perspective." *College and Research Libraries,* 25 (March, 1964): 91-92.

Kuhn, Warren B. "The J. Henry Meyer Memorial Library, Standord University." *California Librarian,* 29 (April, 1968): 93-99.

———"Princeton's New Julian Street Library." *College and Research Libraries,* 23 (November, 1962): 504-8.

———"Summary of the Responses to the Warren B. Kuhn Questionnaire [on Undergraduate Libraries]."*UGLI Newsletter,* 2 (November, 1969): 5-10

———. "Undergraduate Libraries in a University." *Library Trends,* 18 (October, 1969): 188-209.

"Lamont Library, Harvard University." *Architectural Record,* 105 (June, 1949): 86-95.

"Library Service to Undergraduate Collge Students: A Symposium." *College and Research Libraries,* 17 (March, 1956): 143-55. Contains articles by Frank A. Lundy, William S. Dix, and Frederick H. Wagman.

"Library Service to Undergraduates: A Symposium," *College and Research Libraries,* 14 (July, 1953): 266-75. Contains articles by Arthur M. McAnally, Stanley E. Gwynn, Philip J. McNiff, William S. Dix, and Wyman S. Parker.

Logan, Albert A., Jr. "College Libraries Called Inadequate in Meeting Students' Reference Needs." *Chronicle of Higher Education,* 4 (August 3, 1970): 1.

Lovett, Robert W. "The Harvard Union Library, 1901 to 1948." *Harvard Library Bulletin,* 2 (Spring, 1948): 230-37.

———. "The Undergraduate and the Harvard Libraries, 1877-1937." *Harvard Library Bulletin,* 1 (Spring, 1947): 221-37.

Lundy, Frank A. "Library Service to Undergraduate College Students, A Symposium: The Divisional Plan Library." *College and Research Libraries,* 17 (March, 1956): 143-48.

McAnally, Arthur M. "Library Service to Undergraduates, A Symposium: Introductory Remarks." *College and Research Libraries,* 14 (July, 1953): 266.

McCarthy, Stephen A. "The Cornell Library System." Cornell University Library. *The Cornell Library Conference, Papers Read at the Dedication of the Central Libraries, October, 1962.* Ithaca: Cornell University Library, 1964, 25-32.

———. "The Cornell Library System: Present and Future." *Cornell Daily Sun* (Ithaca), October 10, 1962.

———. "Library Provision for Undergraduates in the United States." *College and Research Libraries,* 26 (May, 1965): 222-24.

McKeon, Newton F. "The Future of Libraries in Academic Institutions, Part II." *Harvard Library Bulletin,* 3 (Autumn, 1949): 331-38.

McNiff, Philip J. "The Charging System of the Lamont Library." *Harvard Library Bulletin,* 3 (Autumn, 1949): 438-40.

———. "Library Service to Undergraduates, A Symposium: Lamont Library, Harvard College." *College and Research Libraries,* 14 (July, 1953): 269-70.

———, and Williams, Edwin E. "Lamont Library: The First Year." *Harvard Library Bulletin,* 4 (Spring, 1950): 203-12.

Metcalf, Keyes D. "Harvard Faces Its Library Problems." *Harvard Library Bulletin,* 3 (Spring, 1949): 183-97.

————. "The Lamont Library, Part II: Function." *Harvard Library Bulletin,* 3 (Winter, 1949): 12-30.

————. "To What Extent Must We Segregate?" *College and Research Libraries,* 8 (October, 1957): 399-401.

————. "The Undergraduate and the Harvard Library, 1765-1877." *Harvard Library Bulletin,* 1 (Winter, 1947): 29-51.

————"The Undergraduate and the Harvard Library, 1937-1947." *Harvard Library Bulletin,* 1 (Autumn, 1947), 288-305.

Miller, Robert A. "Indiana's Three-In-One." *Library Journal,* 94 (December 1, 1969): 4399.

Mills, Elizabeth. "The Separate Undergraduate Library." *College and Research Libraries,* 29 (March, 1968): 144-56.

Moss, M. W. "Library Service for Undergraduates." *The Provision and Use of Library and Documentation Services.* Edited by W. L. Saunders. International Series of Monographs in Library and Information Science, vol. 4. Oxford: Pergamon Press, 1966, pp. 85-113.

Muller, Robert H. "Master Planning for University Libraries." *Library Trends,* 18 (October, 1969): 138-49.

————. "The Undergraduate Library Trend at Large Universities." *Advances in Librarianship,* vol. 1. Edited by Melvin J. Voigt. New York: Academic Press, 1970, pp. 131-32.

"A New Intellectual Center." *Michigan Alumnus,* 64 (December 14, 1957): 151-53.

Orne, Jerrold. "The Undergraduate Library." *Library Journal,* 95 (June 15, 1970): 2230-33.

Page, B. S. "Library Provision for Undergraduates in England." *College and Research Libraries,* 26 (May, 1965): 219-22.

Packard, Frederick C. "The Harvard Vocarium Disc." *Harvard Library Journal,* 3 (Autumn, 1949): 441-45.

————. "Harvard's Vocarium Has Attained Full Stature." *Library Journal,* 75 (January 15, 1950): 69-74.

[Packard, James]. "The Undergraduate Library." *Research News* [University of Michigan Office of Research Administration], 15 (May, 1965): 1-12.

Parker, Wyman S. "Library Service to Undergraduates, A Symposium: The Vital Core." *College and Research Libraries,* 14 (July, 1953): 272-75.

Pautzsch, Richard O. "The Classification Scheme for the Lamont Library." *Harvard Library Bulletin,* 4 (Winter, 1950): 126-27.

"Preparations for the Lamont Library." *Harvard Library Bulletin*, 2 (Spring, 1948): 270-71.

Ransom, Harry H. "Academic Center: A Plan for an Undergraduate Library." *Library Chronicle of the University of Texas*, 6 (Winter, 1960): 48-50.

———. "Arts and Sciences: The College Library." *Texas Quarterly*, 2 (Winter, 1959): 7-12.

Reames, J. Mitchell. " 'First in the South' Undergraduate Library, University of South Carolina." *South Carolina Librarian*, 3 (March, 1959): 22-23.

———. "Undergraduate Library, University of South Carolina." *Southeastern Librarian*, 10 (Fall, 1960): 130-36.

Rohlf, Robert H. "The Freshman-Sophomore Library at Minnesota." *College and Research Libraries*, 14 (April, 1953): 164-66.

"A Second Youth for Main Library." *Cornell Alumni News*, 65 (January, 1963): 4-7, 20.

Shepley, Henry R. "The Lamont Library, Part I: Design." *Harvard Library Bulletin*, 3 (Winter, 1949): 5-11.

Shores, Louis. "The Undergraduate and His Library." *The Library in the University; The University of Tennessee Library Lectures, 1949-1966*. Hamden, Connecticut: Shoe String Press, 1967, pp. 199-207.

Sweeney, John L. "A Place for Poetry: The Woodberry Poetry Room in Widener and Lamont." *Harvard Library Bulletin*, 8 (Winter, 1954): 65-73.

Tauber, Maurice F.; Cook, C. Donald; and Logsdon, Richard H. "The College Library" and "The Undergraduate Library Problem at Columbia." *The Columbia University Libraries*. New York: Columbia University Press, 1958, pp. 152-62.

"There Are No Barriers Between Students and Books." *University of North Carolina, Chapel Hill Alumni Review*, 57 (October, 1968): 12-18.

UGLI Newsletter. No. 1, July, 1969-   . [Edited by John R. Haak, University of California at San Diego, La Jolla, California.]

"The 'UgLi' Routine: Student Subculture." *Michigan Daily* (Ann Arbor). February 16, 1969.

"The University of Michigan Undergraduate Library, Ann Arbor, Michigan." *News of the Lite-Weight Concrete Products Industry*, 21 (October, 1958): 1-13.

Wagman, Frederick H. "Library Service to Undergraduate College Students, A Symposium: The Case for the Separate Undergraduate Library." *College and Research Libraries*, 17 (March, 1956): 150-55.

————. "The Undergraduate Library of the University of Michigan." *College and Research Libraries,* 20 (May, 1959): 179-88.

Warner, Charles H., Jr. "The Central Library Buildings." Papers Read at the Dedication of the Central Libraries, October, 1962. Ithaca: Cornell University Library, 1964, pp. 33-40.

Weber, David C. "Stanford: Precision Instrument for Undergraduates." *Library Journal,* 92 (December 1, 1967): 4351-52.

White, Lucien W. "University of Illinois Award Winning Undergraduate Library." *Illinois Libraries,* 50 (December, 1968): 1042-46.

Whitten, Benjamin G., and Wilkinson, Billy R. "A Day of Books and Students." *Cornell Alumni News,* 69 (July, 1966): 7-11.

Wilkinson, Billy R. "The Arthur H. Dean Book Collection Contest." *Cornell Library Journal,* No. 3 (Autumn, 1967): 55-56.

————. "New Out of Old: A Look at Plans for the Undergraduate Library." *Cornell Alumni News,* 64 (January, 1962): 12-13.

————. "A Screaming Success as Study Halls." *Library Journal,* 96 (May 1, 1971): 1567-71.

Williams, Edwin E. "The Selection of Books for Lamont." *Harvard Library Bulletin,* 3 (Autumn, 1949): 386-94.

Wingate, Henry W. "The Undergraduate Library: Is It Obsolete?" *College and Research Libraries* (January, 1978): 29-33.

Reports, Proceedings, Unpublished Material, and Miscellany

Allen, Kenneth S. "Proposed Undergraduate Library — Food Service Building, University of Washington, Seattle." American Library Association, 1967 Library Buildings Institute, Buildings Committee for College and University Libraries, June 5, 1967. Mimeographed.

Braden, Irene A. "The Undergraduate Library — The First 20 Years." Paper presented at the Institute on Training for Service in Undergraduate Libraries, University of California, San Diego, August 17-21, 1970.

————. "The Undergraduate Library on the University Campus." Unpublished Ph.D. dissertation, Department of Library Science, University of Michigan, 1967.

California. University Library. San Diego. "Proposal [to the U.S. Office of Education] for an Institute Entitled Training for Service in Undergraduate Libraries, August 17-21, 1970." Director: Melvin J. Voigt. La Jolla: University Library, University of California at San Diego, 1969. Mimeographed.

Conference on Use, Mis-Use, and Non-Use of Academic Libraries, 1970. *Use, Mis-Use, and Non-Use of Academic Libraries.* Proceedings of the New York Library Association College and University Libraries Section Spring Conference held at Jefferson Community College, Watertown, May 1-2, 1970. Edited by the Committee on the Requirements of the Academic Library Users, John Lubans, Jr., Chairman. (Troy, New York: Rensselaer Polytechnic Institute, 1970).

Cornell. University Library. "Program for the Undergraduate Library." Draft Program, March 26, 1956. Ithaca, 1956. Mimeographed.

————. "Program for the Undergraduate Library." July 13, 1959. Ithaca, 1959. Mimeographed.

————. Committee on Undergraduate Library Service. Minutes of Meetings, 1966/67. Typewritten.

————. Subcommittee on the Undergraduate Library. "First Report of Subcommittee on the Undergraduate Library to the Library Committee." Ithaca [1959]. Mimeographed.

————. Uris Library. "Costs of Remodeling the Building, 1961." [Statement prepared by Harold B. Schell, Assistant to the Director of University Libraries, July 3, 1964.] Ithaca, 1964. Typewritten.

Govan, James F. "The Teaching Library." Paper read before the 55th Conference of Eastern College Librarians, Columbia University, New York, November 29, 1969.

Haak, John R. "Goal Determination and the Undergraduate Library." Paper presented at the Institute on Training for Service in Undergraduate Libraries, University of California, San Diego, August 17-21, 1970.

"It's All Happening at the Zoo." [Anonymous Poem Distributed in Uris Library, April, 1968.] Mimeographed.

Jones, Norah E. "The College Library at UCLA." Paper read before the University Libraries Section, Association of College and Research Libraries, American Library Association, Detroit, June 29, 1970.

Knapp, Patricia B. "The Library, the Undergraduate and the Teaching Faculty." Paper presented at the Institute on Training for Service in Undergraduate Libraries, University of California, San Diego, August 17-21, 1970.

Kuhn, Warren B. "Planning the Undergraduate Library." Paper presented at the Institute on Training for Service in Undergraduate Libraries, University of California, San Diego, August 17-21, 1970.

Lundy, Frank A. "The Undergraduate Library at the University of Nebraska: the Nebraska Hall Project, 1969." February, 1969. Mimeographed.

Lynch, Mary Jo, and Menges, Gary L. "A Proposal for Undergraduate Library Service, 1970-1980." University of Massachusetts/Amherst Library, February 2, 1970. Mimeographed.

McCarthy, Stephen A. "The Cornell Undergraduate Library." [Proposed Draft of Statement for the Use of Arthur H. Dean, Chairman, Cornell Board of Trustees.] Ithaca, December 2, 1959. Typewritten.

————. *Program of the Conference and Dedication of the John M. Olin Library and the Uris Library, October 9 and 10, 1962.* Ithaca: Cornell University, 1962.

Metcalf, Keyes D. *Report on the Harvard University Library: A Study of Present and Prospective Problems.* Cambridge: Harvard University Library, 1955.

Michigan. University Library. Advisory Committee on the Undergraduate Library. Minutes of Meetings. 1954-56. Typewritten.

————. "Preliminary Program for the Undergraduate Library." Ann Arbor, August 18, 1954. Mimeographed.

————. "Program for an Undergraduate Library." Submitted by Frederick H. Wagman, Director of the University Library, for the Advisory Committee on the Undergraduate Library. Ann Arbor, February 1, 1955.

————. *The Undergraduate Library Building of the University of Michigan.* Ann Arbor: University of Michigan Library, 1960.

————. "The University of Michigan Undergraduate Library Audio Room." Ann Arbor, n.d. Mimeographed.

————. "The University of Michigan Undergraduate Library Reserve Information." Ann Arbor, n.d. Mimeographed.

Nelson Associates, Inc. *Undergraduate and Junior College Libraries in the United States, A Report Prepared for the National Advisory Commission on Libraries.* New York: Nelson Associates, Inc., 1968.

Saidel, Cynthia A. "A Survey of the Lamont Library of Harvard College." Unpublished Master's thesis, School of Library Service, Columbia University, 1952.

Stewart, Rolland C. "The Undergraduate Library Collection." Paper presented at the Institute on Book Selection and Acquisitions, University of California, San Diego, August 25-September 5, 1969.

Taylor, Constance M. "Meeting the Needs of Undergraduates in Large University Libraries." Unpublished Master's thesis, Graduate School of Library Science, University of Texas, 1956.

Toombs, Kenneth E. "The Undergraduate Library at South Carolina." Paper read before the University Libraries Section, Association of College and Research Libraries, American Library Association, June 29, 1970.

Voigt, Melvin J. "The Undergraduate Library; The Collection and Its Selection." Paper presented at the Institute on Training for Service in Undergraduate Libraries, University of California, San Diego, August 17-21, 1970.

Wagman, Frederick H. "The Library Situation and the Program of Plant Expansion." Paper presented to the Library Committee of the College of Literature, Science, and the Arts, University of Michigan, Ann Arbor, [October] 1954.

Wilkinson, Billy R. "Are We Fooling Ourselves About Undergraduate Libraries?" Paper read before the University Libraries Section, Association of College and Research Libraries, American Library Association, June 29, 1970.

————. "The Undergraduate Library's Public Service Record: Reference Services." Paper presented at the Institute on Training for Service in Undergraduate Libraries, University of California, San Diego, August 17-21, 1970.

Index

Index